A SHADOW ON OUR HEARTS

A SHADOW ON OUR HEARTS

Soldier-Poetry, Morality, and the American War in Vietnam

ADAM GILBERT

University of Massachusetts Press
Amherst and Boston

Printed in the United States of America

ISBN 978-1-62534-301-7 (paper); 300-0 (hardcover)

Designed by Sally Nichols
Set in Minion Pro
Printed and bound by Maple Press, Inc.

Library of Congress Cataloging-in-Publication Data

Names: Gilbert, Adam, author.
Title: A shadow on our hearts : soldier-poetry, morality, and the American war in Vietnam / Adam Gilbert.
Description: Amherst : University of Massachusetts Press, 2018. | Includes bibliographical references and index.
Identifiers: LCCN 2017038237| ISBN 9781625343017 (pbk. : alk. paper) | ISBN 9781625343000 (hardcover : alk. paper)
Subjects: LCSH: Vietnam War, 1961–1975—Literature and the war. | Vietnam War, 1961–1975—Moral and ethical aspects. | American poetry—20th century—History and criticism. | Veterans' writings, American—History and criticism. | War poetry, American—History and criticism.
Classification: LCC PS310.V54 G55 2017 | DDC 811/.5409358—dc23
LC record available at https://lccn.loc.gov/2017038237

British Library Cataloguing-in-Publication Data
A catalog record for this book is available from the British Library.

To Angela

Ethics grows out of the same root as world- and life-affirmation, for ethics, too, is nothing but reverence for life. That is what gives me the fundamental principle of morality, namely, that good consists in maintaining, promoting, and enhancing life, and that destroying, injuring, and limiting life are evil.

—ALBERT SCHWEITZER

Time may play tricks with human memory. Scholars and politicians, journalists and generals may argue, write and re-write "the facts." But when a poem is written, it becomes a singular entity with an inextinguishable and unalterable life of its own. It is a true reflection of the feelings and perceptions it records, and as such, it is as valuable a document as any history ever written.

—W. D. EHRHART

All this happened, more or less. The war parts, anyway, are pretty much true.

—KURT VONNEGUT

CONTENTS

ACKNOWLEDGMENTS

Historians dream of discovering a long-lost and unread diary written by some particularly insightful observer who lived through a crucial period of the past. I was lucky enough to find thousands of pages. In my case, though, the historical treasure was not a diary but poetry, an abundance of pieces penned by Americans who fought in the war in Vietnam. And the words were not hidden away in a dusty attic somewhere but published in books, journals, and edited collections. While such poetic production had not escaped the attention of literary scholars, it had been largely overlooked by historians. This was a significant oversight because in terms of both quantity and quality, this poetry is an incredibly valuable historical source, a rich repository of the distilled reflections of a group of Americans who participated in one of the most important and controversial events of the twentieth century. My aim in this book is to rectify this gap in the historical record—to examine the American soldier-poetry of the war in Vietnam and, in doing so, to deepen our knowledge of both the conflict and the poetry itself.

In addition to being a remarkable but hitherto neglected archive of historical experience, the poetry written by Americans who served in Vietnam is a vital source of moral insight into the war. A passionate and intelligent engagement with the war's ethical dimension is at the heart of the soldier-poetry. In this book I draw on concepts from moral philosophy to investigate the key ethical issues of the conflict that arise in the poetry, including the impact of the surrounding environment on

American combatants, the complex relationships between these soldiers and the Vietnamese people, the process of injuring and killing in the warzone, and the assessment of responsibility for the harms caused by the war. My goal here is to expand our understanding of this core aspect of the poetry and, at the same time, to explicitly address moral matters that often remain implicit and unexplored in historical accounts of the conflict. By looking at the soldier-poetry through the lens of moral philosophy, then, this book presents a "moral history" of the American war in Vietnam from the perspective of those who fought.

This book would simply not exist without the soldier-poetry, and so my first thanks go to all the writers and veterans discussed here who, through their poems, bear unflinching witness to the American war in Vietnam. I hope I have been able to shed some light on their extraordinary and very necessary body of work. The immense volume and variety of the soldier-poetry has allowed me to quote from almost four hundred poems by over sixty poets in this book, and I would like to express my appreciation to all the poets and publishers who granted me permission to use these poems here (a full list is provided in Appendix B). Jan Barry, Michael Casey, Horace Coleman, David Connolly, W. D. Ehrhart, Yusef Komunyakaa, Gerald McCarthy, and Bruce Weigl were willing to be interviewed for this study, and many have since helped considerably by patiently answering my queries about their writings and the war. I would like to thank these poets in particular for their generosity of time and spirit.

With regard to locating the poems used in this book, I owe a significant debt of gratitude to John Baky and the Connelly Library at La Salle University in Philadelphia, where the Imaginative Representations of the Vietnam War Collection is held. It was in this wonderful collection, the best of its kind in the world, that I found most of the poems I needed for this study. John, the director of the library and curator of the collection while I was there, generously shared his knowledge and experiences with me—a veteran himself, he also agreed to be interviewed for this project—and his help enabled me to make the most of my time working with the collection. Moreover, he was welcoming, friendly, and interested, and he has been a reliable source of assistance ever since. Also at the library, Sarah Seraphin ably aided me in tracking down material and references.

The early stages of this book were completed at the University of Cambridge. The confidence placed in me and in the project by my doctoral supervisor, Tony Badger, was invaluable, as was his sagacious advice and guidance. My doctoral examiners, Andrew Preston and Simon Hall, provided thoughtful and insightful feedback that helped to shape and improve the study. While at Cambridge I greatly enjoyed discussions with and benefited from the support of a number of people: James Cameron, Phil Dow, Jon Earle, Kristal Enter, John Heavens, Sam James, Stephen Mawdsley, Olivia Sohns, Danica Summerlin, Tom Tunstall Allcock, and Brittany Wellner. My time at Cambridge was made possible by funding from the Arts and Humanities Research Council.

The latter stages of this book were completed at the University of Sussex, where I was a Leverhulme Early Career Fellow. I was fortunate to have a trio of excellent bosses in Daniel Kane, Claire Langhamer, and Clive Webb and a fine collection of colleagues in both the Department of History and the Centre for American Studies. Long talks with Tom Adam Davies and long walks with Eric Schneider were among the highlights of my stay at Sussex, and their enthusiastic engagement with my work and tireless encouragement significantly aided in the push to finish the book. My postdoctoral mentor at Sussex, Robert Cook, not only offered constructive comments on an early draft of the book but also taught and supervised my MA at the University of Sheffield and, moreover, fostered my interest in American history when I was an undergraduate there. In his own scholarship and in his support of others, Robert epitomizes the best aspects of academia.

The University of Massachusetts Press was supportive of this book from the outset. Christian G. Appy helped to bring the project to the press. My editor, Matt Becker, skillfully shepherded the study from proposal to publication, diligently answered my innumerable questions, and carefully guided me through the considerable task of securing permissions for the poems—I could not have asked for a better editor for my first book. Carol Betsch and Sally Nichols patiently and proficiently managed the process of preparing the manuscript for publication. Sally also did a wonderful job in designing the cover. The copy editing was completed with the expert assistance and grammatical genius of Annette Wenda. Two anonymous reviewers offered astute comments that aided in the polishing of the manuscript.

While working on this book I was lucky to be surrounded by people who provided me with much-appreciated help, dialogue, and distraction: Kate Anderson, Doug Bridges, Pete Brugger, James Burgess, Mark Crosthwaite, Hilda and Signe Ekström, Claudia Gary, Abby Hone, Sarah Lloyd, Jean-Jacques Malo, Lauren Marchisotto, Lucinda Morcom, Emily Oliver, Andrew Povey, David Rozwadozki, Keith Short, Lee Smith, Emily and Steve Webster, and David West. Much of this study was actually written in Sweden, and I am thankful to my Swedish in-laws—Anette, Bengt, Bibbi, Emil, Malin, Niklas, and Turid—for being so welcoming, hospitable, and generous.

I am extremely grateful to my family, whose care and love nurtured and sustained me during the writing of this book. My brother, Paul, was continually encouraging and affirming. My dad, perplexed that someone could read and write about history, poetry, and philosophy for years and call it "work," was nonetheless unwavering in his willingness and ability to aid and assist when it was most needed. My mum, too, was unfaltering in her support and has always been a wonderfully reassuring presence. A lover of history and literature, she also asked numerous valuable and constructive questions about the study as it developed. Finally, two members of my family were especially close to me throughout this endeavor. My wife, Anna, bore the burden of this lengthy project like no other. There is no way I could have written this book without her kindness, patience, and, above all, her grace. My sister, Angela, who died a few years before I started on the route to becoming a writer and historian, was with me in memory every day. Her bravery and her smile, in the face of adversity, remain a perpetual well of inspiration for me. I dedicate this book to her.

A SHADOW ON OUR HEARTS

INTRODUCTION

In 1967, W. D. Ehrhart went to Vietnam as a United States Marine. In 1985, he went back—this time as a poet. He carried with him hundreds of copies, translated into Vietnamese, of a poem he had written called "Making the Children Behave":

> Do they think of me now
> in those strange Asian villages
> where nothing ever seemed
> quite human
> but myself
> and my few grim friends
> moving through them
> hunched
> in lines?
>
> When they tell stories to their children
> of the evil
> that awaits misbehavior,
> is it me they conjure?[1]

Ehrhart handed out the poem everywhere he went, he recalls, "because I wanted the Vietnamese to see me, I wanted to let them know I'm sorry, I'm sorry for what I did, I'm sorry for what my country did, we shouldn't have been doing this."[2] For Ehrhart, and the many other

American soldier-poets of the war, the conflict in Vietnam was more than just a military defeat for America—it was a moral failure, "a shadow on our hearts."[3]

This book explores the intricacies of that ethical error through the experiences and reflections of American soldiers who fought in the war. In particular, it focuses on a group of former soldiers who returned from Vietnam with a desire and determination to tell the story of their war through poetry. As witnesses, victims, and perpetrators, these soldiers-turned-poets offer an experientially informed, aesthetically rich, and incredibly interesting perspective on the American military intervention. Their exceptionally vast poetic production examines a wide variety of issues relating to the war, including important matters such as trauma, myth, and memory. Perhaps the most powerful and intriguing aspect of the poetry, however, and one that intersects with many other significant subjects, is its engagement with morality. Both implicitly and explicitly, the poets trace the complex and often contentious contours of the war's moral landscape. The account they provide is penetrating, perceptive, and frequently condemnatory of American involvement in Vietnam. The war, many of the poets suggest, was deeply immoral, "as rotten / as the rotting corpses of the dead / peasants lying in the green rice / they would never harvest."[4] In delineating and explicating this poetic position, the following study has two core aims. The first is to gain a better awareness and comprehension of the poetry by looking at it through a historical and a moral lens. The second is to utilize the poetry to achieve a greater understanding of the history and morality of the American war in Vietnam. Thus, this study is concerned with both learning about and learning from the poetry. And, as Ehrhart writes, "these poets are able teachers."[5]

By interweaving history, moral philosophy, and literature, this book investigates pathways of understanding that have been neglected or omitted in each respective approach. Historical accounts of the war are ingrained with the textures of right and wrong, good and bad, just and unjust. The discourse abounds with claims of America's sinfulness and counterclaims of its rectitude, though the use of such strong moral designations is usually avoided. However, these positions are often propounded and accepted as axiomatic assumptions rather than a complex collection of moral beliefs, values, ideas, interpretations, and observations that merit explicit scrutiny and careful contemplation. Additionally, historians, perhaps deterred by the perceived difficulties, uncertainties, and subjectivities of employing a source material such as poetry, have rarely looked to verse for anything other than decorative epigraphs. Moral philosophers have, especially in recent years, contributed considerably to understandings of some of the central ethical issues of war, but in their analyses they still often overlook the illuminative usefulness of historical examples and the elucidatory value of cultural representations. Moreover, many frequently fail to contemplate war from the inside, from the perspective of its participants, and thus neglect the actual moral experience of war, of how, for example, soldiers—and, later, veterans—feel and think about being agents of violence, witnesses of violence, and victims of violence. Certainly, literary studies have given some attention to poetry produced by American veterans of the war in Vietnam, but, possibly out of a reasonable desire to avoid a crass instrumentalization of literature, the literary world can sometimes seem reluctant to draw historical lessons and moral messages from, or apply them to, works of literature. This book addresses these oversights and gaps in history, moral philosophy, and literary studies by using their respective insights to inform each other and by tracing new linkages between them.

With its radical disposition, distilled thought, and imagination rooted in experience, the soldier-poetry presents the perfect opportunity for this synthesis and analysis. Moral concerns are an absolutely vital part of this poetic body. "Ethical questions are unavoidable if you are a thoughtful person and you're engaged in trying to kill people," Ehrhart states, "so if I'm going to write about war in the form of poetry I'm inevitably going to have to deal with ethical questions."[6] Indeed, for Ehrhart, the moral issues of war are deeply intertwined with his poetry: "If you read any of my work, you don't have to read much of it before you discover that war and ethics and poetry are all wrapped up in it together."[7] The same applies to many of the soldier-poets. And it is the voluminous poetry written and published by these American soldiers who served in Vietnam that forms the central source base for this investigation. It is important here to stress the immensity of the poetic production—no other event in the American past has elicited as much poetry as the war in Vietnam.[8] As Ehrhart noted in 1985, "the American experience in Indochina, whatever else it may have been responsible for, produced an outpouring of poetry unparalleled in American literature."[9] Since then, the outpouring has continued largely unabated. Hence, this study is based on a consultation and consideration of thousands upon thousands of poems, published from the 1960s all the way through to the present day. This colossal poetic corpus is a remarkably rich, rewarding, and still relatively untapped historical record of the experiences of ordinary soldiers who, through their writings and reflections, became extraordinary veterans. Additionally, this study utilizes unpublished pieces, archival material, and in-person interviews I conducted with several prominent poets.[10] Taken together, these materials provide significant possibilities for furthering our understanding of the war from the perspective of those who fought.

This introduction outlines the investigative domain of this study, what has been written about the soldier-poetry previously, the relationship between morality and history, the central concepts of rebellion and witness, and the publication history of the poetry. Thereafter, the main body of the book is divided into four thematic chapters that examine the core moral issues with which the poets engage: climates, others, violence, and responsibility. Each chapter begins with a brief philosophical discussion that outlines the ideas most relevant to the poetic reflections on each particular topic. Filtered through my own understanding of the issues, these sections present a synthesis of a variety of pertinent thoughts and theories and introduce readers unfamiliar with moral philosophy to a number of key concepts. The bulk of each chapter then utilizes these ideas to analyze the poetic perspectives on each ethical theme.

The first chapter explores the poetic portrayals of the climates that shaped American soldiers before, during, and immediately after their time in the warzone of Vietnam. The opening section of the chapter looks at the link between morality and climates, defined here as the settings in which we act out our lives, the situations and circumstances in which we find ourselves, and the physical environments and psychological contexts that envelop us. Following this philosophical discussion, the chapter examines the poets' depictions of their childhood and military training, their uneasy relationship with the natural environments of Vietnam, their struggles with the pervasive atmospheres of fear and doubt as they fought, and, finally, their experience of returning to an America that no longer felt like home. This account of the tour of American soldiers in Vietnam establishes a foundation upon which discussions in the subsequent three chapters are built and demonstrates how the poetry offers important insights into the connections between morality and the soldiers' physical and psychological surroundings.

The second chapter investigates the poets' representations of the complex relationships between American soldiers and the Vietnamese people they fought alongside, against, and amongst. The preparatory philosophical discussion outlines how divisive us-them moralities underpin war and reflects on the importance of empathy and imagination in overcoming these divides. Subsequently, the explication of the poetry delineates the us-them moral barrier that separated American soldiers from Vietnamese people in the warzone and explores the racial tensions within the American military. The chapter then details the poetic portrayals of the south Vietnamese military and the Vietnamese revolutionaries and considers how soldiers' perceptions of and interactions with their allies and enemies further compounded the difficult climatic conditions highlighted in the first chapter. The chapter also looks at how the poets address one of the central military and moral issues of the war for American soldiers—the blurred distinction between friend and foe. Last, the chapter examines how the poets, through their poetry and the formation of close personal bonds with the country and people of Vietnam, dismantle the American-Vietnamese us-them barrier. The soldier-poets' depictions of the relationships and encounters between American soldiers and their south Vietnamese military allies, their revolutionary opponents, and Vietnamese civilians reveal many significant moral observations and form a vital part of the poetic record.

The third chapter focuses on the violence of the conflict, which is a core moral concern for the American soldier-poets of the war in Vietnam. The first section presents a philosophical analysis of injuring and killing in war. Thereafter, the chapter explores the poetic depictions of the devastating impact of the war's violence on the human body and examines the poets' insights into killing in war and their repudiation of this ultimate violent act. The poetic representations of atrocities perpetrated during the war are then considered, which the poets imply were an extension, or maybe even an inherent part, of combat in Vietnam. The final section looks at how the poets picture the role of technological violence in the war, particularly their views on killing at a distance and America's use of napalm and Agent Orange. Through their portrayals of bodily destruction, killing, atrocities, and technological violence, the poets bear unflinching witness to their war and offer a powerful moral rejection of the conflict's process of injuring and killing. These first three chapters, then, provide an intimate insight into the American combat experience in Vietnam.

The final chapter offers a broader overview of the conflict by examining the poets' assessments and indictments of those responsible for and complicit in the harms caused by the war. The opening philosophical section articulates a demanding existentialist ethic of responsibility and also explains a commonly held but potentially problematic moral understanding known as the "acts and omissions doctrine." The analysis of the poetry focuses on each of the key groups and factors identified by the poets in their remarkably extensive and uncompromising account of moral responsibility for the American war in Vietnam. The poets consider and condemn a broad range of culprits, including politicians, military leaders, businesses, and the American people. Significantly, the poets do not exonerate themselves or their fellow soldiers. Instead, they offer a radical understanding of soldier responsibility that is particularly interesting and insightful when viewed in the light of recent developments in moral philosophy. The chapter ends by looking at how the poets map similar pathways of responsibility in their reactions to the wars America has fought since the end of the conflict in Vietnam. Each chapter in the book builds on ideas and analyses from the previous chapters, and as the study progresses the issues addressed become more explicitly moral, culminating in the discussion of culpability in the final chapter. Together, the four chapters present, through the lens of morality, the experiences, reflections, stories, observations, and opinions of the American soldier-poets of the war in Vietnam.

Another key aim of this book, then, is to offer an alternative soldier history of the war. It differs from other accounts in two significant ways: the poetic source base and the moral focus. With regard to the former, this study offers an argument by demonstration. The poetry has such value as a historical source, I propose, that it is possible to write a work like Christian G. Appy's *Working-Class War: American Combat*

Soldiers and Vietnam or Kyle Longley's *Grunts: The American Combat Soldier in Vietnam* using the poetry as the main source material.[11] This book is one such work. Beyond that argument, this study offers not so much a central thesis but rather an entangled set of "ethical quandaries."[12] "Moral history," George Cotkin writes, "is valuable precisely because it troubles issues." It can "help create productive confusion, a willingness to recognize that behind all of our moral choices—not to mention choices made in the past—lurks paradox, tragedy, and irony."[13] In agreement with Cotkin, this study seeks to problematize the issues under investigation, to produce complexity and ambiguity rather than simplicity and certainty. As Cotkin suggests, "a little moral muddiness" can prove invaluable.[14] It is also necessary and, perhaps, unavoidable when attempting to understand the American war in Vietnam—an event that offers many difficult questions and few clear answers.

As suggested above, this book approaches these quandaries and questions by utilizing materials and methods that have often been overlooked. It is important here, then, to clearly define the territory explored in this study. The subtitle, "Soldier-Poetry, Morality, and the American War in Vietnam," gives a good indication of this book's fundamental perimeter points, but it is worth explaining each aspect in a little more detail.

First, the term "soldier-poetry" delineates the central selection criterion for this study. It is, however, potentially misleading, since it not only includes poetry written by soldiers but also poetry written by former soldiers. Indeed, although there are pieces in this study penned by people who were soldiers when they actually wrote a particular poem, the overwhelming majority of the poetic body is the work of veterans. To clarify, then, soldier-poetry in this study encompasses poetry written, during the war or more likely after it, by American soldiers who once served in Vietnam.

"Soldier" is used here to refer not only to those people with specific roles in the United States Army but also relevant members of the Marine Corps, Navy, and Air Force. Furthermore, in this study the definition of soldier is restricted by function and, crucially, moral status. Put simply, the focus here is on those members of the American military directly involved in, or very close to, enacting the violence of the war—those who were sent to kill and be killed. The most obvious candidates are combat soldiers, but other specialties are also included. Horace Coleman, for example, was an air traffic controller–intercept director, and he suggests that he "probably helped kill more people than the average guy on the ground."[15] I have also incorporated poetry written by certain medics and military combat correspondents as a result of their proximity to the war's violence and, given that they were often armed, their potential to be perpetrators of that violence as well. However, the focus on soldiers means that the poetic testimony of some Americans who served in Vietnam falls outside the parameters of this study. For example, nurses were not armed and were not "legitimate" targets and, therefore, had a different moral status and experience from soldiers, which places them beyond the domain of this book.[16] Similarly, other poets who are also veterans but who were not soldiers, such as John Balaban, a conscientious objector who volunteered for alternative service in Vietnam, or Bryan Alec Floyd, a chaplain's assistant, are largely absent from my account. This restriction of selection is not absolute—the boundaries are blurred and not always adhered to—but neither is it arbitrary. Its purpose is to center the attention of this study on a group of people whose participation in, and perpetration of, the violence of the war provides them with a particularly interesting and potentially insightful vantage point from which to view the conflict's moral issues.

The experience of being an American soldier during the war in Vietnam, then, is the input criterion; the production of poetry based upon that experience is the output criterion. It is not necessary, and maybe not possible, to define poetry—other than to say circularly that poetry is a specific form of literary expression recognized as such—but it is helpful to expand a little on the sources used in this study. The most frequently considered pieces are those poems that explicitly discuss the war. Poems that implicitly address the war, as well as those that examine and illuminate other relevant and connected issues, are also utilized. Moreover, in the course of constructing this study I have looked at the entire range of each poet's work, including their poetic and non-poetic, war and non-war, related writings. It should be noted that the subjects of this study do not only write "war poems"; they are not exclusively "war poets." Ehrhart, for instance, suggests that "if you go through the poems in my body of published work you will find that fewer than a third deal with war in any way shape or form, let alone the Vietnam War." Yet, he also admits that "all of my writing is politics, *is* the war. Because for better or worse that is the filter through which I now judge the world."[17] That "filter" of wartime experience is a crucial factor in this study. Some of the poems might be understood as works of "fiction." Yet, since each poet in this study went through the experience of being a soldier, their reflections on war, however imaginative or "fictional" they may be, are nonetheless anchored in an experiential actuality of war. As Kalí Tal explains, "*all* of Ehrhart's poetry"—and all of the soldier-poetry in this study—"has passed through the fire of the war." This is a literature "defined by the experience of the poet rather than the nominal subject of the poem."[18] In terms of historical veracity, then, what matters, for this study at least, is that the poets have an authentic experiential base upon which they build their poems about the war and not whether a particular poem portrays a concrete happening. It is this firm anchoring in experiential input that enables the utilization of the poetry as a historical source in this study.[19]

The reason for privileging the historical veracity of input over output is because this book is more interested in the thoughts, emotions, reflections, opinions, and ideas of those who have been to war than in their accounts of specific historical events, although sometimes, of course, that is also a consideration. Ehrhart remarks: "Time may play tricks with human memory. Scholars and politicians, journalists and generals may argue, write and re-write 'the facts.' But when a poem is written, it becomes a singular entity with an inextinguishable and unalterable life of its own. It is a true reflection of the feelings and perceptions it records, and as such, it is as valuable a document as any history ever written."[20] It is these "feelings and perceptions" that this study focuses on. Again, Ehrhart precisely summarizes the significance of the poetry: "The events of the war can be found in any number of chronologies . . . But if one wants to know the essence of the Vietnam War, how it felt and smelled and tasted, what it did to those who fought it and why it will not go away, I believe one is likely to find more truth in these poems than in any history ever written."[21] These poems reach for a different kind of "truth." On the back cover of his poetry collection *Aftershock,* Jim Nye presents a position that applies to many of the poets and their writings: "Some of these things happened, some did not. But that does not matter, because all are true. This is my attempt to realize and communicate that truth."[22]

It should be emphasized that, with regard to approaching and analyzing the main source material, this book primarily presents a historical and moral reading of the poetry. There are, of course, other ways of reading the poetry, including most obviously those that prioritize fundamentally literary concerns. However, since this is a historical rather than a literary monograph, it does not focus on issues such as literary form except in those cases where these issues impact significantly on historical and moral meaning. As discussed below, there have already been some insightful literary examinations of the poetry, so the purpose of this study is to offer a new reading that pays particular attention to the historical and moral dimensions of American soldier-poetry of the war in Vietnam.

Given the vast number of poems and the variety of poets from which to choose, a brief note on the issues of selection, narrative cohesion, and philosophical consistency is necessary. The principal considerations for selection are relevancy, insight, and interest with regard to the particular topic under scrutiny. I have also chosen poems that are representative examples of broader trends within the poetry as a whole. Of course, thought has been given to the aesthetic texture of the pieces as well. Additionally, although several poets receive much more attention than others, an attempt has been made to display and discuss a wide number of poets. However, this presents a challenge for cohesion. Every poet is different; they have different poetic styles and approaches, and they each fought a different war as they were in Vietnam at different times, in different locations, in different services, and in different roles.[23] Stitching together their experiences and reflections to form one cohesive narrative risks the possibility of losing their individual stories and voices and imposing a false unity on a set of individuals. Yet, there are enough similarities, commonalities, and connections between these individuals and their works for the collective phrases "the poets" and "the poetry" to be employed with authenticity and accuracy. Crucially, for this study, they nearly all share a strong moral stance against the war. They may differ slightly on the extent to which the war was wrong and why, but the overwhelming majority agree that their war in Vietnam was immoral.[24] Finally, it must be stressed that although the poets offer profound insights into the moral issues of war, they are not moral philosophers. Their works do not aim for the same sort of consistency, exactness, or rigor for which moral philosophers strive. Although I interweave poetry with the thoughts of moral philosophers and draw connections between the two realms, what emerges is a range of moral ideas, observations, and interpretations, not a complete or necessarily even harmonious system of ethics.

This brings us to the second piece of the perimeter: "morality." This study focuses on issues that involve right and wrong, good and bad, just and unjust, praise and blame, and how these distinctions interact with our beliefs and behaviors. Despite these dichotomized terms, it is vital to emphasize that questions of morality are rarely unambiguous, especially when they are connected to something as complex, contentious, and significant as war. As the philosopher Simon Blackburn suggests, a moral landscape that appears to be "black and white may be an illusion. It may be the result of a moral lens that imposes its black and white on a landscape of different shades of grey."[25] We might feel that certain values are fundamental to morality, as Ehrhart says: "I do believe, have always believed, that there are things that are inherently right and wrong." Nonetheless, there is a difficulty in application, he continues, "because those who think they have a corner on morality tend to start making judgments about other persons, and that gets tricky."[26] Moreover, the process of discernment itself can be problematic. "Funny," Ehrhart writes in one poem, "how the good seems nebulous as fog."[27] Still, as discussed in greater detail in the next section, if we are considerate and compassionate in application and careful in discernment, then a historical exploration of the contours of moral landscapes, however gray and foggy they may be, can offer revealing insights into the American war in Vietnam.

With regard to the third and final perimeter point, "the American war in Vietnam," I use this particular designation for several reasons. As the historian Mark Atwood Lawrence observes, "the fighting that took place in Vietnam between 1961 and 1975 has many names." For most Americans it remains simply "the Vietnam War," or even just "Vietnam." Other labels include "the Second Indochina War" and the revolutionary appellations of "the War of Liberation" and "the Anti-U.S. War of National Salvation."[28] Yet, "the American war in Vietnam" is perhaps the most apposite descriptor of the military events that unfolded in Vietnam during the 1960s and early 1970s. Furthermore, this name serves to emphasize two of the limitations of this study. First, it highlights that this is a story about the American aspects of the war. This in no way means that the Vietnamese aspects of the war are unimportant, but simply that this is a work of American history centered on the experiences and reflections of a group of American soldiers who fought in the conflict. Second, it indicates chronological borders. This study examines poems produced over a range of almost half a century, but mainly insofar as they elucidate what happened in Vietnam, and in America, from the early 1960s until the early 1970s. Although the poets certainly portray significant issues arising in the aftermath of the war, such as the development of a veteran identity or the legacy and memory of the conflict, in order to ensure depth and focus this book mainly examines matters most closely connected to what might be called "the war years."[29]

This book is the first work to use this particular set of parameters. Additionally, this is the first historical monograph to look primarily at the soldier-poetry. Indeed, the poetry is largely absent in the writings of historians about the war. In a handful of the overarching narrative works, some poets and poems are mentioned briefly.[30] In cultural approaches, the poetry is somewhat more present. Yet, even in works such as *The Wars We Took to Vietnam: Cultural Conflict and Storytelling* by Milton J. Bates, attention given to films in particular, and also novels, far outweighs that allocated to the poetry.[31] Thus, in historical accounts in general, there is a scarcity of interest in the poetry that does little justice to either its quantity or its quality and, in doing so, fails to make use of this tremendously rich and potentially revealing repository of soldierly experiences and reflections.

It is really only once we enter the territory of literary studies that an adequate level of attention is given to the poetry. Surveys of the war's American literature, by scholars such as Philip D. Beidler, Philip K. Jason, and Donald Ringnalda, offer glimpses of the poetry rarely available in historical works.[32] In *American Literature and the Experience of Vietnam,* a seminal early study, Beidler argues that the task of those writing about the war, including the poets, is to create "a landscape of consciousness where it might be possible to accommodate experience remembered within a new kind of imaginative cartography endowing it with large configurings of value and signification."[33]

Occasionally, literary studies that examine war literature more broadly, or issues closely connected to war such as trauma, also discuss American soldier-poetry of the war in Vietnam. Here, there are three books particularly worth mentioning that devote considerable space to scrutinizing the poetry. In her perspicacious work *Worlds of Hurt: Reading the Literatures of Trauma*, Kalí Tal dedicates a significant and insightful chapter to understanding the writings of Ehrhart through "the theory of a literature of trauma." "The profound dislocation of combat, the confusion of perpetrator and victim, power and powerlessness," she suggests, "create in the survivors of war a duality of perception characteristic of trauma survivors."[34] Michael Bibby, in *Hearts and Minds: Bodies, Poetry, and Resistance in the Vietnam Era*, also allots a substantial chapter to the poetry. His study analyzes the conception and depiction of the body in "Black Liberation Poetry," "Women's Liberation Poetry," and "GI Resistance Poetry," and his examination of "images of mutilation" in the key anthology *Winning Hearts and Minds: War Poems by Vietnam Veterans* is especially noteworthy.[35] Similarly, Lorrie Goldensohn devotes a large chapter to the poetry in her book *Dismantling Glory: Twentieth-Century Soldier Poetry*, in which she presents an excellent overview of this extraordinary poetic body and locates it within the context of other soldier-poetry from that bloody century.[36]

Additionally, there are three literary monographs that focus exclusively on poetry from the war. James F. Mersmann's *Out of the Vietnam Vortex: A Study of Poets and Poetry against the War*, published in 1974 before Saigon had even fallen, explores the "stateside" protest poetry of Allen Ginsberg, Denise Levertov, Robert Bly, and Robert Duncan.[37] It is certainly an interesting investigation of these four authors and their poetic protests against the war, but given its purely stateside concern, its relevance for this particular study is somewhat minimal. Twenty years after Mersmann's work, the only book to concentrate solely on American veteran poetry was published. In *Radical Visions: Poetry by Vietnam Veterans*, Vince Gotera explores the poetry through the framework of myths, such as the "Wild West," the "city on the hill," "regeneration through violence," and "the warrior against war." Written in the aftermath of the Gulf War, Gotera's call for Americans to "note and heed the warnings contained in poetry of the Vietnam war, particularly through the witness of Vietnam veterans," reads today like a foreboding prophecy in the light of America's recent wars in Afghanistan and Iraq.[38] As Ehrhart notes, *Radical Visions* is a "landmark study," although as a result of timing it misses out on the substantial expansion in poetic output that occurred, alongside the emergence of several important poets, in the middle of the 1990s.[39] Subarno Chattarji's *Memories of a Lost War: American Poetic Responses to the Vietnam War,* published just after the turn of the millennium, has the advantage of including this significant wave of poetic production in its analysis. In an impressively wide-ranging and penetrating investigation, Chattarji looks at stateside poetry, veteran poetry, and also Vietnamese poetry. Few summaries of the poetry are as perceptive and precise as the words that end his last chapter on veteran poetry: "the best of veteran poetry is a testament to past horror and future possibility, a hope for purer words and clearer visions."[40] The works of Gotera and Chattarji, along with those of Tal, Bibby, and Goldensohn, as well as other literary studies, contribute considerably to understandings of the poetry written by American soldiers who fought in Vietnam.

These literary examinations, from Beidler's broad survey of the literature of the war through Chattarji's focus on its poetry, go some way to redressing the poetic absence in the historical record. Yet, they are fundamentally literary, not historical, studies. Furthermore, these works do not focus primarily on morality. Certainly, they sometimes raise and address moral concerns but rarely explicitly or with the analytical aid of moral philosophical tools. Thus, while this study is linked and indebted to these previous explorations, it is also in many ways a significant departure from that which has gone before. As a work of moral history, it pushes into new territory by discussing and confronting moral issues directly and by drawing on connections with and insights from moral philosophy.

Morality and History

Historians often strive to avoid making moral assessments. If they ever opine openly in this regard, it is normally at the beginning or the end and rarely in the main body of a study. Indeed, to indulge in overt moral judgments outside of introductory or concluding remarks is to risk accusations of partiality and polemicism, such is the professional orthodoxy in history writing against explicit moral assessments. It is, of course, important to avoid excessive and unfounded moral judgments of the past. Yet, moral neutrality is an absolute impossibility. Values, beliefs, and assumptions flow through every movement of the historian, from the moment they begin to search for a domain of investigation through all of their reading, research, evidential selections, and, finally, their writings. Moral judgments might not be made openly, or even consciously, but conceptions of right and wrong, good and bad, just and unjust, are present on every page. Certainly, many historians are aware of this. Thus, attempts are made to reduce the unwanted interference of moral bias by abstaining from loaded language, at least aiming at impartiality and fair-mindedness, considering a variety of perspectives, and, in some cases, openly declaring moral assumptions and tendencies. Alongside these laudable efforts, however, there is another way in which historians refrain from making moral assessments of the past: the avoidance of openly discussing and directly confronting complex and contentious moral issues. Their focus is frequently elsewhere, away from the entanglements of ethics. The result is that many important issues are neglected or circumvented; the moral content of parts of the past are left unexplored and unexplained. For some areas of historical inquiry, where moral questions are not so deeply embedded, this is not necessarily such a problem. But in other areas, where historical investigations are inextricably intertwined with moral considerations, this could be a cause for concern. Here, one particularly important example in American history is, of course, the war in Vietnam.

Issues of morality thread throughout historical understandings of the conflict. In 2006, the historian Edward Miller stated: "The past quarter century has seen a great many developments in scholarship on the Vietnam War, but an overall decline in the propensity of historians to make moral judgments about the conflict is not among them."[41] I agree, but with one reservation: the underlying ethical intricacies and specificities of these moral judgments have rarely been expounded directly. Values, beliefs, and assumptions are simply stated—again, primarily in introductions and conclusions—not explicated. Moral positions inform the start and end points of studies but are themselves seldom the focus of deeper investigations. For example, on the opening page of *Choosing War: The Lost Chance for Peace and the Escalation of War in Vietnam*, Fredrik Logevall writes: "That the American decision for war was the wrong decision is today taken as axiomatic by a large majority of both lay observers and scholars, myself included, who see the U.S. intervention as, at best, a failure and a mistake, at worst a crime." After quoting Robert S. McNamara's famous admission that "we were wrong, terribly wrong," Logevall then asks: "So why did the war happen? Might it have been averted? If so, how?"[42] His moral assumption of the war's wrongness declared, Logevall moves swiftly on, free now to focus on these questions. Certainly, they are important questions not necessarily lacking in moral content, Logevall's consideration of them in *Choosing War* is commendable, and he is not aiming at a moral history of the war. Nonetheless, it is a pattern repeated in much historical work on the war: admit a belief in the wrongness or the nobleness of the war and with that out of the way proceed with the rest of the study. The beliefs themselves are discussed and explicated far less often. For example, was the war wrong because of the way it was conducted, or was the underlying intention the main moral failure? Was a confluence of these factors responsible for a particularly disastrous war? Or was it, as Ronald Reagan famously declared, "a noble cause," a just war undertaken with proper authority for right and proportionate reasons with a reasonable chance of success and as a last resort?[43] These are among the most crucial questions of the war, but relative to their significance they have not received the overt attention they deserve. Not all historians can or should focus directly on moral considerations, but a greater awareness and explication of underlying moral assumptions could prove valuable in aiding our understanding of the history and historiography of the war.

Still, there have been some historical attempts to openly and explicitly explore the moral content of the conflict.[44] In recent years, two historians in particular, Kendrick Oliver and George Cotkin, have argued for and demonstrated the efficacy of moral historical approaches to the war. "Intellectual developments since the mid-1960s have served to assist the efforts of those responsible for American policy in the Vietnam war subsequently to empty the history of that conflict of ethical critique," Oliver suggests in his 2004 article "Towards a New Moral History of the Vietnam War?" Against this, he "argues for the necessity of ethically informed historical enquiry and, with respect to Vietnam, proposes that there now exists the best opportunity for a generation for scholars to construct a fresh and credible moral history of the war."[45] Two years later, Oliver published *The My Lai Massacre in American History and Memory*.[46] It is a work sensitive and open to moral considerations, and Oliver's examination of atrocity and culpability demonstrates the effectiveness and force of an "ethically informed historical enquiry" when applied to the American war in Vietnam.[47] The poetry, brimful of moral passion and insight, presents an exciting opportunity to conduct such an investigation from the vantage point of a group of articulate and reflective American soldiers.

The possibilities of moral history are also embraced and espoused by Cotkin, whose article "History's Moral Turn" details the recent opening up of the historical to the ethical. It is a perceptive piece that discusses the complexities and difficulties, but also the potentialities and successes, of moral history: "Historians can, and are at present beginning, to benefit from acquaintance with how philosophers employ and problematize various concepts—intentionality, virtue, character, moral luck, action, and Just War. Moral history, as I conceive it, is valuable precisely because it troubles issues. The moral turn is less about imposing our moral and political judgments on historical events and figures. It looks at historical agents and events to warn us that human motivation is complex and confusing, open and constrained. Morality becomes a process of thinking rather than a pre-digested set of answers."[48] As Cotkin notes, historians are "treading upon a landscape full of moral topics," and moral history offers interesting possibilities for new understandings of well-worn territory.[49] Indeed, Cotkin's book *Morality's Muddy Waters: Ethical Quandaries in Modern America* is an excellent example of how moral history can bring a fresh and enlightening perspective to familiar issues in the American past, including the bombing of civilian targets during the Second World War, the My Lai massacre, racism in the Jim Crow South, capital punishment, and the invasion of Iraq. "By studying historical events, armed with moral concepts and concerns," Cotkin states, "narratives emerge that help us to see how actors in the past have chosen or avoided moral issues, how they have taken the path of evil or refused it."[50] As the historiography of the American war in Vietnam continues to unfold in various different ways—through local or transnational investigations, for example—morally informed historical approaches present a particularly compelling and potentially informative avenue of exploration.[51] This book is a step in that direction, along the beginnings of a track beaten by Oliver and Cotkin.

A key work of moral history, and a significant inspiration and beacon for this study, is Jonathan Glover's *Humanity: A Moral History of the Twentieth Century.* Like this study, Glover's book brings morality and history together: "It uses ethics to pose questions to history and it uses history to give a picture of the parts of human potentiality which are relevant to ethics." As Glover notes, the twentieth century's "history of large-scale cruelty and killing is only too familiar: the mutual slaughter of the First World War, the terror-famine of the Ukraine, the Gulag, Auschwitz, Dresden, the Burma Railway, Hiroshima, Vietnam, the Chinese Cultural Revolution, Cambodia, Rwanda, the collapse of Yugoslavia." *Humanity* offers a compelling moral historical investigation of many of these moments. It is revealing that "Vietnam" is among this list of horrors, and a whole chapter is dedicated to the My Lai massacre.[52] Additionally, in a discussion of Paul Celan and Martin Heidegger, Glover states: "Poets have responded more impressively to the dark events of recent times than—with a few exceptions—have philosophers." In *Humanity,* Glover argues, and demonstrates, that "in understanding the history, philosophical questions about ethics cannot be ignored." Interestingly, he also suggests that inadequate "answers to these questions have contributed to a climate in which some of the disasters were made possible."[53]

Glover's analysis is grounded in his conception of the "moral resources," an important idea threaded throughout this study. The moral resources are "certain human needs and psychological tendencies which work against narrowly selfish behaviour." They include what Glover calls "moral identity" and the "human responses" of respect and sympathy. He pictures moral identity as our "conception of what we are like, and of the kind of person we want to be," the "way we care about being one sort of person rather than another," the "ways we respond to things that happen and to things people do." The two human responses he identifies operate as crucial moral values and restraints: "One is the tendency to respond to people with certain kinds of *respect.* This may be bound up with ideas about their dignity or about their having a certain status, either as members of our community or just as fellow human beings. The other human response is *sympathy:* caring about the miseries and the happiness of others, and perhaps feeling a degree of identification with them."[54] Glover's notions of moral identity and the human responses of respect and sympathy are central to his account, and they provide a simple but firm foundation upon which moral historical analysis can be built, without the need for metaphysical or religious justifications.[55] Unsurprisingly, much of *Humanity* makes for grim reading. Yet, Glover stresses that "the message is not one of simple pessimism. We need to look hard and clearly at some monsters inside us. But this is part of the project of caging and taming them."[56]

In addition to Glover's conceptual framework, this book's moral historical analysis draws on ideas and arguments from the theory at the heart of the moral philosophy of war—just war thinking.[57] There are two "pillars" of just war thinking: *jus ad bellum* (justice of war) and *jus in bello* (justice in war). The former covers the morality of going to war and "is designed to answer the 'when' or 'whether' question: When, if ever, is resort to lethal force justified? The components within this pillar consist of several moral criteria, the satisfaction of which justifies recourse to war." The *ad bellum* criteria include just cause, proportionate cause, right intention, proper authority, reasonable chance of success, and last resort. *Jus in bello* is concerned with moral conduct within war and "is designed to answer the 'how' or 'methods' question: What methods are morally acceptable once recourse to war has been justified? Here the idea is that the justification for entering war does not extend to all methods in war: the ends do not justify the means."[58] There are two key *in bello* criteria: discrimination between the "innocent" and those "involved in harming" or "helping to harm" and the proportionate use of force.[59] Alongside *jus ad bellum* and *jus in bello,* there is also, although it is discussed far less frequently, *jus post bellum* (justice after war), which includes considerations such as punishment, compensation, and rehabilitation.[60] Just war thinking has flaws and inadequacies—and the poets' depiction of the American war in Vietnam reveals some of them—but it is nonetheless a helpful starting point for many discussions about the morality of war.

Just war thinking is certainly not the only moral approach to war but, partly as a result of its assimilation into modern international law, it "has become the dominant discourse on the ethics of war."[61] Michael Walzer's 1977 account of just war thinking, *Just and Unjust Wars: A Moral Argument with Historical Illustrations,* remains a towering work on the moral philosophical landscape.[62] Yet, in the past decade, there has been a significant surge in interest in just war thinking, with the orthodox approach coming under increasing scrutiny and attack.[63] Crucially, core assumptions, such as the moral equality of soldiers or the separation between *jus ad bellum* and *jus in bello,* have been questioned by philosophers like Jeff McMahan and David Rodin.[64] Their revisionist arguments are particularly relevant to this study, especially with regard to the discrimination requirement and soldier responsibility, explored in chapters 2 and 4, respectively. These interesting new developments in moral philosophy have the potential to change the way we think about and understand war—not just present wars and future wars but, if historians are sensitive to such shifts, also past wars.

Finally, it is important to outline how my own morality impacts this book. Moral accounts are often divided into two parts, description and prescription, based on the divergence of what is—or, in moral history, what was—and what ought to be. Thus, descriptive accounts detail what we actually do and believe, while prescriptive accounts suggest what we ought to do and believe. This study is both descriptive and prescriptive, in that it examines and unfolds the descriptions and prescriptions of the poets with regard to the American war in Vietnam in particular and war in general. Several interconnected points need to be noted about my own entanglements in the descriptions and prescriptions in this book. To begin with, the distinct separation between description and prescription is, in any case, a false one. It is not possible to describe without, however implicitly, prescribing as well. Our perceptions and language are filtered through values to such an extent that a neutral description is something of a fallacy. Hence, even in the descriptions of the poets' descriptions, my own morality plays a role—so, too, in the descriptions of the poets' prescriptions. In the latter, my aim is primarily to present the prescriptions of the poets and to limit my own prescriptions. Yet, undoubtedly, the voices sometimes merge. My own values thread throughout this book; I cannot help but project them onto the poetry. Nonetheless, this is not as problematic as it might appear. The formation of my moral position on war has been influenced by my research into the poetry and the poets. At the same time as I was reflecting on the moral philosophical issues of war, I was investigating the poetry, and there was a symbiosis of influence between these two explorations. The understandings and readings of the poetry presented in this study, then, might well be unavoidably filtered through my own moral position on war, but that moral position is, to a certain extent, a product of the poetry itself. Although I have attempted to maintain a critical distance throughout, it would be unwise and dishonest not to admit the impact of the poetry on my own morality, and vice versa. Historians are influenced by what they research. Moreover, when it comes to an issue such as war, there might even be a moral imperative for the historian, at some point, to take a stance. "No one should write bloodlessly / of spilled blood," the soldier-poet Steve Mason insists.[65]

My moral position on war, which, to stress again, has been partly influenced by the poetry itself, could be defined as strict contingent pacifism. In other words, I tend strongly toward the pacifistic, but I cannot reject the possible necessity of violence, or even war, in some extreme circumstances. This stance stems from a "reverence for life," which, as the physician and philosopher Albert Schweitzer suggests, "gives me the fundamental principle of morality, namely, that good consists in maintaining, promoting, and enhancing life, and that destroying, injuring, and limiting life are evil."[66] It is this belief—closely connected to the idea of *ahimsa* (nonharm)—which leads me to agree with the following declaration by Ernest Hemingway: "An aggressive war is the great crime against everything good in the world. A defensive war, which must necessarily turn to aggressive at the earliest moment, is the necessary great counter-crime. But never think that war, no matter how necessary, nor how justified, is not a crime. Ask the infantry and ask the dead."[67] More broadly, I believe that morality is, and should be, difficult. As the philosopher Simon Critchley indicates, morality is "infinitely demanding." I agree with his assessment that "we can never hope to fulfil the radicality of the ethical demand. But far from failure being a reason for dejection or disaffection, I think it should be viewed as the condition for courage in ethical action."[68] Another important and influential moral underpinning in this study is existentialism; Schweitzer's will to life is combined with Viktor E. Frankl's will to meaning.[69] In particular, the work of Albert Camus plays a significant supporting role in this book. His conception of the rebel and rebellion runs through much of the following analysis and, as the next section details, precisely captures a core moral component of the poetic witness to the war.

Rebels and Witnesses

Albert Camus opens *The Rebel,* his extraordinary historical, literary, and philosophical investigation into the nature of rebellion, with the following question and answer: "*What is a rebel? A man who says no: but whose refusal does not imply a renunciation. He is also a man who says yes as soon as he begins to think for himself.*" This is the definition of rebellion that will be utilized throughout this study. But what does this twofold choice, this act of negation and affirmation, signify? According to Camus, the refusal of the rebel "means, for instance, that 'this has been going on too long', 'so far but no farther', 'you are going too far', or again 'There are certain limits beyond which you shall not go.' In other words, his 'no' affirms the existence of a borderline." Moreover, since that refusal is accompanied by a confirmation, "a negative supported by an affirmative," rebellion "says yes and no simultaneously. It is the rejection of one part of existence in the name of another part which it exalts."[70] Rebellion, then, is a simple concept that enables us to identify a profound process, a particular type of awakening and awareness that begins and continues in both negation and affirmation.

Significantly for this study, the act of rebellion can be understood as a moral choice and, in some circumstances, an artistic choice. It is a moral choice because, as Camus argues, "Rebellion cannot exist without the feeling that somewhere, in some way, you are justified," and so the rebel "implicitly brings into play a standard of values." Hence, Camus continues, "Not every value leads to rebellion, but every rebellion tacitly invokes a value." Furthermore, Camus emphasizes that through the act of rebellion, "Knowledge is born and conscience awakened," and, therefore, the movement that initiates and sustains rebellion is both an epistemological and a moral one.[71] From a Camusian perspective, this moral movement, an "awakening of conscience," is absolutely central to our ethical advancement: "Rebellion indefatigably confronts evil, from which it can derive a new impetus. Man can master, in himself, everything that should be mastered. He should rectify in creation everything that can be rectified." For certain people, those whom Camus identifies as "artists," the moral content of rebellion may find expression in artistic form. Here, also, there is a tension between the negative and the positive aspects of rebellion, between negation and affirmation, since in order to "create beauty" the artist "must simultaneously reject reality and exalt certain of its aspects. Art disputes reality, but does not hide from it."[72] Crucially, for Camus, reality is to the artist material for an art.[73] Indeed, with regard to literature, he argues, "Real literary creation . . . uses reality and only reality with all its warmth and its blood, its passion and its outcries. It simply adds something which transfigures reality." Artistic creation and rebellion are thus interlinked: "In art, rebellion is consummated and perpetuated in the act of real creation." Moreover, a literature that "uses reality" as its source material, such as the poetry in this study, is particularly important because, to return to the idea of knowledge and awakening, rebellion "relies on reality to assist it in its perpetual struggle for truth."[74] Thus, rebellion is a choice that, for the artist, represents both a moral stance and an artistic commitment.

The soldier-poets at the center of this book have taken that stance and made that commitment and are very much rebels in the Camusian sense. What does their rebellion entail? The primary "no" of these rebel-poets is a no to war—all else follows from that. This is the very basis of an ethic superior to war.[75] It is a no to war and a no to that which causes, sustains, and perpetuates war. It is a no to war and a no to the consequences, devastation, and death of war. It is a no to war and a no to the glorification, celebration, and sanitization of war. It is also a refusal to accept that the lives of sons should be traded for the lives of fathers, poor for rich, powerless for powerful, them for us. Essentially, it is a rejection of violence and all that is associated with that violence. Indeed, for Camus, nonviolence is a vital aspect of the rebel's choice, for the "positive value contained in the initial movement of rebellion" supposes the rejection of "violence committed on principle."[76] Note that this does not require, to use traditional demarcations, an absolute pacifism but does insist that violence and war should not be pursued for or justified by ideological reasons, that they should not be "committed on principle."[77] The poets' rebellion, too, is not necessarily fastened to an absolute pacifism but rather anchored in a refusal to legitimize violence and war. As the above quotation from Hemingway suggests, war can never be a positive action; at best it is only ever a negative that counteracts a greater negative. A lesser evil is still an evil. Consequently, war might, in some extreme circumstances, be deemed necessary, but "Authentic acts of rebellion will only consent to take up arms for institutions which limit violence, not for those which codify it."[78] In his poem "Notes for Veteran's War Protest," Coleman succinctly expresses the negation of the poets' rebellion: "We did as told but we learned how to / say NO!"[79]

The affirmation of the poets' rebellion, their "yes," represents, above all, a cry for that which war itself negates: humanity. For Camus, the positive aspect of rebellion signifies a solidarity with humanity, since the rebel initially acts "in the name of certain values which are still indeterminate but which he feels are common to himself and to all men," and so he "demands respect for himself, but only in so far as he identifies himself with humanity in general." The yes of the rebel, therefore, "is the affirmation of a nature common to all men, which eludes the world of power . . . the affirmation of a limit, a dignity, and a beauty common to all men." Hence, the rebel realizes that "instead of killing and dying in order to produce the being that we are not, we have to live and let live in order to create what we are."[80] In addition to this vital recognition of our common humanity, the yes of the rebel-poet also signifies an important personal affirmation of his own individual humanity. It is a yes to the new sense of self that has arisen as a result of awakening, as a result of the rebellion itself. Thus, the yes of the poets' rebellion is an affirmation of humanity, both collective and individual.

In concrete terms, it is in and through the poetry that the negation and affirmation of this rebellion finds its fullest expression. It is in the writing of the poets that their no to war and their yes to humanity are combined and realized, given content and form, experiential reality transfigured into literary production, the flesh made word. The moral stance of the poets' rebellion is effected through their artistic commitment, which, in turn, reinforces their moral position. Morality and poetry are thus fused together in this symbiotic relationship. As Camus suggests: "When the most agonizing protest finds its most resolute form of expression, rebellion satisfies its real aspirations and derives, from this fidelity to itself, a creative strength . . . the greatest style in art is the expression of the most passionate rebellion."[81] Alongside the poetry, the negation and affirmation of the poets' rebellion has sometimes been actualized as political activism, particularly antiwar protest. Indeed, Vietnam Veterans Against the War was cofounded by Jan Barry, who contributed to and edited several key poetry collections, and many of the other poets were, and remain, members of this organization.[82] Like the poetry, this political engagement is intimately related to the moral position of the rebel. To summarize, then, rebellion is a specific type of awakening and choice that, for the poets in this study, signifies a negation of war, an affirmation of humanity, a moral stance, and an artistic commitment that all become realized and reified in and through the poetry itself.

That moral stance and artistic commitment, taken together, also form the basis of a type of poetic expression that can be understood as "poetry of witness." Like rebellion, this concept is central to the story of the poetry and is an important thread that runs throughout this book. Carolyn Forché, whose anthology *Against Forgetting: Twentieth-Century Poetry of Witness* offers an eloquent and extensive exploration of this idea, uses the term "poetry of witness" to describe the works of poets who have "endured conditions of historical and social extremity," works that stand "as poetic witness to the dark times in which they lived." They are testimonies to an "experience of extremity," such as political persecution, torture, or war, that a person has endured and chosen to bear witness to through poetry.[83] They are stories that need to be told and stories that need to be heard, stories that signify both an act of remembrance and a call of warning.

As the title of Forché's collection suggests, the struggle "against forgetting" is the central characteristic of poetry of witness. Such poems play a vital role in preventing the terrible events they describe from sinking into "the sea of forgetfulness." Moreover, if, as Carl Gustav Jung argues, our "*capacity to deal with evil*" is diminished by the attempt to "eschew evil and, if possible, neither touch nor mention it," by the "primitive tendency in us to shut our eyes to evil," by the failure of remembering, then the determination of poetry of witness to confront evil, to keep our eyes open to evil, to continue to look at evil even as it recedes into the past, represents a significant and valuable moral act.[84] The idea of warning, the sounding of a cautionary alarm to both the present and the future, is another essential feature of poetry of witness and one that has deep roots in war poetry. As Wilfred Owen wrote in 1918: "All a poet can do today is warn."[85] Furthermore, as Forché emphasizes in her discussion of Bertolt Brecht's poem "To Those Born Later," poetry of witness "writes to the future to remind it of the ease of moral disaster and ethical complacency."[86] Crucially, in the related acts of remembrance and warning, poetry of witness endeavors to speak to and affect us, the readers, in such a way that we, too, may remember and warn, surrogate witnesses who carry within us the seed of another's story. As one American veteran of the war in Vietnam writes: "the nice thing about the story is that now that you have heard it, what happened is part of you, too."[87] Works of witness, Forché insists, "will not permit us diseased complacency. They come to us with claims that have yet to be filled, as attempts to mark us as they have themselves been marked."[88]

The moral significance of poetry of witness has been alluded to above, but it is helpful here to elucidate two key aspects of this: the concept of "moral witness" and the active choice to bear witness. In *The Ethics of Memory*, Avishai Margalit suggests that "to become a moral witness one has to witness the combination of evil and the suffering it produces: witnessing only evil or only suffering is not enough." This must be a direct and unmediated experience of extremity: "A moral witness has knowledge-by-acquaintance of suffering." Additionally, although "observers who are not themselves the suffering victims of evil can serve as moral witnesses," Margalit stresses that the "paradigmatic case of a moral witness is one who experiences the suffering—one who is not just an observer but also a sufferer."[89] Thus, a moral witness often originates in a state of victimhood. However, the status of the witness as victim is complicated in this book by the concomitant position of the poets as perpetrators. The testimony of the poets, therefore, reveals not just their moral courage in the decision to bear witness but also their moral complicity in the events that they describe. Indeed, it is the intricately knotted tension of this victim-perpetrator-witness nexus that gives the poetry much of its vitality and insight. Finally, and essentially, a moral witness is "one whose testimonial mission has a moral purpose."[90] It is the moral content of the message that is the defining characteristic of moral witness, and, of course, it is this particular aspect of the poetry that is at the center of this study.

In addition to the moral content of the poetry, it is important to acknowledge the significance of the active choice that the poets have taken to bear witness to the war. All those who served in Vietnam were observers, witnesses in the narrowest sense, but not all made the decision to actually bear witness, to testify. By telling their story, by remembering, by warning, the poets have taken a stance, chosen not to remain silent, and, in doing so, engaged in a moral act. It is also an act of existential self-creation. The choice to accept the burden of responsibility that is attached to a testifying moral witness can be "viewed as a deliberate effort to make one's life a life of self-definition under the most adverse conditions," to take on "the mission of telling your story, of living with a sense of being a witness."[91] Furthermore, this choice, to bear witness and to live "with a sense of being a witness," may be an important step in confronting an experience of extremity and in constructing a trace of meaning from a traumatic event. Thus, in their poetry of witness, in their status as witness, and in their choice to bear witness, the poets express and demonstrate their moral character and artistic commitment.

There are several noteworthy commonalities and connections between this conceptualization of witness and Camus's understanding of rebellion. As suggested above, for the former soldiers examined in this study, it is through poetry—a poetry of witness—that rebellion finds its fullest expression. Hence, witness can be understood as a form of rebellion, a channel for its communication in concrete terms. Moreover, the reverse also applies, since rebellion can be understood as a form of witness. The new sense of self that arises as a result of the awakening of rebellion is evidence of the impact of the experience of extremity on that individual; the rebel stands as an embodiment of that experience, a living testimony who bears the marks of trauma for others to see. The link between rebellion and witness is also revealed in their parallel rejection of violence. As outlined previously, nonviolence is a vital aspect of Camus's rebellion. Likewise, Forché's poetry of witness represents a "resistance to terror" and a "protest against violence."[92] A further connection between the two concepts can be detected in the idea of warning. The negation of rebellion is similar in sentiment to the warning of witness, for the no to war is, in part, a cautionary call to both the present and the future. Additionally, both rebellion and witness negotiate a complex relationship with their own origin. As the poets separate and distance themselves from experiences of extremity, they are ceaselessly drawn back to these sites of trauma as they struggle to warn, to remember, to confront. Even in negation they must return to that which they negate. Thus, rebellion and witness are inescapably bound to the moment that begat them. As Forché emphasizes, "poetry of witness is itself born in dialectical opposition to the extremity that has made such witness necessary."[93] The same is true of rebellion. However, while this perpetual return to a painful origin is difficult and demanding, it is also a source of strength, a movement that sustains, renews, and empowers the twin acts of rebellion and witness.[94]

Ultimately, the primary shared significance of these two acts is that they both embody a fundamental quality that the poets possess and utilize—an ability to produce meaningful poetry from the wreckage of traumatic experiences of extremity. This is what Frankl describes as "the uniquely human potential at its best, which is to transform a personal tragedy into a triumph, to turn one's predicament into a human achievement." Rebellion and witness are thus part of "the human capacity to creatively turn life's negative aspects into something positive or constructive."[95] The poets have, as the veteran Lamont B. Steptoe suggests, "gathered the darkness / to reap the light."[96] Moreover, as actively taken choices, both rebellion and witness represent an important feat of existential self-creation for the poets. They could have chosen to stay silent, not to rebel, not to witness, but instead they have chosen to speak out, to stand up as rebels and witnesses. The positive and creative momentum of this choice is a testament to the poets and their moral courage. As Frankl states: "Man constantly makes his choice concerning the mass of present potentialities; which of these will be condemned to nonbeing and which will be actualized? Which choice will be made an actuality once and forever, an immortal 'footprint in the sands of time'? At any moment, man must decide, for better or for worse, what will be the monument of his existence."[97] For the poets, who made and continue to make the choice to testify, their writings are a significant monument of their existence, those acts of rebellion and witness set in verse upon the page.

Most of the poets examined in this book, therefore, can be viewed as both rebels and witnesses. Significantly, through their rebellion and witness, they fulfill the task of poetry as conceived by Theodor Adorno. In her exposition of poetry of witness, Forché discusses Adorno's perception of what poetic endeavor requires. It was Adorno who famously declared, "To write poetry after Auschwitz is barbaric," an opinion he partially retracted when he later added: "Perennial suffering has as much right to expression as a tortured man has to scream; hence it may have been wrong to say that after Auschwitz you could no longer write poems."[98] For Forché, a "better expression of his understanding of the task of poetry" is found in one of his meditative reflections in *Minima Moralia,* in which Adorno argues that "*there is no longer beauty or consolation except in the gaze falling on horror, withstanding it, and in unalleviated consciousness of negativity holding fast to the possibility of what is better.*"[99] This conceptualization of the task of poetry clearly mirrors both rebellion and witness. In particular, the first part, that unflinching contemplation of horror, is a precise parallel of witness, and the second part, that combination of negativity and possibility, corresponds closely to rebellion. Adorno's assessment also reflects Frankl's belief that positive potentialities can arise from tragedy. As will be seen at numerous points in this book, the ideas encapsulated in "Adorno's gaze" often map precisely onto the poetic production of American veterans of the war in Vietnam.

As rebels and witnesses, these poets combine a powerful moral purpose with a determined artistic commitment. They show little desire for detachment but rather a strong resolve to enter into an engaged relationship with the world through their poetry. "I can't abide / by words that simply decorate," the soldier-turned-poet Bruce Weigl writes.[100] Similarly, Ehrhart declares:

> I've been to the other side of the world,
> said what I've thought, hedged no bets, had
> no use for comfortable hypocrisies
> or delicate interpretations
> meant to keep the world the way it is.[101]

Bearing active witness is a core motive that spurs these veterans to write, anchored in a belief in the power of poetry and a deep sense of personal obligation to talk about their experiences and their war.[102]

"I think that poetry does play an important role and does fulfil an important responsibility in terms of being a witness to the world," Weigl states.[103] The "world had given me a subject—the American War in Vietnam," he explains, "and it was now my responsibility as a poet, like it or not, to make sense of things again."[104] As his fellow veteran and poet David Connolly insists: "I have an absolute duty . . . to speak, to scream."[105] To return to Camus: "the era of chairbound artists is over." Instead, the artist's "very vocation, in the face of oppression, is to open the prisons and to give a voice to the sorrows and joys of all."[106] This is a stance echoed by Denise Levertov in *The Poet in the World:* "One of the obligations of the writer, and perhaps especially of the poet, is to say or sing *all* that he or she can, to deal with as much of the world as becomes possible to him or her in language."[107] It is, she suggests, the poet's "obligation to be the spokesman for humanity."[108] The poets in this book, as rebels and as witnesses, contribute considerably to this essential undertaking.

Publishing Hearts and Minds

Before further exploring the moral significances of this poetic rebellion and witness, it is helpful here to outline the publication history of the soldier-poetry. The published poetic body is so incredibly vast that it would take an entirely separate book to tell its story in full. What follows, then, is an abridged version that focuses on the key trends, texts, and poets from what remains "an outpouring of poetry unparalleled in American literature."[109]

The crucial breakthrough moment for the poetry came in 1972. As America waged war in Vietnam, a monumental anthology of poems, *Winning Hearts and Minds: War Poems by Vietnam Veterans,* was published.[110] Hitherto, poems about the war had been written predominantly by stateside civilian American protest poets, such as Robert Bly, Allen Ginsberg, and Denise Levertov.[111] In contrast to this abundant body of literary dissent, there was relatively little poetic output by those Americans who had fought in the conflict. Just one anthology and three notable individually authored books of soldier-poetry were published prior to 1972. Released in 1968, *Boondock Bards* was a hyper-patriotic, prowar anthology of soldier-poetry published by the military newspaper *Pacific Stars and Stripes.*[112] As several sources have stated, the poems are "primarily doggerel."[113] The individual collections—Dick Shea's *vietnam simply;* Timothy Clover's *The Leaves of My Trees, Still Green;* and Earl E. Martin's *A Poet Goes to War*—are much more accomplished and penetrating.[114] Still, before 1972, there was only a limited amount of serious soldier-poetry and certainly no collective versified voice for veterans returning from the war.

This situation was dramatically altered by the publication of *Winning Hearts and Minds.* An outgrowth of the antiwar veterans' movement, the collection brought together a selection of poems gathered over four years by members of Vietnam Veterans Against the War. Many of the contributors were actively involved in the organization, as were the editors, Larry Rottmann, Jan Barry, and Basil T. Paquet. Initial attempts "to find a commercial publisher for their anthology met with no success," so the editors decided to establish their own independent publishing house, 1st Casualty Press.[115] Published on 1 April 1972, *Winning Hearts and Minds* was, as Bibby notes, "the first collection of dissident poems in U.S. history produced by soldiers during wartime."[116] Additionally, it introduced a number of noteworthy poets who would go on to contribute even more poems to the poetic body: Barry, Michael Casey, Frank A. Cross Jr., Ehrhart, and Rottmann. Despite limited resources and no commercial backing, the book sold well and received a warm response from the American press.[117] Perhaps the most significant moment of media attention came on 14 May 1972, with John Seelye's "favourable and influential" assessment of the anthology in the *New York Times Book Review.*[118] According to Barry, this "amazing review" helped to launch the anthology "into the 50,000 copies orbit," an extraordinary sales figure for a book of poetry in modern America.[119] Indeed, it was after this praise and positive press coverage that commercial publishers began to take notice, and in the summer of 1972 1st Casualty Press agreed to a contract for joint publication with McGraw-Hill, thus aiding and increasing distribution of the book to that impressive amount.[120] It soon became, as Ehrhart suggests, "a classic: the seminal anthology against which all future Vietnam war poetry would be judged."[121] The production of *Winning Hearts and Minds* was a vital moment in the history of the poetry, and the collection provided a firm foundation upon which the future poetry would build. Hooked into the spirit of

Vietnam Veterans Against the War, the publication of the anthology represented an important initial moment of collective poetic rebellion, a moral stance given form through artistic commitment.

The emergence of a poetic veterans' voice was reinforced by the publication of two other significant works of soldier-poetry in 1972: D. C. Berry's *saigon cemetery* and Michael Casey's *Obscenities.*[122] Both books offer a bleak and uncompromising poetic vision of American involvement in Vietnam. Casey's deeply cynical poems, in particular, hooked into the mood of a war-weary America, and on its release *Obscenities* became a hugely popular work of poetry. With sales exceeding even the fantastic figures of *Winning Hearts and Minds,* Casey's book became the biggest-selling work of American soldier-poetry from the war in Vietnam.[123] Such success generated even more attention, and the *New York Review of Books* printed a joint examination of the two works entitled "Poetry of the Unspeakable" on 8 February 1973, just days after the Paris Peace Accords formally ended America's military involvement in Vietnam.[124] The poetic voice of veterans may have portrayed the seemingly unspeakable, but their rebellion and witness were no longer unspoken or unheard—the poetry had now emerged.

After the end of the war, poetic production by American veterans continued apace. Barry, this time with Ehrhart, edited another significant poetry anthology, *Demilitarized Zones: Veterans after Vietnam.* Again, the editors set up their own independent press, and, timed to coincide with America's bicentennial celebrations, the collection was published on 4 July 1976. A fitting sequel to *Winning Hearts and Minds,* the book is dedicated to "those who refused to honor America's longest war."[125] Its list of contributors includes Barry, Cross, and Ehrhart from *Winning Hearts and Minds,* as well as many other notable poets beginning to emerge in the 1970s, such as Horace Coleman, Steve Hassett, Gerald McCarthy, Perry Oldham, Doug Rawlings, and Bruce Weigl. Although not as successful in terms of sales or attention as *Winning Hearts and Minds,* the 1976 anthology provided a vital collective outlet for the poetic voice of veterans and, like its predecessor volume, created a space in which new poetic talent could flower, the lotus beginning to "grow in places where the fire once burned."[126]

Additionally, several noteworthy individual soldier-poetry collections were published in the immediate aftermath of the conflict, including McAvoy Layne's *How Audie Murphy Died in Vietnam,* Oldham's *Vinh Long,* and McCarthy's *War Story: Vietnam War Poems.*[127] Also among the productions of individual poets in the 1970s were the first books published by two of the poetry's leading lights, Ehrhart and Weigl, whose efforts have been a continual source of strength in the poetry from those early years all the way through to the present day. In 1975, Ehrhart released *A Generation of Peace,* which remains "one of the clearest, most representative poetic representations of the Vietnam combat experience."[128] He published more poetry collections later in the 1970s, and by the end of the decade, as co-editor of a defining anthology and with a growing body of powerful poems, Ehrhart had emerged as one of the soldier-poetry's foremost figures.[129] After writing two chapbooks, Weigl's major breakthrough came in 1979 with the publication of his first book of poems, *A Romance.*[130] The poems in this work, in which the aesthetic is punctuated by the horrifying, embody Weigl's guiding philosophy: "Say it clearly and you make it beautiful, no matter what."[131] This is Weigl's own personal mode of rebellion and witness, an active realization of Adorno's "gaze falling on horror, withstanding it, and in unalleviated consciousness of negativity holding fast to the possibility of what is better."[132]

The 1970s, then, was a decade of beginnings and emergences for the poetry. During the 1980s, with the continued efforts of established poets augmented by the arrival of numerous new poets, the poetic body entered a period of expansion, diversification, and strengthening. Yet again, Barry and Ehrhart edited important anthologies. In 1981, Barry published *Peace Is Our Profession: Poems and Passages of War Protest.*[133] Four years later, Ehrhart produced *Carrying the Darkness: The Poetry of the Vietnam War,* which, as a single-volume collection of poems about the American war in Vietnam, remains unsurpassed. Within ten years of the fall of Saigon, a tremendous mass of poems had been written and published by American veterans of the war, and for this anthology Ehrhart selected just over two hundred remarkable pieces from a possible pool of "well over 5,000 poems."[134] The seventy-five contributors include all of the most important and influential poets to have emerged from the war up to that point.[135] In 1989, Ehrhart edited *Unaccustomed Mercy: Soldier-Poets of the Vietnam War,* a condensed and refined version of *Carrying the Darkness* that focused solely on the preeminent veteran poets, a "'best of' kind of thing."[136] Here, he selected just twelve writers, those who had thus far best represented "the terrible beauty that Vietnam engendered in sensitive hearts, the curious grace with which the human spirit can endow even the ugliest of realities."[137]

Throughout the 1980s, poets who had first emerged in the previous decade, including Ehrhart and Weigl, continued to contribute to the poetic body.[138] In 1988, Weigl's *Song of Napalm* was released. The work is a triumph of rebellion and witness, as Robert Stone suggests in his introduction to the collection: "Bruce Weigl's poetry is a refusal to forget. It is an angry assertion of the youth and life that was spent in Vietnam with such vast prodigality, as though youth and life were infinite. Through his honesty and toughmindedness, he undertakes the traditional duty of the poet: in the face of randomness and terror to subject things themselves to the power of art and thus bring them within the compass of moral comprehension."[139] In addition, a number of new poets emerged in the 1980s, with noteworthy debut collections of war poems published by Richard E. Baker, R. L. Barth, Bill Bauer, D. F. Brown, Jabiya Dragonsun, David Hall, J. Vincent Hansen, David Huddle, and Steve Mason.[140] Perhaps the most significant new versified veteran voice was that of Yusef Komunyakaa, whose work *Dien Cai Dau* stands alongside Weigl's *Song of Napalm* as one of the preeminent individual collections of poetry written about the war in Vietnam.[141] Poems from *Dien Cai Dau,* and other pieces on the conflict, appear in Komunyakaa's *Neon Vernacular,* which won the Pulitzer Prize for Poetry in 1994.[142] Throughout the 1980s, these poets proved that poetry written by former soldiers was more than just an angry reaction to the war and its immediate aftermath in the 1970s. As rebels and witnesses, they combined a determined moral stance with a passionate and engaged artistic commitment to continue to reflect on and attempt to understand the war in which they had fought.

During the 1990s, these poets, and a fresh wave of veteran writers, still had much to say about their war and also about the new wars that were being fought by America. Indeed, in the early 1990s, there was a considerable surge in poetic production. In addition to the stimulus of American military intervention in the Gulf, three key developments that originated in the 1980s and flourished in the 1990s aided this poetic climax. First, there were the return visits to Vietnam of several prominent poets that had commenced in the middle of the 1980s, such as Ehrhart's aforementioned 1985 trip, when he went as part of a poetic trio comprising himself, Balaban, and Weigl.[143] This contact with Vietnam and the Vietnamese offered the American soldier-poets new insights into the country they had fought in and the people they had fought alongside, against, and amongst and, quite simply, provided new material for the poets as well. Many of these cultural exchanges—Vietnamese veteran writers also came to America—were facilitated by the William Joiner Center for the Study of War and Social Consequences at the University of Massachusetts, Boston. This was the second factor in the poetic peak. The birth and development of the Joiner Center, especially its annual Writers' Workshops, helped to bring together veteran writers in a supportive environment, thus stimulating the poetic production of already established poets and encouraging new writers to produce and publish poetry. The third factor, the formation and expansion of Viet Nam Generation, Inc., aided in a similar way. Established by the aforementioned scholar Kalí Tal, this was an organization that arranged seminars and conferences, produced the journal *Viet Nam Generation,* and set up its own press—Burning Cities—to publish books by the poets. Both established and emerging poets, then, had another outlet for their works and another support network through which their poetic voices could develop and be heard. It was an exceptionally important organization in the history of the poetry.[144] Together, these three factors helped to create an atmosphere and an apparatus through which the poetry could thrive, and all three, in terms of both the poets involved and the sense of artistic and moral commitment they exhibited, were hooked into a spirit of rebellion and witness.

Out of this productive climate, a number of particularly noteworthy new poets emerged. Writers such as Doug Anderson, Kevin Bowen, David Connolly, and Dale Ritterbusch, alongside established poets, contributed to an exceptionally fruitful period for the poetry in the 1990s.[145] The level of poetic production peaked in the middle of the decade, but poets continued to write and publish works in the late 1990s. Although anthologies played less of a role in the 1990s, Philip Mahony's 1998 anthology, *From Both Sides Now: The Poetry of the Vietnam War and Its Aftermath,* is a worthy contribution to the poetic body, especially since it includes works from the early 1990s wave and presents Vietnamese poetic perspectives alongside American accounts.[146] In 1999, Ehrhart and Weigl, who were prolific throughout the 1990s, each published an individual compilation—*Beautiful Wreckage* and *Archeology of the Circle*, respectively—containing selections from their previous works.[147] It was fitting that two of the most prominent, prodigious, and powerful poets both published "best of" books at the end of the millennium. While Ehrhart and Weigl certainly differ in poetic approach, form, content, attitude, and many other aspects, they share certain core ambitions and resolutions: to render fragmented experience in fragmented sentences; to bear witness to the war, its aftermath, and its impact on their worlds and the worlds of others; and to continue to write in a spirit of passionate rebellion. Thus, Ehrhart's *Beautiful Wreckage* and Weigl's *Archeology of the Circle* offer an overview of the poetic production of two of the most significant literary and, it is suggested in this study, moral voices ever to speak about the American war in Vietnam.

While the level of poetic production in the new millennium's first decade did not match that of the 1990s, many of the poets continued to write and publish. Viet Nam Generation, Inc., had collapsed due to staffing and funding issues, but the Joiner Center remained, and return visits to Vietnam and cultural exchanges between the two countries still occurred. Furthermore, the events of 11 September 2001 and, in particular, the American military response in Afghanistan and Iraq provoked a vigorous reaction from several poets that demonstrated the enduring relevance, insight, and necessity of their work. Important poets who had first surfaced in the 1990s, such as Anderson, Bowen, Connolly, and Ritterbusch, produced new poetry in the 2000s, as did veteran poets who had appeared all those years before in the anthologies of the 1970s, including Barry, Casey, Coleman, Ehrhart, McCarthy, and Weigl.[148] And, in the first years of the 2010s, both Ehrhart and Weigl published impressive new collections.[149] One poem from Weigl's *The Abundance of Nothing*, which was nominated for the Pulitzer Prize for Poetry in 2013, precisely captures the continuing struggle and desire to bear forceful witness to a painful past that is the mark of all these rebellious poets:

I got my own personal Jacob's ladder,
buddy, reader, listener to this
sad song. I built a temple for the ghosts
because they just kept coming. When I try
to sing, I have a lark in my throat.
I like it when the words are little
daggers, flying through the air like frozen rain.[150]

Decades have passed since the publication of *Winning Hearts and Minds*. While the poets are now in many ways far removed from that first anthology, throughout this long period of prolific poetic production they have maintained a connection to those early years in their determination to write poetry that warns and remembers, that negates war and affirms humanity. This poetic body is an immense repository of insight into the war. It is a vast and valuable historical source that offers interesting opportunities to look at the American war in Vietnam from a soldier's perspective and from a moral perspective. As Ehrhart summarizes: "These poems are what happens when you take a boy and give him a rifle and send him halfway around the world to kill people he's never even met, and somehow he survived and comes back and spends a lot of time thinking about it, then picks up a pen and makes the pain come out of his heart onto the paper, and you have to read it."[151]

1
CLIMATES

In the opening lines of *vietnam simply,* the first individual collection of American soldier-poetry published about the war, Dick Shea writes:

> so for some unknown reason
> i volunteered
> and am suddenly 35 thousand feet over vietnam
> in a military iron bird
> it was all ocean a moment ago
> but now a sandy beach
> and a green land
> peacefully there beneath flowing white clouds
> welcomes me
> sarcastically
> the plane bumps in
> the runway is filled with holes
> and armed guards
> which dispel all the tranquility
> gathered at 35 thousand
> plane door opens
> blast of hot air hits me
> gangway rolls up[1]

These inaugural words in the poetic body indicate Shea's concerned fascination with his impending surroundings.[2] Depictions of this relationship between soldiers and their environment occupy an important position in the poetry, and they offer valuable insights into the connections between climates, morality, and the war. Although conditions varied according to the time period and locations in which soldiers served, their rank, and their role, enough commonality of experience emerges in the poetry to provide a broad overview of the central situational contexts that most American soldiers who fought in Vietnam confronted. This chapter examines how the soldier-poets portray these climates, as well as the environments they encountered before and immediately after their time in the warzone of Vietnam.

Thinking about Climates

Our surroundings play a key role in our morality. Who we are, what we believe, and how we behave are all influenced significantly by the climates we experience. The term "climates" here denotes the settings in which we act out our lives, the situations and circumstances in which we find ourselves, and the physical environments and psychological surroundings that envelop us. Beyond the obvious historical need for contextualization, there are several specific psychological and philosophical reasons for a close awareness and appreciation of these climatic conditions and the ways they can impact us. Crucially, unless we take into account situational contexts when considering moral behaviors, we are in danger of committing the "fundamental attribution error." Also known as "correspondence bias" or "overattribution," this is "the error of ignoring situational factors and overconfidently assuming that distinctive behaviour or patterns of behaviour are due to an agent's distinctive character traits."[3] This tendency "to inflate the importance of dispositions and neglect the importance of situations in explaining behaviour" is a phenomenon that is "certainly among the best documented in personality and social psychology."[4] Interestingly, it has been suggested that while we might make this mistake with regard to explaining the behavior of others, when it comes to explaining our own behavior we nonetheless emphasize the significance of climatic conditions "at the moment of action." There is an actor-observer asymmetry, "a pervasive tendency for actors to attribute their actions to situational requirements, whereas observers tend to attribute the same actions to stable personal dispositions."[5] Although this particular thesis has recently been challenged, it remains clear that a sensitivity to situational contexts is necessary if we are to deepen our moral understanding of actors and events and that both empathy and moral imagination must be employed in any exploration of the moral behavior of others.[6]

Furthermore, such an awareness of circumstance allows us to reconsider our conception of character. It is important to acknowledge that character is not only constrained by situational contexts but also, partly at least, a product of various situational contexts in the first place: "character is itself shaped by genetic and environmental factors beyond our control. Self-creation is at best only partial."[7] More radically, if we move away from the view that it is "character, more than circumstance, that decides the moral texture of a life," toward a position that recognizes that "situational factors are often better predictors of behavior than personal factors" and that "personality is less than robustly determinative of behavior," then, as the moral psychologist John Doris suggests, we might concede that "people typically lack character."[8] Put more bluntly still, as the philosopher Gilbert Harman argues, "it may even be the case that there is no such thing as character, no ordinary character traits of the sort people think there are, none of the usual moral virtues and vices."[9] If this is so, if the determining significance of circumstance so outweighs character, then not only should we pay much more attention to situational contexts, but we must also be willing to contemplate Aleksandr Solzhenitsyn's troubling claim that "it is after all only because of the way things worked out that they were the executioners and we weren't."[10]

Solzhenitsyn's statement also highlights another important climatic consideration, one that can often be overlooked: luck. According to the thinker Thomas Nagel, "it is intuitively plausible that people cannot be morally assessed for what is not their fault, or for what is due to factors beyond their control." Nonetheless, people are frequently judged in such situations. For Nagel, this constitutes the problem of moral luck: "Where a significant aspect of what someone does depends on factors beyond his control, yet we continue to treat him in that respect as an object of moral judgment, it can be called moral luck."[11] For example, one American veteran of the war describes a search-and-destroy mission in a Vietnamese village: "I heard movement in the rear of this hut. I just opened up the machine gun. You ain't wanna open the door, and then you get blown away . . . I killed an old man and a little girl in the hut by accident."[12] Suppose that the hut had been unoccupied or that the bullets had somehow missed the victims—would that alter our moral assessment of the story and the soldier? An awareness of the role of circumstance and chance, therefore, offers the possibility for a more considered, nuanced, and empathetic moral understanding.

A greater appreciation of situational contexts can also help us to identify and scrutinize other influential climatic conditions and their impact on morality, such as the constraints of time; the function of roles; obedience and conformity, which are exceptionally powerful climatic forces and can be viewed as vertical and horizontal pressure, respectively; the idea of moral base lines, which recognizes that moral identity "is often about being a 'good enough' person, in terms of a base line set by others"; and, more generally, the surrounding "climate of opinion," "the unspoken assumptions," and the "networks of rules or 'norms' that sustain our lives."[13] An attentiveness to climates offers insights into the complicated relationship between identity, beliefs, intentions, actions, and outcomes. For instance, climatic considerations, rather than, say, identity or intention, might explain a case where an individual's beliefs and actions diverge. Our surrounding environment affects many aspects of morality, from how we understand moral ideas and concepts themselves through the moral reasons that might compel or commit us to act to the form and content of moral action itself. Thus, a recognition of the significance of the situational context of morality is vital when examining moral issues, particularly ones that arise from a climate such as war.

War is perhaps the most extreme climate any person can endure, and for soldiers the climatic pressures are particularly intense. Not only must they make tremendously challenging life-and-death decisions on a regular basis, but they often do so in conditions of confusion and chaos while facing potential danger to their own lives. The complexities and difficulties of a warzone situation, Jonathan Glover suggests, can be exacerbated when a "sense of unreality blurs habitual guidelines" and the "moral landscape fades" into what W. H. Auden describes in "The Shield of Achilles" as "A plain without a feature."[14] A feeling of unfamiliarity and the absence of normal moral markers—such as the prohibition on killing—contribute to this impression of unreality, as does the distance from home, family, and friends: "Remoteness makes it natural to think all this is not really happening, I am not really doing this." Moreover, this "loss of moral landmarks can be reinforced by the physical landscape of a foreign battlefield."[15] The perceived strangeness or otherness of a soldier's physical surroundings can, therefore, further compound this climate of unreality and impact on morality. Of course, not every person or every extreme climate has this feeling of unreality, but in all extreme climates, by definition, the press of circumstance is especially severe. As such, a consideration of situational contexts is particularly important here, as is an awareness of the common psychological and moral reactions to such climates. Crucially, moral identity and the "human responses" of respect and sympathy for others can often be "overwhelmed, weakened, narrowed or eliminated."[16] In the extreme climate of violence that is war, the consequences of this can be disastrous. Hence, an acute sensitivity to situational contexts is essential in any exploration of war and morality.

Yet, as morally influential as climates are, especially in war, this should not lead to a complete disavowal of the moral significance of choice or, indeed, of character. Surely, even though it may be formed largely by circumstance in the first place, character does matter. In response to Solzhenitsyn's assertion, it must be noted that even in the most extreme climates, not all people choose to become executioners. "Qualities of character," Glover emphasizes, do make a difference: "In similar circumstances, different people [make] different decisions." He concludes: "There are two truths. One is that people with different characters respond very differently to moral crises. There is a difference between those who go along with murder and those who do not. The other truth is that differences of character are, for the most part, not just innate."[17] Furthermore, choice matters, and we always have the possibility of choice. Even when the weight of circumstance is such that it appears as though we are completely constrained, we are still left with the choice of how to face that fate. Viktor E. Frankl, writing from his experiences in the Nazi concentration camps, argues that "everything can be taken from a man but one thing: the last of the human freedoms—to choose one's attitude in any given set of circumstances, to choose one's own way." He insists: "Man is *not* fully conditioned and determined but rather determines himself whether he gives in to conditions or stands up to them. In other words, man is ultimately self-determining. Man does not simply exist but always decides what his existence will be, what he will become in the next moment." And this "residue of freedom, however limited it may be," is a fundamental aspect of not just our morality but also our humanity.[18] As Anthony Burgess suggests in *A Clockwork Orange*, "Goodness comes from within . . . Goodness is something chosen. When a man cannot choose he ceases to be a man."[19]

Making Soldiers

Perhaps the natural narrative starting point for an examination of the climates experienced by American soldiers who fought in the war in Vietnam would be enlistment and military training. Yet, in the poetry the predominant pre-warzone focus is not on military training but on the climates and events of childhood. Many poems depict instances of childhood violence, especially toward animals, and often suggest that these moments foreshadowed the violence to come. In "Military Training in the Very Young," for example, David Hall begins by describing how the curiosity of children can quickly turn to cruelty. He recalls how his childhood self discovered the enkindling potential of a magnifying glass and proceeded to set fire to newspapers, "then sticks / dry leaves / my own clean shirt." Soon enough, "each napping bagworm woke / to nightmares in a smouldering cocoon." Next, Hall moved on to matches and ants: "Ignited / they curled under pebbles / I flicked aside / indignantly." By autumn his weaponry had advanced still further: "No torches by then: / just my father's hammer. / Each corpse in its own round grave." The final lines make explicit the connection between these violent episodes and the war:

> Now
> in another country
> I watch them salvage straw
> from the blazing homes
> whose tenants lie
> scorched
> and crackling

in their yards.
Everywhere
craters gape
in tribute:
my summer of homework shows.[20]

These "scorched / and crackling" victims—identifiable as Vietnamese people only within the larger context of Hall's work, since neither their nationality nor, indeed, their humanness is explicitly stated in this poem—echo the "curled" ants, both burned by American fire, and the craters evoke those earlier round graves. For Hall, the preparatory nature of his "summer of homework" is clear: there is a direct link between the violence of his childhood and the violence of his war.

Often, the poets portray birds as the targets of this childhood violence. For example, in "A Circle of Red," Lamont B. Steptoe describes the "twisted energy" of "a moment of 1960" when he and his childhood friends found a "crippled pigeon" and stoned it "to giblet oblivion."[21] Tellingly, this piece opens *Mad Minute*, Steptoe's collection of war poems, thus establishing this act of boyhood brutality as the starting point in his story of the war. In "Bernard," J. Vincent Hansen writes from the perspective of a mother whose son playacted—practiced, perhaps—as a soldier and "duct-taped / her best paring knife / to the barrel / of his BB gun." The woman "watched / as he gleefully stabbed / the small red sparrow / again and again." At the end of the poem, the mother receives news of her son's death in the war and wonders about the role of that grim incident in his sad fate:

Years later,
when the taller soldier
handed her the telegram,
she tried to recall
when it was
he really died.[22]

At times, the protagonists of these poems, like those of William Golding's novel *Lord of the Flies*, do not seem like children at all, "but something darker, something crazed."[23]

Birds also occupy a noteworthy position in Bruce Weigl's poetry.[24] "Snowy Egret," published in *The Monkey Wars* and reprinted in *Song of Napalm,* is ostensibly not a war poem, but it is a meditation on guilt and violence as powerful and poignant as any piece that examines the war directly. In this work, Weigl describes how his "neighbor's boy has lifted his father's shotgun" and killed a snowy egret. Overcome by the irreversibility of violence and death, as well as fear of his father, the boy cries and shakes "with the weight of what he can't set right no matter what" and "burns with shame for what he's done," for killing "What he hadn't even known he loved, blasting / Such beauty into nothing."[25] Similarly, in "Debris," also from *The Monkey Wars,* Weigl recalls his own childhood shooting of a bird, along with "the physical difficulty and emotional trauma involved in killing it":

> When the gull fell, the air
> Dizzy with feathers went cold
> And the cold drove through my spine like a nail
> So I shot again, and twice more
> To stop the wings from flapping in the garbage.
> I didn't know how easily I could bring it down,
> How hard to finally kill it.[26]

In later poems, Weigl again depicts his younger self as a killer of birds. In "What I Saw and Did in the Alley," he stumbles across a cat killed by another child, "a homemade arrow / nicely through its skull." Weigl details how he studied the cat

> and reckoned our kinship
> of killing
> in that alley and beyond
> where needful of love, and of blood
> I had stunned the brown sparrow,
> the robin and wren,
> the wild canary in spring.

The last lines recall "Snowy Egret" and the nothingness of death: "Don't ask how they felt / in my hands, still warm, / bubble of blood on their beaks; / to nowhere their dead wings unfold."[27] Weigl examines such moments again in "The Happy Land," in which he writes about his "murder in mindless boyhood boredom" of

> so many righteous songbirds
>   that I will never know their forgiveness
> which I had imagined
>
> would feel like their tiny hearts felt
>   sputtering out in my hand because
> I had launched those jagged stones so precisely.[28]

This avian imagery is particularly interesting, since there are a number of works by the poets in which wings operate as a symbol of salvation. For example, in one of his most famous poems, "Song of Napalm," which appears directly after "Snowy Egret" in *The Monkey Wars,* Weigl tries to imagine that the girl with "napalm / Stuck to her dress like jelly" is saved when "wings / Beat inside her until she rises / Above the stinking jungle."[29] Likewise, in James Soular's "The Burning," which contemplates the events captured in that grimly iconic photograph of the burned and naked Vietnamese girl running in terror from "the greedy suck of flames," the girl—Kim Phuc, to whom the poem is dedicated—is pictured with her "arms / flapping as if to fly away."[30] In these poems, wings seem to offer a chance of redemption from the horror of the war. Perhaps the presence of bird killing in the poetry simply indicates that birds are common targets of childhood violence. Perhaps, in the context of the war to come, it also suggests that these children, who would go to that war, could be killing their own possibility of salvation.[31]

In these poetic explorations of childhood climates and events, there is an ominous foreshadowing of the war. Soular remembers the time he shot a deer while hunting, years before he would find himself "in the hunt of war." Looking at the corpse of the deer he killed, the twelve-year-old Soular "marvelled at how the eyes / stayed open, their brown softness, / not yet aware / that men's eyes stay open, too." He emphasizes this portentous connection to the war by explaining how, after his father wiped the blood of the deer across his cheek, "saying, 'Your first kill,'" he "stood there, blinking back tears, / this terrible knowledge an omen, / as overwhelming as the cloying / smell of blood."[32] The use of the phrase "first kill," which is also the title of the poem, further reinforces the idea that this was an inaugural moment in a sequence of violence that would be continued in the war. These poems suggest that some loss of innocence occurred well before the war. "You don't know at the time / just what it is that you're getting yourself into," Weigl writes, "just what doors / you may open, and then never come back."[33] As children, they lacked an awareness of the violence they perpetrated and the violence they would perpetrate, and be victims of, in the future. Looking back, the poets identify a link between the two: "the children don't know why they / are trained to hunt and kill / they will though when / they are 20."[34] As the literary scholar Edward J. Rielly explains, in such poems "the significance of a childhood event, and therefore the completion of it, does not occur until many years later."[35] In "Just for Laughs," W. D. Ehrhart considers "the firecrackers / stuffed down the throats of frogs and lit" and a childhood attack on a snake with sticks and stones, gashes ripping at its "fat thrashing sides until it / finally tired, though it couldn't / run and wouldn't die." "Years later, I volunteered for war," he reflects in the final lines, "still oblivious to what I'd done, / or what I was about to do, or why."[36]

For the poets, these moments, and the climates and characters of violence they came from and contributed to, were not only prophetic but also preparatory. The violent climate of childhood helped ready them for the violent climate of adulthood, including the ultimate violent climate—war. In these poems, Rielly suggests, disconcerting "questions lurk nearby: Could I have been prepared for this? Was I prepared, or somehow, destined for it? Is the future imbedded in the past?"[37] The poets note various childhood rituals related to violence: war games in which "children played with guns, / played at waging war"; fights between gangs that were "like a primer for going to Vietnam"; and sports, especially American football, "where the opponent is sort of dehumanized and you're taught, basically, to fall in love with hurting people."[38] Hence, Weigl suggests, there was "a connection between growing up that way, playing those games, that seemed to be very natural, and then participating in those sports, and then basic training, and then the war, that it seemed a very logical, very reasonable progression of hostility."[39] His shoes were "spit-shined" like those of a soldier, he writes in one poem, "the moment / I learned to tie the bow."[40] Childhood violence, therefore, was the first link in a chain that led these poets to war, and it was in these moments that their military training really began.

Another aspect of pre-warzone contexts explored in the poetry is the "climate of opinion" that surrounded and influenced the poets in their youth. They critique the pervasive Cold War fear of communism and those, particularly their parents and teachers, who believed in and promoted this ideological stance while doing little to examine either its flawed assumptions or terrible consequences. For example, Hall questions the teacher who "said God would never allow / the Communists domination over / a Christian people."[41] "Born in a mushroom cloud," he explains in another poem, "we grew up paranoid."[42] This was not the only shadow the Second World War cast on the upbringing of these nascent soldiers. The myth of the "Good War" significantly shaped their understanding of war during childhood and often played some role in their decision to join the military—or to comply with their draft notice—as well as burdening them with unrealistic expectations about war, which they carried with them into the warzone, homecoming, and beyond. Ehrhart grew up wanting "to be a World War Two fighter ace . . . a Wildcat pilot, / or maybe a ball turret gunner."[43] The allusion to Randall Jarrell's famous poem "The Death of the Ball Turret Gunner," in which the gunner is killed and has to be washed "out of the turret with a hose," highlights the naïveté of the young Ehrhart and how the more horrific aspects of the Second World War, evident in the poetry of Jarrell and many others, were excluded from the sanitized mythological memory of the Good War.[44] Additionally, even those who suspected that the war in Vietnam was a very different affair from the Second World War, that it "smelled bad," found it difficult to resist the pressure emanating from the echoes of the Good War, especially when relatives had participated in that conflict. "I shouldn't have gone; I shouldn't have enlisted," D. F. Brown says, but there "would have been no way to look at my six uncles and my aunt who were all veterans of World War II and say, 'You know, I don't care how the experience played out for you. This is another time.'"[45]

Patriotic duty was another common contributing climatic factor in the decision to join the fight against the supposed communist threat. This idea, instilled in the poets throughout their childhood, included not only the gentle patriotism of "a person / who loves the land" but also the angry patriotism of "a man / who hates another land," as well as the kind of patriotism that spurned reflective thinking in favor of mechanical obedience: "we pledged allegiance, / and never once questioned if it was due."[46] Related to this, the poets grew up in the climate of a culture that venerated ideals such as "Honor, democracy, an American way of life," later identified by one veteran as "words to fill school children's heads as they grew into citizenry to take their places within the confines of the . . . land as unthinking, unquestioning adults."[47] The significance of a childhood climate of unreflective obedience should not be underestimated, since, as Steve Mason suggests, soldiers, not just in America but the world over, go to war "because boy children are taught / to say, 'yes.' For no reason at all."[48] Here, Mason also hints at the significance of gender, and for many poets notions of masculinity played a role both in their decision to join the military and in those moments of childhood violence. Weigl, for instance, suggests that his own acts of violence toward animals stemmed from the boyhood desire "to possess a life not ours . . . our need for blood spilled simply for the sake / of what we thought it took to be a man."[49] These poems, therefore, corroborate the testimony of one participant in the Winter Soldier Investigation who claimed that "our colleges, our high schools, our everyday life is nothing but pre-basic training."[50] As Brown states, "this was the ethical dimension that we were existing in, that we were trying to make choices about."[51]

It should be noted that these factors, from the fear of communism to issues of gender, contributed to a climate of opinion that shaped not just these soldiers-to-be but the whole of American society. Of course, it was American society that produced this climate of opinion in the first place. It was American adults who told these children

> that War
> will bring
> them manhood, wisdom,
> courage, undying fame—
> if they're good
> and march off
> well-behaved.[52]

In a feedback-loop effect, American society was then influenced by its own climate of opinion. Hence, these climatic conditions not only provided the pre-warzone context for the lives of the poets but were part of the very fabric of the society that sent them to war, a war that was, in part at least, a result of these same climatic conditions. If, as Glover argues, "a climate of opinion can make a difference as to whether a disaster is avoided," and if, as the poets strongly suggest, the war in Vietnam was indeed a disaster, then it is possible to understand Philip D. Beidler's suggestion that the war "had been implicit in the American character"—and the American climate—"from the outset, a collective tragedy waiting to happen, a prophetic curse hiding at the heart of a whole mythology of culture."[53]

Although the primary pre-warzone focus of the poets is on the events and climates of their youth before entry into the military, some poets also examine their actual military training. They depict it as a dehumanizing process in which the military urge for conformity demanded an elimination of any differences between individuals. Even simple markers of personal identity, such as hair, were eradicated, succinctly described in McAvoy Layne's "On free haircuts":

> Have
> You
> Ever
> Heard
> Hair
> Hit
> The
> Floor?[54]

In Steptoe's "Before Going," which appears in *Mad Minute* immediately after his poem about the pigeon attack, medical procedures are pictured as a part of this violation of the self:

> before going
> to vietnam
> the united states government
> asked me

to bend over
spread my cheeks
and allow a white male
to insert his finger
up my asshole
only tight virgin rectums
were desired in 'Nam

The racial detail is significant, since it emphasizes that for Steptoe, a black man, the war felt like an abuse perpetrated upon him by white Americans. The use of "virgin" furthers this sense of defilement and hints at the innocence about to be lost. The second half of the poem highlights an even greater loss, that of identity itself:

later
other penetrations
would occur
they said
it was to protect us against disease
but I think
they stole bits of our souls
needle by needle[55]

The training process also aimed at thoroughly reinforcing the climatic norm of obedience. Military education, Peter P. Mahoney writes, "doesn't teach how to think, it teaches how to obey—blindly and unquestioningly."[56] Once the individual had been broken down, forced to conform, and taught to obey, the soldiers could be "transformed / Into a fighting unit" and the central objective of military training could be achieved: "I learn how to kill, maim and brutalize."[57] As the poets suggest, many trainees already had some experience of killing, maiming, and brutalizing through their childhood violence toward animals. Nonetheless, it was still necessary to overcome the constraint against killing other humans. "Combatants," Glover argues, "need to escape the inhibitions of human responses: of respect and sympathy for others. They need to escape the restraints of moral identity: of their sense of not being a person who would wound and kill." Thus, military training attempts to weaken these human responses and reconfigure moral identity. In order to produce "good soldiers," it "has to make people do things which they would not do in civilian life."[58] The significant and calamitous impact of training on morality is summarized by Mahoney in his reflections on William Calley, the only American soldier convicted for the killing of Vietnamese civilians in the My Lai massacre: "I cannot defend him for what he did, but I can understand the circumstances under which it happened. I never participated in any so-called atrocity while I was in Vietnam but that was only a coincidence of time and circumstance. I could have—I had been trained for it. The only guide that confused young men like Lieutenant Calley and me had in Vietnam was morality, and the Army had done its best to eliminate such a defective idea."[59] An awareness of the effects that such training could have, as well as the influence of climatic conditions during their formative years, not only offers insights into the lives of these soldiers before they went to Vietnam but also aids in our understanding of what happened once they finally crossed "through the door of lies / into the greenery's mist."[60]

The Nature of War

During their twelve-month tour—thirteen for Marines, less for the wounded and, of course, the dead—in Vietnam, American soldiers encountered, shaped, and were shaped by a number of different physical environments: military bases, cities, towns, villages, farmland, rice paddies, deltas, mountains, forests, and jungles. The poets examine all of these climates in their writings. For example, Saigon is the setting for many poems, a place often pictured as a moral wasteland, the "Sin City" where "a seemingly neverending war—a series of wars, really—and corruption had turned The Pearl of The Orient into a pig pen," Horace Coleman writes, a place where he "watched devastation and inflation destroy the efforts, savings and morality of a life time."[61] For Steptoe, the capital of south Vietnam was "a lost city / in a lost land . . . a city of orgasms / orgasms of love . . . of lust . . . of death's final grasp . . . of color . . . of noise . . . of troops / gone mad with shell shock."[62] More frequently, however, the poets focus on the "natural" climates of Vietnam, and, as such, this section concentrates on the poetic account of these situational conditions. Certainly, this is not a focal point unique to the poetry; it is a common theme in many representations of the war, particularly in novels and films. Yet, even if it is possible to find a similar emphasis elsewhere, since these natural surroundings occupy such a significant place in poetic considerations of the climates of Vietnam it is essential that they be investigated here, especially as these conditions were fundamental to the experience of so many American soldiers. For those who fought in Vietnam, it was, as Weigl often writes, "the green war."[63]

The otherness of the physical environment of Vietnam, in particular the greenness and the heat, was typically the first thing soldiers noticed upon their arrival "in country" and a key climatic factor recorded in the poetry from the outset. Indeed, in those very first lines of soldier-poetry mentioned above, Shea pictures "a green land" and describes how, as the "plane door opens," a "blast of hot air hits me."[64] This "heat that smacked you like a / battering ram when you stepped off the plane" was also one of Perry Oldham's first impressions, a "swarming / heat, actively oppressive, greasing // everybody with sweat, even at night."[65] David Huddle's "Entry" stresses the stifling temperature, too, as well as its almost dehumanizing impact: "In this heat, more plant than man, I'm breathing / slowly, registering these queer noises, / noticing all around me M-16s / slung like toys on the backs of the ones in green."[66] The "queer noises" underscore the strangeness of Huddle's new environment, and the guns "like toys" emphasize the youthful composition of the American military in Vietnam, as though the war was fought by soldiers who were still only boys. Indeed, the average age of American soldiers in Vietnam was just nineteen.[67] Additionally, the words "in green" suggest both the uniform and the landscape that these soldiers would now wear for a year. To return to Weigl, this was "the green place": "It's the most incredibly verdant green that you'll ever see in your life . . . when I first saw the landscape of Vietnam I couldn't believe how bright everything was, this green, so that's why I called it 'the green war.' And, of course, everything we wore was OD [olive drab] . . . and everything we ate out of was OD, and everything we had was OD, so there's that green too."[68] Thus, from the moment of arrival, Weigl continues, Vietnam "was a completely otherworldly place."[69]

Long after the suddenness of dislocation and the shock of first impressions had passed, the physical surroundings continued to contribute to a climate of strangeness and unreality for American soldiers. The color of the country remained a ubiquitous climatic factor. For example, in what Donald Ringnalda identifies as a "pastoral reversal," Jan Barry's "Green Hell, Green Death" repeats the word "green" almost thirty times in the space of one page, the color overwhelming the poem just as it overwhelmed the soldiers. The last line reads simply: "green jungle: green hellfire: green death."[70] In the warzone of Vietnam, Beidler argues, green was no longer "a color of promise, of expectation," but "a shade of despondency—the color of the jungle, of paddy water, of soaked fatigue uniforms, of crenellated monotonous rows of low hills, of a looming forbidden vine-shrouded mountain."[71] The weather, too, continued to provide a backdrop, and a cause, for the soldiers' sufferings—not only the fierce heat but also the relentless rain.[72] In "Thanksgiving," Steve Hassett offers a meticulous account of the grueling and disheartening effect this intense rain could have on the soldiers, as he describes a patrol lost in a three-day downpour:

> the rain drips from every leaf
> and vine, flows from the arms like
> hatred, turns legs to butter,
> augurs to the leeches, sheaths
> the feet in pyramids of mud

This is a rain, Hassett explains, that "drills imprecise circles in / our faces . . . Each drop severs minutes / from our lives and sets them free, / like grains of rice."[73] For many American soldiers, then, the natural surroundings of the warzone felt unnatural, as well as alienating and unwelcoming. Even the clouds, Stephen R. Hatch writes, "seem to say / we do not belong here."[74] For Weigl, "the stinking jungle" and "the tropical heat like hate" made for an exceptionally "disturbing" world:

> Where black clouds bowed down and swallowed you whole
> And overgrown tropical plants
> Rotted, effervescent in the muggy twilight and monkeys
> Screamed something
> That came to sound like words to each other
> Across the triple-canopy jungle you shared[75]

The difficulties of these climatic conditions were compounded by the difference and distance from America, as Hall summarizes: "How strange to come down / in mud / so far from home."[76] "I felt like I was on a foreign planet, this was so alien to anything I had known," Ehrhart recalls. "I think that was true of almost all of us. It smelled different, it looked different, it sounded different, and it was a scary place because you never belonged anywhere. You knew it was their turf not yours . . . It was foreign and dangerous, it was foreign and deadly."[77] Crucially, the otherness and extremity of the warzone helped to create a sense of unreality or, perhaps more accurately, a strange new reality detached from life, and morality, back in "the world"—a telling phrase that the soldiers used to refer to America. As Beidler suggests, in these literary representations of the landscape, "it is as if reality itself has vanished," and, subsequently, "The war becomes its own reality in a philosophical, a moral, and even a strangely aesthetic sense."[78] Eventually, some soldiers even came to think of this new unreal reality as more real than anything back in "the world." As Corporal Joker states in Gustav Hasford's *The Short-Timers:* "back in the world is the crazy part. This, all this world of shit, this is real."[79]

For American soldiers, and for the entire military endeavor, it seemed as though they were fighting against not just the elusive Vietnamese revolutionaries but also the Vietnamese landscape itself. As Hassett writes in his waterlogged poem, "the earth becomes our greatest enemy."[80] This was not the first American war in Asia in which this was the case. During the Second World War, aspects of fighting in the Pacific also unfolded as a battle against nature, and "Climate and terrain were as much adversaries as enemy forces" during the war in Korea as well.[81] Yet, if this was a lesson that policymakers and military commanders "should have learned" in the Pacific and Korea, it was one "they would have to relearn in Vietnam."[82] For ordinary soldiers, most of whom had never been to Asia before, let alone an Asian warzone, it was a hard lesson they would have to learn for the first time. Unsurprisingly, therefore, this struggle against nature has received significant attention in literary accounts of the war. For example, in almost every novel, Ringnalda notes, "the author underscores America's adversarial relationship with the jungle."[83] Many poems, particularly earlier works, also emphasize this aspect of the war. As Subarno Chattarji argues, in such poems, "Nature seems to conspire to defeat the American enterprise."[84] Weigl's phrase "the green war," then, can be understood to identify not only a key climatic condition the soldiers encountered but also an omnipresent enemy they battled against.

Leroy V. Quintana's poem "Natural History" presents a particularly interesting perspective on this war against nature. In the piece, Quintana associates and conflates the natural surroundings of Vietnam with the North Vietnamese Army and the Vietcong. "A company of NVAs crashing towards you / would be a troupe of baboons," he writes, and "A VC moving slowly in the elephant grass / happened to be a water buffalo." This bewilderment intensified during the nights: "It was said the NVAs carried flashlights. / One night frightening scores of them / turned out to be a swarm of fireflies." Similarly, "One night they overran the compound. / Loaded down with grenades, AK 47s / from North Viet Nam, mines strapped to their chests: / these were only the mosquitos." In one instance, the direction of disorientation is reversed: "The whir of birds' wings / turned out to be artillery rounds."[85] By connecting and confusing the animals and the revolutionaries of Vietnam, Quintana suggests, as many American soldiers felt, that the natural landscapes and the Vietnamese revolutionaries could not be disentangled, that the two were inseparable. Nature was the enemy, and the enemy was nature. Quintana's poem also hints at the perceived otherness of the opposing combatants. For American soldiers, their adversaries seemed strange and, for some, even appeared to be "mystical" warriors whose special connection with their natural surroundings endowed them with "magical" properties, as John F. Howe imagines in "The Land": "They can see in darkness . . . turn to smoke and float over mountains . . . swim for miles under water . . . They are haze in the morning, and distant rippling heat waves across a flat paddy in the afternoon. At night they are shadows that turn into bushes at first light . . . they can do these things because they are the land. It is a philosophy . . . They and the land are one and the same."[86]

Magical or not, the Vietnamese revolutionaries had the simple but exceptionally significant advantage of fighting in a familiar environment they knew and understood well. The Vietcong, in particular, "fought on their own land," a factor that would considerably aid any soldier, as David Connolly suggests: "if the Vietcong had come to South Boston I would've handed them their ass down every alley, just like they did to me going down every trail that I walked down." Additionally, "if an NVA unit moved into the area they had main force Vietcong who grew up there."[87] Given the relationship between the enemy and the enveloping climate, and that the "rotten jungle" was "full of / booby traps / snipers / mines / rockets / and other absurdities," it is unsurprising that many American soldiers, and the American military at large, "came to detest the color green, and defoliation became a primary tactic in the war."[88] Hence, the landscape of Vietnam, as well as the people, became a target and victim of American military tactics and violence—the soldiers' personal struggle against the climatic conditions echoed on an immense and intense military scale. Whether it was the Vietnamese revolutionaries or the Vietnamese landscape, it seemed like, as Quintana writes, the enemy was only ever "a little more than a whisper's reach away."[89]

Yet, if the natural climates of Vietnam were primarily a force sympathetic to, and perhaps sometimes synonymous with, the Vietnamese revolutionaries, they could occasionally appear sympathetic to the plight of American soldiers as well. Steptoe expresses the ambiguity of the relationship between these soldiers and the physical environment:

> In country
> sometimes as you hugged the earth
> to avoid the bullets and shrapnel
> overhead
> you could feel the earth holding back[90]

Numerous possibilities of meaning unfold in the "holding back" of the earth: an unsympathetic refusal to return the hug, a sympathetic reciprocation of the embrace, or an act of fear, as though the earth itself is scared, recoiling from the violent onslaught by holding itself back from the bullets and shrapnel. There is no such polysemy in Hansen's "Wallowing at Tuy Hoa," in which the rain that so often tormented the soldiers offers them the welcome chance for an emotional outpouring, as well as a weeping sympathetic background:

It rained
day and night
for thirty-one days
at Tuy Hoa.

We were thankful
for the opportunity
it afforded us
to cry unnoticed.[91]

In such poems, nature is no longer a strange and threatening other but instead a fellow companion in pain, empathetically connected to the soldier through a shared experience of the suffering and horror of the war.

Furthermore, there were times when American soldiers were able to appreciate the beauty of the Vietnamese landscape. "For many who went there, the landscape was a confusion of crushing heat, monsoons, malaria, bad water, sawgrass, snakes and leeches," John Balaban summarizes, "where ambushes or booby traps lay waiting in flooded rice paddies, in bamboo thickets along canals and slow muddy rivers, and under the triple canopy of the mountain jungles." Balaban, a conscientious objector who volunteered for alternative service in Vietnam from 1967 to 1969 and returned in 1971 to travel the countryside recording Vietnamese oral folk poetry, continues: "But take away the war—*subtract the fear from the landscape*—and it was beautiful, as soldiers often discovered when they were safe and dry and fed, and free, for a moment, to look at another Vietnam."[92] In a diary entry dated 8 April 1968, just weeks before he died from "multiple fragmentation wounds," Bruce Anello describes how, in the "early hour of the morn," there is a sense of "stillness, peace and tranquility . . . It feels so beautiful . . . Just for these few hours I feel the freedom of thought, and the closeness of nature."[93]

The poems of Yusef Komunyakaa also reveal a soldier comfortable with his natural surroundings. "Komunyakaa's poetry is rooted in the jungle, conveying the paranoia of everyday existence amidst a hostile environment," Chattarji suggests. However, while Komunyakaa certainly explores the notion of American soldiers "as an alien presence in a hostile landscape," it is simultaneously possible to trace in his poems a strong thread of familiarity woven through all the warzone's strangeness.[94] The otherness of the surrounding climate is tempered by Komunyakaa's frequent tenderness of description and, in "Camouflaging the Chimera," his observation that American soldiers, too, could become part of the landscape:

> We tied branches to our helmets.
> We painted our faces & rifles
> with mud from a riverbank,
>
> blades of grass hung from the pockets
> of our tiger suits. We wove
> ourselves into the terrain,
> content to be a hummingbird's target.

Although the soldiers have to co-opt nature in order to merge with it, they nevertheless succeed in their attempt to weave themselves "into the terrain." Moreover, later in the poem, Komunyakaa implies that the opposing Vietnamese forces may also have found the landscape challenging: "VC struggled / with the hillside, like black silk // wrestling iron through grass." Even a sense of alienation and unreality is balanced by a connection with nature: "We weren't there. The river ran / through our bones."[95] Nature could also protect American soldiers from enemy combatants, as with the tree that came "between me & a sniper's bullet" and the grass that swayed "seconds before the Viet Cong / raised his soundless rifle."[96] Or, as above, nature could simply seem sympathetic to the suffering of the soldiers, as in his more recent poem "Autobiography of My Alter Ego": "The rice plants trembled / with the dying platoon." In this work, Komunyakaa asks a question that sets nature and death in opposition rather than as enemies allied against the Americans:

> If greenness
> were woven into the weather,
> into jackfruit & lotus
> blooms, how could there be
> death in my mouth?[97]

Two factors in particular may have contributed to Komunyakaa's alternative perspective on his wartime climates. First, as he acknowledges, he was a combat correspondent, not a "typical infantryman," and thus "was able in a way to pull back from things." Second, for Komunyakaa, coming from the relatively rural locale of Bogalusa, Louisiana, the landscape of Vietnam did not seem as different, nor indeed frightening, as perhaps it did to soldiers from more urban backgrounds: "I've thought about this a whole lot, if I had come from a city, such as Philadelphia or New York or a number of other cities in the world, I think Vietnam would've affected me entirely differently. I wasn't afraid of the landscape."[98] In the late 1980s and early 1990s, poets such as Ehrhart and Weigl, inspired and influenced by their return visits to Vietnam, would also begin to "subtract the fear from the landscape" in their writings.[99] Still, during the war, for many American soldiers, the natural climatic conditions of Vietnam seemed, most of the time, like a strange, frightening, and insuperable adversary. Even Komunyakaa sometimes felt as though the "whispers" of the Vietnamese revolutionaries

> sighed through the water
>   reeds & rice shoots, calling
> to the monkeys, the tigers,
>   & the two-step vipers,
> as if summoning the land
>   to march its greenness against us.[100]

Fear

Alongside their struggles with the Vietnamese landscape, American soldiers endured an omnipresent feeling of fear in the warzone. This is depicted by many of the poets, who indicate that it was one of the most significant and stressful factors involved in fighting in Vietnam. Although fear can be understood as a personal psychological phenomenon, it emerges from and is deeply connected to situational conditions. As such, it reveals much about the environments that produce it. Moreover, fear was so pervasive in the warzone that, in effect, it became a climatic condition itself. Indeed, numerous poems suggest that fear was the predominant psychological surrounding, that it permeated almost every environment and moment in the warzone, and that, "bordered on all sides by fear," the soldiers could not possibly escape from it.[101] "I was afraid every single day," Michael Casey states.[102] In "letter to momma #2," Steptoe writes: "I'll be going to the field regularly now and I cannot tell you how frightened I am."[103] "We are," Hassett notes, "the litter of fear."[104]

Through symbiotic cycles of influence, fear both stemmed from and contributed to the above-mentioned climatic difficulties. The otherness, strangeness, and confused reality of the warzone helped to produce fear, and fear made the warzone seem even more other, strange, and confusing. Similarly, the struggles with the natural surroundings of Vietnam generated fear, and fear intensified the perception of those unfamiliar landscapes as threatening, as well as magnifying the extant fear of the enemy combatants so closely associated with those natural surroundings. It seemed as though "everywhere / behind this green curtain / rifles cock" as American soldiers "freeze in terror."[105] Feelings of fear were amplified by the blackness of night, a time so terrifying, Ehrhart admits in his poem "In the Valley of the Shadow," that "we'd rape our mothers, shoot our fathers, / overthrow the government and swear / our innocence to God or Satan / for a single drop of sun."[106] It is important to note the role of perception in such fears, since what *seemed* to the soldiers mattered even more than what actually *was*. As the veteran John Baky says, "fear drives everything in terms of perception."[107]

Many of these fears revolved around one central fear—the fear of being wounded or killed. In Vietnam, violence was an ever-present possibility, and, as such, fear was an ever-present actuality. "The next step you take," Ehrhart writes, might "lead you into an ambush," "hit a wall of rocket-fire," "detonate a mine," "tear your leg off at the hip," "split your belly open," or "send a sniper's bullet through your brain." The repetition in the final lines of this poem emphasizes the ubiquitous closeness of such potentialities:

> The next step you take.
> The next step you take.
>
> The next step.
> The next step.
>
> The next step.[108]

Here, the form of the lines mimics the process of walking in Vietnam: two steps, then another two steps, but then only one step, as though the walking is interrupted halfway through a complete movement, the walker hesitating or, perhaps, wounded or killed by one of the aforementioned horrors. Similarly, in his poem "Mines," Weigl describes the fear produced by this proximity to possible injury and death and details how the presence of such violence transformed the quotidian act of walking into a cautious, uneasy, and even strange exercise of survival:

> In Vietnam I was always afraid of mines:
> North Vietnamese mines, Vietcong mines,
> French mines, American mines,
> whole fields marked with warning signs.
> . . .
> Here is how you walk at night: slowly lift
> one leg, clear the sides with your arms, clear the back,
> front, put the leg down, like swimming.[109]

The warzone, then, was a terrifying climate in which a soldier's life hung in the balance of every step he took.

Some soldiers feared not only becoming victims of violence but becoming perpetrators of violence as well. In "Natural History," Quintana shivers "uncontrollably with fear, / knowing I would have to kill whatever was out there."[110] This particular fear was intimately linked to a soldier's shifting sense of self in the warzone, a fear of the impact on their identity of what they had done, what they were doing, and what they might be capable of doing. They feared for the innocence they had lost and for any remaining innocence that could still be lost. In the aforementioned "In the Valley of the Shadow," Ehrhart considers "the frightened kids / we were and were not anymore, / silent, lost, half-crazed, and deadly." In addition to the biblical allusion to "the valley of the shadow of death," the title of the piece suggests both the darkness of the poem's nighttime setting and the darkness discovered in the self during the war. The final verse stresses the latter, the shadow cast by the shifting sense of self more fearful than even those nights in which these soldiers would have done almost anything "for a single drop of sun": "Something left us slack-jawed, staring / at our own reflections in the dark: / what we were, what we are, and will be. / Bent, we drag it with us like a cross."[111] Fear, then, acted on and emanated from the self, with the soldiers scared of what was outside of them and, also, what was within.

Other fears were related to the social dynamics that existed among American soldiers in the warzone. Some soldiers feared disobedience, some nonconformity; others worried about what their fellow soldiers, the Vietnamese, and even those back home thought of them. This worry arose from not wanting "to appear weak," a kind of fear of fear itself, or at least a fear of showing fear.[112] For the novelist Tim O'Brien, this was "the soldier's greatest fear . . . the fear of blushing," a factor that "had brought them to the war in the first place" and kept them going once they were there: "It was not courage, exactly; the object was not valor. Rather, they were too frightened to be cowards."[113] One method of coping with the climate of fear, which simultaneously operated as a form of psychological distancing from the surrounding violence and death, was to employ an air of nihilistic bravado, to act out the indifferent attitude captured by the oft-repeated phrase—also another signal of the soldiers' sense of unreality—"it don't mean nothing." As Weigl writes, "When bad things happened in the war, / things you couldn't bear to see, or even think about, / we used to say: It don't mean nothing."[114]

For some, this pervasive climate of fear offered disappointing revelations about bravery, masculinity, and the fallibility of parental wisdom, as in Layne's "Conclusions on courage":

Father
Was
In
Error
About
All
Men
Being
Brave.[115]

For others, such as Coleman, it highlighted how "Moral courage is even rarer than physical bravery" and that "You're capable of more than you think you are, positively and negatively."[116] Perhaps the most significant realization was, as Connolly states in a list of the lessons he took from the war, "that you'll be too scared at some time to do what you should do, and learn you're not alone in that by far."[117] As simple as it might seem, this is an exceptionally important insight into the tremendous impact that fear can have on morality. Fear is among the chief causes of the disconnect between our moral beliefs and our moral actions, a fundamental factor in the gap that sometimes exists between what we think we should do and what we actually do, between our best possible self and our actual self. Furthermore, fear is a powerful-enough influence that it can affect not only our actions but, especially if it is internalized, our beliefs as well and, in doing so, can realign our moral identity. This could have the consequence of narrowing the gap between our beliefs and our actions, although not necessarily in a positive direction. Moreover, the extreme climate of war further intensifies the tension that fear can cause between actions, beliefs, and identity. As Soular writes, "over there, in those dark places, / we lost our inner compass."[118] An awareness of the significance of fear, therefore, can aid our understanding of American soldiers and the war in several ways: fear further illuminates those climates it stemmed from and contributed to, fear was a key climatic condition in itself that impacted considerably on how the soldiers felt, and fear is a vital consideration in any attempt to understand how moral actions and beliefs operated in the warzone.

As well as the tremendous psychological burden of fear, the soldiers also faced significant physical demands and challenges, especially those not stationed on military bases.[119] Out in the field, access to water and food could be problematic. "During the war," Jim Northrup remembers, "my overriding thought was about water. There always seemed to be a shortage of good drinking water." In order to reduce the weight they carried, many infantrymen would take only the minimum amount of rations with them, and if "the choppers couldn't come in because of the weather or enemy fire, we'd get hungry."[120] "No rations left. / No water fit to drink," Hassett writes in his poem about the lost patrol unable to be resupplied because of the relentless rain.[121] Even when availability was not an issue, quality could be, with soldiers in the field living largely on C-rations, including the universally reviled ham and lima beans, nicknamed "ham and motherfuckers, usually just motherfuckers for short":

Of the twelve different & interesting meals
Packaged into the 1942 C-ration case,
One was hoarier than the rest:
Ham & little muther fahckers,
Affectionately called,
Ham
&
Mutha's.[122]

And even those who could stomach such food still suffered, as Northrup recalls: "We were living on a diet of C-rations. I learned to like them, though a lot of Marines didn't . . . I went to Vietnam weighing 180 pounds; after thirteen months of C-rations, I weighed 130."[123]

Another challenge, both physical and psychological, was presented, as the title of O'Brien's famous novel indicates, by *The Things They Carried.* "What they carried varied by mission," O'Brien writes, and "was partly a function of rank, partly of field specialty." Yet, whatever their mission, rank, or specialty, an American soldier in the field was weighed down by an enormous amount of equipment, kit, lucky charms, and an assortment of "peculiar little odds and ends." They carried weapons—M-16s, M-60s, M-79s—as well as "whatever presented itself, or whatever seemed appropriate as a means of killing or staying alive . . . They carried all they could bear, and then some, including a silent awe for the terrible power of the things they carried." They even "carried the land itself—Vietnam, the place, the soil—a powdery orange-red dust that covered their boots and fatigues and faces," just as they carried the "whole atmosphere . . . the humidity, the monsoons, the stink of fungus and decay, all of it." And they carried "each other, the wounded or weak," along with "their own lives" and "all the emotional baggage of men who might die. Grief, terror, love, longing—these were intangibles, but the intangibles had their own mass and specific gravity, they had tangible weight."[124]

These were soldiers pushed to the point of physical and psychological exhaustion. The thirst, the hunger, the fatigue, and the weight of everything the soldiers carried were all exacerbated by the climatic conditions examined in the previous section, especially the weather and the natural landscapes of Vietnam. In "Heat Casualties," Frank A. Cross

Jr. describes the equipment the soldiers shouldered and how "the men / Who carried all this / Had melted in the sun," how their

> Knees buckled
> And they went down
> Under seventy-eighty
> Pounds of
> 		Rucksack,
> 		Sixteen,
> 		Bandoliers,
> 		Steel helmets,
> 		Grenades,
> 		Machine gun belts
> And humpin two klicks outa water.[125]

In another poem, "Jungle Rot," he portrays the sheer exhaustion and painful physical toll of "sloggin / Through nine foot elephant grass."[126] Indeed, the arduousness of the conditions was such that, for Cross, a firefight was almost a welcome respite:

> We stagger on line
> With seventy pound rucks,
> Till we drop
> (Almost with relief)
> When we take fire,
> And casualties.[127]

Others "found relief in cigarettes, / Dry socks, or no patrol today."[128] But such moments of reprieve were usually only temporary, and before long the soldiers would be back out "humping the boonies." Moreover, the harshness of these physical conditions, as well as their attendant psychological impact, heightened the soldiers' sense of alienation from the surroundings and the self, intensified the impression of an unreal reality, and increased the feeling of distance from home and their pre-warzone identity. An early poem by Ehrhart precisely captures all of these considerations:

The long day's march is over.
Ten thousand meters through the bush
With flak jacket, rifle, helmet,
Three hundred rounds of ammunition,
Three days' rations, two canteens,
Hand grenades, a cartridge belt;
Pack straps grinding at the shoulders,
Feet stuffed in boots that stumble forward
Mile after hour after hill;
The sun a crushing hundred-and-two,
Sweat in the eyes and salt on the lips;
And always aware that Charlie only waits.

The march is over for today.
Now, heaped against a paddy dike
And fighting back the sweetness of exhaustion,
I close my eyes, and struggle
To recall another life.[129]

Doubt

In addition to their encounters with the landscape, fear, and physical hardships, many American soldiers experienced doubts about the war and increasingly questioned both the war itself and the country that had sent them to fight it. Like fear, doubt was a personal phenomenon that arose from the conditions of the war and, again, was so embedded in the milieu of the warzone that it can be understood as an important part of its climatic texture. In particular, the surrounding presence of other American soldiers who also doubted and questioned the war reinforced and further contributed to any one soldier's own doubts and questions, an interdependent relationship in which the individual fed from and into a shared state of disillusionment.

Here, a similar narrative of evolving doubt emerges in many of the poems. Shortly after their arrival in the warzone, soldiers began to question the beliefs and assumptions they held with regard to both the war and America. Sooner or later—depending on a number of variables, including the time period when they were in Vietnam, where in Vietnam they served, rank, specialty, and their preexisting identity and beliefs—many soldiers lost faith in the cause they were fighting for, or perhaps lost faith that there even was a cause. This was accompanied by the feeling that they had been lied to and betrayed by their country—by politicians, of course, but also by their parents, teachers, and upbringing, as well as by American society as a whole. Finally, with no cause left to believe in and fight for, yet nonetheless stuck in the trap of war, soldiers realized that they fought only for their own survival and for their friends. In some respects, this is the standard soldier story of the transition from innocence to experience.[130] However, the poetic account does differ in certain key aspects, most notably in the poets' unconventional conception of the start point of the decline of innocence and the end point of experience, their unorthodox interrogation of the culprits and factors responsible for the war, and their radical examination of their own role in the conflict.[131] Furthermore, this process of shifting beliefs marked the origin of the poets' rebellion and the beginnings of an antiwar moral identity.

From the perspective of situational conditions within the warzone, this breakdown of beliefs and sense of betrayal can be understood as part of a climate of doubt, since these personal revelations resulted from and augmented the atmosphere of confusion, uncertainty, and questioning that prevailed in Vietnam. As Christian G. Appy states, from the moment of their arrival, American soldiers encountered an interconnected chain of "the war's most troubling questions: Where are we? What are we doing here? Where is the enemy? Whom can we trust? Where is it safe? What is our mission? The answers received provided little comfort or clarity. Instead, the green troops faced a series of confusing and incongruous experiences—ominous portents of a yearlong tour of duty against enemies they could not identify, among allies who did not welcome their presence, and on behalf of a policy that was neither meaningful nor realizable."[132]

One of the most common inaugural incongruities portrayed in the poetry is the soldiers' discovery of the widespread Vietnamese hostility toward the American presence. Neither the people nor even the military of south Vietnam, it seemed, welcomed the American involvement, and they appeared resentful of the American soldiers who were supposedly there to fight for their freedom: "they do not want us here / they do not want to fight this silly war."[133] A people whom American soldiers "had thought they were going to liberate treated them with apparent indifference or outright hostility," Ehrhart recalls.[134] For the soldiers, this was difficult to grasp, at least early on in their tour, before they came to understand and share the Vietnamese hostility to the war. Shea, who was in Vietnam during the first half of 1965, writes:

> the situation here
> is one of frustration   loneliness   and wonder
> in the midst of a war
> a war that involves us all
> and yet does not involve us

Later in the poem he offers a cynical assessment of the motivation of America's military allies in Vietnam:

> they are not fighting for their beliefs
> or for their country
> they are fighting because they are mercenaries
> and america is paying them
> to fight for america's beliefs[135]

If many Vietnamese people did not really want to fight the war, then, American soldiers quickly came to ask, why was America fighting it? "Official explanations of the American mission in Vietnam failed to match the reality experienced by U.S. soldiers," Appy notes. They may have arrived in Vietnam with the belief that they were there to help south Vietnam, contain communism, aid democracy, preserve American credibility, and generally make the world a better place, but "the actual nature of the war so fundamentally undermined these explanations that most American troops did not find in them a meaningful sense of purpose or legitimacy." Although doubt, questioning, and confusion intensified as the war continued, "there was, from the beginning, significant disillusionment."[136] Ehrhart summarizes "the predicament in which they found themselves": "Who in the hell was fighting whom? Why?! And for what?" He continues: "the explanations given by those who'd sent the soldiers to fight in Vietnam became ever more surreal and absurd until they were revealed for what they were: nothing but empty words, bereft of reason or any semblance of higher moral authority."[137] As Mason writes, the American soldier in Vietnam "looked for a reason. / And found none."[138]

Furthermore, not only did the war seem unwanted and unjustified, but it often also appeared to be unwinnable. Connolly arrived in Vietnam on 2 February 1968, in the midst of the Tet Offensive, and as he saw streets lined with the bodies of "American soldiers, dead for days, in full bloat," he explains, "I knew right there and then that the war, which we were winning when I left the States, yesterday, was as lost as I was."[139] Once they suspected that people were "giving up their lives in a senseless war," many soldiers came to the unnerving realization that they would "change nothing / save the tally of dead men / in a dying cause."[140]

Another incongruity occurred because of a discrepancy between the soldiers' expectations of war and their experiences once they were in Vietnam. "I mean really, we didn't know how to act," Brown suggests. "The war we were raised for and / Something going on they didn't tell us."[141] For the soldiers, brought up on the mythical glory of the Good War, the war in Vietnam was very different from what they thought war would and should be like. They desired the perceived moral clarity of the Second World War, not the moral ambiguities that came with fighting against guerrilla revolutionaries in a war with no discernible reason in which they increasingly came to identify themselves as perpetrators. As Hall writes:

> In my father's war
> the young men knew who was wrong
> and blazed into death
> with clear consciences.
> Here
> under monsoon clouds
> it is grey all over
> and no one looks guilty
> but me.

At the heart of this doubt and uncertainty was a difficult and problematic relationship with the Vietnamese—the focus of the next chapter—in which American soldiers struggled to distinguish friend from foe. As his poem continues, Hall expresses a yearning for a return to earlier innocence and naïveté, before the emergence of questioning, doubt, and moral ambiguity: "I would lift these boots backward / if I could / through each mudprint / to a simpler time."[142] Hansen describes a similar desire in "Uncertain Notions":

How
I long
for that time
when
right and wrong
and truth
were mine.
That day
before
black and white
gave way
to gray
and left me
with
uncertain notions
only.[143]

In this climate of doubt, some soldiers began to regret their decision to join the military or to submit to the draft. "Give us this day / a plane ticket back to San Francisco," Hall pleads, "give us another chance / to size things up / just one more low-pitched whine / before the draft board."[144] Alongside this regret at their own involvement in the war—as though the present self had been betrayed by the past self—they wondered about those who had sent or allowed them to go to this "senseless war" to fight and possibly die for "a dying cause."[145] They felt betrayed by the president—whichever president it might be—and his "myriad of advisors / To help him determine right from wrong"; "Sleek senators and bored bureaucrats" who "Sent lean soldiers to their duty"; the "rich . . . sons-of-bitches / that rule our lives"; the "silent" bystander apathy of the American people; teachers, such as Hall's communist-fearing Mrs.

Porter, who "grows old and fat / on her porch back home / unmolested / by the yellow horde"; and the mothers and fathers "who bequeathed to us / this rotten patch of earth, this fate."[146] From these feelings of bitter betrayal emerged an understanding of the failure of political, economic, national, and generational responsibility, as examined in chapter 4. The climate of doubt, therefore, altered the beliefs of the poets about the war and all those whose actions and omissions had placed them and millions of other American youths in the maelstrom of a seemingly unwanted, unwinnable, and unjustifiable war.

With their beliefs in the war and America shattered, the poets suggest, many soldiers continued to fight for survival and for their comrades. They may have wanted, like Oldham, "to go home / to go home only to go home," but, as Ehrhart recalls, "it never occurred to me to lay down my rifle and quit. Instead, you develop a survival mentality. You stop thinking about what you're doing, and you count days."[147] Even those who pondered the possibility of quitting were trapped in a warzone with few viable escape routes: "that just wasn't an option . . . there was no way to desert in Vietnam. What are you going to do? It's not like you can hitchhike home."[148] There were instances of disobedience, resistance, and, as the scholar and peace activist David Cortright documents, "quasi-mutinies."[149] But most soldiers just kept going, "counting the year / in days, one by one," as "each morning ritual marks / one more, one less," Brown notes, and feeling, as other soldiers had in previous wars, resentful, powerless, and what Glover identifies as a "sense of helpless resignation."[150] Soldiers persevered because no matter how betrayed they might have felt, they still did not want to disappoint those back home and also, quite simply, because they wanted to survive: "He fights for the approval of his loved ones. / And he fights for his life."[151] Moreover, they fought on from a sense of duty—not to a tarnished cause or country, but a duty to themselves and those around them. Partly, this was just another aspect of the climate of fear, as the soldier was afraid of "letting his comrades down, or being labeled a coward."[152] But in a world where time was "measured / by the Xing of the days / like the labored wall-scratchings / of condemned men," it was also a vitally reliable and honorable replacement justification once "their original sense of purpose became clouded by doubt."[153] "When we had no other reason to fight / in Vietnam," Mason writes, "we fought for each other."[154] As R. L. Barth reflects:

> I learned what soldiers learn: neither a flag
> Nor brassy phrases count much, under fire.
> Men fight from pride, grief, fear of censure; mostly,
> Though, it's closest buddies who evoke
> Some kind of courage, if only hanging on.[155]

Perhaps, too, he suggests in "Why We Fight," they even fought for those beliefs that had died during the war:

> We fight for no
> Slant domino,
> Ragged-assed flag,
> Or body-bag;
> Say, rather, for
> Buddies—but more,
> Even, for grief
> And lost belief.[156]

In Barth's precise and perceptive two-line "Epitaph," he situates this "lost belief" among the above-mentioned burdens of physical hardships and fear: "Tell them quite simply that we died / Thirsty, betrayed, and terrified."[157]

For some American soldiers, particularly the poets examined in this book, this doubting and questioning marked the beginning of a significant shift in identity. The war "was a huge part of my life," Ehrhart states, and it "changed the way I see myself, my country, the world in which I live."[158] Their experiences during the conflict undermined certain core beliefs, those ideas and assumptions about "myself, my country, the world." Consequently, they had to reassess and reconfigure the entire belief system that underpinned their identity. As soldiers, the poets had suffered a painful and irretrievable loss of innocence, a source of deep regret for Gerald McCarthy: "I think we are never the same for what happened. That's what you lament . . . you can't get back your innocence, I'd give anything to be innocent again and . . . naive."[159] Yet, they had also gained an awareness that laid the foundations for poetic rebellion and an antiwar moral identity. "Knowledge is born and conscience awakened," Albert Camus writes of the rebel.[160] The war altered their moral beliefs about what, and who, was right and wrong, good and bad, and evinced the uncertainty and ambiguity of these categories. Ehrhart summarizes the transformation:

> what happened to me in Vietnam is that I had the entire framework by which I live, we all do, we all have a framework, a structure around us that we live in, and mine was completely destroyed, just completely, utterly destroyed. Everything I ever thought I knew, everything I ever believed in, everything I thought about what was right and what was wrong, and how I personally and my country should be in the world, was all completely destroyed. And that was a terrible, terrible feeling, and it took me a decade before I even began to be functional again. But the one thing that that did was it stripped away everything and I had to rebuild some kind of framework, some kind of ethical belief system that I could live in. And it left me open to rethinking, to thinking in ways I never would have thought in had that not happened.[161]

And so: "Almost all of us came back to a homeland which bore little resemblance to the one we left—not because it had changed, but because we had."[162]

The New World

When their time in Vietnam was up, whether they had all "365 days / blacked out on a hopeful calendar" or whether the violence of the war had shortened their tour, the soldiers went back to America.[163] Vietnam was a place almost "too incomprehensible to exist," a place so strange, unfamiliar, unreal, disturbing, alienating, terrifying, and confusing that American soldiers "did not go home"; they went back to the place they called "the world."[164] Yet, if they expected or hoped that the world of America would be without such arduous and distressing situational conditions, many were quickly disappointed and further disillusioned as they faced yet another cluster of challenging climates. The difficulty of this return to "the world" and the interrelated problem of coming "home" are well documented in the works of the poets.

As well as noting the soldiers' relief and joy of leaving "that mean year of black nights / spent wide-eyed in foxholes" behind them, the poets also portray a sense of shifting realities as the survivors boarded the "freedom bird" that would fly them back to America.[165] Peter Ulisse's "Captain Windslow" sits on the plane, stares out at replacements, wonders "who will catch syphilis, / how many will die," and then reflects: "All seems unreal / as dress khakis I now wear, / low quarter shoes / like paper mache."[166] The ambiguity of these lines, in which "All" might refer to the unreality of the year just endured, the unreality of leaving the warzone, or the unreality of the transition between the two, echoes the feeling of shifting realities—shifting unrealities—that exiting soldiers experienced. For instance, for Andrew Gettler, "even the sky / looked different" on his "redeye special" flight, "though more real— / or less— / i couldn t know."[167] B. D. Trail's "With My Shield or On It" also addresses this perceptual shift in realities, as well as the difficulty of returning to America. "Everything rolled by like a grim silent movie," Trail writes of his last impressions of Vietnam: "The whirring blades . . . The little people . . . The pock-faced land" as "the Danang chopper plucked me out of Tam Ky." The surreal and alienating sense of watching "this final film clip" seems to end as Trail boards the plane back to America, but in hindsight he notes that the replacement reality will prove just as painful and problematic as the one he is leaving behind:

> No one laughed or even talked much on the plane.
> The stewardesses seemed disappointed in us.
> But, as I heard one man say,
> "At least nothing will ever be as bad as what
> We've been through,"
> He was wrong, of course.
> Home was still ahead.

"When I flew out of that Inferno," Trail reveals a few lines later, "I did not suspect I was entering into another one."[168] Similarly, Soular's book of war poems is split into two sections, "In Country" and "Back in the World," and the last line of the former reads simply: "this nightmare ended, another beginning."[169]

The poets also record the sense of loss that soldiers felt as they boarded their flights and thought about friends who had died during their tour, those the First World War poet Siegfried Sassoon called "The unreturning army that was youth; / The legions who have suffered and are dust."[170] Gettler pictures the scale of this loss when he explains how, on his flight back, "if i d have bought / a seat for / everyone i d left / behind" then "we d have been flying / mighty light / and filled the skies / with ghosts."[171] The climate of fear that had enveloped soldiers throughout their tour persisted even on the departing runway, with soldiers scared they might still be added to this sad sum of ghosts. This was followed by an immense feeling of relief when the plane flew safely out of the warzone, as Jon Forrest Glade, who "left Vietnam aboard a hospital plane," recalls:

> I remember everybody was nervous
> as we turned and taxied,
> afraid we might catch a rocket
> or one last mortar round.
> Everyone held their breath
> as the plane gathered speed.
> When we felt the wheels
> leave the ground,
> someone yelled out,
> "Good-bye, you rotten nasty motherfucker."[172]

Likewise, Ulisse's "Captain Windslow" registers the elation of leaving Vietnam, as well as the exhaustion and emotion of survival for those returning to "the world":

> Wheels lift,
> higher and higher we soar
> over the trees infested with VC
> till our pilot announces, "Gentlemen,
> we have just left the Republic of Vietnam"
> and with three hundred GIs
> I scream unashamed,
> foot stomping yells till my voice
> goes hoarse
> and I slump in my seat
> living, living.[173]

As these new veterans landed back in America, one of the first challenging climates they encountered was the immediate absence of a warm welcome. When Ehrhart arrived at San Francisco airport, there were

> No brass bands;
> No flags,
> No girls,
> No cameramen.
>
> Only a small boy who asked me
> What the ribbons on my jacket meant.[174]

The poem ends there, the reader, like the boy, offered no answer to the question, as though Ehrhart cannot bring himself to speak about the war or simply cannot say what the ribbons mean, his silence indicative of the impossibility of finding meaning in, making meaning from, or expressing meaning about a seemingly meaningless war. In the first poem of his "Back in the World" section, Soular describes the lack of an amiable welcome along with the realization that the war was now an inextricable part of his identity and how being ignored and even deprecated by others while simultaneously alienated from his altered self produced a sense of existential doubt:

> No friendlies in San Francisco.
> No cheers, no welcome.
> In the sterile bathroom you choke back tears
> and scrub futilely to rid the shriek
> of Nam from your crippled face. Your reflection
> in the clean mirror says you exist.

In the final line of the poem, Soular urges himself to accept the event of his own survival and future: "Now dare to believe you will live."[175] As Coleman suggests: "The shock of survival can be / worse than other wounds."[176]

Furthermore, the absence of a warm welcome again conflicted with expectations established by perceptions of the Second World War. As

Kyle Longley highlights, a common complaint was that "unlike their fathers and uncles returning from World War II, the Vietnam veteran merely arrived, often alone and with little fanfare," and they felt they "received little of the respect afforded other generations of veterans."[177] The romanticized image of the American soldier who fought in the Good War returning to a rapturous welcome and a happy homecoming was, however, far from accurate. As Kenneth D. Rose documents in *Myth and the Greatest Generation: A Social History of Americans in World War II,* some of these veterans also faced difficult homecomings and immediate reintegration problems.[178] Yet, American veterans of the war in Vietnam often contrasted their homecoming experiences to the pleasant myth rather than the complicated actuality of this earlier conflict.

Nonetheless, there were some crucial differences between the two sets of veterans that did indeed contribute, in certain aspects, to a more problematic and distressing return for veterans of the later war. Unlike many veterans of the Second World War, most veterans of the war in Vietnam returned not in units but as individuals, thus further exacerbating a sense of loneliness and isolation. Additionally, while most of the former returned by sea, most of the latter returned by air, and the suddenness of this transition from the warzone back to America left little "time for decompression."[179] Above all, most veterans of the Second World War returned after the end of a victorious campaign, whereas most veterans of the war in Vietnam returned while their war was still raging, a faltering war that promised little hope of a clear victory and one that was the source of bitter debate and struggle in a tumultuous America that seemed to be tearing itself apart. "Thirty-six hours ago you were at war / and now find a new one festering / back in the World," Soular writes.[180] And while stories of veterans being spat on by antiwar activists—the "spitting image"—were largely a myth "perpetuated by government outlets," some returning soldiers did encounter hostility from some members of the antiwar movement.[181] Soular, for instance, remembers being called a "baby burner."[182] Primarily, though, it was the apathy of the American people that most disconcerted returning veterans on their arrival. "Younger on the average by seven years than their World War II counterparts, having endured a war far more complex and confusing," the historian George C. Herring summarizes, "Vietnam veterans by the miracles of the jet age were whisked home virtually overnight to a nation hostile to the war and indifferent to their plight. Some were made to feel the guilt for the nation's moral transgressions; others, responsibility for its failure. Most simply met silence."[183] As Baky explains, "people would look at returning GIs and all they would see in these returning kids was another reason to feel guilty, and so people just put it away from them, didn't want to hear about it, didn't want to talk about it."[184] A short piece in the anthology *Demilitarized Zones: Veterans after Vietnam* captures this discomforting quiet: "I'm home America . . . / . . . Somebody I'm home. / Welcome home Self."[185] Hence, the immediate climate of homecoming was, like the warzone itself, challenging, confusing, and alienating.[186]

After the flight back and the disappointing and confounding welcome upon arrival, the next climate returning veterans encountered in their transition back to "the world" was the new strangeness of the place they had once thought of as "home." Our sense of reality, and our sense of morality, depends heavily on the quotidian. Thus, just as American soldiers experienced a shock of difference when they arrived in Vietnam, they experienced a shock of difference when they returned to America. If, as mentioned above, some soldiers came to believe that the warzone of Vietnam was more real than anything back in "the world," and others never shook the feeling of unreality, for each of them the climates of Vietnam were part of their daily life for a considerable time and so the change to the American environment was necessarily one of difference and shifting realities. As Steptoe writes in "Returnee": "This post-'Nam reality continues to / shift and change."[187] The sense of dislocation was intensified by the expectation that they would be returning to a familiar place, but, instead, many found that they had simply traded one unreality or strange reality for another or, as Trail and Soular suggest above, one inferno or nightmare for another. As Ehrhart recalls: "it's like I spent thirteen months just hoping to escape from Mars and then I end up on Jupiter, because by the time I came home this wasn't home anymore, it too had become an alien place." It was also "in many ways a hostile place," and not in this instance because Ehrhart was denigrated for being a veteran of the war but because the war and its impact on his beliefs and identity had so drastically changed his perception of America. As well as coping with another shift in reality, then, veterans had to adjust to this shift in the self: "Really the place hasn't changed at all, you have."[188]

In "the old guard," a poem dedicated to Ehrhart, Gettler describes how the difference between life in the warzone of Vietnam and life back in America alienated veterans by making them strangers in "the world":

> the world had changed;
> so central to our lives
> had been the fact of death,
> the counting of the days
> and their minutest portions,
> that to see each sunrise
> come -then go in peace-
> without the need to mark
> its passage with relief,
> made of us strangers,
> intruders in the normal
> course of things . . .[189]

"We went to Vietnam as frightened lonely young men," William Jayne explains. "We came back, alone again, as immigrants to a new world. For the culture we had known dissolved while we were in Vietnam, and the culture of combat we lived in so intensely for a year made us aliens when we returned."[190] In Jonathan Tran's work *The Vietnam War and Theologies of Memory,* he suggests that it was as though the returning veteran was banished from "the world," cursed "to wander a moral landscape he no longer recognized."[191] As Weigl writes in "And we came home": "we did not know / how to live in the new world."[192]

It was not only the strangeness of this new world and the strangeness of the self that contributed to yet another unsettling, confusing, and uncertain climate for many veterans; the strangeness of their relationship with the people they returned to also confounded them. In his poem in which he expresses the moral problem of not knowing "how to live in the new world," Weigl ends with the following lines: "No one / understands how we felt. / Kill it all. Kill it all."[193] The repetition of "Kill it all" emphasizes the difficulty of returning from the violent climate of the warzone, where "Kill it all" was a common refrain, and along with the preceding lines indicates the bitterness, resentment, and frustration veterans could feel toward the wide gap of understanding between them and the American people. Likewise, in the aforementioned poem "Coming Home," the question the boy asks Ehrhart about the meaning of his ribbons underlines the divide between those who fought and those who did not, between experience and ignorance. In another poem, Ehrhart writes that he had been sent "back alive among a people / I can never feel / at ease with anymore."[194]

Veterans found their relationships with friends and family particularly strained and, again, strange. When Richard E. Baker arrived home, "The war was not mentioned," and his parents assured him "that little had changed." For Baker, of course, much had changed, and the awkward avoidance of the war only aggravated the sense of distance between him and his parents. Later in the piece, Baker describes the difficulty of resuming his relationship with his girlfriend and his frustration that the American people seemed unburdened by the war, that they continued to live a life of comfort that contrasted with the hardships he had just suffered and others still endured in Vietnam: "She ate too well. Everyone ate too well."[195] For Mahoney, a central problem of homecoming stemmed from his family's proud but simplistic image of him as "Soldier-son, hero-brother," and their misplaced belief that just because he had not sustained physical injuries, he was not wounded. They could not yet detect the psychological damage wrought by the war, the impact it had on his identity that meant he would not long be able to maintain this role of "Soldier-son, hero brother," that the hidden harms caused by the war would soon surface and spread:

They think me whole
Grateful I am unscraped
By war's steel
I wince at their sympathy
All wounds do not pierce the skin
Control! Control!
I must play my role
With precision
My pain will be theirs
Soon enough[196]

For Gary Rafferty, even the articulacy of poetry struggled to bridge the gap of understanding between veterans and their relatives:

> Although poets
> we're wordless to explain,
> we stammer:
> "I grew up on a different planet
> than this one."
> They think us mad.[197]

Rafferty's poem also highlights the potential mutuality of this perception of strangeness. It was not only that the American people seemed strange to returning veterans but also that returning veterans could seem strange to the American people. Veterans had been changed by their wartime experiences, and the sometimes dramatic difference between the person who went to war and the person who came back, as well as the psychological and emotional issues they now carried with them, made some veterans appear alien to the people to whom they returned. As Gerald McCarthy writes:

> A voice of strangers
> knocking politely
> on doors.
> The soldiers are coming home,
> they carry the sadness with them
> like others carry groceries
> or clothes in from the line.[198]

"I didn't come home," one veteran explains, "I just came back. Home had changed so much that I didn't recognize it. And no one recognized me, either."[199] Yet again, these young men found themselves in a confusing and seemingly foreign climate.

This feeling of alienation was further intensified by isolation, since veterans lacked the strong support network and friendships that had kept so many of them going during the war. In the warzone they had belonged

To a Squad
  a Platoon
  a Company
To a Battalion
  a Division
  an Army
We were cloaked
rag-lady deep in belonging then.

There was always, Hansen continues, "someone nearby to say: / 'You did the right thing.' / 'I would have done the same thing.' / 'Anyone would have done the same thing.'" Back in America, there was no such moral support and confirmation. "We had come from different places / to bond," Hansen explains, but in homecoming "the layers of belonging / fell . . . and we stood naked and alone. // Naked and alone / we went back / to our different places."[200]

The alteration of identity and questioning of beliefs that occurred for many soldiers during their time in Vietnam were also important contributing factors to the tensions and problems of homecoming. "Inside me the war had eaten a hole," Weigl explains. "The wind blew through me to the green place / where they still fell in their blood."[201] "Someone told me, / Let it go, boy," he writes in another poem, "let the green / untangle from your body."[202] But for Weigl, as for so many returning veterans, the green war and the green place were now inextricable parts of his identity, and such an untangling was simply not possible. These ex-soldiers had been irreversibly altered by that aspect of their past. This was another reason the happy homecoming they might have hoped for was unattainable. As Kalí Tal argues, that fantasy required "returning not only to a place, but to a time where they were innocent of war."[203]

For some veterans, the extremity of their wartime experiences established an almost complete disconnect between their prewar and postwar identity. As early as the flight home, Bill Bauer realized the significance of the change in self that the war had produced: "After my plane lands / I'll step onto a freeway . . . so turned around I won't remember / what I was like back then."[204] Veterans, Weigl suggests, identified "a change in themselves and in others who fought," a transformation that included an important moral aspect: "Those who fought and returned home from the war came back to discover a complete collapse of their moral identity."[205] The questioning that arose in the warzone, with regard to both the war and America, along with the attendant doubt and moral ambiguity, undermined the belief systems of many soldiers and impacted significantly on their sense of morality. For Mason, this breakdown of prewar beliefs and morality is a phenomenon that all veterans confront upon their return:

> From any nation
> each man
> returning from war
> stands alone in the rubble
> of his personal Homecoming.
>
> In victory or defeat,
> his former life has collapsed
> under the undeniable weight
> of debunked values.
> His cultural upbringing is in ruins.
> He enters a world of his own creation.

The belief system and moral identity of the veteran have "collapsed / under his rude questioning," Mason indicates, and they must be restructured and reconfigured. Since there is little left of "his former life," this is an existentialist project in which the veteran "enters a world of his own creation" in order to produce a new set of beliefs and values.[206] In other words, because the beliefs and values of others—those that were instilled during his "cultural upbringing"—no longer hold true, for the veteran to live authentically he must establish his own belief system and moral identity anchored in his own experiences and understandings.

Furthermore, the questioning that developed in the warzone continued back in "the world." "For a time, most veterans turn inward— / 'one man' awareness patrols / searching for a truth to believe in," Mason writes, as they "question / why they fought, / for whom they fought / and the true identity of the real enemy."[207] This line of investigation led to some uncomfortable and disturbing realizations, as Weigl suggests:

"what they thought had been heroic battle, they came to realize, had actually been a dark absurdity perpetuated by the rich and powerful in ignorance and at the sake of a vast prodigality."[208] Such questioning and such realizations led some veterans, and many of the poets, to join the antiwar movement, especially the group Vietnam Veterans Against the War, to fight against the war they had fought in:

> We harnessed our terrible knowledge
> And we joined the demonstrations
> And became the soldiers
> For peace
>
> And we marched
> And we prayed
> And we marched
> And we marched
>
> Till the din subsided
> In one small corner of the world[209]

However, for some veterans, this questioning and rebellion further distanced and alienated them from those to whom they returned. "We are the ones you sent to fight a war / You did not know a thing about. / Those of us that lived / Have tried to tell you what went wrong," Ehrhart writes. But, he continues, this was not a critique the American people wanted to hear: "Now you think you do not have to listen."[210] These veterans realized that family, friends, and the public might not agree with or understand them fully. After all, they had held similarly unquestioning and uncritical views before their wartime ordeal altered their beliefs and values. Nonetheless, being ignored was a frustrating, disheartening, and dislocating experience. Returning veterans desired at least an acknowledgment, if not necessarily a wholehearted acceptance, of the influential impact the war had on them, rather than apathy, inattention, or silence. "It may be we cannot change you / but we hope to make you see / How we have changed," Landon Thorne declares.[211] And as painful as these changes could be, for some veterans they also signaled the end of playing false roles and the beginning of a movement toward a more authentic mode of being—and, for the poets, a rebellious way of writing—anchored in an ethic of love:

> I went to Viet Nam a man and I came back
> a boy. I am very thankful for that. As
> a man I played many roles. In Viet Nam
> I saw the ultimate result of role playing.
> As a boy I loved a lot, very simply and
> without fear. This is the first and last
> thing about war that I will do. From
> now on I'm going to write about things like
> love as seen through the eyes of a boy.[212]

The cumulative impact of all these immediate homecoming issues that veterans confronted, the poets suggest, meant that there really was no "home" left to come back to. Their perceptions of themselves, the place, the people, and the feelings of familiarity, closeness, and comfort that constituted home had been so shaken by their wartime experiences that home no longer existed. For many returning veterans, the absence of home in homecoming was a deeply shocking and alienating realization, as Ehrhart explains: "I expected Vietnam to be foreign, I didn't expect the land of my birth to become a foreign place, and it was. That's a fairly common experience for veterans."[213]

Many of the problems veterans encountered in their return to "the world" are encapsulated by Dale Ritterbusch in his poem "Geography Lesson." "I have little sense of place / having grown up on the other side / of the world and returned home / to foreigners on foreign soil," Ritterbusch begins. He then notes his family's awkward avoidance of the war: "Not once does the family ask questions— / as if I'd gone off for the weekend / to fish or hunt." On the surface, it appears as though little has changed—"My place at the table / is the same, same chair, same silverware"—but the war's impact means that he no longer recognizes "the family portrait / hanging on the wall—their faces unfamiliar, / their eyes from another time or country, / another race." As his father "stands on the front porch / staring at the lawn I had so often mowed / and played on as a kid," Ritterbusch senses the disconnect between his prewar and postwar identity and the distance this transformation has created between him and his family. In the final lines, he describes what he and his father still share and his somber realization that he has not and never will come back home:

> We share the dark and the silence,
> the silence of the world
> in response to inarticulate horrors; I flick
> a lighted cigarette, watch its red glow
> as it traces an arc over the front yard,
> land I cannot recognize as home.[214]

The poetic account, then, offers an interesting and insightful picture of the climates American soldiers lived in before, during, and immediately after their time in the warzone of Vietnam. In many ways, their childhood climates prepared them for war long before they entered the military. Once in the warzone, American soldiers found Vietnam a strange and frightening place. Within this difficult environment, they endured psychological and physical exhaustion and the emergence of significant doubt about the war and the country that had sent them to fight it. When they finally went back to America, the new veterans discovered that they had exchanged one strange world for another. Hence, these pieces of poetic witness present a valuable perspective on the climates that enveloped American soldiers during childhood, training, the warzone, and homecoming. The poems show what it meant to send these young boys to fight in a foreign land far away from a home to which they never returned, even if they survived.

2
OTHERS

"This ground is indifferent / It does not recognize me," Jim Nye writes of his experience of the conflict in Vietnam. Yet, as difficult as the climatic conditions of the warzone were for American soldiers, their relationships with those they fought alongside, against, and amongst were even more disconcerting. The people of Vietnam, Nye continues, "look at me / I do not know them."[1] The complex and often confusing encounters between American soldiers and their south Vietnamese military allies, their revolutionary opponents, and Vietnamese civilians constitute a significant part of the poetic record. This chapter explores the ethical intricacies of these interactions, as well as the racial tensions within the American military. In particular, it focuses on how the soldier-poets describe and dismantle an American-Vietnamese us-them moral barrier and, in doing so, demonstrate the importance of empathy and imagination in overcoming the dehumanizing divides of war. This is a key aspect of their rebellion and witness.

Thinking about Others

War necessitates, inculcates, and is even caused by a divisive morality that separates *us* from *them.* In such a morality, those who share a particular characteristic—nationality, race, religion, gender, class, generation, political ideology, and so on—are included within the moral space of us. Outside of this moral space are the others, those not a part of this constructed commonality whose exclusion confers on them a different and often lower moral status than those inside the grouping. "Many moralities are 'internal,'" Jonathan Glover explains, "giving weight to the interests of those inside a community, but doing little against the common indifference or even hostility towards those outside."[2] This us-them moral barrier is predicated on perceived difference: *they* are not the same as *us*. Moreover, this polarizing tendency portrays the other as holding characteristics that are opposed and potentially threatening to the defining characteristics that ostensibly unite us. Here, difference is danger. This division, and the desire to maintain it, may simply stem from a lack of contact with and understanding of the other. An absence of familiarity strengthens the sense of strangeness. It also prevents the possibility of gauging the accuracy of assumptions about the other and allows us to continue to project preconceived notions onto them. Indeed, this moral divide is linked to psychological projection, that "operation of expelling feelings or wishes the individual finds wholly unacceptable—too shameful, too obscene, too dangerous—by attributing them to another."[3] Our deepest fears are projected outside of the space of the self and, beyond that, outside of the space of us onto a site of otherness that this same projection helps to establish and reinforce. "Strangely, the foreigner lives within us: he is the hidden face of our identity," the thinker Julia Kristeva writes in *Strangers to Ourselves*. "And when we flee from or struggle against the foreigner, we are fighting our unconscious."[4] This is a process that also constrains our ability to think clearly, as the psychoanalyst Carl Gustav Jung suggests: "fear of the evil which one does not see in one's own bosom but always in somebody else's checks reason every time."[5]

Crucially, to return to Glover, "this moral gap is a human disaster." Us-them barriers result in "far weaker social pressures against hostile treatment of members of other groups," and the moral resources of respect and sympathy "also have less power."[6] In some instances, the moral status of the other can be reduced to such an extent that they are perceived and treated as subhuman. This dehumanization enables us to do to them what we would not have them do to us; it allows us to violate the Golden Rule. A divisive morality is the foundation upon which many moral atrocities are built. It is an "ethic gone wrong," the philosopher Simon Blackburn indicates, "an essential preliminary to the sweat-shop or the concentration camp and the death march."[7] It is also a vital part of war.

The us-them moral barrier is at the center of war. Paul Fussell outlines this "gross dichotomizing" in his examination of the First World War: "'We' are all here on this side; 'the enemy' is over there. 'We' are individuals with names and personal identities; 'he' is a mere collective entity. We are visible; he is invisible. We are normal; he is grotesque. Our appurtenances are natural; his, bizarre. He is not as good as we are."[8] This simplified oppositional morality is a key component of the climate of war. It is a biased and adversarial ideology utilized to justify war and, as the literary scholar Janis Haswell emphasizes, sees evil only in the other, "instead of providing adequate ways of sorting out moral right from wrong."[9] Furthermore, in war this divide delineates a boundary of violence. As the enemy, the other is a dehumanized and objectified target of permitted and encouraged violence. In reflections penned during the Second World War on Homer's *Iliad,* the philosopher and mystic Simone Weil stresses that violent force "turns anybody who is subjected to it into a *thing.* Exercised to the limit, it turns man into a thing in the most literal sense: it makes a corpse out of him."[10] Moreover, for the perpetrator of violence, this dehumanization is a necessary prelude to killing, as the poet Yusef Komunyakaa asserts: "one has to dehumanize before one can kill another."[11] Hence, as another poet, David Connolly, suggests, the denial of the humanity of the enemy plays a crucial role "in all war."[12] In both a practical and a moral sense, then, war is a mode of violent interaction in which strangers kill strangers. Che Guevara, in *Guerrilla Warfare,* offers a precise summary of war and the us-them barrier: "War is always a struggle in which each contender tries to annihilate the other."[13]

Yet, as potentially divisive as us-them barriers can be, they can also be weakened and even removed through the exercising of empathy and moral imagination. "Putting yourself in the place of others," the ethicist Peter Singer argues, "is what thinking ethically is all about. It is encapsulated in the Golden Rule, 'Do unto others as you would have them do unto you.'"[14] Empathy acknowledges the moral status of other people and prevents them from being dehumanized. It can reveal that certain us-them dichotomies are based on a false sense of separation and demonstrate what Komunyakaa calls "the fact that we're all connected."[15] Through empathy, we encounter other people not as objects but as subjects.[16] Empathy also acknowledges that "the foreigner lives within us," as Kristeva suggests, and through "recognizing him within ourselves, we are spared detesting him in himself."[17] In the face of the other, we glimpse the self reflected back—the Golden Rule incarnate.

This empathy is rooted in moral imagination, in the ability to picture ourselves in the position of other people, to see the suffering of others through the shroud of difference. "You never really understand a person until you consider things from his point of view," Harper Lee writes in *To Kill a Mockingbird,* "until you climb into his skin and walk around in it."[18] According to the psychologist Rollo May, empathy is the fundamental basis of moral courage: "It is highly significant, and indeed almost a rule, that moral courage has its source in such identification through one's own sensitivity with the suffering of one's fellow human beings."[19] Conversely, a lack of empathy weakens respect and sympathy for others. Moreover, in Simon Baron-Cohen's recent study of empathy, he suggests that an erosion and absence of empathy may be the root cause of human cruelty and "evil."[20] Of course, the relationship between empathy and us-them barriers is deeply entwined and somewhat circular: empathy can break through us-them barriers, but us-them barriers often exist because of a lack of empathy in the first place.

War, then, feeds from and into a failure of empathy and moral imagination deeply connected to us-them barriers. Indeed, Robert S. McNamara, who served as secretary of defense from 1961 to 1968, notes that one of the "fundamental failures" of the American war in Vietnam was a "failure of empathy" and admits that the conflict was "filled with examples of monumental misunderstandings, projections, and other failures of assessment and judgment."[21] In the Oscar-winning documentary *The Fog of War: Eleven Lessons from the Life of Robert S. McNamara,* the first lesson listed is "Empathize with your enemy."[22] Still, although war often involves a lack of empathy and moral imagination, its conditions are such that it can sometimes also engender a moral sensibility that transcends all us-them barriers, as the philosopher Simon Critchley explains: "there is a total risk of the self in battle, an utter emptying of the self, that does not produce egoism, but rather a powerful bond of compassionate love for one's comrades and even for one's enemy. The inhumanity of war lets one see through the fictions of a people, a tribe or a nation towards a common humanity. The imponderable question is why it should require such suffering to bring us to this recognition."[23]

The poetry examined in this book stresses both this inhumanity of war and our common humanity. Moral imagination and empathy are an integral part of poetic imagination, and, therefore, poetry often rejects us-them barriers and perceived differences. In his exploration of stateside protest poetry, James F. Mersmann highlights the strength of this sensibility in the American poetry that emerged after the Second World War and observes that it intensified during the war in Vietnam. He remarks that Galway Kinnell, for example, "believes that all poetry . . . attempts to break through, rend, or transcend the barriers and veils that separate men from one another." The roots of this inclusive moral and poetic imagination, Mersmann argues, stretched back to that angel of American poetry, Walt Whitman, and as American involvement in Vietnam deepened this "voice of American poetry made itself heard with a new insistence" in a "Whitmanesque rebellion" of "all-embracing love."[24] Although the work of the soldier-poets is often cynical, especially toward those who maintain and profit from us-them barriers, it is nonetheless infused with a similarly inclusive spirit of love. As Kate McLoughlin concludes in her investigation of war writing, this is a prevalent feature in many literary representations of war: "war literature reveals and recommends love," including, she adds, "love for the enemy." She notes that, for the philosopher Emmanuel Lévinas, "himself a Second World War veteran and concentration camp inmate" and a key interpreter of the idea of the other, "Perceiving and embracing the alterity of the Other is the beginning of not killing, of acceptance, of non-totality, of pluralism." This is the basic "requirement for love and peace: the embracing of alterity," and by "affording glimpses of the face of the Other, texts of war can facilitate similar embracings."[25] As Viktor E. Frankl suggests: "Love is the only way to grasp another human being in the innermost core of his personality. No one can become fully aware of the very essence of another human being unless he loves him."[26]

Finally, it should be noted that such moral and poetic imagination can be understood in terms of the Camusian rebellion outlined in the introduction: it is a negation of us-them barriers and perceived difference and an affirmation of our interconnectedness and common humanity. For Albert Camus, "the affirmation implicit in each act of revolt is extended to something which transcends the individual," and thus "rebellion is not, essentially, an egoistic act." The rebel "demands respect for himself, but only in so far as he identifies himself with humanity in general . . . When he rebels, a man identifies himself with other men." Camus insists that "Man's solidarity is founded upon rebellion," for "from the moment that a movement of rebellion begins, suffering is seen as a collective experience—as the experience of everyone." It is a moral stance that gives rise to a collective ontology: "Rebellion is the common ground on which every man bases his first values. I *rebel*—therefore we *exist.*" An artistic rebellion, such as that present in the poetry, reveals this "We are." Above all, Camus suggests, rebellion "is the refusal to be treated as an object" and the refusal to treat others as objects, too. "It is the affirmation of a nature common to all men."[27] In their versified witness of American-Vietnamese relationships and encounters in the war, the poets articulate and demonstrate this crucial collective and connective aspect of rebellion.

Us and Them

For American soldiers who fought during the war in Vietnam, the primary us-them moral barrier was not a separation between allies and enemies but rather a racial and national divide between American and Vietnamese people. This contributed to and derived from complex, confusing, and often hostile relationships with various sections of the Vietnamese population, including the soldiers' south Vietnamese military allies, their revolutionary opponents, and civilians. The specific intricacies of those particular relationships are examined later in this chapter, while this section offers a more general overview of the American-Vietnamese us-them barrier, especially as it related to the process of dehumanization that occurred during the war.

Of course, the segregation and dehumanization of others based on race was part of the social, cultural, legal, and moral climates of the country in which these soldiers grew up. There were, and remain, deep racial divides within America. "The men did not become racists when they entered the service. They grew up with it. It was taught to them," one participant in the Winter Soldier Investigation testified. This particular witness also suggested that the same applied to an American nationalism that expressed itself via an imperialistic impulse: "The idea that the United States has a God-given right to go into any country and take out its raw materials at an advantage to ourselves is not something that they learned in Vietnam." Rather, the soldiers "learned it in our schools," he continued, "from their mothers, fathers, their sisters and their brothers, their uncles. They learned it from all of us." Certainly, it must be stressed that not all American soldiers, nor indeed all American people, supported or sympathized with such racism and nationalism and also that the extent of their exposure to and acceptance of these ideas and values was heavily dependent on personality, location, family, and other influential situational factors. Yet, as suggested in the previous chapter, what surrounds us shapes us, and this certainly holds for the construction of us-them barriers: "We start taking it in, if by no other process, at least by osmosis, from the day we are born in this country."[28]

Nonetheless, it was primarily during military training that the particular us-them barrier between American and Vietnamese people was instilled in the soldiers. Indeed, the dehumanization of the Vietnamese was a vital part of priming these young Americans for the forthcoming violence of the warzone, as Bruce Weigl suggests: "the entire process of training that you go through before you go to the war has to do with dehumanizing the enemy because it's much easier to kill people that you don't think of as really people than it is to kill people who you think of as your fellow human beings."[29]

Here, as with many moral divides, language was a fundamental mechanism of inculcation. As Connolly remembers: "through all my training I probably heard the word 'Vietnam' ten, fifteen, twenty times a day . . . but I never heard 'Vietnamese,' I heard 'gook,' 'dink,' 'slope,' 'zipperhead.'" Hence, Connolly explains, "now he holds a tag that dehumanizes him, that puts him in the target . . . that's how they get all these nice, sane, young men and women to kill other young men and women because they're not humans anymore they're 'gooks.'" Connolly was aware of this attempt to establish an us-them barrier, although he did not fully realize its devastating impact until he was in the warzone: "I knew that this was a part of my training, that I was being taught to think . . . of these people as different but didn't really relate it to a course of brainwashing . . . until I started to watch it happen, until I started to see people just indiscriminately firing into groups of Vietnamese . . . because they're just 'gooks.'" Thus, Connolly came to conclude that "war is racism, war is the denial of another person's humanity through racism . . . you have to use racism, you have to use some form that separates him apart, that denies him the same humanity you hold."[30] As a key carrier of moral meaning, language plays a vital role in this. Such "verbal dehumanization," Komunyakaa suggests, imparts "signals embedded in language." The moral message might be explicit or implicit, but even in the latter case, "People still act on it, and they are acting on it when they're not fully conscious that they're acting on it." As Komunyakaa argues: "We internalize it, we internalize the spirit of language." This linguistic othering is not only a necessary part of war's violence—"one has to dehumanize before one can kill another"—but a causal contributor to war, too: "there's a kind of verbal dehumanization that leads to war even before there's war."[31] Through this process of military training and the use of dehumanizing language, then, recruits were taught the central idea and aim of the American-Vietnamese us-them barrier: "The only good gook is a dead gook."[32] Thus, this dividing line of morality and violence was firmly established before the soldiers even entered the warzone.

The construction of this us-them barrier was reinforced upon arrival "in country." Just as the physical environments of Vietnam initially seemed strange to many American soldiers, so, too, did the people. The perceived otherness of the people echoed the perceived otherness of the place, and, as the previous chapter outlined, the two often seemed inseparable. In W. D. Ehrhart's "Making the Children Behave," translated copies of which he took with him on his 1985 return trip to Vietnam, he wonders:

> Do they think of me now
> in those strange Asian villages
> where nothing ever seemed
> quite human
> but myself
> and my few grim friends
> moving through them
> hunched
> in lines?

When they tell stories to their children
of the evil
that awaits misbehavior,
is it me they conjure?[33]

In the first stanza, Ehrhart recalls a strange place in which only those on his side of the us-them barrier seemed fully human. In the second stanza, however, he questions the moral status of this divide through a perceptual reversal that indicates the possibility that it was actually him and his "grim friends" who were "the evil." As the literary scholar Renny Christopher notes, in this poetic turn, "Americans change from human to monster, while Vietnamese change from nonhuman to human."[34] It is a work, the cultural historian H. Bruce Franklin suggests, that highlights the distilled power of poetry: "it takes Ehrhart precisely forty-eight words to demonstrate that all those perceptions of Vietnam and the Vietnamese as alien, unreal, and unknowable actually invert reality while revealing the opposite of what they profess."[35] In this poem, as in many other pieces, as the us-them barrier is depicted, it is simultaneously questioned and destabilized.

Like many us-them barriers, the dichotomy was predicated on perceived difference and a gap of understanding that, in turn, contributed to fear, frustration, and hostility. This was not the first time that America had fought an Asian adversary, yet "Orientalism" and its attendant assumptions and miscalculations still figured in the thought and tactics of Americans during the war in Vietnam.[36] Dick Shea summarizes his early impressions: "orient is strange / different perspective / different people." This perceived strangeness and difference of the Vietnamese hooked into established conceptions of an Oriental other, a divide derived from a line supposedly separating East from West. Shea then emphasizes the lack of empathy and imagination involved in such us-them barriers and how ignorance and fear of difference fed into the war and fueled a brash and ineffective American imperialism:

the american
he can not understand
life other than his own
he tries to convert other peoples

to his way
and he does not do it subtly
in fact he does not do it at all[37]

"Our misjudgments of friend and foe alike," McNamara retrospects, "reflected our profound ignorance of the history, culture, and politics of the people in the area," and America's failure to appropriately adapt and apply its military tactics to the Vietnamese context was a "major [cause] for our disaster in Vietnam."[38] Hence, what George C. Herring identifies as "the chasm of ignorance that separated us from our Vietnamese allies and enemies at the time," and an "inability as a nation to make this cultural leap," contributed to both the moral and the military failure of America in Vietnam.[39]

For some American soldiers on the ground, the divide between us and them could provoke intense feelings and actions of frustration, fear, and hostility toward this other. As Connolly notes: "In all the senseless acts of racist hate, / I felt the growing fears."[40] "I hate you / with your yellow wrinkled skin— / and slanted eyes, / your toothless grins," Igor Bobrowsky writes. "I can't stand your children— / cowering or begging— / or staring blankly, / void of any comprehension," he continues. "And I despise your men, / Indifferent to my curses— / passive before my kicks and shoves / like shadows." This hatred is compounded by the enveloping climate of violence in which his close comrades are injured and in pain: "Always when the time is wrong; / while my friends bite at the air / and press their palms / against the earth." Bobrowsky cannot connect to these people with their physical differences, cannot comprehend their perceived passivity and apparent apathy. "Why / do you not respond, / resist or fight?" he asks in the poem's final lines. "It would make hating you / so very much easier."[41] As in Ehrhart's "Making the Children Behave," the twist at the end questions the us-them barrier. Subarno Chattarji's astute analysis of Bobrowsky's poem explicates its interesting and revealing tension: "Herbert Marcuse's idea that language creates the enemy not 'as he really is but rather as he must be in order to perform his function for the Establishment', is borne out by the manner in which the poet attempts to maintain, and simultaneously realizes the futility of maintaining, the oppositional framework."[42] Again, as it portrays the us-them barrier, the poetry simultaneously undermines the structure of the divide.

One particularly revealing aspect of the othering that occurred during the war was the belief among some Americans that Vietnamese people did not place the same high value on life that Occidentals supposedly did. For example, in three different poems, Shea comments that "life is cheap here," "life is not much to them," and "here death is a part of a short life / war is constant / bodies are cheap / death is accepted."[43] One source of this dehumanizing conception was the immense scale of the sacrifice of the Vietnamese revolutionaries. As American soldiers "peered in disbelief at the piles of torn and twisted enemy corpses following an engagement," the journalist and historian Stanley Karnow states, "they had no explanation for such sacrifice except to dismiss them as 'gooks' for whom the Western concept of life was alien."[44] The notion that the Vietnamese held life in low regard was a way of coping with and justifying the death that the American intervention was causing. It was also a case of projection. It was not that the Vietnamese did not value life, but that the Americans did not value the life of the Vietnamese, a belief they projected onto the other. This was an idea embodied in military practices and policies like the body count and free-fire zones and in the use of devastating weaponry such as napalm and Agent Orange. As John Kerry, speaking as a member of Vietnam Veterans Against the War, asserted in his appearance before the Senate Foreign Relations Committee on 22 April 1971: "We learned the meaning of free fire zones, shooting anything that moves, and we watched while America placed a cheapness on the lives of orientals . . . We fought using weapons against 'oriental human beings,' we fought using weapons against those people which I do not believe this country would dream of using were we fighting in the European theater or let us say a non-third-world people theater."[45] Hence, race and "Orientalism" were significant factors in the construction of this us-them barrier and also in how America acted on it. Moreover, the methods of war employed further ingrained and sustained the belief that the lives of those on the outside of this boundary were worth less than those on the inside. In a downward spiral of dehumanization, military and moral climates developed that both stemmed from and continually reinforced this divide.

The language of dehumanization that American soldiers were taught during their training played a vital role in the maintenance and application of the us-them barrier in the warzone. Derogatory names that excluded the Vietnamese from the moral space of the Americans were a key part of the "verbal climate of war."[46] A glossary in the poetry anthology *Carrying the Darkness* defines one particularly prevalent appellation: "gook: disparaging GI slang for a Viet Cong or any Vietnamese person."[47] It is a revealing description. Although the term applies to and identifies an enemy combatant, it also includes "any Vietnamese person," the American violation of the discrimination requirement encapsulated in one word.[48] Similarly, during the war, one American veteran noted that the "universal designation for the people of Vietnam, *friend or enemy,* is 'gook.'"[49] A variety of other epithets were also attached to the Vietnamese. As one poet suggests, these names eased the process of dehumanization and objectification:

> Put a label on the victims of our crimes.
> Call them commies, dinks or dupes.
> They're not human anymore.
> They must [die] or be degraded.
>
> They have no dreams.
> They feel no pain.
> They're just gooks and slopes,
> Objects for our jokes.[50]

The intimate connection between language, difference, dehumanization, and the war's violence is perfectly captured in Jan Barry's "Memorial For Man In Black Pajamas":

> Trinh Vo Man was a poet
> in his own land a scholar
> to his own people a venerable
> and wise old man
> in his village
> throughout his native land
> a warm and kind man
> to his wife and children
> and grandchildren
> a humorous and tolerant man
> to his neighbors
> an hospitable man to all

til the blue-eyed visitors
came uninvited
and shot him

because a Man wearing
black pajamas
to them
was just a slope, a dink, a gook
was "Vietcong"[51]

Barry simultaneously describes and subverts the us-them barrier. Set against the dehumanizing language and violence of the war it portrays, the poem maintains and remembers the humanity of the victim. The naming, the first act of the poem, is particularly significant, as it resists the stripping of individual identity caused by this language and violence. Perhaps it is simply actuality, perhaps just a coincidence, or perhaps poetic choice that the word "Man" appears in the victim's name. Whatever the reason, as Barry details the character and attributes of the victim, the word "man" is repeated several times, and the "Man" in the final stanza is capitalized, thus linking back to the victim's name and also strongly emphasizing his humanity. Additionally, Barry highlights the simplistic and inaccurate cultural assumptions of an us-them divide that saw those "wearing / black pajamas" as an uncivilized other; indeed, in this poem it is "the blue-eyed visitors" who seem uncivilized. Hence, Barry's poem can be understood as an act of artistic rebellion: it negates the us-them barrier and instead affirms humanity.

Divisive and derogatory language was a crucial part of the process of killing in the warzone. Verbal dehumanization weakened respect and sympathy for the Vietnamese and helped to create the moral distance necessary for killing. In Komunyakaa's "Autobiography of My Alter Ego," the speaker states: "I called the Vietnamese / gooks & dinks / so I could kill them."[52] "A thousand / words of hate," J. Vincent Hansen writes, "employed / to dehumanize / and incite."[53] In another poem, "Hate," he emphasizes the link between dehumanizing language and violence and suggests that a divisive and hateful vocabulary can lead to tragedy and atrocity when applied and actualized in a military climate:

Naked
he sires
little words
like
gook, kike
and *spik.*
Then
puts on
his
uniform
and
gives birth
to
big words
like
holocaust and
genocide.[54]

Similarly, Peter Berenbak indicates that racial othering and the language of dehumanization were vital factors in the violence perpetrated by Americans in Vietnam:

Wanting to cry out in anger!
At the racism so
Blatantly accepted as
Part of our daily existance [*sic*].
Black
        As well as
            White
Skillfully play the game.
Blacks just learning;
Whites practicing for home.
Gook,
        Dink,
            Slope.
Colorful words for a
Less than human race.

The stage is now set
For the triumphant third act.
Kill them all.
Everything!
Since they're not really people
It can't be murder[55]

Thus, the construction and application of an American-Vietnamese us-them barrier, significantly aided by linguistic dehumanization, was a central aspect of the American war in Vietnam and one that is frequently depicted and condemned in the poetry.

The Stranger Within

Before exploring further intricacies that occurred in the American relationship with the other side of the us-them barrier, it is helpful to consider poetic portrayals of the tensions and complexities that existed on the inside of that divide. As Berenbak's poem intimates, there were racial issues within the American military during the war, internal cracks in the moral space of us. "For African Americans, Latinos, Native Americans, and Asian Americans, the Vietnam War created some significant challenges," Kyle Longley notes, and the diversity of America's soldiers contributed to complicated and sometimes discordant racial dynamics in the warzone.[56] There were other internal frictions, too—between "grunts" and REMFs (Rear Echelon Mother Fuckers), for example, or between enlisted men and officers, hence the rise of "fragging," "the attempted murder of officers and NCOs by their own troops."[57] These divisions were also linked to the stratifications of education and class.[58] All of these strains and partitions stemmed from the conditions of American society itself; the military simply echoed, and in some instances exacerbated, the fractured state of the country as a whole. There are a number of poems written by American veterans, from a variety of perspectives, that address each of these fissures. Still, perhaps the most significant internal rift, and one that receives noteworthy attention in the poetry, was that involving black Americans.[59] Through the work of Lamont B. Steptoe and Yusef Komunyakaa, this section focuses on that particular tension.[60]

In a piece located and dated "Chu Chi, Vietnam 1969," Steptoe summarizes his understanding of both American society and the war: "a victim of racism, i now fight a racist war. i, a black man, am told to kill a yellow man."[61] Language and labeling are integral to this racism: "they want to take my life . . . they, the gooks, so named by the white man, want to kill me, a nigger, so named by the white man." He feels his life threatened by two separations. First, the divide between him and the people and country of Vietnam: "i want to live but they want to take my life, the Vietcong, the NVA, malaria, the heat." Second, the divide between him and his own countrymen: "they want to take my life, those white GI's who feel that i'm not a necessary implement of their security and they can quelch [*sic*] a bit of that 'American homesickness' by bringing to the fore a little bit of the Blackman prejudice. they want to take my life."[62] Hence, for Steptoe, "they" included not just the Vietnamese but "white GI's" as well. Conversely, it appears that for these white soldiers, black Americans were an excluded other. Steptoe's depiction dismisses any idea of America as a united if diverse and strained space; there were no internal divisions subsumed within a larger us-them construction, just a multitude of us-them barriers in which racial difference preceded state-based similarity. Indeed, in one poem, he writes: "In country / Black men were a nation." Later in the same poem, Steptoe hints that the "bones" of black soldiers were a "White man's price" in a "White man's war."[63] Certainly, in the early stages of the American escalation, black casualty statistics were disproportionately high, with the death rate in 1966 close to 21 percent, "compared to their 12 percent share of the population. This led to a concerted effort by the military to reduce African American deaths, which leveled off by the end of the war to 13.1 percent."[64] Still, Steptoe's poem concludes with the suggestion that those who survived the war continued to face a fatal threat when they returned to America:

> Black men are a nation
> under siege
> if you lived to fight another day
> the White man will try to kill
> you in the U. S. of A.[65]

In Steptoe's poetry, then, black Americans encounter hostility, racism, and violence whether they are in Vietnam or in America.

Komunyakaa also considers the experience of black Americans who fought in Vietnam, although he provides a more complex and nuanced account of the racial issues they confronted.[66] Like Steptoe, he expresses a keen awareness of the ability of language to dehumanize. "I never used the word 'gook,' I never used the word 'dink,'" Komunyakaa states, "because coming from Louisiana and being conscious of my situation as an American I thought it paralleled other derogatory terms in the American lexicon." Yet, "I knew black soldiers who did," he continues, "and sometimes I would check them on it . . . other times it just became part of the climate . . . it was just the, you could say, verbal climate of war." Unlike Steptoe's poetic portrayal, here was the American-Vietnamese us-them barrier in action, as American soldiers united against the Vietnamese: "there is a kind of verbal dehumanization that happens, and it happened with black and white soldiers, side by side, dehumanizing the Vietnamese." Nonetheless, Komunyakaa acknowledges that the American military was still fractured internally along racial lines: "how could it not be, it was in the social fabric of the American, so how could it change?"[67]

Several pieces in Komunyakaa's collection *Dien Cai Dau* explore the links between the war in Vietnam and "a war back in America," as well as the way in which the Vietnamese revolutionaries attempted to utilize racial issues to undermine the morale of black soldiers in the warzone.[68] In one poem, the voice of "Hanoi Hannah" speaks to black soldiers:

> "You know you're dead men,
> don't you? You're dead
> as King today in Memphis.
> Boys, you're surrounded by
> General Tran Do's division."
> Her knife-edge song cuts
> deep as a sniper's bullet.
> "Soul Brothers, what you dying for?"[69]

This psychological warfare may have been practiced by the revolutionaries, but the ammunition was provided by the reality of American racism: "leaflets tell us / *VC didn't kill / Dr. Martin Luther King*."[70] Similarly, in "The One-legged Stool," the revolutionaries exploit internal racial tensions and the death of King to disturb and demoralize a black POW Komunyakaa imagines: "Those white prisoners didn't say what you say they said. They ain't laughing. Ain't cooperating. They ain't putting me down, calling me names like you say. Lies. Lies. It ain't the way you say it is. I'm American. (*Pause.*) Doctor King, he ain't dead like you say. Lies." The black prisoner, like the reader, cannot be sure what those white prisoners are actually saying, but his insistence that "They ain't putting me down" and "I'm American" is checked by the news of King's assassination. "You've pitted me against them. Against those white troops," the black prisoner realizes, but he is also aware of the actuality of the racial divide in America. "Yeah, VC. I've been through Georgia. Yeah, been through 'Bama too. Mississippi, yeah. You know what? You eye me worse than those rednecks," he states. "They used to look at me in my uniform like I didn't belong in it . . . My brass, my ribbons, they would make their blood boil. They'd turn away, cursing through their teeth," he continues, as he recognizes that some white Americans despise him just as much as his captors do: "All I have to go back to are faces just like yours at the door."[71]

For Komunyakaa, his own experience as the other within the borders of America impacted on his understanding of and relationship with the Vietnamese. As the previous chapter emphasized, Komunyakaa "wasn't afraid of the landscape," and, he explains, "not being afraid of the landscape consequently I wasn't really detached from the people." To him, as a combat correspondent rather than a "typical infantryman," and coming from a relatively rural location, Vietnam did not seem quite so strange, frightening, or hostile, and so neither did the people. Moreover, as a black American, an awareness of what it meant to be in the position of the other helped him to empathize with the Vietnamese: "coming from the Deep South, from Louisiana . . . my whole life had been I suppose shaped by the idea of the other, because I was . . . So I knew the situation of the Vietnamese as the other as well." Hence, "I could empathize to an extent with the Vietnamese and their situation."[72] For example, in one poem, Komunyakaa looks through a "starlight scope" at an "old, bowlegged" Vietnamese revolutionary and expresses a desire to embrace him: "you feel you could reach out / & take him into your arms."[73] Another poem depicts an act of compassion in which the speaker turns over the body of an enemy who has just been killed, "so he wouldn't be / kissing the ground." In the context of *Dien Cai Dau*, it might be assumed that the victim is Vietnamese and the compassionate soldier American, but the ambiguity of the poem is such that these roles could be reversed. Either way, it is an empathetic moment in which the us-them barrier is breached.[74] Empathy, especially for the other, is a thread that runs throughout many of Komunyakaa's poems, and much of his work is filtered through an understanding and belief that "we're all somehow connected."[75]

Crucially, Komunyakaa suggests that constructions of us and them, insider and outsider, friend and foe, are never fixed but always dependent on and shaped by contextual considerations. Thus, just as climatic conditions for American soldiers could be influenced by factors such as the time period and locations in which they served, their rank, and their role, so too could their notions of difference and otherness. This fluidity underpinned a particularly important aspect of internal racial dynamics in the warzone: differences and divisions mattered considerably less, if at all, out in the field and during combat operations. When there "was more of a social situation, like for instance back at the rear—if we can say that there was a rear—there was always tension," Komunyakaa explains, but in "a combat situation everybody fended for each other."[76] In "Phantasmagoria," he writes: "We slept side by side in the sand-bagged bunker, with arms around each other, too scared to see black and white. We didn't know how deeply hearts took sides on foreign shores, that only the metallic whine of rockets broke down barriers." However, these same barriers were rebuilt when they returned to America: "We'd lay down a fire that melted machineguns, but back in The World we threw up fences laughter couldn't shake. The bridge we rigged with our bodies, did we know it would crumble into dust and light?" Still, even as old differences and identities were reconstructed, remnants of those moments of unity remained: "When we stepped off the plane, you kissed the ground and disappeared. I put on my time-woven mask. But wherever you are, please know I won't say I heard you cry out in your sleep those burning nights—like you didn't hear me."[77]

This pattern of shifting internal divisions outlined by Komunyakaa is also portrayed by Connolly, a white American, in his poem "Brotherhood." "The Klan was there, / maybe in your platoon . . . And in the midst of ours / they waged their own war," he writes, a war that mirrored "one older, / for many unfinished, / and . . . one recent, / the war at home." In the warzone's extremity, though, divisions faded and a strong unity emerged:

> We were scared,
> and the combination
> of fear and youth,
> and death and injury,
> along with
> the realization
>
> that we were on our own,
>
> turned a reluctant,
> tennuous [*sic*] acceptance
> into true brotherhood.[78]

In these circumstances, "we're all Americans," Connolly says. Whereas in America a black person might have been perceived as the other and labeled a "nigger" by some, in the realm of combat "that word that he was tagged with . . . he no longer carries anymore."[79] Yet, as Komunyakaa indicates, the old antagonisms reappeared once the soldiers returned to America, a separation that Connolly urges against:

> It is harder here,
> back in the world,
> without the danger
> and the death
> and the despair
> to hold that feeling,
> but I ask you,
> Brothers,
> to try.

Connolly hopes that the wartime bond has impacted on those who previously "knew only / what our side / had told us / of the other" and that the word "brotherhood," "because of / our experience there, / has a different meaning." For him, veterans can choose to maintain those connections they forged in the war as soldiers:

> The next time
> you say,
>
> "I hate,"
>
> because of
> the color
> of a face,
> remember you had,
> and still have,
> if you want them,
> Brothers that color.

This feeling of unity that they shared in the warzone is one that Connolly suggests they "can surely / use" and "may need" back in America.[80]

In his poem "Tu Do Street," Komunyakaa eloquently summarizes these complex linkages between race, America, and the war in Vietnam. "Music divides the evening. / I close my eyes & can see / men drawing lines in the dust," he begins. "America pushes through the membrane / of mist & smoke, & I'm a small boy / again in Bogalusa. *White Only* / signs." Back in the poem's present, in Vietnam, he walks "into a place where bar girls / fade like tropical birds" and where the "mama-san" does not seem to understand why a black soldier is in a bar full of white soldiers. "We have played Judas where / only machine-gun fire brings us / together. Down the street / black GIs hold to their turf also," he continues. The final lines of the poem trace connections between prostitution and the war, between the Vietnamese and Americans, and between Americans and Americans:

> Back in the bush at Dak To
> & Khe Sanh, we fought
> the brothers of these women
> we now run to hold in our arms.
> There's more than a nation
> inside us, as black & white

soldiers touch the same lovers
minutes apart, tasting
each other's breath,
without knowing these rooms
run into each other like tunnels
leading to the underworld.[81]

Additionally, the internal tensions that existed during the war influenced not only how Americans related to other Americans but also how they related to the Vietnamese. In a letter written during the war, one veteran summarized the situation: "The analogy is depressingly clear between our failure to relate successfully to the Vietnamese and to the black people who comprise an 'underdeveloped nation' within our own society. In both cases our behavior is racist in the true sense of opposing the overwhelming forces generated by a people's search for pride and identity. The price of our lack of perception is defeat abroad, and, if not corrected, may be the dissolution of society at home."[82] Thus, an absence of empathy and imagination contributed to moral and military failure in Vietnam. Moreover, if, in certain times and places, some of those supposedly inside the American-Vietnamese us-them barrier were mistreated and dehumanized, then it is perhaps unsurprising that so too were those outside the boundary. As Shea reasons: "the americans do not respect each other / how can they respect the vietnamese."[83]

Allies and Enemies

Despite these internal tensions and difficulties, the primary us-them barrier for American soldiers during the war was, as indicated above, between American and Vietnamese people. That this preceded a divide between allies and enemies is evidenced by the poetic depictions of the south Vietnamese military and the Vietnamese revolutionaries. Moreover, these portrayals reveal much about the climatic conditions discussed in the previous chapter. In particular, the doubt, questioning, and confusion of American soldiers were entwined with their impressions of and relationship with those they fought alongside, and the fear, frustration, and the strange and adversarial physical landscapes they endured were connected to those they fought against. Their perceptions of and encounters with these two sets of people on the outside of the us-them barrier were a significant part of the experiences of American soldiers in the warzone.

For many of the poets, one of the most disconcerting aspects of the warzone, and a particularly influential contributor to the development of doubt and questioning, was their south Vietnamese military allies. Although the Americans had other military accomplices during the war, including South Koreans, Australians, and New Zealanders, it was their interactions with the Army of the Republic of Vietnam that proved most problematic and disturbing. The poetic account of Shea, who observed the ARVN closely in 1965 as "a paid american advisor," abounds with concerns about these allies.[84] As mentioned in the previous chapter, Shea was suspicious of the ostensibly mercenary motives of the south Vietnamese military and also of their apparent unwillingness to fight: "we pay them to fight their war / and they mostly collect / and mostly don't fight."[85] Additionally, he frequently portrays the ARVN as weak and overreliant on American support: "they are too dependent on americans / they cannot combat their guerrilla enemies / because they are pampered / and have no fighting spirit." This leads Shea to the conclusion—one that could be used as an argument for either the necessity or the undesirability of American involvement—that "they would crumple / and capitulate to communism / as soon as america pulled out of here."[86] Shea portrays his Vietnamese allies as "grinning nothings" who "learn to lie / in order to tell the american what he wants to hear," and he expresses disillusionment at the detrimental impact of the American presence on the behavior and character of the south Vietnamese: "some of them are really brave good people / most are not / some of these might have been / if the american personality had not subordinated them."[87] As Shea's chronological account progresses, he reveals an increasing awareness of just how many of the seemingly negative aspects and traits of the behavior and character of both the civilians and the military of south Vietnam stemmed from the climate created by the American intervention. This subservience, as well as corruption and favoritism, not only was problematic in itself but also hindered those who displayed characteristics that could actually have helped in the fight against the revolutionaries, such as the south Vietnamese officer Shea meets "who thinks" and "is not afraid of me / or any american / or his superiors":

he believes in principles
fights for what he believes is right
and is not greatly concerned with money
and yet
this man is held down by his superiors
and can not achieve his goals
because he doesn't kiss ass[88]

The outcome of all of this was an ineffective fighting force. In one poem, Shea describes a fishing trip with some of his military allies in which their dismal attempts at catching fish, even using explosive charges, echo their unsuccessful efforts at fighting the revolutionaries, even using American support and technology. He "will try to avoid all such fishing parties in the future," Shea decides dejectedly, "although many of them do better at fishing / than they do at killing viet cong."[89]

Not all of the poetry offers such a negative portrait of the ARVN. In "War Stories," for example, Horace Coleman elicits sympathy for "the ARVN who lost his arm to the NVA, / his wife to a free fire zone, / and his kid to disease and / American medicine."[90] Yet, an attitude similar to Shea's skepticism does thread through much of the poetry, with the ARVN frequently derided as apathetic, unwilling, incompetent, cowardly, corrupt, disloyal, untrustworthy, and opportunistic. "We fought outnumbered in Hue City," Ehrhart writes of his experience during the Tet Offensive, "While the ARVN soldiers looted bodies / In the safety of the rear."[91] Above all, Longley notes, for American soldiers it often seemed like they were the ones putting themselves in danger while the ARVN "avoided fighting and let the Americans bear the burden."[92] In "ARVN Rangers," Leroy V. Quintana describes a strong feeling of resentment for this, "of my having to be there fighting his war."[93] As Longley summarizes, the consequence was "an ambivalent relationship at best, a dysfunctional one at the worst," and "negative perceptions of the ARVN remained throughout the conflict despite efforts by American propagandists to portray them in a positive light."[94] For American soldiers, it was almost as though their Vietnamese allies were as much of an impediment as their Vietnamese enemies.

It was this perplexing situation that prompted many soldiers to doubt and question the war. If the south Vietnamese, as Kerry noted in his 1971 congressional testimony, "were hard put to take up the fight against the threat we were supposedly saving them from," then, American soldiers wondered, who were they really fighting for, what was the true nature of this threat they were meant to be fighting against, and was this supposed threat really so dangerous for America or even for Vietnam itself?[95] In sum: if the south Vietnamese did not seem so concerned, why should Americans worry, fight, kill, and die?

These questions and doubts were further provoked by the perceived contrast between the apathy and incompetence of the ARVN and the conviction and determination of the opposing revolutionaries. The former may have had the apparent advantage of being able to rely on American support and technology, "on trucks for transportation / and well oiled weapons for fighting / and money," but the latter "has a belief . . . and he has spirit / while the south vietnamese has comfort," although, as Shea acknowledges, "it is not comfortable to have a spirited enemy."[96] For Shea, this was a reflection of the political and ideological underpinnings of each side: "democracy is fighting with money / communism is fighting with controlled spirit."[97] As Ehrhart recalls, "one side had massive support from [the] Americans, was equipped by the Americans, trained by the Americans, supported by the Americans, had everything going for them and they wouldn't freaking fight." Conversely, the "other side has nothing going for them," he continues, "they got nothing, and yet they won't quit. And yet, they're the same people. These guys won't fight with all the advantages, these guys won't quit with all the disadvantages." From this contrast, doubt, questioning, and an incipient if confused awareness arose: "I'm eighteen-years old and I'm looking at this and thinking, 'who believes in what here?' These guys clearly believe in what they're fighting for, these guys don't and these guys are supposedly the guys I'm helping. Well I don't know how to make sense of that but I'm certainly aware of it." For Ehrhart, and for many other American soldiers, this was one of the central factors that made them begin to think, "what the hell is going on here?"[98] Their relationship with and perceptions of their south Vietnamese military allies, therefore, contributed significantly to the enveloping doubt, questioning, and confusion in the warzone.

Simultaneously, the fear, frustration, and apparently otherworldly and hostile physical environments the American soldiers endured were substantially shaped by their engagement with and impressions of those they fought against. If it seemed as though the ARVN would have fared poorly in comparison with any other fighting force, they had the added misfortune of being contrasted with the Vietnamese revolutionaries, who garnered respect and even admiration from American soldiers for exactly those characteristics the ARVN appeared to lack: skill, ingenuity, spirit, courage, determination, and steadfast dedication to a cause. For example, Ehrhart states that while he had "increasing contempt" for his military ally, his admiration for his military opponent grew the longer he was in Vietnam.[99] This wartime respect and admiration for the enemy, sometimes given grudgingly, appears in many poems. Nobody "could disagree— / we had fought the finest, light infantry / in the world," Steve Mason suggests.[100] The poets do not always clearly distinguish between the North Vietnamese Army and the Vietcong—the content of the poems perhaps reflecting the form of the war—but when they do, as is common in other soldiers' accounts of the war, the former are especially respected. With regard to the latter, the respect was tempered by "a sense of frustration of fighting an elusive enemy" who employed guerrilla tactics and, in doing so, also confounded American soldiers' initial expectations of what they thought a war and a soldier should be.[101] This was not just a military frustration but a moral one, too, as American soldiers desired the perceived moral clarity of fighting a more conventional and identifiable military force. In one poem, Ehrhart describes how he "was green / with envy . . . rice shoot green" the day a friend of his "flew to Tam Ky":

> This wasn't going to be just one more
> chickenscratch guerrilla fight:
> farmers, women, boobytraps and snipers,
> dead Marines, and not a Viet Cong in sight.
> This was hardcore NVA . . .[102]

For Connolly, the "widespread belief that the Vietcong were nowhere as good a soldier as the NVA" did not correspond to his experience in the warzone, where he soon discovered "that the people who had told me in training that the Vietcong were a bunch of farmers and mama-sans, that they were full of shit . . . these were people who had grown up at war . . . these people were soldiers 24/7 and had been for years."[103] Of course, an individual soldier's specific impressions and experiences of the enemy, as in many other instances in the war, depended on where, when, and whom they fought. Yet, wherever the place, whenever the time, and however the NVA and the Vietcong compared with one another, taken as a whole the Vietnamese revolutionary forces were a formidable foe.

The poets emphasize how the enemy sowed fear, frustration, and doubt among American soldiers. As mentioned in the previous chapter, some soldiers imagined the revolutionaries to be mystical and magical warriors. Partly, such mythological accounts stemmed from their sheer elusiveness. They were, Hassett writes, "the enemy / we can't find."[104] Nonetheless, somehow they seemed constantly close, rarely seen but always felt, pictured by the poets, Chattarji notes, as "a shadowy absent presence."[105] Moreover, if the revolutionaries were "an enemy we couldn't see," the poets suggest, they had no such problems locating American soldiers: "see, they always knew where we were."[106] They appeared to be able to decide where and when military engagements occurred, and so American soldiers, "always aware that Charlie only waits," came to feel as though they were as much the hunted as the hunters.[107] Connolly recalls one particular encounter in which this pattern of control was reversed and how he reflected on the rarity of such an event: "I settled back, wondering, / would I live to remember / this time that *we* caught *them*."[108] This was an exceptionally uncommon occurrence. Throughout his entire tour, Connolly states, "there was only half a dozen times that we actually caught the enemy, the rest of the time we were just out stumbling around like morons, bait . . . waiting for somebody to trip a booby trap, waiting to spring the next ambush . . . I maintain that the American soldier in Vietnam was just bait anyway, just bait."[109]

To many American soldiers, then, the revolutionaries seemed both ominously omnipresent and dangerously omniscient. "They can see everything and they know everything," John F. Howe writes.[110] Layne describes how "Charlie got the word" when a group of American soldiers was

> bogged down
> Without much ammunition.
> Charlie

Always
Got
The
Word.[111]

In another poem, he expresses the unnerving and claustrophobic sensation of being in a warzone in which the enemy always seemed to be watching:

When the M-16 rifle had a stoppage,
One could feel enemy eyes
Climbing
His
Bones
Like

Ivy.[112]

Even nighttime provided no respite from the all-seeing revolutionaries, who were apparently also aided by enhanced sensory faculties: "Everyone knows Charlie can see in the dark / And smell Americans."[113] Additionally, the link between the revolutionaries and the natural climates of Vietnam, especially the jungle where "the foe takes root / like palms / like sticky ferns / like weeds in the garden / of our innocence," and their utilization of the physical environment as a weapon in their guerrilla arsenal heightened American soldiers' feelings of fear and their dread of the dangers of and in the Vietnamese landscape.[114] The revolutionaries "used the land as part of the fight," Komunyakaa explains. They "knew how to hit the American soldiers and fade back into the landscape because they were so familiar with the land."[115] "From the ferns they emerge," Hall writes of an ambush, "like awful butterflies / from the earth's cocoon."[116]

Eventually, some American soldiers began to believe that the revolutionaries might even be unbeatable. Just as the bamboo they "hacked down" would grow back "chest high" within weeks, their opponents could never be completely cut down either, for such a committed and determined force "always comes back."[117] And they did. The revolutionaries "fought back, and fought back again, and again, and again," the historian James Pinckney Harrison stresses, "until finally they indeed 'got the better of fire with water,' in Ho Chi Minh's phrase."[118] This tenacity and determination led some American soldiers in the warzone to ask why it was that the revolutionaries were so committed and "endured the hardships and battering inflicted on them by the technologically superior American forces," to "question their commitment to the South Vietnamese, both the troops . . . and the civilians," to reassess both militarily and morally the notion of American superiority and supremacy, to wonder whether the war was winnable at all, to reflect on what winning the war would even mean, and to query which side was right, which side was wrong, and what their own role was in "the entire disaster that was America's war in Indochina."[119] The Vietnamese revolutionaries, then, not only were a dangerous and skilled military adversary but also frustrated American combatants with their elusiveness while simultaneously instilling a fear in these soldiers through their ghostly omnipresence, mythical omniscience, and intimate connection with the physical landscape. Furthermore, through their indefatigable determination to fight for their cause, they made many American soldiers question their own cause and, as a result, considerably intensified the doubt and moral confusion these soldiers experienced in the warzone.

Distinctions

As difficult and troubling as their encounters with those they fought alongside and those they fought against were, for American soldiers it was those they were supposed to be fighting for—the Vietnamese people, that is, rather than the American public safely ensconced thousands of miles away—who generated the greatest degree of moral tension in the warzone. Although the poets indicate that the relationship between American soldiers and the civilians of south Vietnam could be amiable and friendly, the predominant atmosphere portrayed in the poetry is one of mutual fear, misunderstanding, suspicion, distrust, and hostility.[120] Frank A. Cross Jr. summarizes the feelings of the Vietnamese people: "They stood before us, / Frightened, bewildered, hateful."[121] Hence, fear was an important factor not just for American soldiers but for all those in the warzone. As Connolly states: "everybody was scared to death."[122] Confusion, too, affected both soldier and civilian. And, if to American soldiers the Vietnamese people seemed as unfamiliar and strange as the physical landscape in a mutually reinforcing otherness between people and place, to the Vietnamese these Americans were an alien presence in a familiar environment. As Shea observes, "everything in their atmosphere meshes / except for one clog / the american."[123]

Above all, it was the apparent hostility, or at least apathy, of the Vietnamese civilians that most shocked and disconcerted American soldiers. Many were initially confused and resentful that those they had been sent to save did not seem to welcome or even want their presence. As Ehrhart recalls: "When I'd first arrived in Vietnam, I had expected to be greeted by thankful peasants lining the roads, waving and cheering like the newsreels I'd seen as a kid of American GIs liberating French villages from the Nazis." However, this was not the "Good War." Ehrhart soon discovered that he had been misled by expectations derived from both the past and the present. "What I found in Vietnam bore no resemblance to what I had been led to expect by Lyndon Johnson and *Time* magazine and my high school history teachers," he continues. "The peasants of Vietnam had greeted me with an opaque silence that looked for all the world like indifference or hostility."[124]

Indeed, soldiers did not meet a grateful population but, instead, encountered a people who had endured years of violence and instability, much of it caused by the American military intervention and support of a corrupt, repressive, and unpopular regime against a revolutionary force fighting for national liberation, unification, and communism. The final lines of Michael Casey's poem "A Bummer" concisely capture the terrible impact of the war on the country and people of Vietnam: "If you have a farm in Vietnam / And a house in hell / Sell the farm / And go home."[125] It was, therefore, unsurprising that some American soldiers came to feel like oppressive invaders rather than the liberating saviors they had hoped and expected to be. As Connolly writes: "I fought to keep a nation / and a people divided"; "I saw very quickly / that we were the invader"; "I was hated / by the people I fought for."[126] Kevin Bowen's poem "Temple at Quan Loi, 1969" carefully describes the enmity some Vietnamese people harbored for American soldiers:

> Outside the gate
> the old woman
> walks up the hill
> from the temple.
> Her pace
> deliberate as a procession.
> From the corner of an eye
> she stares.
> She must wish our deaths.
> Beneath the white silk band
> breasts ache for a husband.
> She passes in mourning,
> counting each step.
> Her prayers rain down like rockets.[127]

The piece hints at an important reason for Vietnamese animosity—the death of loved ones in the war—and also suggests that the soldiers were both aware of and hurt by such hatred. This hostility was a significant contributor to the doubt, questioning, and confusion American soldiers experienced, as their beliefs about the war, their own country, and their own identity began to unravel. "What had damaged our morale," Ehrhart stresses, "was the discovery that the people we had been sent to defend did not want us there—and indeed, more often than not and with good reason, hated us."[128]

Within this confounding, disheartening, and hostile context, American soldiers struggled with one of the most difficult and serious moral problems of the war: the distinction between the civilian population and the Vietnamese revolutionaries. The discrimination requirement, which along with the principle of proportionality forms the central basis of the *jus in bello* aspect of just war thinking, is traditionally stated as follows: "in our conduct of the war we must not deliberately attack the innocent. In this formulation 'innocent' means . . . 'not involved in harming us, or helping to harm us.' It does not refer to personal moral culpability . . . By 'deliberate attack' is meant attack in which the harm to the innocent is the direct aim of the attack, or essential to achieving its purpose."[129] It is this formulation that "underlies the almost universally accepted claim that the distinction between legitimate and illegitimate targets coincides with that between combatants and noncombatants," a claim "so widely accepted that many just war theorists substitute the term 'principle of noncombatant immunity' for 'requirement of discrimination,' on the assumption that they are synonymous."[130]

Yet, as Jeff McMahan highlights in his groundbreaking work *Killing in War,* there are several serious problems with the standard just war conceptualization of the discrimination requirement. These issues include the difficulty of actually defining combatant status; the question of noncombatants who are involved in "helping to harm," such as scientists who develop napalm or villagers who hide weapons for local soldiers; whether those who engage in "morally justified self- and other-defense . . . forfeit their right not to be attacked or killed"; and whether it is plausible that an aggressor retains a "right of defense against a threatened harm to which he has made himself liable."[131] There is also the matter of intention, since the discrimination requirement states only that the innocent must not be the *intended* target of attack. Just war thinking, therefore, allows for some actions that have the unintended, even if foreseen, consequence of harming the innocent. Such exceptions are permitted on the basis of the "doctrine of double effect," according to which, Glover explains, "the morality of the act is tied to whether the bad effect is merely foreseen or actually intended. A merely foreseen bad effect may be permissible, so long as the badness is not out of proportion to the good being pursued."[132] Depending on one's personal position, this could be understood as a flexible and pragmatic necessity in warfare, a disingenuous piece of sophistry that reveals a shortcoming in the just war approach, or something in between.[133] Clearly, a central problem is distinguishing between what is "actually intended" and what is a "merely foreseen" side effect, as well as weighing the proportionality of that "bad effect" and "the good being pursued." Yet, as Glover emphasizes, the doctrine does have "intuitive appeal," since, at the very least, it acknowledges the importance of intention in morality, although, as with the doctrine itself, opinions concerning the moral significance of intention vary widely.[134] As abstract as these philosophical considerations might seem, they were incredibly important on a practical level in Vietnam, where the American military and its soldiers struggled to distinguish, and act in accordance with, the blurred line between those they were fighting for and those they were fighting against.

Often, many poets observe, the civilian population of south Vietnam was caught in the middle between the Americans and the revolutionaries. Ehrhart portrays this precarious predicament in "Farmer Nguyen":

> When we swept through farmer Nguyen's hamlet,
> Some people said that farmer Nguyen
> Had given rice to the Vietcong.
>
> You picked the wrong side, farmer Nguyen.
> We took you in, and beat you,
> And put you in a barbed wire cage.
>
> When the Vietcong returned to farmer Nguyen's hamlet,
> Some people said that farmer Nguyen
> Had given information to the Round Eyes.
>
> Wrong again, farmer Nguyen.
> They took more rice, and beat you,
> And made you carry supplies.[135]

Whether it be actuality, coincidence, or poetic choice, Ehrhart's use of the name "Nguyen," the most common Vietnamese family name, underlines the prevalence of this problem, as though it could happen to any farmer in south Vietnam.[136] This was a war in which the civilians were forced to choose sides, even if that meant choosing both sides. As Kerry stated in his congressional testimony, "they practiced the art of survival by siding with whichever military force was present at a particular time."[137]

Consequently, American soldiers frequently suspected civilians of being revolutionary "sympathizers," even if the Vietnamese people sometimes had little choice but to cooperate with the revolutionaries. Moreover, given the elusiveness of the revolutionary fighters, these civilian "sympathizers" were often the closest thing American soldiers had to a tangible enemy. R. L. Barth describes "sweeping a ville / For sympathizers" and his discomfort at guarding two "POWs" they found: "A hunchbacked mama-san and her child, who / Squat, fingers quick, blindfolded, loosely bound. / It's odd, but neither makes the smallest sound, / Kneading this silence that I cannot fill."[138] In another poem, Barth illustrates the difficulty of fighting guerrillas amid civilian habitations. When American soldiers took fire near a village, by the time they closed in on the enemy position the revolutionary combatants had often melted away or been pushed back by returning fire, leaving only civilians to face the soldiers' frustration and wrath. And so, Barth recalls, "we swept, our rifle butts / At ready, through civilians left to us."[139] Any sign that civilians were friendly to or aiding the revolutionaries, by hiding food or ammunition or even harboring revolutionaries themselves, could lead to significant problems for the villagers, who would be interrogated, sometimes brutally, and the village itself might be torched and destroyed. "Democracy on Zippo raids, / Burning hooches to the ground," notes Ehrhart.[140] The fear, frustration, confusion, and sense of unreality, as well as the death of friends who may have been killed just minutes before, further contributed to the desire for and severity of reprisals. As Barth writes:

> Rice caches and dead buddies—God's grim sign
> To His Elect—prompted us when, on line,
> We judged the sympathizers, righteous
> With Zippos.
>   Torching their thatched homes, we built
> Altars, then scattered ashes, scattered guilt.[141]

As the poets demonstrate, in Vietnam the discrimination requirement shifted from the usual combatant-noncombatant divide as Americans "set up a new distinction: between loyal and disloyal, or friendly and hostile noncombatants." Yet, according to the philosopher Michael Walzer, "political hostility does not make people enemies in the sense of the war convention," and these villagers "have done nothing to forfeit their right to life, and that right must be respected as best it can be in the course of attacks against the irregular fighters the villagers both resemble and harbor."[142]

Additionally, American military policies and actions during the war pushed even more Vietnamese people onto the wrong side of the discrimination divide, both on paper and in actuality. The use of free-fire zones—"an American military term used to designate a defined geographical area in which all life is considered enemy"—stripped away innocence and identified "legitimate" targets solely on the basis of location, while curfews did the same solely on the basis of time.[143] These seemingly arbitrary designations demonstrated and reinforced American suspicions of and hostility toward the Vietnamese population and were internalized by some soldiers as true markers of enemy activity, as Perry Oldham, adopting here the voice of a gung-ho helicopter gunner, reveals:

> the dumbfuckers in the sampan
> who wouldn't get off the canal after curfew—
> you and me both know they're out there
> for one reason—
> so we hovered overhead and sunk their ass.[144]

Any Vietnamese civilians who disobeyed American instructions were also considered and treated as the enemy: "Over the paddy a chopper calls out / to the hamlet, *Do not run! Those who run / will be shot as VC.*"[145] And if they did run, then it could be assumed that they were the enemy: "Son of a bitch wouldn't of run if he wasn't a Cong!"[146] The emphasis on kill ratios and the "glorification of body counts" created a climate in which killing was encouraged, and since any dead Vietnamese person could be counted as a dead enemy, the restraints against the killing of civilians were loosened still further, as described in this grim song composed by American soldiers in Vietnam:

> We shoot the sick, the young, the lame,
> We do our best to kill and maim,
> Because the kills count all the same,
> Napalm sticks to kids.
>
> Ox cart rolling down the road,
> Peasants with a heavy load,
> They're all VC when the bombs explode,
> Napalm sticks to kids.[147]

Included in Barry's poetry anthology *Peace Is Our Profession*, this song highlights a deadly retroactive logic in which the deaths of Vietnamese victims justified their being killed in the first place, the principle that only legitimate targets can be killed reversed so that all killed targets are legitimate. As the writer and monk Thomas Merton explains in an essay published during the war, "the killing of the people earn for them a final and official identity . . . They were thought to be Vietcong and were therefore destroyed. By being destroyed they became Vietcong."[148] Hence, the attitude that "if it's dead it's VC" rendered the discrimination requirement useless and, indeed, harmful.[149]

Furthermore, such policies and actions not only created enemies on paper and increased civilian casualties but also actively engendered support for the revolutionaries and provided them with numerous new members and a key recruiting tool. Since Vietnamese civilians were perceived as and treated like sympathizers and enemy combatants, it was not surprising that, as a result, some became sympathizers and enemy combatants. Ehrhart describes a typical outcome of the hostile encounters and interactions between American soldiers and Vietnamese civilians, one that could be seen as a reflection of the entire intervention: "if they weren't pro-Vietcong before we got there, they sure as hell were by the time we left."[150] Thus, there was a link between the American failure to carefully distinguish between the civilian population and the revolutionary combatants and the support of some civilians for the revolutionaries.

Yet, if the Americans struggled to discriminate between the civilians and the revolutionaries of Vietnam, that was partly because the demarcation was indeed ambiguous in actuality. This was primarily a guerrilla war, in which the ability of the revolutionaries to operate amongst and blend in with the people was a key tactical advantage and one of their most important weapons. Just as American soldiers might have mistaken a civilian for a revolutionary, they might also have mistaken a revolutionary for a civilian, a factor the guerrilla fighters depended on and utilized in their fight against the Americans. Hence, it was not only the Americans who blurred these boundaries, and while such obfuscations were a significant problem for the American war effort, they were considerably helpful for the revolutionaries. Additionally, the guerrillas were reliant on the cooperation, support, and help, or at least the acquiescence and acceptance, of Vietnamese civilians. In such a climate, it was not only the distinction between civilians and combatants that was confusing and problematic but also the unclear distinction between the various shades of supporters and combatants. For example, Ehrhart describes the war as one "where women / carried rice for soldiers, children / threw grenades in jeeps," and Peter Ulisse, adopting the persona of a general, writes: "They hide VC on their farms / make ten-year-old-daughters / grenade my men."[151] In both cases, a supporting but nonetheless noncombatant act is portrayed directly alongside and so conflated with a combatant act: carrying food for or hiding revolutionaries is connected and associated with, and considered on a similar level of seriousness as, throwing a grenade. These two poems also highlight a further difficulty, both practically and morally, that American soldiers encountered in the warzone: child combatants. How can and should a war be fought in which even children might be considered enemy combatants?

American soldiers felt, perhaps with some justification, that any Vietnamese person could be a sympathizer or enemy combatant. David Huddle, who was a military intelligence specialist, "spent long days in that hot office hooch . . . tracking down everybody's hunch / that somebody was V.C. or had been one / or was kin to one or maybe they dreamed / they were one once."[152] And, since this was "a war with no fronts," the enemy could be anywhere, too.[153] All this contributed greatly to the fear, frustration, confusion, and uncertainty that American soldiers experienced, and from these burdens an attitude of apathy arose toward the discrimination requirement. Ehrhart's poem "Guerrilla War" precisely summarizes the complications of fighting against the Vietnamese revolutionaries and the resulting impact on the moral behavior of American soldiers:

> It's practically impossible
> To tell civilians
> From the Vietcong.
>
> Nobody wears uniforms.
> They all talk
> The same language
> (And you couldn't understand them
> Even if they didn't).

They tape grenades
Inside their clothes,
And carry satchel charges
In their market baskets.

Even their women fight.
And young boys,
And girls.

It's practically impossible
To tell civilians
From the Vietcong.

After awhile,
You just quit trying.[154]

Such confusion and uncertainty are central characteristics of guerrilla war. Clearly, the traditional just war emphasis on the division between combatants and noncombatants, with its corollary principle of noncombatant immunity, does not adequately address the complexities of this type of warfare. Rather than thinking of a simplistic dichotomy of innocent civilian noncombatants and dangerous revolutionary combatants, it would be more helpful to our understanding of the conditions of the American war in Vietnam to instead picture a spectrum, with civilians completely uninvolved in harming or helping to harm at one end, armed revolutionary fighters at the other end, and many degrees of sympathizing and support in between these extremes.

Still, although such a spectrum might be more conceptually and historically accurate, the moral and practical problems of where to draw the line between an illegitimate and a legitimate target—if there even is such a thing—remain. If "helping to harm" is a core consideration, then that line must extend beyond traditional conceptions of combatant status to include some sympathizers and supporters. The "most widely accepted" distinction comes from Thomas Nagel, who argues that the harmfulness and "threat presented by an army and its members" stem from "the fact that they are armed and are using their arms in the pursuit of certain objectives," and so "Contributions to their arms and logistics are contributions to this threat; contributions to their mere existence as men are not."[155] Similarly, Walzer states that the "relevant distinction" is between "what soldiers need to fight" and "what they need to live, like all the rest of us."[156] To use the aforementioned poetic examples, carrying food for enemy soldiers, which is simply something we all need to live, might place a person on the safe side of the line, while hiding enemy soldiers, since it can be understood as a logistical contribution, might place a person on the other side of that divide. Yet, since there are cases that may involve contributions to both life and logistics, and since this distinction is itself ambiguous, as McMahan suggests, "this gloss on the moralized notion of combatant status does not solve the problem."[157] Moreover, given the significance of intention in just war thinking, the extent to which such contributions are intended and freely given must also matter. A villager might be forced to hide soldiers, for example, or they may be hidden without that villager's consent or knowledge. Judging such intentions, especially in the midst of a warzone, would be exceptionally difficult. And even if an appropriate and applicable line of discrimination could be drawn, there would still be, as in Vietnam and any other guerrilla war, the significant challenge of actually identifying which side of that line a particular individual is on. "Nobody wears uniforms," as Ehrhart writes. In *Killing Civilians,* the scholar Hugo Slim shows that "marking out a special category of people called civilians from the wider enemy group in war is a distinction that is not, and never has been, either clear, meaningful or right for many people pursuing and fighting a war."[158] Indeed, any attempt to distinguish between civilians and soldiers, noncombatants and combatants, nonthreatening and harmful supporters, illegitimate and legitimate targets, the innocent and the condemned, is fraught with moral and practical problems.

This was a central challenge and difficulty faced by American soldiers during the war in Vietnam, at a time when and in a place where their own lives were constantly threatened. Nagel admits that the line of discrimination is not "a sharp one, but it is not so difficult as is often supposed to place individuals on one side of it or the other."[159] Even if this were valid from a philosophical perspective—and recent work by moral philosophers such as McMahan suggests otherwise—it certainly does not hold in the confusing circumstances of guerrilla war, where the problem of discrimination is often at the heart of the conflict. It also overlooks the significance of the intense and influential situational pressures faced by soldiers in a warzone. For instance, for American soldiers during the war in Vietnam, a range of factors, such as frustration, doubt, confusion, and fear, both stemmed from and further complicated the difficulty of discerning dangerous combatants from harmless civilians. As Karnow emphasizes in his introduction to the poetry anthology *From Both Sides Now:* "Baffled in a strange environment in which they could not distinguish between friend and foe, they were prompted by fear to conclude that every Vietnamese was hostile."[160] Hence, frequent violent violations of the discrimination requirement occurred.[161] This is what the author Samuel Hynes, in his analysis of modern war, locates as "what was most wrong about the Vietnam War: the *indiscriminate* killing of civilians."[162] For Ehrhart, such an outcome is unsurprising: "when you send armed, scared kids into an alien and hostile environment they will never ever understand, bad things happen."[163] Perhaps, too, as Coleman suggests, such transgressions are a part of all war: "Well, hell yeah, I killed babies, killed women, killed old people, that's what war is about, that's what happens when you go to war, you don't just kill soldiers in uniform."[164] The particular conditions of the American involvement in Vietnam meant that this was an absolutely central aspect of the war in which the poets fought.

Breakthroughs

During the war, then, an us-them barrier existed that separated American soldiers from the Vietnamese, whether they were allies, enemies, or civilians. Those on the other side of the divide were not necessarily seen as a monolithic block, since there were attempts to distinguish between, for instance, competent and incompetent allies, the NVA and the Vietcong, or friendly and hostile civilians. Nonetheless, that allies and civilians could be, and often were, perceptually and practically placed among a grouping of others that also included the enemy was a crucial military and moral failing of the American intervention in Vietnam. For many Americans, the allies and civilians of Vietnam were often located, in terms of moral spacing, closer to the enemy than to themselves.

In the poetry, however, this American-Vietnamese us-them barrier is frequently breached. As outlined above, through their depictions, the poets question, subvert, undermine, and ultimately condemn this divide. In the case of Komunyakaa, for example, it was suggested that his own experience as the other in America, as well as less fear of and detachment from the Vietnamese people, helped him to empathize with the Vietnamese and bridge the separation. Additionally, in the poets' portrayals of the relationships between American soldiers and the allies, enemies, and civilians of Vietnam, they expose the factors that contributed to the us-them barrier and the problems that followed from this dichotomy. In such poems, the poets utilize moral and poetic imagination to stress the distortions, deceptions, and dangers of "the barriers and veils that separate men from one another" and affirm instead our common humanity.[165] This poetic breakthrough is epitomized in Weigl's poem "Him, on the Bicycle." "In a liftship near Hue, / the door gunner is in a trance," he begins. Then:

> The door gunner sees movement,
> the pilot makes small circles:
> four men running, carrying rifles,
> one man on a bicycle.
>
> He pulls me out of the ship,
> there's firing far away.
> I'm on the back of the bike
> holding his hips.
> It's hard pumping for two,
> I hop off and push the bike.
>
> I'm brushing past trees,
> the man on the bike stops pumping,
> lifts his feet,
> we don't waste a stroke.
> His hat flies off,
> I catch it behind my back,
> put it on, I want to live forever!
>
> Like a blaze
> streaming down the trail.[166]

As Christopher notes in her analysis of this poem, Weigl's "surreal journey . . . bridges the seemingly unbridgeable gap between the American soldier and the Vietnamese soldier." Their ride together "is a model of cooperation," and in putting on the hat, "the speaker experiences a sort of fusion of identity." It is a life-affirming moment of solidarity: "It is in his union with the 'enemy' soldier that the speaker finds life." Christopher concludes: "This poem's attempt to bridge the gulf between an American in a helicopter and a Vietnamese on a bicycle reaches across distance, across cultures, and across the politics of the war for a symbolic fusion that proclaims the necessity of communality."[167] In his account of the war's literature, Philip D. Beidler also highlights the significance of the unifying impulse in Weigl's poem: "In some new dimension of consciousness where memory and imagining can at last be reconciled, he calls us to a breakneck, thrilling race, an ecstasy of flight toward a vision of our common humanity."[168]

For Weigl, like Komunyakaa, this ability to see through the veil of difference and connect with the other stems partly from a lack of fear and detachment. "I wasn't particularly afraid," he explains, "and the contact that I had with the people and with the culture [was] positive and I liked it a lot." The result was an absence of hostile feelings: "I didn't hate the Vietnamese, I really didn't have any reason to . . . I didn't feel any personal animosity toward anyone."[169] Yet, given the conditions of the warzone and, quite simply, the desire to survive, for many other poets it was only once they had returned to America that they began to permanently dismantle this us-them barrier.

As suggested in the previous chapter, the questioning of assumptions and beliefs that had begun in the warzone continued apace when the new veterans came back "home." Part of this reconfiguration of beliefs and identity involved a reassessment of those they had fought alongside, against, and amongst. From the confusion of the warzone, clarity emerged with regard to who the actual "enemy" was. Like veterans of other wars before them, the poets realized, as Dalton Trumbo argues in his classic antiwar novel *Johnny Got His Gun,* that "the menace to our lives does not lie on the other side of a nomansland that was set apart without our consent it lies within our own boundaries here and now we have seen it and we know it."[170] The greater danger was inside the us-them barrier, not outside. "Well, then you come back, and . . . once

I begin this process of trying to figure out what the hell hit me back there," Ehrhart explains, "and the more I learn about the real history of the Vietnam War and the country of Vietnam . . . I realized that they weren't my enemy. My enemy was my own goddamn government, that was the enemy."[171] The poets' wartime experiences and their postwar reflections on them, therefore, resulted in a strong contempt for those whom Trumbo identifies as the "masters of men" who "plan the wars and point the way."[172]

The poets also acquired an awareness of the fallacious and morally deficient nature of the American-Vietnamese barrier and, moreover, of all the pernicious dividing lines that separate humans from each other. Indeed, many came to see and believe in what Connolly calls "a community of man."[173] This is an important aspect of the poets' rebellion: a negation of divisive boundaries in favor of a "cosmopolitan conviction of the oneness of humanity." It is a moral stance, Kwame Anthony Appiah explains in *Cosmopolitanism: Ethics in a World of Strangers,* that expresses "the idea that we have obligations to others, obligations that stretch beyond those to whom we are related by the ties of kith and kind, or even the more formal ties of a shared citizenship." Here, there are no us-them barriers: moral space is all-embracing. This cosmopolitan perspective does not deny that differences exist but insists that they should not be the basis for an exclusionary morality and, furthermore, suggests that they can open up possibilities for understanding: "People are different, the cosmopolitan knows, and there is much to learn from our differences."[174]

This all-embracing spirit and cosmopolitan conviction is present throughout much of the poetry.[175] In "Viet Nam," for instance, Barry expresses this ideal and describes how wartime experiences led to a deep connection with the Vietnamese, a replacement of hate with love, a determination to resist unthinking obedience, and a new postwar identity rooted in a belief in our common humanity:

> Once you were a strange, alien name
> far across the seas somewhere.
> Then you were a small, damp, green
> hostile land
> where for a lifetime lived in a year

I sweated, stank, drank, struggled
to survive, stumbled
and nearly died.

Now you are my foster, second home;
a place I've left forever
a part of me.

The best part: the part that cries
when your peoples cry,
that part that suffers when
you suffer.
. . .
Best, you have taught me to love
those whom I fought
and was once taught to hate
and question that love
which I used to blindly obey,
and to serve no one or no thing
blindly ever again.

You have taught me, foster land,
to be not just a man
but a human being.[176]

As Vince Gotera suggests, Barry, like many of the poets, "traces his political and perhaps human awakening to the Vietnam war." This particular poem reveals that he "is keenly aware that he owes his compassion and his personal freedom and realization of choice to the Vietnam war."[177] "In the beginning, I was an American fighting man who fought and killed for the concepts of 'duty, honor and country,'" Mason writes in his poetry collection *The Human Being: A Warrior's Journey Toward Peace and Mutual Healing.* "Today," he continues, "I am a man who has extended his citizenship to become a human being. I am still a fighter, yet I do not kill. I have become a warrior for peace and my commitment is to conscience, human dignity and the concept of one world."[178] Thus, out of the wreckage of the war, the poets have built a more collective and connective morality, and, in doing so, they embody Frankl's belief in "the human capacity to creatively turn life's negative aspects into something positive or constructive."[179]

In the aftermath of the war, the poets disassembled the American-Vietnamese us-them barrier in their writings. Since the 1980s, these poetic breakthroughs have been coupled with, and consolidated by, the return visits of some of the poets to Vietnam and the establishing of friendships with "yesterday's enemy."[180] A small group of poets, including Ehrhart and Weigl, returned to Vietnam in 1985, a whole decade before America finally decided to normalize diplomatic relations with the country.[181] This was the first of several postwar return trips for Ehrhart and Weigl, and it was a crucial moment in the evolution of their relationship with their former foes, as Weigl explains: "The trip changed me forever . . . the Vietnamese taught me this lesson: there was a war, we were soldiers so we had to fight, and now the war is over so we can be friends. It's that simple and that complicated at the same time."[182]

In addition to Ehrhart and Weigl, a number of other poets have gone back to see the country they fought in and to meet the people they fought alongside, against, and amongst. In 1990, for example, Komunyakaa and Larry Rottmann joined Ehrhart and Weigl, along with a small number of other American authors, including Larry Heinemann and Philip Caputo, for the First International Conference of United States and Vietnamese Veteran Writers, held in Vietnam.[183] This was an outgrowth of work undertaken at the William Joiner Center for the Study of War and Social Consequences at the University of Massachusetts, Boston, led by another poet, Kevin Bowen. In an interview published in 1992, at the height of the POW/MIA "myth"—the belief that there were still Americans held captive in Vietnam—which both prevented the American government from normalizing relations with Vietnam and distorted the memory of the conflict by demonizing the Vietnamese and diverting attention away from the war itself, Weigl commented on the role of these return visits, the Joiner Center, and authors in nurturing a more positive American-Vietnamese relationship: "All my efforts now are towards normalization. That's why I work with the Joiner Center; that's our goal. Our government won't do it, so the writers are doing it."[184] Still active today, the Joiner Center has also often arranged for Vietnamese veteran writers to visit America. These cultural exchanges have fostered a bond between former adversaries, anchored in a shared experience of suffering and a common belief in the moral necessity and desirability of bearing witness. "What I've done with my life and my writing makes perfectly good sense to them," Ehrhart writes of the Vietnamese. "They see it, as I do, as a duty and an obligation, a way of turning disaster into hope. All of us learned things that are too important to be ignored or forgotten or left behind."[185]

Over time, a number of the poets have developed a close relationship with the people and country of Vietnam, a connection that has impacted on their poetry. It has influenced their understanding and representation of the Vietnamese and, indeed, has itself become a theme in the poetry. Bowen's book of poems *Playing Basketball with the Viet Cong* is a particularly good example of this, a work that, according to Carolyn Forché, "reinscribes the humanity of a former enemy."[186] This relationship has also allowed the poets to see the war from the other side, to explore the Vietnamese perspectives and give voice to them, as in, for instance, Rottmann's collection *Voices From The Ho Chi Minh Trail.*[187] It should be noted that this willingness and ability to give voice—to give humanity—to the Vietnamese is much more common in the poetry than in other cultural depictions of the war. For example, in her work on American representations of the Vietnamese, Christopher notes, "More poets than prose writers seem to have made the imaginative leap over the stereotypical boundaries that constrain most Americans' understanding of the Vietnamese."[188] Additionally, poets such as Bowen and Weigl have been involved in translating the poetry of the Vietnamese who fought, renderings that provide "insights nowhere else available in English" and that "humanize the soldiers who fought on the side of the revolution in such a way as to dispel the stereotypes created by the United States military and the American media during and after the American war in Vietnam."[189]

Connolly's poem "Reconciliation," written "For Nguyen Ngoc Hung, once an infantryman in the People's Army of Vietnam," summarizes the importance of this American-Vietnamese bond. "I stand, looking that way / over the water / and let go the hawser of hate," he writes. "And across the pond / stands someone much like me / weary of the weight / of old hate." Connolly contends that their shared past can be the basis for a warm and mutually supportive relationship in the present: "Take my hand, Brother; / we'll keep each other afloat."[190] In his depiction of this shift from other to brother, Connolly suggests that the experience of the war unites all veterans, American and Vietnamese, and that this solidarity can be a source of sustenance and salvation. "When we use the word 'reconciliation,'" Wayne Karlin declares, "what we simply mean is peace: a true peace with our former enemies, and a true peace with ourselves, both of which depend not simply on a lack of hostilities but on a process of recognition, mourning and transformation."[191]

Numerous poems document this postwar solidarity. Indeed, Chattarji devotes significant attention to such poems in his account and notes: "Some of the best poets sketch not merely a political solidarity . . . but a human one, the ability, as Grace Paley puts it, 'to imagine the real—the lives of other people.'"[192] Certainly, these poems display and enact a deep and enduring connection that was simply not possible during the war and are a vital part of the poetry and its affirmation of "the possibility of what is better."[193] Yet, although the postwar dismantling of the us-them barrier occupies a prominent position in the poetry and represents a significant moral achievement, it is also important not to overlook the wartime breakthroughs depicted by the poets. They may seem relatively small and transitory, especially when compared with the postwar developments. However, given the climatic conditions and the strength of the us-them barrier in the warzone, these breakthroughs are particularly remarkable and, furthermore, highlight the importance of the moral resources of respect and sympathy—those "human responses" Glover identifies as vital to our morality and our humanity.[194]

It is possible to observe these wartime breakthroughs in the first book of poems produced by an American veteran of the war in Vietnam. Dick Shea begins *vietnam simply*, which was published in 1967 during the midst of the war, by recording his initial suspicions, skepticisms, and fears of the Vietnamese. On his first night in a hotel room in Saigon, for instance, he writes: "locks on doors to hall and balcony / not sufficient / for my state of mind / slept with pistol near pillow."[195] And as outlined above, Shea's poems reveal a particular distrust of his south Vietnamese military allies. However, as the poems unfold in chronological order, they indicate a shifting attitude, a growing fondness for the Vietnamese, and the occasional small but significant breakthrough of the us-them barrier. The first of these occurs at a "vietnamese party / welcoming me to their country / and life," in which Shea partakes in food and drink provided by his hosts. Interpreters are needed at first, but by the end of the night and after indulging in "wild rice rum," Shea notes: "we needed no interpreters / we parted / shaking hands."[196] Although this brief breaching of the American-Vietnamese barrier is aided by alcohol, it is nonetheless noteworthy as the first authentic human interaction between Shea and the Vietnamese, and also one that manages to overcome the difficult separation of language. In a later piece, he shares a meal with a Vietnamese family and leaves "wanting to return."[197] These poems demonstrate the significance of simple acts of sharing and the influence they can have on perceptions of the other. The sharing of food and drink is a simple but effective method of bridging divides. Even though the particular type of food and drink, or the way it is shared, may vary across cultures, the act of sharing food and drink plays an important role in all cultures. Both culturally specific and universally practiced, then, it is an act that allows for the possibility of breaching barriers.

Sharing, generosity, and kindness all contribute to breakthroughs, for they signify a recognition of the humanity of other people. In one poem, Shea describes how he "found vietnamese worker / shaving" without lotion, soap, or a razor, just with "finger through hole in center / of old gillette blue blade." He continues: "i offered him my electric razor / his eyes sparkled / and he shaved for five minutes / though he had no whiskers."[198] Although there are possible connotations of difference and even effeminacy in that final line, the act of giving itself is an example of a sharing and generous breakthrough. Notice, too, that Shea writes "*my* electric razor"; he might just have easily written "*an* electric razor," but, crucially, this is an "offer" from one person to another, and it is a gesture that is clearly appreciated. In another poem, Shea asks an old Vietnamese man if he would like a ride in his jeep: "his eyes lit up . . . he thanked me many times / when i left him / he was a good old man."[199] Such moments are scattered throughout *vietnam simply.* As Gotera summarizes: "These are small acts of kindness, but, in the context of what the war would become after the military-adviser period in which Shea went to Vietnam, these are significant acts."[200] Additionally, taken as a whole, *vietnam simply* details a process of de-othering in which the American-Vietnamese divide narrows the longer Shea stays in Vietnam. Toward the end of the book, Shea expresses regret for some of his early assessments of the Vietnamese: "in reflection / have expressed here / some rather strong cutting feelings / against some vietnamese people."[201] Just four words long, the final poem set in Vietnam undermines the very basis of the us-them barrier and reveals Shea's attitudinal transformation: "i like the vietnamese."[202] Back "home," he stresses the need to act according to our common humanity and urges us to exercise imagination and empathy:

> we are the same
> we are all people
> we have to feel for each other
> we have to do for each other
> we have to respect each other
> mostly
> we have to understand each other[203]

Wartime breakthroughs can be found in many of the poetic portrayals of the warzone. In Coleman's "I don't suppose I'll ever forget," for example, he remembers "the night they brought the VC in." Initially, as he "scoped the little skinny fuckers out real good," Coleman focused on apparent differences and pondered the possibility of violence: "not one came up to my shoulder or had any real meat. / I could have punched them all out real easy." Yet, what followed was an overcoming of differences and the antithesis of violence. "I just kept / watching me watching them until one laughed / and put a 'V' of fingers and then a thumb and forefinger / to his mouth," Coleman recalls, "so I tossed them a canteen and some 'Say-Lems' / and we all smoked and I didn't even ask for the pack back."[204] This sharing of drink and smoking of cigarettes together was a unifying moment, an act of rehumanization set against the dehumanization of the war. In that instant, there was no us-them barrier: "we all."

Certainly, such moments are fleeting and may even seem trivial, but their value should not be underestimated. "I remember how one day a foreman secretly gave me a piece of bread which I knew he must have saved from his breakfast ration," Frankl writes of his experiences in a

Nazi concentration camp. "It was far more than the small piece of bread which moved me to tears at that time. It was the human 'something' which this man also gave to me—the word and look which accompanied the gift."[205] "I have forgotten nothing, including the few brave people I encountered," the writer Jean Améry states in his reflections on surviving the Holocaust. "They are with me: the disabled soldier Herbert Karp from Danzig, who in Auschwitz-Monowitz shared his last cigarette with me; Willy Schneider, Catholic worker from Essen, who addressed me by my already forgotten first name and gave me bread . . . the *Wehrmacht* soldier from Munich, who tossed a burning cigarette through the cell bars after I had been tortured in Breendonk."[206] Acts of sharing, generosity, and kindness embody and enact the moral resources of respect and sympathy that us-them barriers weaken and erode. A "small human gesture," Glover argues, "can be enormously important. These small acts reinforce the ordinary, everyday human decencies, out of which the large heroic acts grow."[207] Just as dehumanization is part of a downward moral spiral, then, rehumanization can be part of an upward moral spiral. Such human gestures, rooted in respect and sympathy for others, can therefore be understood as acts of rebellion that, however briefly, negate false separation and affirm our common humanity.

From dehumanization to rehumanization, the poets' story of their relationship with the Vietnamese people is full of moral questions and insights. In their depictions of the American-Vietnamese us-them barrier, they simultaneously dismantle it and reject its divisive and dehumanizing underpinnings. They also explore the internal tensions within the moral space of the American military. The poetic portrayals of America's allies and enemies not only shed more light on the disconcerting climatic conditions American soldiers faced in the warzone but also hint at fundamental problems with the entire American intervention. The difficulty of discriminating between dangerous enemy combatants and harmless civilians, as well as degrees of sympathizers and supporters, was a core military and moral issue for the American war effort. Here, the poets raise serious questions about America's adherence to the discrimination requirement and, moreover, about the capacity of just war thinking to adequately address the complexities and confusions of guerrilla warfare. After the war, through their poetry and the formation of close personal bonds with the country and people of Vietnam, the poets disassembled the American-Vietnamese us-them barrier. This is a crucial aspect of their rebellion—a negation of false separation and an affirmation of our common humanity. The roots of this significant breakthrough can, perhaps, be traced back to those small human acts that mattered a great deal in the midst of the warzone's violence.

3
VIOLENCE

In his "Addendum: 1970" to his unforgettable 1939 novel, *Johnny Got His Gun,* Dalton Trumbo suggests one way of trying to understand the violence of the American war in Vietnam: "An equation: 40,000 dead young men = 3,000 tons of bone and flesh, 124,000 pounds of brain matter, 50,000 gallons of blood, 1,840,000 years of life that will never be lived."[1] Given that the war continued along this sanguinary path for several years after 1970, until almost another twenty thousand Americans had died, it is necessary to update Trumbo's grim equation: 60,000 dead young men = 4,500 tons of bone and flesh, 186,000 pounds of brain matter, 75,000 gallons of blood, 2,760,000 years of life that will never be lived.[2] This takes into account only the American war dead. About 1 million Vietnamese people died in battle—over 200,000 from the south and 800,000 from the north—and maybe as many as 2 million Vietnamese civilians died. The war also caused the deaths of hundreds of thousands of Cambodians, tens of thousands of Laotians, and thousands of American allies from South Korea, Australia, and New Zealand. And forget not the missing and, of course, the wounded. It was, as the historian John Prados laments, "a huge butcher's bill."[3]

The terrible violence of their conflict is a core moral concern for the American soldier-poets of the war in Vietnam. Indeed, taken as a whole, the content of the poetry reflects the form of the war—violence and death are everywhere. This chapter examines how the poets represent and reflect on this key aspect of their wartime experience. Through their portrayals they offer a firm moral rejection of the war's process of injuring and killing. This is a crucial part of their witness, of their "gaze falling on horror, withstanding it, and in unalleviated consciousness of negativity holding fast to the possibility of what is better."[4] It is also at the heart of their rebellion, of their negation of war. During the conflict, a disillusioned medical veteran pleaded, "There must be some among us who can yet remember that the most eloquent word in the language, the loudest moral expletive, the final refuge of a besieged conscience is still . . . No."[5] In their depictions of the war's violence, the poets voice this "moral expletive"—the first word of Albert Camus's rebel—with intelligence and imagination, power and passion.

Thinking about Violence

Violence is the primary instrument and product of war. As Elaine Scarry emphasizes in *The Body in Pain: The Making and Unmaking of the World:* "The main purpose and outcome of war is injuring." Yet, although "this fact is too self-evident and massive ever to be directly contested," it often "disappears from view" by being overlooked or omitted. For example, it is possible to read a historical account of a particular war "without encountering the acknowledgment that the purpose of the event described is to alter (to burn, to blast, to shell, to cut) human tissue." Such injuring might also "disappear from view" if war is redescribed simply as "disarming," or even "disarming by injuring," since the latter "still misrepresents war's activity by misidentifying injuring as the subordinate activity." Instead, it would be more accurate to view both the "substance and purpose" of war as not "to disarm by injuring" but rather "to out-injure by injuring and disarming." As Scarry explains: "each side works to out-injure the other and does so in two ways: first, by inflicting injury on the bodies of the opponent; second, by resisting injuries to themselves . . . To say that each side in a war wishes to disarm the other only expresses the fact that each side wishes to increase its own immunity while inflicting damage on the other."[6]

Through such a formulation, we can comprehend the reciprocal and relative structure of this injuring—war is a contest of violence. As each side inflicts injury on the other, "the side that inflicts greater injury faster will be the winner; or, to phrase it the other way around, the side that is more massively injured or believes itself to be so will be the loser." As Scarry notes, "believes itself" is an important qualification, since each side "will differ in the level of injury that represents the borderline between tolerable and intolerable damage." Thus, through these two premises—"that the central activity of war is injuring" and "that war is in its formal structure a contest"—war can be described as a process of violence in which "each side works to bring the other side to the latter's perceived level of intolerable injury faster than it is itself brought to its own level of intolerable injury."[7] Or, in the words of the poet W. D. Ehrhart, the object of war, "in the end, is to kill, maim, cripple, and destroy until the people whose lives you are deliberately making miserable either give up or all die."[8]

For those not committed to an absolute pacifism, there are certain circumstances in which this process of violence might be justified or necessary. Just war thinking, for example, rests on the beliefs that, in some cases, violence can be justified and that injuring the human tissue of others can be a morally appropriate method of achieving justice. Here, violence is not strictly the intended aim of war—as it might be in, say, a genocidal campaign—but a policy tool utilized in the service of other aims, such as "protecting the innocent, restoring rights wrongfully denied, or re-establishing just order."[9] Thus, those willing to inflict and sustain injury in war accede to the "structural logic of an event in which alterations in human tissue can come to be the freedom or ideological autonomy or moral legitimacy of a country." Other concerns outweigh the concerns of injuring. As Scarry details, in war each side starts "by perceiving physical damage as acceptable and ideological and territorial sacrifices as unacceptable," and "through the war each side tries to bring about in the other the fundamental perceptual reversal—damage as unacceptable and sacrifices as acceptable."[10]

In order to enable and enact this process of violence, the everyday moral restraint against injuring others must be removed, and, given the possibly fatal outcome of injuring, so too must the prohibition on killing. War is a climatic extremity that reverses one of the most fundamental and widely held moral beliefs. In religions, societies, and legal systems throughout the world, killing is prohibited, but, as Jeff McMahan highlights, "as soon as conditions arise to which the word 'war' can be applied, our scruples vanish and killing people no longer seems a horrifying crime but becomes instead a glorious achievement." It is this prevailing view—"that in a state of war, the practice of killing is governed by different moral principles from those that govern acts of killing in other contexts"—that McMahan argues against in his work *Killing in War.*[11] Hence, the violent contest of war is not just a violation of human tissue; it is also a violation of a fundamental principle of human morality.

Like all processes of violence, war has interconnected physical and psychological impacts. Physical injuring forces us to confront our corporeal materiality; it pushes upon us, through an unwanted imposition, the fact of our own body. In doing so, it emphasizes our vulnerability and attests to the power of the physical. It also highlights the tension in our relationship with the physical, as both that which we need to sustain us and that which can unmake us at any moment and will, ultimately, undo us all. The acts of injuring and killing reveal "Snowden's secret," that somber message of materiality that haunts the protagonist Yossarian throughout Joseph Heller's renowned Second World War novel, *Catch-22:* "He felt goose pimples clacking all over him as he gazed down despondently at the grim secret Snowden had spilled all over the messy floor. It was easy to read the message in his entrails. Man was matter, that was Snowden's secret. Drop him out a window and he'll fall. Set fire to him and he'll burn. Bury him and he'll rot, like other kinds of garbage. The spirit gone, man is garbage. That was Snowden's secret. Ripeness was all."[12]

Jean Améry, who worked in the resistance movement during the Second World War, was arrested and tortured by the Gestapo, and subsequently sent to and survived the concentration camps, offers further insights into the impact of violence on the self. Although his reflections on torture are not always directly transferable to the situation of war, they can nonetheless tell us much about what violence is and what violence does. Améry explains how violence can destroy our "trust in the world," specifically "the certainty that by reason of written or unwritten social contracts the other person will spare me—more precisely stated, that he will respect my physical, and with it also my metaphysical, being."[13] He continues: "The boundaries of my body are also the boundaries of my self. My skin surface shields me against the external world.

If I am to have trust, I must feel on it only what I *want* to feel." In an asymmetrical person-on-person injurious encounter, such as torture or abusive interrogation, the victim is made to feel the fact of their own body, against their will, through the fact of the perpetrator's physicality. Améry describes his own experience as one in which the torturer "forces his own corporeality on me . . . He is on me and thereby destroys me." In this moment, "trust in the world breaks down . . . a part of our life ends and it can never again be revived."[14]

While not all aspects of injuring in war are precisely analogous to this, the violent attempt to alter the other is central to the structure of war. As the pacifist theologian James W. Douglass stresses, "the object of war is to change the enemy's mind by making him suffer."[15] War's process of violence aims to violate the boundaries of the body and the self of the opponent in order to produce a change in that opponent. The logic of war is that of "bringing physical pressure to bear on the body so that its brain says: 'To avoid further misery I will give in and concede to the victor what he demands.'"[16] So, even though the primary mechanism of injuring in war is physical, its aim and impact are both physical and psychological. "Violence is an action contrary to the nature of man," Douglass writes, an "action which violates man in his being, that unique union of spirit and matter for whom an injury is that which affects the whole person."[17] Furthermore, although violence "affects the whole person," its impact on spirit often outlasts its impact on matter. For instance, Améry notes that the violent injuries he endured "left no conspicuous scars on my body," but as his translator Sidney Rosenfeld suggests, "their psychic imprint remained indelible" and Améry's "loss of trust in the world" was "irrevocable."[18] He committed suicide on 17 October 1978.

Since the process of violence "violates man in his being," it can result in "ontological death." Injuring may lead to killing, where death, to use the Heideggerian distinction, is an "ontic phenomenon," that terminal biological point of demise we normally recognize as dying. Yet, violence may also lead to "ontological death," the end of a way of being caused by "the loss of what gives meaning to one's world" and "the collapse of our way of life."[19] In the case of Améry, this phenomenon of "world collapse" occurred "with the very first blow that descend[ed] on him," when he experienced that irreversible loss of trust in the world.[20] The process of violence, Janis Haswell argues, "turns a person into an object of contempt and degradation" and "radically alters one's self-identity and sense of personal value and meaning."[21] As the psychologist Aphrodite Matsakis details in *Vietnam Wives*, during the violation of injuring, "one almost becomes a thing, a vulnerable object subject to the will of a power of force greater than one's self," and when the perpetrator "is another person, the victim's faith in other human beings, and in society in general, can be severely shaken or shattered entirely."[22] Since violence "impacts victims' relations to the world they once trusted, it marks 'the undoing of character' and the destruction of the belief that 'one can be oneself in relation to others.'"[23] This is what Haswell describes as "moral trauma" or "moral shock . . . a violation of right relations to the outside world that supports personal integrity."[24] Moreover, ontological death and moral trauma can affect not just victims of injuring but also witnesses and perpetrators, for while they might be spared direct physical harm, they must nonetheless reconceptualize the world and their own relationship with it as a result of witnessing or enacting violence. All those who encounter violence are altered in some way by its destructive process.

As victims, witnesses, and perpetrators of violence, soldiers are particularly prone to ontological death and moral trauma. Hubert Dreyfus and Camilo Salazar Prince utilize the Heideggerian distinction between ontic demise, or actual physical death, and ontological death, or the end of a way of being, to analyze Terrence Malick's Second World War film, *The Thin Red Line*. They present the example of an American soldier who shoots and kills a Japanese soldier at Guadalcanal and suggest that, at the moment of the Japanese soldier's death, the American soldier "realizes he has murdered more than just one man; the normative structure of the world as he knows it has ceased to exist." Here, the ontic demise of the other has caused the ontological death of the self. Dreyfus and Prince identify two ways in which soldiers confront the phenomenon of ontological death: "through identity failure and the collapse of an unconditional commitment." In the former case, there is a "complete existential ontological breakdown," in which an individual's world crumbles as "the light that shed meaning on his . . . life suddenly becomes dim." In the latter case, the soldier loses the commitment that had sustained him in the warzone, such as a commitment to a cause or country "that defines who he is and what is essential in his world." If this commitment collapses, so too does the soldier's world and his way of being. Here, total despair can be avoided "by converting his defining commitment" to something else—a commitment to his comrades, for example.[25] These two cases represent the questioning of the self and related shift in identity and the sense of betrayal and connected change in beliefs and fighting motivation outlined previously in this book.[26] Furthermore, ontological death is intimately linked to moral trauma, a "trauma born of betrayed trust, producing a moral void when sustaining faith proves hollow and the meaning of one's actions, one's purpose, one's life, is shattered."[27] The violence of war, therefore, destroys a number of worlds: physical worlds, ontological worlds, and moral worlds.

Of course, in any discussion of the destructive impact of violence, it is important not to overlook or omit the fact that injuring can sometimes be fatal, that it can lead to the biological phenomenon of ontic demise. Indeed, killing is the ultimate act and consequence of violence. It is the final denial of the world, an absolute negation of the other.[28] This annihilation of persons is one of the defining features of war. "At its core, perhaps, war is just another name for death," Tim O'Brien writes.[29] As Scarry explains, death is the complete "unmaking" of a person. It is not just the destruction of bodies but "in each case the unmaking of the civilization as it resides in each of those bodies." So, in wounding and death:

> The arms that had learned to gesture in a particular way are unmade; the hands that held within them not just blood and bone but the movements that made possible the playing of the piano are unmade; the fingers and palms that knew in intricate detail the weight and feel of a particular tool are unmade; the feet that had within them 'by heart' (that is, as a matter of deep bodily habit) the knowledge of how to pedal a bicycle are unmade; the head and arms and back and legs that contained within them an elaborate sequence of steps in a certain dance are unmade; all are deconstructed along with the tissue itself, the sentient source and site of all learning.

In the event of wounding, only particular aspects of embodied culture are unmade, but in the event of death, all aspects of embodied culture are unmade; they are all simultaneously and totally destroyed in one moment of unmaking. Hence, Scarry writes, "the roll call of death" for

America in their war in Vietnam "is not 57,000 names but names, bodies, and embodied culture."[30] Moreover, death marks not only the complete unmaking of a person's past but also the final point of their present and, with that, the vanishing of their future. This is, above all, what death means—the end of a person's possible future. Since killing involves the premature conclusion of life, it takes away, as Trumbo suggests, all those "years of life that will never be lived."[31] This destruction of the past and denial of the future is the mechanism through which war operates.

There is, however, a significant phenomenological problem with studying death: it is not possible to experience death oneself. In "death the world does not alter, but comes to an end," the philosopher Ludwig Wittgenstein, himself a veteran of the First World War, notes. "Death is not an event in life: we do not live to experience death."[32] Similarly, Albert Camus suggests that "in reality there is no experience of death. Properly speaking, nothing has been experienced but what has been lived and made conscious." We might witness the death of another person, but even then "it is barely possible to speak of the experience of others' deaths. It is a substitute, an illusion, and it never quite convinces us."[33] Indeed, the representation of death is one of the impossible challenges of war writing. As Bruce Weigl states, "in the case of war and the terrible consequences of war, words finally fail. Remarkably though, it's that failure of language to say a thing straight, what Dante felt when he came out of hell, that compels us to write poetry." It is the *attempt* to write about war, despite the "impossibility of the act," that is valuable and necessary, with the literary imagination capable of stretching the boundaries of our understanding of death.[34] The poetic medium may be particularly well suited to this unfulfillable task and also to the related exploration and representation of how "violence wreaks havoc on our physical and conceptual worlds."[35] According to the poet Robert Pinsky, the "two most interesting things in the world, for our species, are ideas and the individual human body, two elements that poetry uniquely joins together." It is this "dual concern, bodily and conceptual," that enables poets to offer such significant insights into the injuring and killing of war.[36] Additionally, as former soldiers, the poets in this study speak as the victims, witnesses, and perpetrators of injuring, and although as survivors they cannot ever speak as the dead, their closeness to the death and the dead of war does give them the opportunity, as well as the responsibility, to speak for those who did not survive, for those who were silenced forever by the war's violence. As David Connolly insists: "I owe people who no longer have voice."[37]

Bodies

The violence of the war is a central issue for the poets. One of the key focal points here is the devastating and destructive impact of the conflict on the human body. The poetic depictions of injuring and killing detail the vulnerability of the body to the violations of violence and reveal how another generation of American boys discovered firsthand Snowden's grim message of materiality: "Muddy body bags . . . sagging with their emptiness . . . spilling out life's secrets."[38] The poets also examine the psychological influence of this alteration of human tissue and explore how our relationship with the world is affected by violence. "They marched without knowing / how the air would be sucked from their lungs, / how their lungs would collapse," Weigl writes, "how the world would twist itself, would / bend into the cruel angles."[39] Those affected by violence, Weigl suggests in another poem, are "betrayed by the world / like birds by false spring."[40]

Perhaps unsurprisingly, former medics supply many of the most insightful and interesting poetic accounts of the war's path of destruction and dismantling. Among those who gagged "from puke / blown into their mouths / while trying to blow fleeing souls / back into shattered bodies," Basil T. Paquet, D. C. Berry, and Doug Anderson are particularly noteworthy poets.[41] Both Paquet and Berry published poetry during the war, and the direct brutality of their descriptions bears the marks of a proximity to a process of violence that was ongoing as they wrote. While Anderson's work, published some years after the end of the conflict, lacks this temporal immediacy, his explorations of violence are equally penetrating and perceptive. These three medic-poets detail, reflect on, and ultimately reject the violence of a war that produced vast numbers of "fleeing souls" and "shattered bodies."

Paquet was drafted into the Army as a conscientious objector and served in Vietnam from 1967 to 1968 with the 24th Evacuation Hospital.[42] His portrayals of the war's horrors, then, have an added texture of poignancy, since this was a war in which he was forced to serve; he was against the war's violence even before he was made to witness its terrible impact firsthand. In the opening poem of the seminal anthology *Winning Hearts and Minds*, published in 1972, Paquet pictures the war's violence as a process of unmaking. He describes how "The half-dead comatose / Paw the air like cats do when they dream" and notes that the violence that causes this animalistic regression also destroys embodied culture, memory, and identity as "their multiplication tables, / Memories of momma, and half their id / Lies in some shell hole / Or plop! splatter! on your jungle boots."[43] That this mutilated "id" could signify military identification, personal identity, or Freud's instinctual id is an intriguing and revealing ambiguity of meaning. Subsequently, Paquet portrays the impact of the war's violence as a de-evolutionary unmaking of the human being:

> It must be some atavistic angst
> Of their muscle and bones,
> Some ancient ritual of their sea water self,
> Some blood stream monsoon,
> Some sinew storm that makes
> Their bodies rage on tastelessly
> Without their shattered brains.[44]

Here, although the body remains animate, any human sense of self has been destroyed by the war's violence; biology outlasts being. This highlights the extent to which our mental self is reliant on our physical self, if such a distinction can be made. We need the body to sustain a mental self, but the body has no such requirement; it can "rage on" even when the mental self is "shattered."[45] It is almost as though the mental self is betrayed by the physical self that outlives it, although the direction of betrayal is reversed if we perceive instead the abandonment of the physical by the mental, what Weigl calls "the soul's revenge / on the body."[46] In another poem by Paquet, biology and being are annihilated simultaneously:

> The bullet passed
> Through his right temple,
> His left side
> Could not hold
> Against the metal,

His last "I am" exploded
Red and grey on a rubber tree.[47]

This poem also emphasizes our vulnerability to violence—just a small piece of metal is enough to completely unmake us and all that we are.[48]

In "Mourning The Death, By Hemorrhage, Of A Child From Honai," Paquet illustrates the impact of the war's violence on the bodies of Vietnamese children. "I could only wonder what ideology," Paquet writes, "The child carried in her left arm—necessity / Must have dictated an M-16 round / Should cut it off, and her gaining the roll of martyrology." Here, Paquet exposes the mechanism through which war operates: the attempt to alter human thinking through the violent alteration of human tissue. The body of the young girl becomes an object, a means to an end for each side in their fight for ideological supremacy. In life, her body is a site upon which a physical battle is waged. In death, her body is a tool used in a propaganda struggle. Paquet cynically suggests that the "slaughter" of this girl "was for the greater / Glory of all concerned."[49] This is a poem that forcefully reminds us that, as stated in the film *Notre Musique,* "To kill a human being in order to defend an idea is not to defend an idea, it is to kill a human being."[50]

Paquet's poem "Morning—A Death," accurately identified by Ehrhart as "a masterpiece," encapsulates this medic-poet's perception of war's violent impact on people.[51] For the victim, death is the ultimate end, and there is no possibility of redemption or resurrection: "The bullet barks apocalyptic / And you don't unzip your sepulchral / Canvas bag in three days." Death is a process of dehumanization, a "demotion / To lower order, and you wash out pure chemical." When Paquet shifts to the viewpoint of the victim, he emphasizes that war's violence is a forced alteration of the human form and that suffering ceases only with death: "I'm thinking, as I hear my chest / Sucking air through its brand new nipple, / I bought the ticket, I hope I drown fast, / The pain is all in living." From his own perspective, Paquet stresses the harrowing effect of violence on himself, as medic and witness: "I have thumped and blown into your kind too often, / I grow tired of kissing the dead . . . I grow so tired of . . . washing / Your spittle down with warm beer at night, / So tired of tucking you all in." In the final lines of the poem, he explains how he would sooner be

Lightly fondling breasts and kissing
Women's warm mouths than thumping
Your shattered chests and huffing
In your broken lips or aluminum windpipes,
Sooner lift a straying hair from her wet mouth
Than a tear of elephant grass from your slack lips
I'd so much rather be making children,
Than tucking so many in.[52]

Through this juxtaposition, Paquet asserts a moral position that favors creation over destruction, a belief implied by the catalog of the horrors of war detailed in all of his poems. He negates violence and death and affirms instead love and life.

Berry, like Paquet, served as a medic in Vietnam from 1967 to 1968, and his poems share a similar concern with the corporeal and with the influence of injuring on the individual. In the first poem of his collection *saigon cemetery,* also published in 1972, Berry suggests that violence not only alters the body of the victim but also alters their relationship with the world:

The sun goes
down
a different way when

you
are lungshot in a rice
paddy and you
are taking a drink of
your own unhomeostatic
globules each

Time

you swallow a pail
of air pumping like you
were

bailing out the whole

world throw
ing it in your leak
ing collapsible lung

As the victim's lung collapses, so too does their world. Indeed, they really are "bailing out the whole / world," a world that ends when "the sun / goes down // Bang // ing the lung completely / flat."[53] Like Paquet, Berry exposes our corporeal vulnerability and our reliance on a physicality that will ultimately unmake us. The same point is made in another poem in *saigon cemetery*, where Berry depicts the process of injuring as one in which human biological systems are unorganized, in this case to the point of destruction:

The way popcorn pops is
the way punji sticks snap
into your skin and stab

pricking urine
into cardiovascular
systems and apparatus
apparently
unorganizing then demonstrating
it.

then you die
either from the spike,
the p,
or the

sun gone to grain
expanding

in your eye.[54]

In both poems, the shifting sight of the sun seems to signify the changing and terminating relationship between the victim and the world, and in each case the victim is undone by their own physical self, by their "own unhomeostatic / globules" or their own "p."

In other poems, Berry focuses on the absolute finality of death. In this piece, for example, he pictures death as the end of thought and even time itself:

> Tangerines and white
> marshmallows pop before the
> soldier's eyesbriefly   with the pop
> of the AK-47
> Assault Rifle's speedy mind
> expanding bullet,
>
> then a black canvas bag is stretched across
> his thinking
> . . .
>   —closing Time
> for
>
> Forever.[55]

"This is the end where the begin / ning starts with the zing / ing unacrobatic / bullet," he writes in another poem:

>   the end
>
> where
> absolute
> zero
>
> begins
> to
> begin[56]

Interestingly, Berry notes, this simple undeniable nothingness of death is subverted by the American military practice of the body count, in which death marks not an absence but a presence:

The gasping redness touches
out of the gunmouth
        blasting wretchedness
death   making
        zeros
counted one
        by the
death editing
lieutenants[57]

Although Berry offers no direct proclamations about the wrongness of war, his moral rejection of the process of injuring and killing is evident in his stark and detailed descriptions of the dehumanizing and deadly impact of war's violence.

Given its conspicuousness, it is worth briefly noting the role of form in Berry's poetry. Throughout *saigon cemetery*, the typography and lineation are fractured and fragmented, the form of the broken words reflecting the content of the broken bodies, "truncated, staggered lines that visualize disfigurement."[58] "In many of Berry's poems," Ehrhart highlights, "lines, pieces of lines and words are scattered across the page like dismembered body parts, mimicking that all-too-frequent reality of the war."[59] As Carolyn Forché suggests in her account of poetry of witness, this fracturing and fragmentation is "a standard feature of literary modernism. But the fragment gains urgency in the aftermath of extremity." The reader, Forché explains, "is strangely aware of what has been left out, what cannot or has not been said." This is a procedure, she continues, the French call "*recit éclaté*—shattered, exploded, or splintered narrative. The story cannot travel over the chasm of time and space. Violence has rendered it unspeakable." Hence, such poetry of trauma "is itself traumatized, and bears witness to extremity by its inability to articulate directly or completely."[60] As Vince Gotera argues, "Berry's poetry is a heroic attempt to come to grips with an experience that seems beyond any ability to be reproduced."[61] Still, Gotera agrees with Philip D. Beidler's assessment that Berry's book concludes by presenting the "possibility that serviceable meaning can be made, the memory of things at least at times assimilated into common imaginative terms that consciousness can bear."[62] Indeed, the final poem of *saigon cemetery* reads:

A poem ought to be a salt lick
rather than sugar candy.
A preservative.
Something to make a tongue
tough enough to taste
the full flavor
of beauty and grief.[63]

Anderson's poems were published almost two decades after those of Paquet and Berry, yet his "gaze falling on horror" is no less intense for that temporal gap. Like them, he reveals the fragility and vulnerability of our body and shows how our identity is tightly interlinked with and reliant on the functionality of our physicality. In "Short Timer," Anderson tells the bad-luck story of a soldier shot by a sniper, "Twelve hours before his plane was to lift off for home." He recalls:

Inside we saw how bad it was.
I syringed the long gash in the parietal with sterile water,
the doctor with a flashlight looking close,
the man saying, *Oh God,* and already the slur,
the drool. He would live. Go home.
Sit the rest of his life in front of a television set.

Afterward, Anderson wonders about the relationship between our body and our identity: "What was in the 20 cc's of brain he lost?" Echoing Paquet, Anderson demonstrates how dependent being is on biology, how just a small alteration of human tissue can have a dramatic impact on the self. In the final lines of the poem, he emphasizes that the hurt caused by war's violence is not confined to the initially wounded person, but that their loved ones also become victims of this process of injuring: "Somewhere a family, a girlfriend, prepared for his return. / Somewhere a telegram raced toward them into Pacific Time."[64]

Anderson's poem "Mine" is another powerful piece that examines the effect of war's violence on identity. He begins by describing the dismembering force of an exploded mine on the body of the initial victim:

> the man two up in front of me steps on a mine,
> loses both legs at the hip, and that's not all.
> He's stunned, doesn't know how bad it is.
> Can't give him morphine in that much shock.
> He'll die if he's lucky.[65]

In the unexpounded "that's not all," Anderson hints that the wounding has led not only to other biological losses—genital mutilation, perhaps—but to the victim losing something else as well, something indescribable. While the destruction of biology can, at least partially, be put into words, the destruction of being evades expression. Anderson also highlights the instantaneousness of the violent moment in which the victim's biology and being are both irreparably altered forever. As the body is immediately dismantled, so, too, is a way of being; pieces of the self are left forcibly and irretrievably behind in the past. In this case, the unmaking seals its terrible finality in the process of its own action: "I have less work than I thought: / the blast's heat has cauterized his wounds." Instantly and permanently the new amputated body and identity are sealed. Furthermore, it is not only the initial victim who is violated by this injuring; the witness is also altered as a result of their proximity to this process. Psychologically wounded, they become a secondary victim of the war's violence. The witness may also, as in this poem, be physically wounded:

> I'm bleeding too, a rivulet
> of my blood blends with one of his.
> When he's gone, I wash my wound.
> It's not shrapnel. A shard of his
> shattered bone is sticking in my arm.[66]

The violence enacted on the victim also marks the witness. The two are forcibly connected through the process of injuring, and each individual suffers a rupturing and changing of their own personal boundary. Indeed, Anderson reveals violence for what it is: the unwanted opening up, violating, and altering of human boundaries.

This portrayal of the war's violence as a transgression of human boundaries is present in many poems written by American soldiers who served in Vietnam. For example, the intermingling of the victim and the witness of violence is succinctly stated in R. L. Barth's epigram "One Way to Carry the Dead": "A huge shell thundered; he was vaporized / And, close friends breathing near, internalized."[67] For the medics who grew "tired of kissing the dead," such as Paquet, these interpersonal boundary transgressions were a common feature of the war: "This dead boy is on my hands / My thighs are wet with the vomit of death / His blood is on my mouth / My mouth My mouth tastes his blood."[68] The repetition of "my" highlights the sense of personal violation as the dead boy's body irrupts onto and into Paquet's body. The frequent use of the possessive pronoun signifies a need to restore and reinforce the broken boundary of the body, to reclaim possession of the self. However, even in death, the boundaries that separate human bodies are violated by the process of war, as Gerald McCarthy reveals:

> They brought the dead
> in helicopters and trucks
> and tried to piece the bodies back together,
> shoved them in plastic bags
> to be sent home.
> Sometimes there was an arm or leg
> leftover,
> it lay around until the next shipment;
> they made it fit in somewhere.[69]

Stan Platke's poem "Gut Catcher," a particularly memorable piece from the collection *Winning Hearts and Minds*, describes the desperate and often futile attempt to maintain the boundary of the body against the war's violent unmaking. "Have you ever seen / A gut catcher? / Perhaps not / If you never had to use one," Platke begins, before explaining for the uninitiated what a "gut catcher" is:

> There is no patent on them
> They're makeshift
> Depending upon time
> And place

I've seen ponchos used
And a pack
And a canteen cover
Or your hands

You catch the guts of your buddy
As they spill out of his body
And try to stuff them back in
But they keep sliding out

For a face blown in
For an eye blown out
For an arm blown off
For a body blown open
. . . A gut catcher.[70]

Despite the universal quality of violence's unmaking, each individual incident of violence, as Platke suggests, has a temporal and spatial specificity. Violent happenings often occur within larger structures of violence, but each event of violence is always a specific act that affects specific persons in a specific "time / And place." And in each case, as specific human boundaries are violated, the victim and sometimes, as in this poem, the witness struggle to mitigate the terrible influence of injuring. Often, however, the momentum of unmaking cannot be restrained, and so "the guts of your buddy . . . keep sliding out." This is the instrument and outcome of war: "a face blown in . . . an eye blown out . . . an arm blown off . . . a body blown open." Rather than offer a direct polemical condemnation of this violating process, Platke simply details its horrific impact on humans and, in doing so, clearly and effectively rejects that which he describes.

These unflinching portrayals of injuring and killing, which carry with them an implicit moral repudiation of the war and its violence, are ubiquitous in the poetry. In the warzone, violence and death were both immanent and imminent, inherent in the nature of the war and seemingly the place, woven into the very fabric of Vietnam, always happening and always about to happen. Hence, depictions of booby traps and their brutal impact on the body are particularly common in the poetry;

not only were they actually a frequent feature of the warzone, but their presence and description in a poem also allows the poet to emphasize the omnipresent possibility and fear of being injured or killed. Booby traps were the unsurprising surprise; always expected, they were nonetheless shocking in their sudden ability to wound or annihilate, astonishing in their instant power to change or end the world. As D. S. Lliteras writes in his short piece "Booby-Trap": "Sparkle in the grass / Invites a touch . . . / To oblivion."[71] And, of course, there was a strong link between these pervasive booby traps and the prolific bodily destruction inflicted during the war, as Weigl highlights in "Mines":

> A Bouncing Betty comes up waist-high—
> cuts you in half.
> One man's legs were laid
> alongside him in the dust-off,
> he asked for a chairback, morphine,
> he screamed he wanted to give
> his eyes away, his kidneys,
> his heart. . . .[72]

This poetic focus on booby traps also underlines the significant extent to which survival in the warzone was dependent on luck and stresses that American soldiers had little control over the constant threat to their body and being. This was a world defined by violence and its ultimate product. "Death was the context and the only fact," Barth states in a poem that begins with the following lines: "And all around, the dead! So many dead! / So many ways to die it hurt the heart."[73] For some soldiers, this climate of death heightened the sense of unreality, as Yusef Komunyakaa notes: "I wasn't on earth because death / was all over me, from head / to feet, first word to last song."[74] For others, death was the event that finally shattered that feeling and ushered in a terrifying new reality. "Death is so ever present. I'll be going to the field regularly now and I cannot tell you how frightened I am," Lamont B. Steptoe writes in "letter to momma #2." He continues: "It took me awhile to recognize the reality of this place until I saw my first dead man and saw two guys from my platoon get wounded. Also, a guy I went to Dog School with and flew over on the same plane with got killed last week . . . I think his death made me realize the reality and horror of this place."[75] "Because we experience certainty by way of the body," the scholar Franny Nudelman suggests, "the corpse provides a sign of uncontestable reality."[76] Indeed, this helps to explain the corporeal focus of so many of the poems, as the poets attempt to anchor their experiences and their writings in the perceived certainty of physicality. The presence of the body in the poetry may also indicate, as with Paquet's repeated use of "my" in the above-mentioned work, the need for the victims and witnesses of violence to maintain a sense of self in the face of a process of violation and unmaking, to reassert and maintain the human boundaries that are broken by the war's violence. Enveloped by the omnipresent threat of wounding and death, it was unsurprising that soldiers attached themselves to a corporeality that could, as evidenced by the human wreckage that surrounded them, be destroyed at any moment.

Two final interrelated points should be noted with regard to the poetic depictions of the war's violent impact on the human body. First, in much of the poetry, as in the works of Paquet, Berry, and Anderson, the national identity of the victim of the war's violence is unstressed, ambiguous, or simply unstated. Certainly, in some poems it is clear, as a result of either direct description or context, that the victim of a particular violent act is American or Vietnamese, but often this detail of nationality is omitted or else not emphasized. Even when the poets do clearly identify the nationality of the victim, there is little difference in the way they describe the process of violence—it is inflicted on, alters, and destroys the bodies of American and Vietnamese people alike. This is an important moral stance given form through artistic commitment. By not asserting a significant difference between American and Vietnamese victims of the war's violence, the poets reject, however implicitly, the American-Vietnamese us-them barrier, which designates only the former as worthy of mourning and only the latter as deserving of violence. By examining the injuring and killing of each group side by side, the poets refuse to picture the sufferings and violations of Americans above those of the Vietnamese and, in doing so, deny an America-centered hierarchy of moral and mortal meaning that underpinned many of the validations and tactics of the war in Vietnam.

Second, in their portrayals of the influence of injuring and killing on individuals, the poets also expose a fundamental feature of the process of violence: the destruction of identity itself. Indeed, another reason for the ambiguous or unstated identity of the victim in some poems is that the impact of violence can be so severe that it eradicates any identifying characteristics, as Ehrhart observes:

> The bodies beneath the table
> had been lying there for days.
> Long enough to obliterate their faces,
> the nature of their wounds.
> Or maybe whatever killed them
> ruined their faces, too.
> Impossible now to tell.
> Only the putrefying bodies
> bloated like Macy's Parade balloons,
> only unrecognizable lumps on
> shoulders where heads should be.[77]

In cases such as this, the identity of the victim is destroyed because it is simply not possible to discern who that person was. Yet, when, for example, David Hall writes "O God / O Jesus / this boy has no face," he is noting not only the physical devastation of the war's violence but also the unmaking of the victim's identity.[78] The poetic focus on bodily destruction is necessary because that was a common occurrence in the warzone, but it also serves to symbolize the simultaneous destruction of identity that accompanied this violence, regardless of whether the damage to the victim's physicality renders them beyond recognition—for even when the victim of violence can be identified, and even if they survive with physical wounds that will heal, they are dehumanized in the moment of violence, and so some part of their identity is forever altered or lost. Since their relationship with the world has changed—perhaps they have lost trust in it—and since their own personal boundary has been violated, they are no longer the same person. The harming of human tissue impacts both biology and being. In a context defined by the destruction of bodies and identities, by the unmaking of persons, the identity and identification of individuals almost lose their meaning. "I cannot believe anymore / that names count," Paquet writes.[79] Through their detailed depictions of this process of violence, the poets present a powerful moral rejection of it: "only unrecognizable lumps on / shoulders where heads *should* be."[80] This denunciation of the war's violence and death is a fundamental aspect of their rebellion and their witness.

Killing in War

American soldiers in Vietnam, then, were victims of the war's violence and also witnesses to its destructive impact on American and Vietnamese people alike. Additionally, they were perpetrators of this violence. Of course, they were not the only perpetrators in the warzone; their enemies and their allies were also participants in this process of injuring and killing. The poetry depicts the violence committed by all sides during the course of the war. Yet, it is the violence enacted by the Americans—by themselves—that the poets detail most often and examine most intensely. From their firsthand perspective, the poets explore not just what violence does but also what it means to be a doer of violence. They do not shirk from investigating and acknowledging the most brutal aspects of their own role in the war, including the ultimate act of violence—killing.

Killing is what soldiers are sent to do; it is their task and their technique. However, it is not just the frontline soldier who attempts to completely and permanently unmake other persons, for the entire military apparatus is devoted to this pursuit of annihilating. As Horace Coleman suggests, "Military jobs fit into two broad categories: Killing or in some way helping people who do kill."[81] Nonetheless, despite the vast military structure that supports killing, every act of killing has a specific victim and a specific perpetrator. "An enemy does not die in collective numbers," Haswell notes. "Each death is the death of an individual; each death is the result of a decision made by a soldier to take action."[82] In order to make this decision and take this action, the soldier must first dehumanize the victim, as Komunyakaa emphasizes: "one has to dehumanize before one can kill another."[83] That is, the perpetrator must think the victim dehumanized before they can totally and irreversibly dehumanize them in the final fatal moment. Dehumanization is both anterior and interior to the terminal act. The process of killing, then, relies on and acts out a moral negation of the other.

With regard to the poetry, one of the most interesting and insightful ways in which the poets envision the killing of war is by comparing it to hunting. Through this connection to an activity usually associated with the killing of animals, the poets stress the dehumanizing nature of the process of killing in war.[84] In a poem included in *Dear America: Letters Home from Vietnam,* James McLeroy describes an "Ambush": "Aching, filthy, weak, afraid, / Creeping through the dripping shades, / Searching forms through jungle haze, / We stalked those men as prey."[85] He recognizes the humanity of "those men," but simultaneously indicates that the search to kill them strips away their humanity; the hunt of war turns "those men" into mere "prey." In one of his earliest poems, entitled "Hunting," Ehrhart also recognizes that he has become a hunter of other humans. "Sighting down the long black barrel, / I wait till front and rear sights / Form a perfect line on his body, / Then slowly squeeze the trigger," the poem begins. The next lines present the reflective revelation: "The thought occurs / That I have never hunted anything in my whole life / Except other men."[86] Jon Forrest Glade's "Blood Trail" is another poem that pictures war as a hunt:

I had a man in my sights
and I pulled the trigger.
I knew he would fall,
but I didn't think
he would get back up
and run like a wounded deer.

As above, although the poet describes the dehumanization that the hunt of war produces, he also recognizes the humanity of his victim: "I shot a man." By doing so, Glade resists the process of war's dehumanizing violence even as he perpetrates it. Moreover, by openly declaring his participation in this process, he acknowledges and accepts responsibility for his own act of violence: "*I* shot a man."[87] These poetic depictions of the war as hunting, therefore, demonstrate the dehumanizing of the enemy that killing in war necessitates, inculcates, and perpetuates, and through exposing this element of the war, and admitting responsibility for their own role in it, the poets also reject it.

The comparison to hunting also helps to highlight the structure of war as a contest of violence, since the poets emphasize that they were not just the hunters but also the hunted. As suggested previously, American soldiers perceived their revolutionary opponents as ominously omnipresent and felt constantly watched, "always aware that Charlie only waits."[88] He "prayed fervently" and shivered "uncontrollably in the mud" with fear, Leroy V. Quintana confesses, when he felt the proximity of his own pursuers: "As men whose duty it was to kill me filed by / only a little more than a yard away."[89] American soldiers, too, were dehumanized by becoming the hunting targets of other humans. As McLeroy explains: "we next go out again / At night to kill more killer men, / Or else be hunted to our end."[90] Yet, the dehumanization of the perpetrator in war is more complex than simply a case of the hunter also being the hunted, for, as the poets attest, in the process of killing other human beings, the perpetrator loses something of his own humanity as well.

The impact of killing on the killer is an important and recurring theme in poetic depictions of the war's violence. At the moment of killing, the killer is altered both by the act itself and by being a witness to that act. Victims and perpetrators, in addition to their primary roles, are also witnesses: the victim witnesses his own victimization; the perpetrator witnesses his own perpetration. However, in the event of ultimate violence, the victim does not witness the final act, since, to recall Wittgenstein, "we do not live to experience death."[91] But the killer does witness the final act, and they have to live with being a witness to their own act of killing. As J. Vincent Hansen suggests:

> They will say:
>   you should be
>   willing to die
>   for your country.
> They will not say:
>   you should be
>   willing to kill
>   for your country.
> But always remember:
>   you will never
>   have to live
>   with having died.[92]

Crucially, the killer must live with the interrelated changes that occur in both his relationship with the world and his own identity. At the moment of killing, as Dreyfus and Prince argue, the killer experiences ontological death: "he has murdered more than just one man; the normative structure of the world as he knows it has ceased to exist."[93] "I have a theory that once you have violated the most sacred law and taken another life," one of the contributors to the anthology *Demilitarized Zones* writes, "the structure that permitted it, that encouraged it, rings kind of hollow ever after."[94] The immediate insinuation in the context of this piece is that this structure is the American military, but the openness of the statement allows for the possibility that this structure might also be the war in Vietnam, war in general, American society, or a morality that strictly prohibits killing in one situation but strongly encourages it in another. Whichever structure the writer is referring to, it is clear that his relationship with and trust in the world has been significantly and permanently altered as a result of his violation of "the most sacred law." Indeed, when McLeroy encounters the Vietnamese enemy and engages them in a fatal firefight, he realizes that at that moment, the world has changed: "the very Earth was torn." And the surviving hunters find that they have killed not only the enemy but something of themselves as well: "Now jungle covers the stench and sight / Of the wrecks we left behind that night. / Yet we, too, die, while winning such fights, / From a sickness caused by slaughter."[95]

James Soular, whose "first kill" was that deer he shot when he was twelve, also describes this killing of the self that results from the killing of others.[96] In "Letter to Billy," he starts by detailing the bodily destruction and death of a Vietcong soldier he shoots from his helicopter, as "the bullets jerked / and slapped him until there wasn't enough / meat and bone to hold him up anymore." Subsequently, in a repeating dream, Soular pictures the position of victim and perpetrator reversed: "that VC / is firing at me . . . until I feel the sudden snap / of bullets breaking bone." He concludes:

> I try to fall down and rest
> but the bullets hold me up
> like a scarecrow until a final blast
> spins me around and I see the VC
> only it isn't him, it's me,
> and I come up to me and put the barrel
> of the gun to my forehead and pull the trigger.[97]

The killer has become the victim of his own perpetration; when he killed "the VC," he also killed himself.

This alteration of identity caused by being a killer can, as with the victims of violence, be understood as an unmaking of the self. In war, the moral prohibition against killing—"the most sacred law"—is reversed. Killing, therefore, "requires the soldier to 'unmake' himself as a moral human being."[98] As Scarry explicates, "in consenting to kill, he consents to perform (for the country) the act that would in peacetime expose his unpoliticalness and place him outside the moral space of the nation." It is an undoing of moral identity and beliefs and also an undoing of that morality as it is embodied in the individual: "What in killing he does is to wrench around his most fundamental sanctions about how within civilization (and this particular civilization, his country) another embodied person can be touched; he divests himself of civilization, decivilizes himself, reverses not just an 'idea' or 'belief' but a learned and deeply embodied set of physical impulses and gestures regarding his relation to any other person's body . . . He consents to 'unmake' himself, deconstruct himself, empty himself of civil content 'for his country.'"[99] By participating in killing, therefore, the soldier changes his way of being, alters his relationship with the world and with other people, and, in doing so, loses part of himself in the process. As Bill Bauer writes:

> The boy who swung
> on a Missouri porch
> to summer wind
> and an ice cream bell
> lost it, lost it all
> the minute he spotted a figure
> in his sights,
> pulled the trigger
> and meant it.[100]

In these depictions, then, the poets demonstrate that the process of killing not only dehumanizes the victim but also dehumanizes the perpetrator. War unmakes the humanity of all those involved, and it is the rejection of this dehumanizing process of violence that underlies both the rebellion and the witness of the poets.

Rejection and Resistance

The poets reject the killing of war in several ways. As with their descriptions of bodily destruction, simply through their determination to bear unflinching witness, to provide an open, honest, and unsanitized account of the process, they highlight the devastating impact of killing on both the victims and the perpetrators. They show war for what it really is: the mutual hunting of humans. In doing so, the poets "dismantle the glory" of war and oppugn those institutions, especially the military and perhaps even the state itself, and those ideas, particularly the notion that in war "the practice of killing is governed by different moral principles from those that govern acts of killing in other contexts," that legitimize and support it.[101] Moreover, in their emphasis on the dehumanization that war produces, the poets renounce such dehumanization and, like Camus, reject killing for what it stems from and leads to: "the depersonalization and trivialization of human life."[102] They question whether the dehumanizing logic of war, and its world-shattering impact on all those involved, is really necessary: "Must we kill them, as beasts must fight, / Until the Earth is torn?"[103]

In "Choking," Soular depicts an American soldier who refuses to accede to the attitude of hate that the dehumanization of war requires and perpetuates, even as he realizes that he is being held in the sights of a Vietnamese revolutionary's rifle:

> You look down a tube of light, eye-to-eye,
> with gutshot understanding
> that your twenty years
> have come to this man
> you do not know, do not hate.[104]

In "Keeping My Distance," Ehrhart describes an ambush in which four Vietnamese men were killed and notes that "All of them were armed / for once: bodies with weapons— / a rare thing" in this confusing guerrilla war. He was, he remembers, "elated . . . one of those rifles was mine. / A custom ancient as the art of war." Yet, in the final lines of the poem, Ehrhart rejects the act of killing:

I kept that rifle
long enough to understand
I hope to God I never
have to find myself
in need of one again,
and one too close at hand.[105]

By tracking this shift from elation to rejection, the poem highlights the transformative impact of the war on Ehrhart's identity, that move from innocence to experience that resulted in this abjuring of violence.

These poetic rejections of killing, it should be noted, are postwar rejections. For a soldier fighting during the war, resisting or even reflecting on the climate and process of killing could be difficult and dangerous. Yet, for a poet writing after the war, much greater possibilities, and perhaps responsibilities, exist for rejecting the war's killing.[106] Put simply, even if as soldiers they did not reject killing, as poets they can—and they do. George Mizo, for instance, recalls how his church, teachers, parents, friends, and country had all "told me it was wrong to kill - except in war." However, following his experiences in Vietnam, he denounces this prevailing ethic: "It is not wrong to kill - except in war. / It is wrong to kill - period."[107] These poems not only represent a morally significant stand in the present but also operate as a moral intervention into the poet's own past; they say "no" for a past self that had little possibility of such a negation at the time. As Ehrhart explains: "my poetry is an ongoing attempt to atone for the unethical, for my loss of a moral compass when I was a young man."[108] Sometimes, the depiction and renunciation of a violent past extends beyond in-war violence to prewar violence, as evidenced by the poetic portrayals of childhood violence. For example, in his reflections on soldiering and war, Peter Ulisse's "Warrant Officer Tadduni" concludes by expressing his regret at a moment in childhood when he killed a fish. Through this moral intervention into his past, he presents a simple negation of killing and affirmation of life that he has learned through his wartime experiences:

When I was thirteen
I scooped this trout

as he was about to swim
to open stream.
I wish I'd thrown him back.[109]

The poets' rejection of killing is a central aspect of their rebellion against war.

Yet, although killing is morally resisted in the poetry, such a stance was much harder to maintain in the warzone. "In war the moral resources—respect, sympathy and the sense of moral identity—are often neutralized," Jonathan Glover argues, "but, even when they still exist, the trap of war can make them largely ineffective."[110] Caught in this trap of war, the soldiers had few options but to acquiesce and participate in the climate of killing. Hansen pictures the sudden transformation of an American child into an American soldier and killer: "In eight short weeks / he went from altar boy to ammo bearer / and in the course of the following year / killed seven people." He explains:

It was never so much
that he said yes to murder
as it was that he was unable
to say no to the way it was
in 1965.[111]

All wars establish an irresistible climate of killing. In Vietnam, however, this was exacerbated by American policies that further encouraged and promoted killing, such as the use of the body count and kill ratios to measure success and the emphasis on this grim arithmetic for "military reward and advancement" or the concept of free-fire zones that distorted and even ignored the discrimination requirement.[112] Such policies both contributed to and exploited the strange situational context of the warzone. They made the warzone seem even more unfamiliar and otherworldly, and they relied on this sense of strangeness and distance from home for the perpetration of policies and attendant actions that would be considered morally unacceptable back in "the world." Moreover, as Glover suggests, this sense of alienation from normality could make "killing in battle seem unreal," which, in a mutually reinforcing spiral, also intensified the soldiers' overall sense of unreality and detachment in the warzone.[113] "Goddamn, it was just like in the movies," Soular exclaims in his above-mentioned description of killing in war.[114] Additionally, the feeling of fear, a crucial contextual consideration, further constrained the soldiers within the trap of war and the climate of killing: "When the bullets / Hissed round, the will contracted to brute zero."[115] Above all, the soldiers had to kill to stay alive. They were being hunted by a determined enemy, and killing was sometimes simply a matter of self-preservation; killing the other might lead to ontological death, but at least it could possibly prevent the ontic demise of the self.

Nonetheless, despite this factor of biological self-survival, and despite the virtually inescapable climate of killing, the poets still depict the hesitation and concern they felt about killing, even in the midst of the warzone:

> Somewhere, near here, there are
>   men who don't know me
>   that want to kill me.
>
> I do not particularly want
>   to kill them, but I will.
>
> The men stir,
> I see the signal to move out—
> I do not want to do this.[116]

Here, Jim Nye presents the moral dilemma of soldiers in war as kill or be killed. Given the context of this stark choice within the trap of war, his repeated declaration of his reluctance to kill is particularly significant. It is a form of moral resistance, even if practical resistance is not feasible.

Connolly's poem "Corporal Thach: First Confirmed NVA Kill" is a particularly important piece on killing in war. He writes:

> I see you still;
> your shining, black hair,
> your high cheekbones
> and bared teeth,

your glowing, searching eyes,
testing each step
as if it were your last.

After describing his shooting of this man, Connolly states:

Your last reflex
killed the man next to me
but it's your death
I remember.

There's no pride, no regret,
no way I'll forget
your death until mine.[117]

The first key point to note is the title of the poem, which resists the dehumanizing process of killing by naming the victim, thus maintaining his human identity. Connolly's detailed and careful description of Thach also reinforces and retains the victim's humanity, as does his insistence that he will not forget Thach's death until his own. While Connolly does not feel proud of his action, neither does he regret it, as he explains: "there was no way around killing a . . . soldier who's holding an AK-47 . . . I don't have any regret, I had no choice about killing Thach, I had no choice about killing anyone who had a weapon in their hand."[118] Yet, although Connolly was caught in the trap of war with "no choice" but to become a perpetrator and to kill, in this poem, by emphasizing his victim's humanity and human identity, he nonetheless rejects the dehumanization at the heart of killing in war. At the time, actualized resistance was impracticable, but Connolly's poem operates as an important postwar rejection of the mindset and process of killing. Like the poetic breakthroughs discussed in the previous chapter, it is a rehumanization set against the dehumanization that occurred during the war.

Connolly also discusses Thach in another piece, "Heart Attack," which examines the impact the killing had on his own self. Years after the war's end, Connolly suffered a heart attack. "My first thoughts were not of my wife and family," he recalls, "but of a young man named Thach, an NVA grunt, I killed when we were both nineteen." Connolly highlights the vulnerability of our physicality, the small things that can unmake us: "our lives held in the balance of a few centimeters deep in our chests, mine by my clotted blood, his by the bullet I put there." Unlike Thach, Connolly survived. "So I'm still here to smell the rain, to feel its touch on my face, to look into the eyes of my wife and children, my grand-children, to hold them all close," he writes as he pictures killing as the denial of a person's possible future: "I'm still here to revel in all that I stole from Thach." Connolly concludes by rejecting the us-them distinction that underlies the killing in war and suggests that perhaps he, as well as Thach, lost something in that moment, even if he did not realize it at the time: "It no longer matters to me that Thach and I were on different sides. All I can really see now is what was lost on that trail so many years ago, when I was young, and my heart was too hard to notice."[119] As he explains: "I killed people . . . I'm an agent of this violence but I'm also a victim of it."[120]

Atrocities

The process of injuring and killing in war is supposed to be enacted only upon those who present a military threat and are "involved in harming . . . or helping to harm."[121] However, given the confusing climatic conditions, the elusiveness of the revolutionaries, and the difficulties of discrimination discussed in previous chapters, it was not only enemy combatants who felt the force of American violence. Indeed, acts of violence in Vietnam sometimes stretched far beyond the boundaries of the "rules of war," and representations of such atrocities permeate much of the poetry.

Before examining the poetic depictions of wartime atrocities, however, four important points need to be noted. First, it should be stressed that the majority of American soldiers did not participate in large-scale killings of civilians, such as the infamous My Lai massacre, or indulge in the barbarisms that have become part of the mythological memory of the war. As Ehrhart emphasizes: "most people who went to Vietnam didn't cut off ears and didn't throw people into ditches and shoot them." Second, it is necessary to keep in mind the extreme climatic pressures American soldiers faced: "Most of us did the best we could under really difficult circumstances."[122] An awareness and appreciation of the difficulty of the conditions in the warzone in no way excuses or justifies atrocities, but it might help us to understand certain aspects of such acts. Third, the Vietnamese revolutionaries also committed atrocities against the civilian population—"cutting the head off the mayor's daughter and doing same same to his / arm"—and against the south Vietnamese and American soldiers:

> Bates was sent out as FO that night.
> Then came his pleas.
>
> The VC waiting; his screams tempting us.
> Until at first light,
>
> when his company swept the area,
> found his skin beside him like a twin.[123]

Finally, although for the sake of analytical and narrative clarity atrocities are addressed here in this separate section, it must be emphasized that in the poetry such incidents are often portrayed side by side with, and in similar terms to, "legitimate" uses of violence in the warzone. In this descriptive closeness, the poets imply that these atrocities were really just an extension, or maybe even an inherent part, of combat in Vietnam.

The indistinctness of the line between "legitimate" and "illegitimate" violence, between combat and atrocity, is depicted by Anderson in his poem "Infantry Assault." The title of the piece is suggestive of combat, yet what he portrays does not seem much like a contest of arms between opposing sets of combatants, but, instead, appears more like an unfettered frenzy of violence and destruction. The poem begins with an account of the bodily destruction of the dead, death itself not enough to end the personal boundary violations caused by war. Anderson remembers watching an American soldier:

> The way he made that corpse dance
> by emptying one magazine after another into it
> and the way the corpse's face began to peel off
> like a mask because the skull had been shattered, brains
> spilled out, but he couldn't stop killing that corpse

In the next verse, Anderson describes a violation of the "rules of war" that protect prisoners and the officer's failure of command responsibility: "the way they dragged that guy out of the stream, / cut him to pieces, the stream running red / with all the bodies in it, and the way the captain / didn't try to stop them, his silence saying *No Prisoners*." Subsequently, the momentum of violence seems unstoppable, as the soldiers extend their killing to anything left living: "the way when all the Cong were dead, lined up in rows, / thirty-nine in all, our boys went to work on all the pigs / and chickens in the village until / there was no place that was not red." The poem concludes with the complete destruction of this village and the soldiers' deep sense of guilt for the violence they had just perpetrated:

> finally, how the thatch was lit, the village burned
> and how afterwards we were quiet riding back
> on the tracks, watching the ancestral serpent rise
> over the village in black coils, and
> how our bones knew what we'd done.[124]

Anderson's poem, to borrow from Michael Walzer's analysis of similar moments, "suggests a kind of killing frenzy that begins in combat and ends in murder, the line between the two being lost to the mind of the individual soldier."[125] Indeed, Anderson's sequence of events unfolds in one long sentence, each act linked to the next, the desecration of the dead to the killing of prisoners to the destruction of the village, and there is seemingly no separation between these atrocities and the killing of "the Cong" in this "Infantry Assault." Furthermore, perhaps Anderson insinuates that such moments should not only be understood as an extension of the violence of combat as it spiraled out of control into violence beyond the boundaries of battle but also viewed as an intrinsic part of American combat in Vietnam. An "Infantry Assault" did not just mean a military encounter with armed combatants but an entire process of destruction. This was written into the "rules of engagement" in Vietnam, as the stark warnings given to Vietnamese villages highlight: "The U.S. Marines will not hesitate to destroy immediately any village or hamlet harboring the Vietcong . . . The choice is yours. If you refuse to let the Vietcong use your villages and hamlets as their battlefield, your homes and your lives will be saved."[126] Hence, the line between combat and atrocity could sometimes be "lost to the mind of the individual soldier" because the rules of engagement in Vietnam, coupled with practices such as search and destroy, body counts, kill ratios, and free-fire zones, meant that the American military failed to properly establish such a demarcation in the first place. "Legitimate" violence became simply that which was allowed, rather than that which adhered to stringent *jus in bello* criteria. Under such conditions, along with climatic pressures and discrimination difficulties, it was unsurprising that sometimes combat and atrocity bled into each other.

The sense of guilt that Anderson describes in the final lines of "Infantry Assault" is depicted in many of the poetic accounts of atrocities. Such guilt can be understood as a moral awareness of having perpetrated a past wrong, as in this poem by Hansen:

> Still hitched,
> the huge beast
> looked down
> in bovine awe
> at the old man
> mangled and moaning
> in monsoon mud.
>
> Later that night
> on guard
> Tyus whispered:
> "It ain't good, what we done."[127]

In an earlier poem in Hansen's collection, he identifies Tyus as being uneducated but possessing a judicious moral identity: "Tyus was a barely literate black kid from Alabama who didn't know much, not much, that is, except right from wrong."[128] Tyus's simple assessment and admittance of wrongdoing is, therefore, particularly damning. Yet, the feeling and expression of guilt is a morally appropriate reaction to such events. As Haswell notes in her investigation of moral trauma, although it may seem paradoxical, "moral trauma is a sign of moral health insofar as the soldier (in this case, both perpetrator and victim of trauma) realizes the damage being done and attempts to articulate his/her own moral disintegration."[129] "Bear in mind," Ehrhart states, "that while guilt can be a terribly destructive emotion, a person who has done things he or she should feel guilty about but doesn't is a frightening and dangerous person."[130]

Repeatedly in poetic representations of the war's violence, it is not revolutionary combatants who are the victims of American injuring and killing but vulnerable Vietnamese civilians. "There are no young men: / they are hiding, Viet Cong, or dead," Barth writes. "Only the old folk, children, / and empty-breasted // mothers still remain." It was these old people, children, and women who often bore the brunt of the war's brutality, and depicting the violence inflicted on them is an important part of the poets' testimony, as Barth continues: "I become one of their witnesses / to history."[131] In "'Snips and Snails and Puppy Dog Tails'"—the title of which is the answer given in the nursery rhyme "What Are Little Boys Made Of?"—Hansen depicts the deaths of seven Vietnamese children. Contrasted against this nursery rhyme image of childhood, he offers a horrifyingly vivid vision of what little boys are made of when they become unmade by war's violence:

Seven
school-bound
boys
opened
claymore wide,
spread thin
like strawberry jam
onto
a slice
of Asian meadow.
Seven boys
revealing now;
all had lied.
Everyone had lied,
even his mother.[132]

It is a moment of violence so devastating that Hansen loses faith in everyone he once trusted, with this breakdown of belief unlikely to be limited to the veracity of nursery rhymes.

Often, as in Hansen's poem, Vietnamese children were the victims of accidental atrocities, where they were not the intended target of injuring and killing. Soular tells one such story in "Voices," in which he describes a night ambush gone horribly wrong. A group of American soldiers "lie in wait / to light up the night and Charlie," and on hearing "a rustle that is not wind," they detonate claymores "and everyone opens up with their weapons." Soon, though, they realize their awful error: "Then the cries, tiny voices. / Children." The poem continues:

> He and his men lie
> with hands over ears, eyes shut
> but nothing can keep the children out.
> He hurls a grenade, the sudden blast
> drenching the jungle with silence.
> Morning brings a body count:
> one adult, seven children.[133]

In the following verses, Soular details the traumatic postwar struggles of Tim, the man who threw the grenade. He describes how Tim eventually becomes a victim of the incident himself as one final act of violence ends his suffering—suicide. In addition to portraying this tragic chain of violence, Soular's poem also highlights the role of moral luck in such events. If those killed had been enemy combatants, it would be considered not an atrocity but a legitimate—perhaps to some even praiseworthy—act of violence in accordance with the rules of war. Hence, the line between legitimate and illegitimate injuring and killing in war, and the commendations or condemnations that follow, can sometimes simply be a matter of luck.

In the short poem "A Child Accidentally Napalmed," Barth offers the perspective of one of these child victims of the war's violence: "'Why waste your tears on me? Give over grief. / If I knew horror, yet my life was brief.' / Some poet will perhaps say that for me. / I'd say, 'I suffered an eternity.'"[134] It is a poem set against platitudes that might seek to assuage the pain of these atrocities. Few such sanitizing views are to be found among the poets in this book, and the briefness of a child victim's life, along with their complete innocence, only adds to the horror and pathos of such incidents. In "It's Too Late," for example, Jim Nye emphasizes the absolute finality of a life cut so drastically short, as well as the anguish inflicted on those close to these children:

The dumpy, toothless woman
    Mouth and gums red from betel nut
Screamed and cried
    Kneeling over the body
The kid got caught in a cross-fire
    Spun around and dropped
Other villagers joined the keening
    And the wailing
And I thought,
    Lady, it won't help
    It won't bring him back
    If I thought it would
    I would kneel beside you
    And weep
But it's too late
There is nothing in this world
    As dead as a dead child[135]

For American soldiers, these young victims of the war's violence were a deep source of grief and guilt. Richard E. Baker remembers "Burying the Children," "wrapped / tight and stiff in slick tied ponchos," and confesses that "we counted the children / like sins."[136]

Women, too, are frequently portrayed in the poetry as victims of the war's atrocities. Few accounts of the violent unmaking of women in the warzone are as harrowing as B. D. Trail's "The Grenading." In this poem, which Trail thought of as "my best war poem," it is the Vietnamese on both sides who commit atrocities, with Trail and his fellow Americans complicit bystanders to the unfolding violence.[137] He begins by depicting an abusive interrogation, as an "ARVN Major beat the boy / with the captured rifle sling / glancing proudly at us, / his American advisors." Trail describes this as "An uninteresting event to everyone / except the boy who silently cringed / and shook from blow to blow," such was the quotidian nature of these scenes: "In the madness of the war / today was near-to-normal." Yet, this desensitization was soon shattered. "The stick grenade was lobbed out of a bunker . . . towards / a cookfire," presumably by a hiding revolutionary, and "A village woman heavy in her pregnancy / caught the rolling blast of the grenade," with it "slicing, filleting, cutting / deep, deep into her belly." Trail remembers how, in "a switch to surreal slow motion," he watched "her baby, / her corded baby, / easeooze / from her fish-gutted belly / and fall into the fire." The terrible event, however, did not end there:

> The madness was not just the fetus in the fire.
> No, that was just a novelty-of-horrors.
> to men who had seen minings and other mutilations.
>
> The madness was the mother was still alive.
> Split from throat to crotch,
> the mother was alive and
> screaming screaming screaming
>
> I didn't shoot her and I don't know why.
> No one shot her. And she kept on
> screaming screaming screaming.
>
> Dragged over the white-hot sand
> on a red-wet poncho,
> she screamed for two hours on the landing zone.
>
> She died before a helicopter came.
>
> I died back at the fire.[138]

The impact of the war's violence on the woman, and her unborn child, is excruciating and appalling. Furthermore, as a witness to this terrible ontic demise, Trail himself experiences ontological death. A way of biology is ended for the victims; a way of being is ended for the witnesses. And, decades later, a way of biology ended for Trail, too—he committed suicide on 1 January 1992.[139]

In their depictions of the atrocities committed against Vietnamese women during the war, the poets explore the intersections of violence, gender, and sexuality. In one of the vignettes from McCarthy's poetic series "War Story," he writes:

> They shot the woman in the arm,
> four of them

raped her
and killed an old man
who tried to interfere;
and later killed the woman too.
She was the enemy.[140]

Was she "the enemy" because she was a revolutionary, or simply because she was Vietnamese, or even because she was a woman? Whatever the answer, it is clear that her injuring, raping, and killing stemmed, in part at least, from a misogynistic impulse.

Similar incidents of violence against and sexual violations of Vietnamese women appear in many of the poets' works. "More than war poems of any other era," Lorrie Goldensohn highlights, "Vietnam war poems try to tell the individual stories at the flashpoints clustering around gender and violence, within the flammable arenas of power, desire, fear, and sex."[141] In particular, numerous poems address the prostitution that was prevalent in Vietnam during the war. A later piece from McCarthy's "War Story" reads:

Hot sun,
I walk into a whorehouse
pay the girl
unbuckle my pants
and screw her
sweat sticking to my fatigues
small legs grasping my back
her slanted eyes look up at me
as I come.
Outside the tin-roofed hut
another GI waits his turn.[142]

Vietnamese women were the other other: othered by race, with "her slanted eyes," and othered still further by gender. Some of the poetic depictions of prostitution explore its role within the larger breakdown of Vietnamese societal and familial structures caused by the American presence. Other poems trace the link between the violence of the war and the violence inflicted on these women through their commodification and exploitation: "kept my hand on the 25 caliber pistol in my pocket / paid the madam lady less than she asked / but more than she would have accepted / took my choice."[143] And almost all of these poems emphasize that the process of prostitution was dehumanizing and alienating for these women, as in Soular's "Numbah One," in which a "nineteen-year-old boy . . . rocks hurriedly, / drunkenly, on top of her while she, / smothered by his hugeness, diminishes."[144] Although it might seem slightly anomalous to include prostitution among the atrocities of the war, its position and portrayal in the poetry indicates that it can certainly be considered a part of the web of violence in Vietnam that breached the boundaries of any rules of war.

Another atrocity depicted by many of the poets is abusive interrogation, sometimes of identifiable revolutionary combatants, often of people whose status, beyond simply being Vietnamese, is hard to discern, the difficulty of discrimination both cause of and supposed justification for such inquisitions. In "Interrogation," Baker describes the brutal beating and killing of an old Vietnamese man, his hands "bound in prayer behind / his back, and swollen black, tied / to his chipped and bleeding ankles." Nowhere in the poem does Baker indicate why this man was being interrogated. Indeed, the title of the piece is the only clue to the ostensible purpose of the unfolding violence, since any actual questioning is completely absent from the poem. The act, then, does not seem like an attempt to extract information at all but torture for the sake of torture or vigilante punishment for some crime unknown to the reader, possibly to the victim himself, and maybe even to Baker. "Over eighty years of blood filled / his upturned eyes as the sergeant / beat him in the belly," Baker writes, with the old man dehumanized, reduced to an animal state as "he swung // and ticked like a clock, inverted, / clinging like a bat to the wooden backbone / thrust between the V of his knees." The final verse links this atrocity back to America: "When he died, they threw him in the lake / where he floated in tiny circles, spread-eagled / like the seal of American Justice."[145] For Baker, atrocities such as this revealed what American justice in Vietnam really looked like.

Significantly, like Baker's piece, several poems suggest that atrocities sprang not only from conditions within the warzone of Vietnam but could also have deep roots back in America itself. In another poem about abusive interrogation, Quintana begins by describing a violent method of questioning in Vietnam:

One
way the Army
got a gook
to talk
was to take
two
up in a chopper
and throw
one
of them
out.[146]

"Got a gook who wouldn't talk," Quintana continues as he explains another technique of examination. "Wired his dick / to a G-47 / and cranked like crazy. / Would talk then." In the final example in the poem, the process of interrogation recalls a form of torture from supposedly more barbarous times while simultaneously drawing a link between such atrocities and America itself:

Tied arms and legs
to four tanks.
Stretched him tight,
tighter till he talked.
After all said,
or, if a woman,
after all said and
done,
then revved the engines,
hauled ass as if
heading to

Chi Town

Frisco Philly

Houston[147]

Here, in both content and form, Quintana connects these transgressing acts of violence to all four corners of America. Both Baker and Quintana, among others, hint that atrocities stemmed not only from conditions and factors internal to the warzone, or solely from individual soldiers, but also from the society that sent them to fight. What happens in a warzone is not disconnected from but, rather, inextricably bound to what happens back at home. Put simply, the violent acts of Americans in Vietnam were as much a part of America as they were a part of Vietnam.[148]

Unsurprisingly, the poets morally reject the atrocities they describe. Often, as in several of the aforementioned examples in this section, they were bystanders rather than perpetrators. Most of the poets did not participate directly in atrocities within the warzone, and this is mirrored in the narratorial distance they establish in the poems between themselves and the acts portrayed. Perhaps, too, this narratorial distance signifies their moral desire to dissociate themselves from such violence. Nevertheless, the poets display an understanding that as bystanders they were, to some extent, complicit in such acts through their passivity and inaction. "I was barely in country," Weigl recalls, and was being driven "into the jungle" when "we came upon a mama san":

> I have no excuse for myself.
> I sat in that man's jeep in the rain
> And watched him slam her to her knees,
> The plastic butt of his M-16
> Crashing down on her.[149]

It was not Weigl who committed this act of "illegitimate" violence, yet in that declared refusal to exculpate himself, he claims some responsibility for what happened. It is, he suggests, "a kind of confession" for one of those "should've, could've, would've kind of situations," although he adds that there were other times "that I did act and . . . sometimes those actions made a difference, sometimes they didn't."[150] Additionally, in those poems in which the poet is a perpetrator of an atrocity, the sense of guilt displayed is also an admission of responsibility. In both cases, either as bystanders or as perpetrators, the poets acknowledge and denounce the moral wrong that was committed: "It ain't good, what we done."[151] As with their broad rejection of the war's process of injuring and killing, their poetic witness to atrocity also operates as a moral intervention into the past. If they were a bystander, the poet transforms passive witness into active witness.[152] If they were a perpetrator, the poet bears witness to his own transgression and through the display of remorse morally rejects this past action. In their depictions of atrocities, then, the poets fulfill the first half of Adorno's poetic task: that unflinching "gaze falling on horror."[153]

Finally, it is helpful to briefly summarize some of the key contributing factors to these atrocities. Certainly, the climate of the warzone in Vietnam played a crucial role. Fighting in a frightening, frustrating, and confusing guerrilla war, close to and amongst the civilian population, especially when some of those civilians could even be guerrillas or sympathetic to and supportive of the guerrillas, made atrocities more likely. The prohibition against killing was, as it is in all wars, reversed, but more than that, killing was encouraged in a way that made little moral or practical distinction between killing combatants and killing civilians. Military policies and practices such as free-fire zones and, in particular, the body count blurred the boundary between "legitimate" and "illegitimate" killing. "I am convinced," the psychiatrist Robert Jay Lifton asserts, "that the ethically sensitive historians of the future will select the phenomenon of the body count as the perfect symbol of America's descent into evil." As the poets demonstrate, and as Lifton stresses, a great moral corruption occurs when "the amount of killing—any killing—becomes the total measure of achievement."[154] The us-them barrier and related dehumanization of the Vietnamese, as discussed in the previous chapter, were also integral parts of this climate. As William Calley said: "We weren't in My Lai to kill human beings, really."[155] Thus, the climate of the warzone helped to produce these transgressing acts of violence. As Glover argues, "atrocities themselves do not just happen: people commit them. In a different moral climate, it could be harder to take part."[156] Moreover, as the poets suggest, the moral climate of Vietnam could not be disconnected from that of America. To rephrase Glover, then: coming from a different moral climate, it could also be harder to take part.

Nonetheless, despite this multiplicity of contributing factors, the poetic depiction and moral rejection of atrocities does imply at least some possibility of individual choice in these moments. The sense of responsibility and admission of guilt portrayed in both the bystander and the perpetrator poems indicate that there was some room, however small, for a better, more moral choice. By highlighting these feelings of accountability and remorse for watching or participating in atrocities, the poets suggest that they could have and should have acted otherwise—"I knew right, and I chose wrong."[157] Certainly, "There were times when all we could do was watch / The unfolding atrocity, observe, under the stern masters, / The civilized restraints disintegrate."[158] Yet, by indicating that there was, in some moments, a chance of choice, the poets fulfill the second half of Adorno's poetic task. They display the horror of these atrocities, and "in unalleviated consciousness of negativity" they hold fast, with hands slightly bloodied, "to the possibility of what is better."[159]

Technology

The violent processes of the war—the bodily destruction, hunting, killing, and atrocity—were aided and augmented by the vast technological might of the American military. As Stanley Karnow notes, the war ended "the lives of at least two million Vietnamese soldiers and civilians, the majority of them slaughtered by U.S. artillery, bomber planes, and other ultramodern weapons."[160] Of course, many American lives were also terminated by the war. Almost sixty thousand names are carved into the Vietnam Veterans Memorial in Washington, DC, each etching on that 150-meter-long black wall a sign of a future denied. Still, Ehrhart suggests that "if all the names of all the dead from the war in Indochina were carved into a wall, it would stand nine feet high and run from the Lincoln Memorial to the Washington Monument."[161] Actually, this interesting attempt to visualize the terrible magnitude of the war's dead is an underestimation; such a wall would most likely stretch all the way from the Lincoln Memorial to the steps of the Capitol, if not farther.[162] It is also a question Anderson ponders: "My face reflected, I watch the wall's / perspective vector into earth and wonder, how long a wall, / if we inscribe three million Vietnamese . . . how long a wall?"[163]

Technological violence was a key contributor to the immense scale of this tragedy. The term "technological" could include most tools of modern warfare; it might be suggested that in Vietnam, "the Zippo lighter was a piece of American technology as destructive as the B-52."[164] In this section, however, "technological" is used specifically to identify the weaponry utilized outside of close combat, those instruments of war that allow injuring and killing to be done at a distance. Certainly, this apparatus was not used only by the Americans, and much of it was not new to this particular war, yet the American access to and employment of technological violence far surpassed that of their opponents and of any previous wars. It was a defining feature of America's war in Vietnam and provokes significant moral questions in the poetry about bombing, distanced killing, and the use of chemical weapons. Also, in their depictions of "the murder of unarmed peasants / with our modern technology," the poets highlight the role of technological violence in violations of the discrimination requirement.[165] Moreover, it is in the poetic portrayals of technological violence that America's considerable transgression of the proportionality principle—a core strand of *jus in bello* that, simply stated, requires "the likely military benefit" of an act of war to be weighed against the harm it produces—is most apparent.[166] Indeed, the massive level of destructive force unleashed on the people and the country of Vietnam raises the question of whether American violence in Vietnam was the means to an end or an end in itself.

Bombing was at the forefront of America's onslaught. James William Gibson summarizes the key details in his account of the "technowar": "During World War II the United States dropped over two million tons of bombs and other munitions from aircraft. From 1965 through 1973, the United States dropped *at minimum* over eight million tons of munitions from aircraft onto Southeast Asia. The air war over Southeast Asia was thus the largest air war in world history. The United States did not use atomic weapons, but eight million tons is the equivalent in explosive force to 640 atomic bombs of the size used at Hiroshima."[167] This volume of violence stretched well beyond military necessity and surely violated the *in bello* proportionality principle that applies to the particular acts and tactics of a war: "excessive force is wrong."[168] The magnitude of the destruction caused by this bombing may also have contributed to the status of the entire war as unjust, for there is also an *ad bellum* proportionality principle, "which says the destructiveness of war must not be out of proportion to the relevant good the war will do."[169] Moreover, since hundreds of thousands—maybe millions—of Vietnamese civilians were killed during the war, many of them by American bombs, this technological violence was a significant part of the breaching of the discrimination requirement: "High civilian casualties were an inevitable feature of the nature of the war and the sheer volume of firepower used by the American military."[170] The bombing of Vietnam can thus be understood as a mass atrocity, although it is rarely conceived of as such, as Ehrhart explains:

> one can certainly recognize that what took place in a village that Americans remember as My Lai in March of 1968 went beyond what anyone would consider ethical in war. To take unarmed men, women and children and throw them into ditches and shoot them is not okay by anyone's code of ethics. But at the same time I witnessed repeatedly . . . massive aerial bombardment and artillery bombardment of targets that were heavily populated where civilian damage vastly exceeded anything that was done in My Lai and no one ever tried those pilots for murder. No one ever said that they had stepped beyond the bounds of what is acceptable in war.[171]

Yet, in their depictions of technological violence, the poets do reflect on what this type and level of killing might mean for the morality of war.

One particularly important and effective way in which the poets highlight the horror of the bombings is to present the perspective of the Vietnamese victims. It is difficult to comprehend the statistics, to understand the impact and the meaning of those eight million tons, but by giving voice to the victims, the poets employ empathy and moral imagination to demonstrate the human cost of this violence. They rehumanize those dehumanized by the bombing, a moral intervention that resists, through poetic representation, the us-them boundaries of the war. One of the best examples of this is Kevin Bowen's collection *Playing Basketball with the Viet Cong*, in which many of the poems explore various Vietnamese viewpoints. "The Arts of Love and Hydrology as Practiced in Hà Nội" begins with a delicate description of the morning routine of a Vietnamese woman—possibly "Thuy," to whom the poem is dedicated—before depicting the time she tried to save her brother from the annihilation of American bombs:

> It seems so distant now
> that day she dove and dove
> for him. She'd been
> among the first pulled

back from the canal,
the bombs still falling.
They couldn't understand her
as she gestured
back to the water.
Then she left them, dove back in,
found him, drew him
up the bank where she pumped
the brackish waters
from her brother's chest.
Some of the children trampled,
she later learned, rushing from road
and school into the flooded ditch.

Even though that day "seems so distant now," when Bowen details the protagonist's evening routine in the final verse of the poem, he writes: "Some nights the hues of crimson / in the rice will trouble / her."[172] This work highlights the powerful violence of the bombing and hints that such acts violated both the proportionality and the discrimination requirements of *jus in bello,* with the unrelenting "bombs still falling" and children attacked. Furthermore, the poem emphasizes the humanity of the Vietnamese people harmed, physically and psychologically, by American firepower. Rooted in the experience of a former other, poems like this illuminate the human dimension of the above-mentioned statistics. When numbers verge on the unimaginable, poetic imagination offers the possibility for a greater and more empathetic understanding of the suffering that such violence produces; it gives a sense of what bombing really means, of what it is like for those individuals who live and die under a blackened sky.

The poets also present their own perspective as participants in this technological violence. For example, Horace Coleman, who served as an Air Force air traffic controller–intercept director in Vietnam from 1967 to 1968, reflects on what it means to be involved in distanced killing. "Sitting before the height-finder radar / we see the blip/shapes of unseen bombers / miles high and away," he writes in "The Raid Near Saigon." He continues:

Thick as mosquito eggs
on the circled surface of a pond,
bombs drift like dying fireflies,
like murderous ghosts
falling in green streaks.

At the bottom of the screen,
electronic dust spills upward
and before we can speak,
the floor rumbles.[173]

Coleman's description captures a strange simulacrum of violence played out on the radar screen—the bombs only ghosts, the destruction just electronic dust. Yet, despite the technological veil and physical distance between Coleman and the bombs dropping "miles high and away," he nonetheless feels a close connection to the act of violence, with the rumbling floor both event and symbolic link.

In another poem, "Saigon Warrior," Coleman begins by suggesting that although his job may have been different from that of a combat soldier on the ground, it was nonetheless difficult and, given the omnipresence of violence in a war with no frontline, dangerous. Moreover, it was a role that implicated him in the war's process of violence as much as any combat soldier, as indicated by an interesting and honest attempt to evaluate his participation in killing: "I figure you could have two lines—like a weekend showing at / a theater with popular movies—and one would be / those I've helped kill and one those I've helped save / and there might be more women, children and old people in one." He wonders "if all the napalm and white phosphorous that make / 'Crispy Critters' or turn flesh into puddles and cluster bomb units . . . or simple high explosives . . . and the ghosts they made equal / the living bones from the times I played junior guardian angel." Coleman's moral reckoning demonstrates a sensitivity to both discrimination and proportionality considerations. With regard to the former, he acknowledges his involvement in the killing of "women, children and old people," who, although "they can take you out of here too," are more likely to have been harmless. With regard to the latter, he is aware that the bad he did in terms of lives ended might outweigh the good he did in terms of lives saved. Perhaps, though, this is not a calculation that he can work out, since in the final line he writes that "some one else can see which way my scale tilts." This could be seen as an evasion of personal responsibility, yet it is clear that Coleman does not shirk such responsibility, even if he cannot determine the exact extent of his accountability. It would be easy for him to attempt to morally exculpate himself from the violence from which he was physically removed, but he refuses to do so—"*my* scale."[174] He sees himself as much a part of the war's violence as those in the planes who dropped the bombs or those on the ground who fired the guns. "I mean the distinction in terms of the action you do is different," Coleman says, "but in terms of the moral responsibility I don't see any. I probably helped kill more people than the average guy on the ground."[175]

Furthermore, even some American soldiers on the ground participated in distanced killing. In the poem "Time on Target," which is military terminology for "artillery saturation fire," Ehrhart explains how "We used to get intelligence reports / From the Vietnamese district offices. // Every night, I'd make a list / Of targets for artillery to hit." He describes the powerful thrill of being able to control this violent technology: "It used to give me quite a kick / To know that I, a Corporal, // Could command an entire battery / To fire anywhere I said." Such weaponry may be directed and triggered at a distance, but the impact on victims is the same as violence enacted at close range: bodily destruction and death.

> One day, while on patrol,
> We passed the ruins of a house;
>
> Beside it sat a woman
> With her left hand torn away;
>
> Beside her lay a child, dead.
> When I got back to base,
>
> I told the fellows in the COC.
> It gave us all a lift to know

That all those shells we fired every night
Were hitting something.[176]

It is, as the literary scholar Lorrie Smith suggests in her astute analysis, a poem that relies "on ironic understatement" to make moral judgment, and Ehrhart's "kick" of power "is exposed as immoral by the war story at the poem's heart." Yet, the poem also intimates that the conditions of the war influenced soldiers' perceptions of and relationships with violence: "soldiers *were* frustrated by not being sure of what they were firing at; they *were* just doing their jobs; dead bodies *are* a fact of life in a war zone; it *is* necessary to numb yourself to daily atrocity." Hence, Smith concludes, Ehrhart's piece "allows for the soldier's feelings while also rendering them specious in the face of the woman's throat-catching agony."[177] And it is through this juxtaposition that the poem delivers much of its emotive and moral power. The final three lines shock the reader, who might have expected an expression of sadness or horror; instead, the soldiers are lifted by the news. The poem reveals how their sense of morality has been altered by the war, in which climatic conditions, the American-Vietnamese us-them barrier, and the physical and psychological distance enabled by technological violence turn the injuring and killing of any Vietnamese person into an accomplishment. Here, Ehrhart does not explicitly state his disapproval, but the implied military and moral failure he presents is as forceful and damning as any direct denunciation.

Just as the physical and psychological distance enabled by technological warfare can obscure the reality of violence and warp morality, so too can language. By helping to disguise and sanitize the process of injuring and killing, the language of war, especially its euphemisms, can act as a form of psychological and moral distancing.[178] In his piece "Politics and the English Language," George Orwell offers a germane example: "Defenceless villages are bombarded from the air, the inhabitants driven out into the countryside, the cattle machine-gunned, the huts set on fire with incendiary bullets: this is called *pacification.*" As he explains: "Such phraseology is needed if one wants to name things without calling up mental pictures of them."[179] For soldiers, this might be a necessary coping mechanism for enduring the horrors of war. For military and political leaders higher up the chain of command, it is a helpful masking of meaning for practices and policies that might be considered objectionable, even abhorrent, if they were to be described honestly. By concealing the brutal reality of violence, such veiled language aids not only the perpetration but also the perpetuation of war. Additionally, when coupled with the language of dehumanization, euphemisms provide a strong sense of detachment from the reality of killing another person, one that can be as significant as physical and technological distance. "I wasn't going to 'kill' them, I was going to 'zap' them, I was going to make 'body count' out of them . . . I was going to 'waste' them," Connolly recalls. What occurs is a "nasty little bit of brainwashing," he explains: "to 'zap a dink,' that doesn't make a picture in your mind . . . 'shoot a Vietnamese' and . . . in your mind you see an Asian person fall and not get up again, but 'zap a dink' are meaningless words, unless you've been to Vietnam."[180] These are the forms of language necessary to facilitate the process of killing in war.[181]

In "Bad Semantics (B.S.)," Hansen examines the role of both language and technology in killing. A note at the top of the page defines "*The Systematic Reduction of Enemy Cadre*" as "Army euphemism for killing." The short poem then reads:

> So hygenic [*sic*], so stainless,
> So innocent, so painless.
>
> No blood, no gore,
> No feces on the Huey floor.
>
> No endless rows of
> Charred bodies to dispose of.
>
> As if it could all be done
> in the living room, without
> setting off the smoke alarm.[182]

Both euphemism and technological violence sanitize killing. Sterilized of meaning and blood, the language and modern weaponry of war make the process seem clean and easy. Psychologically and physically, they insert an important degree of distance between the perpetrators and the victims. Yet, if language can distort and disguise moral meaning, it is also the medium through which the poets operate, and they resist and reject these obfuscations by exploring and exposing moral meaning. For example, the title of Hansen's poem plays with language by itself using a euphemism to underline the lies involved in military terminology. "B.S." might denote "Bad Semantics," but it is also a sanitized form of "bullshit." Just as military euphemisms, since they distort the meaning of words, are a case of bad semantics, they are also bullshit—lies and nonsense—for the same reason. And, Hansen indicates in the body of the poem, just as the bad semantics and bullshit of the military distance the dirty violence of war, so too does the use of technological weaponry. Moreover, given that military terminology is quite often used to refer to technological violence, the two are deeply intertwined. Their success in sanitizing the perception and actuality of the process of injuring and killing is a vital part of war.

One of the most significant aspects of America's technological violence in Vietnam was the use of chemical weapons, especially napalm and Agent Orange. During the course of the war, America dropped 400,000 tons of napalm on Vietnam and 18,850,000 gallons of herbicide, including 11,220,000 gallons of Agent Orange.[183] With regard to the latter, this meant that "over a nine-year period 20 percent of South Vietnam's jungles and 36 percent of its mangrove forests were sprayed," and agriculture was also attacked, with, for example, "42 percent of the 1965 spraying being allocated to food crops."[184] Here, it was not just the people of Vietnam but the landscape itself that was the enemy. The supposed purpose of this drastic defoliation was to deny the revolutionaries cover and food, but in the violent unmaking of nature with these chemicals, America also committed ecocide on a vast scale.[185] This was "the green war," to use Weigl's phrase.[186] Certainly, landscapes are harmed in all wars, but as Samuel Hynes suggests, "Vietnam was different; there the destruction was not simply a consequence of war, it was a *policy*."[187] Many poets detail this aspect of the war by portraying the natural landscape of Vietnam as the victim of this violence. "In country / many trees were wounded," Steptoe writes, "shot through with rifle fire / warped and charred with chorus / lines of napalm."[188]

Yet, if the Vietnamese landscape was the intended target and frequently the victim of chemical warfare, the Vietnamese people were also often harmed by this mode of technological violence. Weigl's "Song of Napalm" is a particularly memorable and powerful poem about this raining fire. He remembers the girl "Running from her village, napalm / Stuck to her dress like jelly, / Her hands reaching for the no one / Who waits in waves of heat before her." Weigl desperately tries "to imagine she runs down the road and wings / Beat inside her until she rises / Above the stinking jungle and her pain / Eases, and your pain, and mine." However, "the lie swings back again":

> The lie works only as long as it takes to speak
> And the girl runs only as far
> As the napalm allows
> Until her burning tendons and crackling
> Muscles draw her up
> Into that final position
> Burning bodies so perfectly assume.[189]

Agent Orange used during the war also inflicted terrible damage on the human body, and it continues to do so. Both the Americans and the Vietnamese were exposed to the chemical in the warzone, which led to victims "feeling dizzy, bleeding from the nose and mouth, and suffering from debilitating skin rashes and violent headaches."[190] Even worse were the long-term effects of exposure, "including cancers, diabetes, and birth defects in Vietnamese civilians, U.S. and Vietnamese war veterans, and their progeny."[191] The legacy of America's chemical warfare in Vietnam "has been maiming and killing people for decades," a violent unmaking of humans that will likely continue for some time yet: "No one can be sure when, if ever, this calamity will end."[192] For the American veterans affected, they were betrayed a second time by their own government as they were marginalized and mistreated. "The war in Vietnam was not the first time that a nation resorted to a scorched earth strategy against an enemy in war," the author Fred A. Wilcox notes; "however, it was the first time in human history that, in the process of trying to defeat an adversary, a government inadvertently poisoned its own army, then waited for this army to die." As for this "adversary," they are still "enduring the aftermath of a chemical holocaust," one that has "destroyed the lives of several million Vietnamese adults and children."[193] As the Vietnamese scientist Ton That Tung states: "In the abominable history of war, with the sole exception of nuclear weapons, never has such an inhuman fate ever been reserved for the survivors."[194]

This awful legacy of Agent Orange, particularly the impact on American veterans, is examined in numerous poems. "Some / rotted away internally / dying in orange light," Steptoe writes. "Ten thousand baths / never reach bone marrow / where the toxic waste / of war lives."[195] In "The Agent," Soular explicates this process of biological destruction: the "defoliant / sucks at your life like a leech / and mad glands and cells / devour themselves in a frenzy." The spraying of the chemical occurred in the past, but its process of altering and injuring human tissue operates as an act of violence in the present:

> Your skin turns yellow
> and your body rots before your eyes.
> You bleed *under* your skin
> from exploding capillaries,
> angry, purple islands, fierce contusions
> as if you were the victim of a severe beating.

It is an unmaking that appears as a reversal of human development: "You are almost a baby again / with loved ones cleaning you / and turning you gently / while they change the soiled sheets." The war may have ended, but its violence still kills: "No body counts these days / but the toll still mounts."[196] Quintana wonders whether this might be "The curse of a country that endeavored / to paint the jungle a resplendent orange."[197] Similarly, in a poem dedicated to "my brothers dying from Agent Orange," Connolly, adopting the voice of a veteran victim, asks if this agonizing aftermath is a punishment for what Americans did in Vietnam:

> I risked my life ten years ago,
> lived through danger, death, and pain.
> Since then I've been slowly dying
> from our aircraft's milky rain.
>
> Is this retribution,
> for doing what they sent me there for?
> I'm dying a slow death from "friendly fire"
> ten years after the war.[198]

Steve Mason examines the American government's ignoring and shirking of responsibility for this "cancerous time bomb." For Mason, it is a second betrayal for these veterans: "He dies from unseen wounds / drawn deep into his blood . . . He trusted his country as did you and I. / It sent him to Vietnam—way up in I Corps. / They deny that Agent Orange is killing him."[199] For Mason, the whole tragic issue of Agent Orange almost refuses poetic representation:

> . . . the green disappeared from the trees—
> attacked by the one word in his language
> which refused to rhyme;
> Orange.
>
> Years later,
> it would bleach the rainbows
> from his children's eyes
> and then, nothing rhymed.[200]

Mason himself was exposed to Agent Orange during the war, and thirty-seven years later "his doctor informed him that as a result of this exposure, he had developed terminal lung cancer."[201] He died on 25 May 2005.

Finally, although this book focuses primarily on the war years, it is nonetheless necessary to note that, just as with their depictions of the impact of Agent Orange, the poets detail the "slow violence" that has unfolded in the decades since the war officially ended and that will persist for decades to come.[202] Among other issues, they portray the long-term ruination of the natural landscapes and ecosystems as well as the destruction of the villages, towns, and cities of Vietnam; the exodus of the Vietnamese "boat people"; the destabilization of Cambodia and the subsequent genocide there; the many physically wounded and disabled veterans from all sides of the conflict; the reintegration difficulties of some veterans; and the deep psychological issues many veterans encountered.[203] Just as some poets ponder the inclusion of the Vietnamese dead on the Vietnam Veterans Memorial in Washington, DC, others consider the memorialization of those who perished, physically and psychologically, in the war's aftermath. Steptoe, for example, imagines

A
second wall
for those who cracked
like weathered stone
split open like gutted fish
by the knife
of memory and nightmare

A
second wall
for those who landed
on American shores
hit the trip wires
the punji pits
got caught in the most concealed
ambush of all
the one that waited
secretly for years
to slay its final victims
the one that hid
in the tunnels of the spirit[204]

Some of those who returned from the war nonetheless experienced the end of a way of being—ontic survivors subject to ontological death. As Hansen suggests, such victims have been largely absent from official accounts of the war's violent impact:

So
many names
were
missed
on
your tidy list,
when
you
too narrowly defined
survive
and

assumed
all those
who walked away
were
still
alive.[205]

War kills not only biology; it kills something deep inside as well. "We lost more than just a war," Connolly says to his fellow veterans.[206] "War is a brutish and vile business," Ehrhart argues. "It does things to the lives of those who survive it, and to their souls."[207] As D. F. Brown suggests: "nobody / comes away in one piece."[208]

The process of a war's violence, then, does not end when the last shots are fired. As the years pass and new wars begin their own processes of violence, old wars continue to inflict harm. In Gary Rafferty's poem "Last Asylum," set in "a psychiatric ward in a VA hospital," he writes of the legacies of the war's violence:

The funniest part?
When Howard, our Korean Vet asks
in perfect innocence,

"Do you guys know how fast
a grass hut burns?"

We make zippo motions
with our hands
& tears roll down our cheeks.

"Do we know how fast
a grass hut burns?!"

Shit, Howard,
half of 'Nam
is STILL on fire
because of us!
& so are we.[209]

Through their portrayals of bodily destruction, killing, atrocities, and technological violence, the poets bear unflinching witness to their war. In doing so, they reject the violence of which they were both victims and perpetrators. This is a fundamental part of their rebellion—a negation of violence and war and an affirmation of humanity and life. These are poems, then, that embody "the gaze falling on horror, withstanding it, and in unalleviated consciousness of negativity holding fast to the possibility of what is better," written by those "who were warriors in their youth / and learned that was not the way."[210] Furthermore, through such works, the poets give voice to those completely unmade by the conflict—the dead, who "are lashed / to nothingness, like blood / spilled on our living hands"—and to those, including themselves, not fully unmade but still irreparably marked by the war's violence.[211]

4
RESPONSIBILITY

"The Vietnam War didn't just happen," W. D. Ehrhart emphasizes in a piece entitled "Who's Responsible?" "It didn't gather cosmic dust somewhere out in the universe until it gained enough mass to come crashing down on Planet Earth like some sort of random bad luck." The war happened, he continues, "because distinct individuals made distinct choices over a discrete period of time . . . Virtually all of those decisions were wrong."[1] The result of all those wrong decisions, the poets strongly suggest, was a war that was a significant moral failure. As previous chapters have outlined, the poets indicate that the American intervention in Vietnam breached both the discrimination and the proportionality requirements of *jus in bello*. It can also be understood to have violated almost every *jus ad bellum* criterion: just cause, proportionate cause, right intention, reasonable chance of success, and last resort. Thus, according to a mode of thinking that allows for war, and possibly even obligates war in certain circumstances, it was unjustifiable.[2] Even those who would seek to validate the war might struggle to completely exculpate the scale of death and devastation it left in its wake. More pacific philosophies would, of course, be condemnatory and likely to adjudge the war a terrible moral crime. Whatever the viewpoint, it is clear that the war caused a great deal of harm. This raises one of the central moral questions of the conflict: Who was responsible for that harm? This final chapter examines the poetic responses to that question.

Before that, though, it is necessary to note the poetic position regarding the responsibility of the Vietnamese for the war. As the historian David W. P. Elliott argues, an "American-centered approach tends to put the spotlight on Lyndon Johnson and his advisors as the initiators, while downplaying the role played by the revolutionary leadership (and the Saigon government)." Crucially, with regard to responsibility, "it also tends to deny agency to the Vietnamese side of the conflict and glosses over the role that decisions taken by the Vietnamese had on the war."[3] As preceding chapters have detailed, many poets present a deep suspicion and mistrust of their south Vietnamese allies. Certainly, they place part of the blame for the war on "the old regime / rotting like a corpse from the inside out."[4] They also condemn particular acts committed by the revolutionaries, such as those atrocities mentioned in the previous chapter. Yet, beyond this, there are few poems that directly address the blameworthiness of the Vietnamese.

There are two key reasons the poets do not emphasize Vietnamese culpability. First, despite their empathy for the Vietnamese and considerations of various Vietnamese viewpoints, the poets offer an American perspective. It is, therefore, unsurprising that they focus primarily on aspects of American responsibility. Second, the relative absence of blame placed by the poets upon the Vietnamese, especially the revolutionaries, should not be seen as a denial of Vietnamese agency. Rather, it reflects the widespread belief among the poets that the Vietnamese revolutionaries were fighting for a moral cause; just as there is little in the poetry that blames the revolutionaries, there is rarely any suggestion that they were fighting in anything other than a justifiable campaign. "I admire the spirit of the V.C.," Bruce Anello noted in his diary during the war. "But who wouldn't have spirit? They have a cause to die for, it's their country."[5] A similar view runs throughout much of the poetry. This lack of blame in the poets' work, therefore, is a revealing silence; they refuse to condemn the revolutionaries' cause of liberation, unification, and communism. The poets do not necessarily exculpate the revolutionaries from the violence they perpetrated. But the poets understand that it was not the revolutionaries of Vietnam who placed them and other Americans in the way of harm and asked them to be agents of harm as well. As David Connolly explains: "I've come to know that my former foe, / he's not the man I should blame."[6] "Interestingly enough, as soon as I went home, the Vietnamese communists stopped trying to kill me," Ehrhart notes sarcastically.[7] The poetic account of responsibility for the harms perpetrated in the course of the war, therefore, is directed predominantly at Americans.

Thinking about Responsibility

The assignment of responsibility is dependent on the confluence of choice and causation. In the simplest terms: when a person's choice causes some harm, they are responsible for that harm. To trace the pathways of responsibility, therefore, is also to inquire into causal connections. It is helpful here to remember that the chain of causation can be influenced by many aspects outside of a person's control, such as the simple but significant factor of chance. As the legal scholar and philosopher Larry May argues in *Sharing Responsibility*, although there is "a tight relationship" between responsibility and causal agency, "moral responsibility is not the same as causal responsibility, for people are not responsible for all of the things they cause. With a few important exceptions, people are generally morally responsible only for those things they *voluntarily* cause."[8] This connection between choice and causation is at the heart of moral responsibility.[9] Of course, it should be noted that people can be morally responsible for harms beyond those which they immediately or directly cause. Additionally, May suggests, "Defects, especially in states of mind or character, that make it more likely that someone will cause harm are also things for which a person can be responsible." He argues that people can be held responsible for various attitudes "and not just for the effects of their explicit behavior." This is still rooted in choice, since, May posits, "states of mind are themselves often effects of what a person voluntarily chooses to do, although these are effects on a person's own self rather than effects on other selves."[10]

This emphasis on choice, with regard to both external and internal effects, is anchored in an existentialist ethic of responsibility. This draws not so much from early existentialism, which generates what May calls a "*personal* existentialist account of responsibility," as from later existentialism, which provides a "*social* existentialist account of responsibility" that "sees the self as a social construct, as a function of the interplay of history, social conditioning, and the chosen behavior of the individual person." In this view, derived from Karl Jaspers and the later works of Jean-Paul Sartre, a person may be "a product of society," but it is nonetheless possible for them "to choose which societal influences he or she will be exposed to, and hence which kind of self he or she will become (at least within certain limits)."[11] As discussed in chapter 1, a person is conditioned and constricted by situational contexts, but within those confines there remains what Viktor E. Frankl identifies as "a residue of freedom." In that space, "however limited it may be," a person has the capacity for choice.[12] A pertinent example from Sartre's *Being and Nothingness* highlights the centrality of choice in an existentialist ethic of responsibility: "If I am mobilized in a war, this war is *my* war . . . For lack of getting out of it, I have *chosen* it. This can be due to inertia, to cowardice in the face of public opinion, or because I prefer certain other values to the value of the refusal to join in the war (the good opinion of my relatives, the honor of my family, etc.). Anyway you look at it, it is a matter of choice."[13] The existentialist emphasis on choice, even within the restrictions of circumstance, results in a demanding ethic of responsibility, in which "attitudes as well as explicit behavior must be scrutinized to see if the individual is living up to his or her responsibilities." And as May stresses: "Even when there is seemingly nothing that one can *do* to prevent an evil in the world, one has a responsibility to distance oneself from that evil, at the very least by not condoning it." Hence: "Existentialist responsibility is a heavy burden on all of us."[14] As Sartre writes: "man being condemned to be free carries the weight of the whole world on his shoulders; he is responsible for the world and for himself as a way of being."[15]

People are also responsible for harms caused by the groups to which they belong. For example, the citizens of a particular country can be held accountable for the behavior of their country. In terms of group responsibility, it is possible to draw a distinction between "collective responsibility" and "shared responsibility." "When a group is *collectively* responsible for a harm, the group as such is responsible," May explains. Here, it is the whole group that is responsible. "When a group of people *shares* responsibility for a harm," however, "responsibility distributes to each member of the group." With shared responsibility, then, "Some or all members of a group may be assigned less than full responsibility for a harm," although they are still "subject to blame, punishment, or shame for what has occurred." The concept of shared responsibility is particularly helpful, since it "calls attention to the way in which the actions or attitudes of a group of people resulted in a harm" and focuses "on the way in which each of us interacts with others" without losing a sense of individual moral agency and responsibility. Thus, May argues that "the members of communities should come to see themselves as *personally sharing* in responsibility for the harms of their communities."[16]

As with individual responsibility, this understanding of shared responsibility is based on a social existentialist perspective. And again, "Emphasis is placed as much on the attitudes we choose to have, or choose to endorse, as it is on our outward behavior." May suggests: "If we focus only on personal responsibility for what we fully control, proper attention is not given to the fact that many people contribute indirectly to a harm, or that many people have the same attitudes and dispositions as the people who cause harm. These people may share responsibility for the harms . . . even though they do not have full control over the harms." May claims that "people who share certain attitudes, such as racist attitudes, share responsibility for harms that result from their attitudes, even if the individuals in question do not directly cause the harms themselves." This is because people who hold certain attitudes "share in the production of an attitudinal climate," and so "they participate in something like a joint venture that increases the likelihood of harm." By "contributing to a climate that influences others to cause harm," a person may therefore share responsibility "for the harms perpetrated by others who are influenced by that climate."[17] This conception of shared responsibility dovetails with the idea of a symbiotic relationship between the moral climate and the morality of an individual. Just as an individual's morality—including both behaviors and beliefs—is shaped and restricted by the surrounding moral climate, their morality contributes to that climate. In other words, moral agents are simultaneously influenced by and constitutive of moral climates. In that space in which an individual has the capacity of choice, they have the chance to alter, however slightly, the surrounding moral climate for themselves and for others. If that moral climate causes harms, they share, along with the other individuals who contribute to that climate, some responsibility for those harms and, furthermore, the obligation to utilize whatever choice they might have to alter that climate for the better.

Accounts of responsibility, therefore, focus on choice and causation and also consider the role of chance, circumstance, and climatic conditions. The locus of both personal and shared responsibility is in chosen acts and attitudes. Crucially, chosen omissions also matter. What people fail to do—that is, choose not to do—is an important aspect of responsibility. "One way of inflicting harm on others is to do something which results in their being harmed," the ethicist John Harris argues in *Violence and Responsibility.* Another way, he continues, "is to fail to do something the consequence of which is that they are harmed, in short, to fail to prevent harm." The distinction between the two can be described in various ways: "between acts and omissions, or between positive and negative acts, between harming and failing to help or, where life and death are at issue, as a distinction between killing and letting die." For Harris, much of the harm caused by negative acts can "be directly attributed to the wide acceptance of the view that the distinction between positive and negative actions marks a distinction both in the causal efficacy of what we do, and in its moral significance."[18] This commonly held view is known as the "acts and omissions doctrine," which, put simply, is the belief that "there is a morally important difference between *doing* something and *allowing* something to happen."[19] This doctrine suggests that "it is always worse to cause harm or death positively rather than negatively and, often, that the causal connection between an act and its consequences is necessarily somehow *closer* than that between an omission and its consequences." Yet, as Harris asserts, "there can be no moral difference between positive and negative actions with the same consequences."[20] Similarly, May argues "for responsibility based on failures to act, both individual omissions and collective inaction, especially as those failures increase the likelihood and scope of harm that one's community perpetrates."[21] Other moral philosophers, including Jonathan Glover, also suggest that "we ought to reject the acts and omissions doctrine."[22] Certainly, there are situations where blaming a person for inaction would be unjustified, such as if a harm occurs and "my ignorance of the whole episode meant I had no opportunity to intervene, and this ignorance was not itself the result of negligence." But blame can be justified if such an omission is "the result of ignorance that is negligent, where the agent could and should have avoided being ignorant."[23] A full account of moral responsibility, therefore, requires an attention to both acts and omissions. Ignorance, apathy, indifference, and other cases of inaction can be just as pernicious as positive acts that cause harm. As Glover concludes: "It is arguable that indifference plays as large a part in causing the world's misery as positive hostility. The existence of wars, poverty and many of the other things that destroy or stunt people's lives may be as dependent on widespread unconcern as on any positively bad motives. It may well be because of tacit acceptance of the acts and omissions doctrine that we acquiesce in the worst evils in the world."[24]

As with the existentialist perspective, a rejection of the acts and omissions doctrine leads to a demanding ethic of responsibility. "If we are responsible for harm which we could have prevented and if we believe that we should not harm others," Harris emphasizes, "we will find ourselves committed to a morality which challenges many of our basic beliefs and one which makes disturbing demands."[25] It would seem, as that forefather of existentialism Fyodor Dostoyevsky writes, that "each of us is guilty before all for everyone and everything."[26] Yet, this is why shared responsibility is so important. May's "expanded notion of responsibility" also suggests a "notion of shared agency" that captures "the idea that people are empowered by, and also aid in the empowerment of, their fellow community members." Thus, "all of the members of a community share in what each member does, and each member should feel some responsibility for what the other members do . . . Here sharing responsibility and taking responsibility for one's community merge."[27] But this also allows for the sharing and merging of agency. Isolated, the burden of morality might be too much for an individual to bear. Together, it might be possible to make choices that rise to the difficult demands suggested by a sense of morality anchored in a desire to avoid and minimize harm.

A rejection of the acts and omissions doctrine also alerts us to the accountability of "bystanders." It is clear that people who cause harm through positive acts are responsible for that harm, but it is vital not to overlook the responsibility of bystanders—those who choose not to act when they might be able to prevent harm by acting. Jaspers, in his discussion of German guilt in the aftermath of the Second World War, declares that "each one of us is guilty insofar as he remained inactive . . . passivity knows itself morally guilty of every failure, every neglect to act whenever possible, to shield the imperiled, to relieve wrong, to countervail."[28] As Glover summarizes: "bystanders look away." The first step in refusing to be a bystander, therefore, "is not to look away."[29] The poets in this study, with their "gaze falling on horror" and "withstanding it," take that step, and in their acts of poetry they suggest, and also accept, a demanding ethic of responsibility.[30]

The Usual Suspects

Poetic depictions of the American war in Vietnam, written by Americans who fought there, suggest a multiplicity of culprits who share in the responsibility for the immense harms caused by the war. With their broad vision and deep moral imagination rooted in a firsthand experience of the horrors of the war, the poets identify agents and factors—discussed in subsequent sections of this chapter—that have often remained outside the purview of historians. Nonetheless, they still denounce the most obvious candidates for blame, including those who have frequently been the focal point for historians: politicians, especially presidents. In Peter Ulisse's *Vietnam Voices,* "Doctor Able" reflects on the personal impact of the potent words of presidents:

> I often think about
> words,
> the way John F. Kennedy
> ("ask not what your country
> can do for you.. . . .")
> glistened and gleamed
> on a January podium.
> I understand how syllables
> can make some able
> and willing
> "to bear any burden, meet any
> hardship."
> I hear Johnson
> blistering and badgering
> congressmen like ants:
> Gulf of Tonklin [*sic*], minimum
> essential force,

winning the hearts and
minds of the people.

But words fail me now
looking into my wife's eyes
simply trying to say,
"I have orders for Vietnam."[31]

There is a painful contrast between the powerful words of presidents and the mute powerlessness of those they send to war. The significant influence of political leaders, including Johnson's manipulation of the Gulf of Tonkin incident, is also explored in a poem by D. C. Berry: "LBJ gets Congress to attack North Vietnam / because of twenty phantom torpedoes. / North Vietnam supposedly shoots them // at the US Navy." However:

according to the US Navy, "Freak weather effects
and overeager sonarmen may have accounted

for many of the reports.
No actual visual sightings
by *Maddox* . . .

Turner Joy also reports no actual visual sightings
or wakes. Entire action leaves many doubts."
Nevertheless, President Johnson

gets sixteen wise men. They push
two long tables together, two oak tables
mightier than aircraft carriers. The guns

are a dozen ash trays.
It's the Year of the Dragon—time, dammit, to nail
Ho's pecker to the wall, boys, and do it today.[32]

Again, the poem emphasizes the degree of control and choice, and thus responsibility, that Johnson and his advisers—"wise men" like Secretary of Defense Robert S. McNamara and National Security Adviser McGeorge

Bundy—had with regard to the decision to pursue the path of war.[33] Berry's representation of Johnson's distinctive diction and the reason for fighting in Vietnam—"We can't let Uncle Ho shoot the bird / at John Wayne"—suggests the absence of any wisdom around those tables.[34] Steven Hassna also mocks Johnson while simultaneously exposing his tremendous power. "When seeing what was happening," he writes:

> fearless johnson yells fear not I'll help/ and being
> a man of his word and because he just like sticking
> his nose in things that have no concern of his he
> sends 500,000 with orders to stop whatever it is
> that's happening there . . .[35]

These poems, then, appear to agree with the historian Fredrik Logevall's argument that "it seems undeniable that Johnson, fated to be president when the key Vietnam decisions had to be made, could have chosen differently. He could have avoided this war."[36] Thus, since Johnson *chose* war, he must be held morally responsible for the harms that followed from that decision.

While Johnson appears as the primary political perpetrator of the war's escalation and intensification in some poems, it is his successor, Richard Nixon, who attracts the most animosity and condemnation in the poetry. This enmity stems, in part, from the antiwar movement in which many of the poets participated when they returned from Vietnam. "Everyone hated him, / and that / brought us all together," Bruce Weigl recalls in his poem "Nixon":

> Nixon,
> whom we had seen
>
> in all of his flesh,
> standing
> on the White House balcony,
> Apollonian
> above the half-million
> citizens who had come
>
> to stop his killing . . .[37]

Through the ownership indicated by the words "*his* killing," Weigl stresses Nixon's responsibility for the war's harms. If it was Johnson's choice to escalate the war, it was Nixon's choice to continue it.

It is important to remember that during the 1968 presidential campaign, Nixon had pledged to end the conflict in Vietnam. In the time it took him to stop the war and bring about "peace with honor," another twenty-two thousand Americans were dead; many more Vietnamese allies, enemies, and civilians had been killed; and Cambodia had been destabilized to such an extent that it paved the way for the rise of Pol Pot and the Khmer Rouge genocide.[38] In his testimony before the Senate Foreign Relations Committee in 1971, John Kerry stated: "Each day to facilitate the process by which the United States washes her hands of Vietnam someone has to give up his life so that the United States doesn't have to admit something that the entire world already knows, so that we can't say that we have made a mistake. Someone has to die so that President Nixon won't be, and these are his words, 'the first President to lose a war.'"[39] As Hassna summarizes: "dick wins and in seeing what he / has won he says we want peace but let's not lose face / we must change but not too fast, etc."[40] By attempting to "not lose face," Nixon prolonged the war and, in doing so, significantly increased the harms of the conflict. In a piece written and published during the war, veteran Charles M. Purcell pictures the human impact of this deadly delay:

Streets—quiet and wet
Green bags of garbage and leaves
Neatly placed by the road.

Abruptly another scene pierces my mind
Other green bags are remembered
Neatly placed by the road.

Green bags made from ponchos
Bags with legs sticking out the bottoms
A nightmare awaiting the man from glad.

In the quiet dignified houses Nixon flashes on T.V.
Smiling his asinine smile and waving his asinine wave
While men lie along the road like so much garbage.[41]

To Nixon, the lives of these men, not to mention the lives of Vietnamese people, were disposable, an expendable commodity to be traded for the sake of political and personal pride. For the poets, Nixon was a politician who, as David Connolly suggests, did not "know right from wrong."[42]

Johnson and Nixon are the two most frequently named political perpetrators in the poetry, but the poets also condemn politicians as a whole for their role in the war. As indicated above, there were those who advised the presidents. In "On deference," McAvoy Layne suggests mockingly: "The President has a myriad of advisors / To help him determine right from wrong."[43] Bill Bauer lists McNamara among "the worst of the century," those responsible for "the most casualties, massive injuries": "Stalin, Hitler, Tojo, Mao, Khomeini, / Sukarno, Franco, McNamara, Saddam, / Pol Pot, Karadzic, Syngman Rhee."[44] The inclusion of McNamara in this roll call of the twentieth century's most infamous moral villains is a particularly damning indictment.[45] Above all, the poets are angered by the political structure of war, by "the grandiose hypocrisy of those who sell it, promote it, and command it compared with the reality of those who do the fighting," by "the fatal bluster of those who try to lead without knowing the way first hand."[46] As one poet notes: "Those that make the decisions / don't do the fighting over here; / They don't see what it is really like: / the blood, the death, the fear."[47] "I hate not these people, / I hate not the land," Anello wrote of the Vietnamese and Vietnam just months before he was killed in action, "I hate but the person / with his peace waving hand / starts a war and wants / everyone else to fight it."[48]

In many poetic accounts, soldiers appear as pawns used by politicians far removed from the actuality of war. "Now, show me a leader / with a weapon in his hand / as they chess us about / from land to land," Horace Coleman demands.[49] Politicians are frequently depicted as incompetent fools and duplicitous liars. In "Casualties," for example, J. Vincent Hansen writes:

> The "Best and the Brightest"
> proclaimed:
> "Peace with Honor."

Sometimes in war
words become
casualties too.[50]

They are also viewed as hypocrites, as Ehrhart states: "The beliefs worth dying for / are not the ones practiced / by the people who order your children / to die for them."[51] Lamont B. Steptoe offers a simple but clear denunciation:

I spit in the eye
of the lie
that sends sons
to die
and causes families
to cry

These people are killers, he suggests: "Washington / is a town of morticians / otherwise why / the big black limousines?"[52] Thus, the overall poetic perception of politicians is of a group of people whose combined ignorance and power placed the poets and many other young Americans in an arena of violence. This view is neatly summarized by Yusef Komunyakaa: "we played some deadly / game for blind gods."[53] Decades later, as new wars unfold, those who witnessed the horrors of war firsthand, like Ehrhart and his friend Lynda Van Devanter, who was a nurse, are still "frightened by the posturing of presidents // and statesmen who have never heard the sound / of teenaged soldiers crying for their mothers."[54]

Of course, American politicians could not have implemented their choice to make war in Vietnam without the willingness, machinery, and manpower of the "caterers of violence"—the American military.[55] Indeed, they were the immediate cause of much of the violence described in the previous chapter, and, as such, the poetic record suggests that the military should also share significant responsibility for the war and its tremendous harms. In particular, many of the poets strongly condemn America's military leaders. Hansen's piece "The Generals" stresses the power these men held over the lives of ordinary soldiers:

Late at night,
in dim-lit tents
they stick pins
into voodoo maps.

Half-a-world away,
blood spurts out
in little places

like Willow Bend,
Cedar Falls and
Popple Creek.[56]

Again, such poems underline the human impact of the choices made by those in positions of control. Similarly, D. F. Brown's "Poem (Westmoreland)" highlights the tragic human cost of military decisions, this time with regard to the apparently absurd tactics employed in the warzone:

I'm talking about boys
who die for nothing
or at best
some damned hill
Command abandons
next day.

I'm talking
blood
you suckers.

Some kid
19
from Alabama
just lost his legs
and
no bandage big enough.[57]

The tactics and dubious demands of military leaders also contributed to the questioning and doubt that affected American soldiers in the warzone and further undermined their belief that they were fighting for a worthwhile and moral cause. "I need *just* war, a people's sense of mission," R. L. Barth declares, "And not some general's arrogant ambition."[58]

As with the discrepancy between politicians and those they sent to Vietnam, the poets also emphasize the gap between the upper levels of the military and its soldiers. A stark contrast of experience existed even when these military men were in the warzone. As Dick Shea states:

> in the papers you see many photographs of rank officers
> getting awards for bravery in a combat area
> bullshit mostly
> the poor bastard who does the ducking
> gets a can of c-rations
> while the rank flies overhead
> visits safely and briefly
> and collects the medals
> it is an unjust world[59]

Although they were actually in Vietnam, these military leaders, like the politicians, were far removed from the dangers and discomforts in which they placed their soldiers. "Major Gordon Granger," Leroy V. Quintana writes, "Volunteered his line doggies anytime, / kept them in the boonies trying for a higher body count." He went home with "rows of medals," although "He never left basecamp except for quick scouting trips / on his chopper, always with a gunship or two along."[60] Unsurprisingly, many soldiers became resentful of military command and also their officers, sometimes to the point of violence, as depicted in Komunyakaa's poem about the killing of a superior: "Five men pull straws / under a tree on a hillside . . . 'We won't be wasting a real man. / That lieutenant's too gung ho.'"[61] Connolly recalls the time "we got drunk, on our ass drunk," and after "smoking a lot of Cambo dope, / we dipped the LT, / head first, into the pisser." They blamed him, Connolly explains, "or rather, his uniform, / because we were there."[62] Connolly "went to Long Binh jail over it," and although he regrets the act, his contempt for the role of military leaders in the war remains:

LT, you were KIA in June, at twenty one,
trying to save one of us from death,
I'm sorry for what I did to you.
You didn't deserve that.
But your uniform, for killing you
and so many others, for nothing,
it deserved worse.[63]

Thus, the poets indicate that the military, especially its leaders, should shoulder significant responsibility for the harms caused by the war.

America's political leaders chose to make war in Vietnam. America's military leaders supported their decisions and also chose, along with those politicians, how that war would be made. Yet, although they share a large degree of responsibility for the war's harms, politicians, advisers, and military leaders acted within the confines of conditions not entirely of their own choosing or control, and they inherited a set of possible choices that had been limited by the choices of those who had gone before. To give a simple example, Nixon's available choices were, to a certain extent, restricted by previous choices made by Johnson, just as Johnson's available choices were restricted by previous choices made by Kennedy, and so on. They also made such choices within the complex international context of the Cold War.[64] Furthermore, taken as a whole, and viewed from a long-term historical perspective, the American intervention in Vietnam can be understood as an imperialistic inheritance. Indeed, numerous poets portray the war in which they fought as part of a chain of attempts by foreign aggressors with imperial ambitions—China, Japan, France, and then America—to impose their will and authority on the people of Vietnam. Americans, Jan Barry writes, were "walking in the footsteps / of Genghis Khan," as well as more recent occupiers:

There, where a French legionnaire
once walked patrol
around the flightline perimeter of the airfield
at Nha Trang,
ten years later I walked,

an American expeditionary forces
soldier on night guard duty
at Nha Trang,
occupied even earlier,
twenty years before
(a year more than my nineteen),
by the Japanese.[65]

The poets acknowledge these inherited aspects of the conflict. Nonetheless, that does not soften their scorn for the political and military leaders who chose to make an American war in Vietnam.

The Business of War

According to several poets, those who chose to profit from the war should also be held morally accountable for its harms. These profiteers and businesses were deeply entangled in the political and military structures that pursued and supported the war.[66] Steve Mason observes:

Everywhere I look,
from government building
to government building,
I see merchants. Businessmen.
Who are these fucking accountants
who manage our destinies
as if mankind were the private stock room
of the trilateral commission
and the pentagonal shoe clerks?

This confluence of politics and business reminds Mason of his grandfather's words: "Boy, crime don't pay on a small scale, / it pays on a Big one. / And if that crime becomes big enough / it begins to govern."[67] Similarly, in Steptoe's poem "Gulf of Tonkin," "the faces of Congress" represent corporations rather than the American people:

Damn
you rich

lawyer sons of lawyer
sons-of-bitches
that rule our lives
like Roman Patricians
. . .
You're not America
and never will be just GM
Ford and IBM
and Tri-Lateral Commission lackeys
dancing to the tune
of Magicians of darkness
hell-bent on importing
the flames of Hades to earth's
surface[68]

"In the names / of the Vietnam / dead I curse you," Steptoe writes, just as he curses "Pentagon Generals / at the controls / of the video arcade / of the world" and the technowar they perpetrated in Vietnam:

You frigid
unemotional
computer-prick
assholes
I survived
your Vietnam
charade

In Steptoe's vitriolic piece, political and military leaders are seen as part of a morally reprehensible corporate establishment that acts against the interests of America:

You're not America
just big business
and robber barons
and la Costra Nostra
evil polluting our
amber waves of grain[69]

As Steptoe issues forth his damnations and excoriations, the powerful men of politics, the military, and business who "rule our lives" become almost indistinguishable from one another—and all of them, according to Steptoe and a number of other poets, are worthy of condemnation.

These former soldiers are angered by the realization that as they fought in Vietnam, and as American and Vietnamese people were maimed and killed, other people and businesses were making money from that suffering. As Connolly suggests, "there should be corporate responsibility."[70] Just as politicians relied on the military to implement their policies in Vietnam, they and the military relied on businesses to manufacture some of their deadly weaponry. Certainly, these businesses may not have chosen to make war, but to the extent that they chose to make war possible, and profited as a result, they share some responsibility for the harms caused by the war.

Connolly states that "one of the most glaring things from the Vietnam War in general is Dow Chemical," and this particular company is a good example of the shirking of corporate responsibility that occurred during and after the war.[71] "In addition to manufacturing Agent Orange, Dow was the principal supplier of napalm to U.S. forces in Vietnam," David Zierler notes in his account of the ecocide in Vietnam, "and it was that weapon that first made Dow one of the most notorious members of the 'military-industrial complex' in the eyes of antiwar protestors." Given "Dow's onerous record of supplying U.S. forces with napalm and herbicides," it came to be viewed "as the corporate embodiment of American atrocities in Vietnam."[72] "We are not . . . dealing with trivialities, but with monstrous deeds," the historian and activist Howard Zinn wrote in an essay supporting demonstrations against the company in 1967. Although he noted that the "root issue . . . is not simply napalm; it is the Vietnam war as a whole," Zinn argued that "the use of napalm is one particularly bestial tactic in this war" and "is one of the cruelest acts perpetrated by any nation in modern history."[73] Dow responded to such condemnations and demonstrations by stating: "Our position on the manufacture of napalm is that we are a supplier of goods to the Defense Department and not a policy maker. We do not and should not try to decide military strategy or policy. Simple good citizenship requires that we supply our government and our military with those goods which they feel they need whenever we have the technology and capability and have been chosen by the government as a supplier."[74] Yet, this was an attempt to evade moral responsibility by hiding behind the decisions of the government and the military. What "simple good citizenship" really required in this case was to question why the government and the military needed napalm, what they were doing with that napalm, whether it was right to supply them with that napalm, and, more broadly, whether it was right to manufacture napalm at all. A verse from a song composed by American soldiers in Vietnam, included in the poetry anthology *Peace Is Our Profession,* captures the company's lack of concern with regard to the consequences of the weapons it chose to supply and also its complicity in the crimes of the war: "A baby sucking on his mother's tit, / Children cowering in a pit, / Dow Chemical doesn't give a shit, / Napalm sticks to kids."[75] For Mason, the horrors of Agent Orange, and Dow's role in its production, are almost beyond poetic comprehension: "nothing rhymed . . . least of all, DOW."[76]

The company, then, was complicit in causing horrific harm during and after the war. Yet, in considerations of "corporate responsibility," it is vital to remember that it is not some faceless entity that is to blame, but rather all those individuals working for Dow who contributed to the production and supply of these weapons. This includes those at the very top, such as the company chairman Carl A. Gerstacker and president Herbert D. Doan, as well as the scientists and other workers involved in the manufacturing and distribution process. While the extent of attributable moral responsibility might be mitigated slightly by ignorance that "was not itself the result of negligence" of the devastating long-term effects of these chemicals, all those who make weapons of war share some responsibility for the harms they cause.[77] Businesses are composed of individuals, and ultimately those individuals are accountable for the acts and omissions of which they are a part.

Of course, Dow was not the only company that contributed to and profited from the injuring and killing of the war. The Honeywell Corporation and its workers, for example, produced cluster bombs, "deadly packages of exploding pellets which left machines untouched, but people—mostly civilians—severely wounded and in agony."[78] Furthermore, such businesses were part of the whole system of profiteering and capitalism, in which "Peace is consumers . . . consuming. / It plots nicely on a graph. / Peace is tons of napalm falling, / A gamble where it lands."[79] The poets depict a world in which "carpet bombing civilians / stimulates the stock market" and men "pay for life with money."[80] "Putting a price on Life and I'm sick of it," one poet laments.[81] "Power, Politics, and Profit! / What a reason to die! / Now that I know the truth, / it's difficult not to cry," G. P. Johnson writes.[82] It is a point he reiterates in another poem:

> In God we trusted—
>   this was the American Dream.
> What I see now,
>   Lord, it makes me want to scream.
>
> Power, Politics, and Profit!
>   What a reason to die!
> Power, Politics, and Profit!
>   What a reason to live![83]

According to Mason, the pursuit of profit is a central causal factor in war:

> Hundreds of millions
> of men under arms
> have killed millions
> of men, women
> and little children
> with nails and clubs,
> bullets and bombs.
>
> They did it and continue to do it
> in the name of gods,
> for the sake of governments
> and in the cause of nationalism.
> But especially they do it
> for the thousand nameless men
> who control the world of business
> and have not yet found the profit
> in peace.[84]

Perhaps Mason's suggestion that the people "who control the world of business" are "nameless" exonerates individuals who could actually be named rather easily, such as Gerstacker and Doan of Dow. It also overlooks the role of workers who support this system. Nonetheless, his identification of the profit motive as a significant cause of war is valid. Moreover, Mason also hints, as do other poets, that for certain businesses, there might be more profit in war than in peace.[85]

The position of these poets with regard to the profit made as a result of war echoes the stance of Smedley D. Butler. A highly decorated Marine Corps major general who participated in numerous campaigns during his thirty-three years of service, Butler left the military and in 1935 published *War Is a Racket,* a work that describes and criticizes war profiteering. He declares: "War is a racket. It always has been. It is possibly the oldest, easily the most profitable, surely the most vicious . . . It is the only one in which the profits are reckoned in dollars and the losses in lives . . . Out of war a few people make huge fortunes."[86]

David Connolly is a particularly powerful poetic voice on this issue. The events that transpired while he was "on an operation in the Michelin Rubber Plantations, near the town of Dau Tieng, in what was called South Vietnam," highlight the moral failings that could occur when business mixed with the war and also reveal the real priorities of the American government.[87] On a "warm, May morning" in 1968, the Second Squadron of the 11th Armored Cavalry Regiment entered the plantation.[88] They were "ambushed by an entrenched, numerically superior force," and a brutal and deadly firefight ensued.[89] It was, Connolly recalls, "a bloodbath. Of the seventy men that had moved into that grove, eleven left alive." As for their Vietnamese opponents: "There were one hundred and three enemy bodies."[90] But Connolly's harrowing experience did not end once the firefight had finished. When the "medevacs started to land," one helicopter had its doors closed and "didn't have the red cross brassard on it," and as it touched down the doors opened "and all of these officers started to get out." These men "still had creases in their fatigues, their boots were shined," Connolly remembers, and "they told us that they couldn't take our wounded out, they were there from the General Accounting Office of the United States Army and they were there to count the trees that had been damaged so the U.S. could pay reparations to Michelin Incorporated." Connolly states: "if you ever want to feel like you are just a fucking number have somebody say that to you." One of his comrades told the auditors, "'we've been killing people for about two hours, we'll shoot you,' . . . and luckily one of our officers intervened and said, 'get off the bird, we're using it to take wounded out.'" As Connolly asks: "Who should've been put first in that situation, the corporate interest or the guy bleeding to death?"[91] The intense anger Connolly felt then has not lessened over the years, and it never will, as he notes in his poem "Into the Michelin Rubber Plantations": "One Huey was full of officers, there to count the damaged trees, / so the US could pay off Michelin and they tried to ignore our pleas / to get our wounded out of there; see, they had a mission to fulfill. / I still taste the bitterness of that day; you can bet I always will."[92]

Connolly's experience in the Michelin Rubber Plantations is the basis for his poem "Thoughts on a Monsoon Morning," an especially fierce denunciation of the role of business and profiteering in war. Originally written after a memorial service for those fifty-nine American soldiers "who were killed in action or who died as a result of wounds received" in the plantation, the piece begins with Connolly questioning his own moral complicity: "Wondering, with the things I've done, / can I ever make amends?" He also reflects on the difficulty of returning to America: "Wondering, how will I ever fit in / with people who just don't know?" Connolly notes his betrayal by the rich and powerful who sent him to war and ponders the possibility of informing unreflective patriots of what he has seen: "Used by the rich of my country. / Duped by those I looked up to. / Wondering, how can I tell those / who blindly wave the red, white, and blue?" At this point, the tone of the poem shifts considerably, as though Connolly's rage can no longer be restrained. He unleashes a torrent of condemnation, as an antagonistic refrain identifies those who profited from the war as complicit in the deaths from which they made money. These final three verses of Connolly's poem, anchored in a painful and unforgettable wartime experience, perfectly capture the widespread hostility in the poetry directed toward those who benefited financially from the tremendous suffering during the war:

> I hate every fucking one of you
> who make dollars from our deaths.

I hate every fucking one of you
for my friends' dying breaths.

I hate every fucking one of you
banker or corporation head.
I hate every fucking one of you
for so many, so young and dead.

I hate every fucking one of you
with your pin-striped, dark blue suits.
I hate every fucking one of you
for all those empty boots.[93]

America and Americans

Politicians chose the war, the military executed it, and some businesses and people profited from it. Yet, the war could not have occurred, or continued for so long, without the support of the American people. Johnson and his advisers, for example, may have taken the final decision to significantly escalate American military involvement in Vietnam, but, even so, to identify them as the only persons worthy of blame—if, as the poets strongly suggest, the war should be condemned rather than commended—would be to overlook the vast network of moral agents and structures within America that enabled this decision to be made in the first place. Rather than looking solely at the most direct or immediate causal thread, then, a fuller account of moral responsibility must also examine the large web of interwoven and interdependent threads that supported the weight of such choices. It is just such a complex and multilayered picture that emerges in the works of the poets, especially in their considerations of national responsibility.[94]

While the poets sternly criticize those at the end of the causal chain who made the final decisions, they also explore how the deeply entangled acts and omissions of the American people and the values they built up and lived by contributed to situations and structures in which the war became possible and actualized. This comprehensive conception of national responsibility is neatly summarized in a letter written in response to the aftermath of the My Lai massacre, published in the

New York Times on 27 March 1970: "The war is the primal atrocity. The crime belongs to the *nation*. The war criminals are all of us." The author acknowledges the responsibility of "President Kennedy through Johnson, Nixon, Congress, the Pentagon on down—or up" for "the daily slaughter we wreak on that far away land," but stresses again: "The criminals are all of us. The war itself is the great atrocity that spawns the lesser atrocities."[95] Similarly, the editors of the first key poetry anthology, *Winning Hearts and Minds*, note the attempted avoidance of this responsibility by the American people: "Americans are desperate to believe they do not share in the complicity of the acts committed by their sons and their leaders."[96] But the editors of and contributors to the collection, and many of the other poets who have written since then, attack this belief and insist that the American people do share in the complicity for the war's harms.

Taken together, the works of the poets offer an extensive examination of how the American people contributed to the war. Their reflections on national responsibility range far beyond the most direct and explicit aspects, such as democratic and taxpayer responsibility, to offer a remarkably broad account of the many elements of American life that were complicit in the war's harms. Indeed, it is here that they are particularly penetrating and critical. As discussed previously, the poets examine the significance of American racial structures, and they are also concerned with other societal structures, including class and gender. They reflect on the role that religion, anticommunism, patriotism, and distrust of dissent played in the war, as well as the values imparted, implicitly or explicitly, through culture. Additionally, many poets consider the failure of generational responsibility that the war represented. They also present a scathing critique of bystander apathy among the American people. These structures, beliefs, ideas, attitudes, and values provided the framework within which American policy in Vietnam was formed and executed. To the extent that this national framework supported the weight of the choices taken to make war and continue to make war, its constituent parts share in responsibility for the war's harms. Hence, just as the poetry offers insights into the climatic conditions of the warzone in Vietnam, it also offers insights into the climatic conditions of American society that contributed to the war. The poets remind us that this was a war rooted deeply in American life. As Weigl writes: "If you think there's no blood / in the streets / then you live in a dream."[97]

While American politicians chose to make war in Vietnam, it was the American voting public who chose those politicians. In his seminal work *Just and Unjust Wars: A Moral Argument with Historical Illustrations,* Michael Walzer utilizes the example of "The American People and the War in Vietnam" to explore the intricacies of this issue of democratic responsibility. "Democracy is a way of distributing responsibility," he notes. "But that doesn't mean that all adult citizens share equally in the blame we assign for aggressive war. Our actual assignments will vary a great deal, depending on the precise nature of the democratic order, the place of a particular person in that order, and the pattern of his own political activities."[98] Moreover, the imperfections and practicalities of democracies also affect attributions of accountability. For example, it is important to consider factors such as the significant deficit of both knowledge and power between citizens and politicians; the duplicity of politicians; the lack of real choice between politicians, policies, and ideologies; the role of the media, which may be politically controlled or biased; and the relative impotence of any one individual's political participation, "only our one vote each, / only our small voices."[99] Still, as members of a democratic society, however imperfect, American citizens during the war in Vietnam exerted some degree of influence over which politicians were elected and what policies they pursued once they were put in the path of power, including the military decisions they made. Thus, Ehrhart, preeminent among the poets with regard to the issue of national responsibility, writes that American soldiers were "Democracy on Zippo raids, / Burning hooches to the ground, / Driving eager Amtracs through a farmer's fields."[100]

Additionally, as taxpayers, the American people funded the war.[101] As Arthur S. Blank Jr., who served as an Army psychiatrist in Vietnam, suggests: "we are all in this together. Most obviously, all of us who were there; but everyone else too, who worked to earn the money to pay the tax to buy the gun and ammunition, and the airplane and the fuel which got the soldier there. Every American taxpayer paid an average of $3300 for the Viet Nam war. If you don't yet quite see how connected you were, eventually you will."[102] Ehrhart examines the issue of taxpayer complicity in a poem tellingly titled "Responsibility," which begins with an apposite epigraph from the United States Constitution: "The Congress shall have power to lay and collect taxes . . . to . . . provide for the common defense and general welfare of the United States." Although the piece refers specifically to the American involvement in El Salvador in the 1980s, it could apply equally well to all of America's military machinations:

> Friday, payday, security:
> money in my pocket for the weekend;
> money for my government;
> money for the soldiers of El Salvador,
> fifty bullets to the box.[103]

That which provides Ehrhart and other taxpayers with "security" also contributes to the perpetration of violence and war. A consideration of what our taxes are used for is, therefore, an important aspect of national responsibility. With regard to war, this demands an acknowledgment of and engagement with the terrible reality that, as Weigl writes, "children / are terrorized out of their minds by bombs we pay for. You can only / cover your mouth, so you won't scream out loud."[104]

Although the poets denounce the visibly direct contributions of votes and taxes to the war, their attention is more often focused on exposing the underlying climatic conditions of American life that helped to make the conflict possible and to shape its contours. Here, class was an important factor, particularly with regard to the composition of America's fighting force. "Roughly 80 percent came from working-class and poor backgrounds," Christian G. Appy notes in his history of American combat soldiers in the war. "Vietnam," he argues, "more than any other American war in the twentieth century, perhaps in our history, was a working-class war."[105] Or, as the poet D. F. Brown suggests somewhat sardonically: "Nam was / a theme park for working class kids."[106] Yet, while the burden of fighting may have fallen on working-class Americans to an exceptionally large degree, it was the same structure—in which the poorer parts of society provide a higher proportion of the soldiers—that undergirds most wars. "I'm the same as me Da and my GrandPa; / we answered our country's call, / the working poor who were never quite sure / that what we did was right after all," Connolly writes in "War Song." It is a song he sings "for the Viet Cong, / for the IRA and for me, / for every young kid who didn't know what he did / just maintained the powers that be."[107] Connolly's concern with class and power structures is perhaps unsurprising given his perspective on profiteering and war. Similarly, Mason's suspicion of the profit motive hooks into his understanding of the role of class in war:

> War is a surrealistic penal colony
> for young patriots of the real world
> who, as sons of poor men,
> must pay the price
> for the believable myths
> of national furors and private enterprise.[108]

In the poetry, a concern with class often expresses itself via a twofold resentment of the rich. First, there is anger at the use of privilege to avoid the draft.[109] Second, many poets convey a sense of disillusionment that they fought on behalf of the rich who themselves avoided fighting. Both of these issues provide the material for several particularly acerbic short poems by Barth. In "Social Darwinism," he notes: "Professionally aided, / The Privileged became, / Until the danger faded, / The weak and halt and lame."[110] This leads to a "Grunt Fantasy": "Another war and, swabbing tears with sleeves, / Over the coffin a rich mother grieves."[111] While some veterans in the aftermath of the war blamed the Vietnamese, Barth locates the responsibility closer to home: "Tonight you bitch, under too many drinks, / 'Fucked over! Got our asses kicked for dinks!' / I leave the obvious alone—in fact, / For wealthy children, to keep theirs intact."[112] This intersection of class and the war is precisely summarized, again by Barth, in "A Brief History of the Vietnam War": "The essence was economy: / How wealthy was your family?"[113]

The poets also consider gender and war. With regard to responsibility, a key concern is how conceptions of masculinity and the myth of "What Makes a Man" contribute to war.[114] Boys are told, Barry explains, "that War / will bring / them manhood, wisdom, / courage, undying fame."[115] From their earliest years, then, and throughout their life, males have to "wade through several tons / of social excrement / wearing testicle-high value systems," Mason writes, which act "as prophylactics against the responsibility / to be people (instead of simply men)."[116] In "Unaccustomed Mercies," Ehrhart argues that war is "what men do to be men / to the white bleeding bone." This poem begins with him kissing his fellow veteran and author Larry Heinemann, the dedicatee of the piece, as "a way of saying thanks / for surviving, for writing." So many veterans, Ehrhart notes, are "unable to find a way out of the past, / angrily vacant, calling themselves men. / Someone ought to kiss them too." As the poem continues, Ehrhart wonders whether a failure to offer these men tenderness, compassion, and love as they were growing up and the inability of men to be open to and receive these gifts of the heart play a part in war:

> Someone ought to have kissed them
> years ago, before the war, before
> their first football game, before
> the last time they saw their fathers
>
> naked. Think of it: all that steel,
> the hatred, the generations consumed
> for want of unaccustomed mercies men
> might receive, if only they knew how.

The poets suggest that there is a need for these veterans, and for American society as a whole, to decouple war from conceptions of manhood, to replace its violence with a "kiss, / my weaponless hands, your smile."[117]

Another factor identified by the poets in their explorations of the framework that helped to support the weight of the war is religion. Some poets demonstrate an awareness of the religious content of the struggle within Vietnam itself, especially the tensions between the Catholic and Buddhist populations. For example, Kevin Bowen depicts "President Diem's Motorcade":

> Two hours now
> since the President took communion.
> The car rocks just a bit;
> the President turns,
> wonders, all the monks in the streets,

> then something he'd meant
> to ask in confession.[118]

Several poets note the dramatic self-immolating Buddhist protests, including that of Thich Quang Duc, who "burned like a bundle of black joss sticks" on the "2527th Birthday of the Buddha," Komunyakaa writes. The terminal point of such events may have been Vietnam, but, as Komunyakaa hints, the causal chain connected back to America: "A high wind that started in California / fanned flames, turned each blue page, / leaving only his heart intact. / Waves of saffron robes bowed to the gasoline can."[119]

More often, however, the poets focus on the impact of Christianity—or the lack thereof—on the American side of the conflict. For many poets, the professed Christian values of love and peace were significantly compromised by the war. Certainly, there is the occasional poetic piece that emphasizes the potentially positive and pacifistic effects that such an ethic could have when it was maintained. Hansen's poem "Sgt. Royster Meets Pvt. Stanley," for instance, tells the story of a recruit who, despite repeated orders, refuses to kill even a rabbit. Here, a moral belief in the wrongness of killing anchored in a religious conviction provides the recruit with the strength to resist the military's climate of killing: "Sgt. Royster retorted: 'Why won't you kill the damn rabbit, Pvt.?' / Pvt. Stanley replied: 'Because it is wrong to kill, Sgt.' / Sgt. Royster shouted: 'Wrong to kill? Then what in God's name are you doing in this man's army, Pvt.?' / Pvt. Stanley replied: 'Nothing in His name, Sgt.'" The piece concludes with a note explaining what happened next: "After six months of side sink, Pvt. Stanley was discharged with what was called a personality disorder. (i.e., He would not kill.)"[120] Much more frequently, however, the poets offer a negative assessment of the role of Christianity in the American intervention. In another poem, Hansen writes:

> This "7 times 70" God,
> this "Love your enemy" God,
> this "Thou shalt not kill" God,
> we take Him along.

Turn Him
from a breaking-bread God,
into a breaking-starch God,
from a "turn the other cheek" God,
into a "MAKE MY DAY" God
and take Him along.

Make Him fall in.
Make Him salute.
Make Him march.
Make Him shoot.
This "Thou shalt not kill" God
and take Him along.[121]

Here, the moral demands of Christianity are twisted to fit military demands, and the prohibition on killing, which Hansen stresses through repetition, is disregarded. It is, Hansen implies, an eviscerated version of Christianity that the American military takes along to war.

The poets expose the hypocritical involvement of alleged Christians who, in the course of the war, betrayed the core values of their faith. As representatives of the religion in the warzone, military chaplains are a particularly common target of such condemnations. There is a recognition of their bravery, the comfort they could provide, and the good they could sometimes do, as well as sympathy with the difficulty of their task, of making those in the midst of horror "aware of the purity of / God's love, / His infinite wisdom and saving grace."[122] But, more often, poetic portrayals emphasize the hypocrisy and complicity of chaplains who "Preach love of the enemy" while simultaneously leading prayers "in the names of the Joint Chiefs of Staff / and fixed-wing aircraft / and the napalm's orange glare / so help you God."[123] "Priests blessed weapons in the mist of Ca Lu," Weigl states sadly.[124] It was a faith-shattering moment that he still remembers decades later. Weigl realized then he "couldn't count on the priesthood . . . I thought, 'this is my church? Wait a minute, what is this? It doesn't make sense.'"[125] Similarly, Komunyakaa found it strange for supposed men of love and peace to be so deeply intertwined with the ways of war. "I could never understand what a chaplain would be doing in a situation of war . . . as a military man, wearing a uniform," he reflects, "that was very difficult for me to understand, especially looking at sacred documents."[126] In the final line of Barth's "Chaplain to Bishop," the chaplain speaker dejectedly concedes the contradictions in his role: "I see my self-deceit."[127] For many poets, then, chaplains share in the moral burden for the war. They became embroiled in a military endeavor that often negated the very values they were meant to affirm. In sum, the picture presented in the poetry suggests that the complicity of chaplains in the war, not to mention many other American Christians, represented a significant failure of Christian responsibility and a betrayal of a Christian ethic of nonviolence.[128]

Back in America, an interconnected group of beliefs, which also included versions of Christianity comfortable with the use of military force, helped to support the war. As discussed in the first chapter, the poets critique the Cold War fear of communism that underpinned America's crusade in Vietnam. Given the supposedly atheistic nature of communism, and the purportedly Christian character of American life, it was not unusual for the language and justification of the war to take on a religious texture: "America's saving the world from godless Communism!"[129] In "Free Fire Zone," Doug Anderson describes how "The eighteen year-old who thinks / Christ is about to rain death on commies / kicks the family altar to pieces in an old mud hut."[130] Perhaps the roots of, and therefore part of the responsibility for, such beliefs and behaviors can be traced back to people like David Hall's eighth grade history teacher, who said, "God would never allow / the Communists domination over / a Christian people."[131] "We had prayed the entire school year / for peace, and for the fall of communism," Quintana writes, as though he had been taught to believe that communism was the primary cause of conflict in the world.[132] There is no awareness that America's blustering attempts to "contain" communism and to maintain its own sphere of influence might have been a key causal factor in the war. Hence, good intentions, such as the desire for peace, and even sincerely held concerns about the possible spread of tyranny and totalitarianism throughout Asia and beyond were clouded in this Cold War climate by an almost hysterical fear of communism. It was a fear fostered and used by politicians, one they may have become trapped in themselves. In "Gulf of Tonkin," Steptoe condemns both the people and the politicians for this anticommunism: "I curse / the fools who / believe your rhetoric / of Red lies."[133] As a central foundation of the American war in Vietnam, and the American people's support of it, this ideology of anticommunism must share significant responsibility for the harms perpetrated in its name.

Similarly, the poets suggest that unreflective patriotism must shoulder some responsibility for the war. As with anticommunism, some American people combined patriotism with a hawkish religiosity. Ehrhart, for example, writes that he grew up "in a town that / Feared God and raised sons / Willing to die for their country."[134] After his experiences in the war, he finds this common cause of conflict almost inexplicable: "How explain a world where men / kill other men deliberately / and call it love of country?"[135] Uncritical patriotic beliefs are often an integral part of a belligerent moral climate, and Ehrhart eschews such jingoism: "You can just keep your rockets' red glare."[136] For him, the American flag symbolizes "blood, stars, an ocean of ignorance."[137] "So take some care; tell your sons to beware, / about blindly following flags," Connolly warns.[138]

Climates marked by a suspicion of questioning and distrust of dissent can also aggrandize prowar voices, or at least undermine antiwar opinion and activity. Indeed, as the political scientist Adam J. Berinsky outlines, there was a positive correlation "between levels of war support and the probability of advocating a restriction on the right of protest," with surveys suggesting that "supporters of the Vietnam War were the most enthusiastic about restricting the liberties of its opponents."[139] Ehrhart's poem about the Kent State massacre, in which four college students were shot dead by the Ohio National Guard during an antiwar protest on 4 May 1970, reveals just such an atmosphere during the war:

> The girl kneels in the parking lot,
> her face uplifted, mouth so twisted
> she appears to be hysterical.
>
> . . .
>
> She doesn't understand
> the gray-haired men who've done this
> or the millions more who think
> the dead boy at her feet has gotten
> just what he has asked for and deserves.[140]

These societal attitudes seem to stem from a self-righteousness and certainty that devalues dissent in favor of unreflective conformity, as in the town where Ehrhart grew up: "so smug it was, so self-content, / its point of view so narrow one could / get a better field of vision peering / through the barrel of a shotgun."[141] Thus, currents of Christianity, anti-communism, and patriotism were a vital part of the American climate at the time of the war in Vietnam. If, as Glover indicates, the "climate of opinion conditions everything," and if the beliefs and values of the citizens of a nation impact on where, when, why, how, and with whom their country goes to war, then these factors must be considered in any account of responsibility for the war.[142]

Furthermore, beliefs and values can be transmitted through culture. The cultural productions and consumptions of a nation—the books its people write and read, the films they make and watch, the sports they play and watch, to name just a few examples—are a crucial part of its moral climate and, as such, share in the responsibility for harms that flow from that climate. The relationship between American culture and American society, and more specifically between American culture and the war in Vietnam, is a concern that threads, implicitly and explicitly, throughout many poems.

This poetic consideration of cultural responsibility is perhaps best epitomized by the portrayals of one American icon in particular: John Wayne. "Vietnam vets seem to love to feature or at least mention John Wayne in their poetry," the veteran and author David Willson notes.[143] For many American soldiers who fought in Vietnam, Wayne had been an important cultural presence throughout their childhood. Even during military training, Ehrhart remembers, he was "talking tough, eating from cans, / wearing my helmet John Wayne style."[144] Indeed, the result of "growing up on a steady diet of his westerns and World War II movies," Tobey C. Herzog suggests, "was the John Wayne Syndrome: Wayne's widespread role in shaping the romantic illusions about Vietnam embraced by the young American combat soldiers entering the conflict."[145] Yet, these illusions were shattered when American soldiers arrived in Vietnam and quickly realized that Wayne, along with so many others they once trusted, had deceived them. Barth describes watching a film at base camp: "We scoff at John Wayne's gung-ho ways, / His works and pomps and matinees."[146] In another poem by Barth, the "Duke" becomes the "dupe": "John Wayne— / 'America's embodiment?' Straight scoop: / Embodied the know-nothing or the dupe." There is a sense of resentment at being misled, and Wayne is mainly a despised figure in the poetry, ridiculed and reviled for "Perverting combat on a movie screen."[147] According to one contributor to *Winning Hearts and Minds,* Wayne is simply "A paunchy worn out movie hero . . . Parading / Patriotic / Obscenities."[148] For some soldiers, this loss of faith in Wayne accompanied a larger loss of faith in the American cause and American values. Shortly after returning from the war, while recoiling from a parade of veterans, Gerald McCarthy found himself outside a cinema, almost startled by the demise of old myths and the beginning of new beliefs: "The movie marquee says: John Wayne in . . . / I realize / I am a communist."[149]

For Willson, Jim Northrup "has written the most immediate and powerful of them all about that ultimate American icon."[150] "Just before we set out to go beyond the wire, the platoon commander told us to wait," Northrup remembers.[151] Soon, a helicopter landed, and out stepped "a large green clad man. / 'It's John Fucking Wayne,' one grunt said." Northrup describes how Wayne smiled, posed for pictures, and signed autographs. Then:

> He was enjoying himself until
> the Indian patrol leader
> invited him for a walk with the grunts.
> The Duke patted his ample belly and said,
> "Heh, heh, heh, I'll leave that to you
> professionals."
> John Fucking Wayne, who killed
> Indians by the dozens
> with his movie sixshooter, refused.
> . . .
> Derisive laughter lifted the chopper away
> from the young grunts.
> "What a pussy, wouldn't even
> go on a little walk with us."[152]

As these soldiers realize, Wayne offers nothing but empty macho bravado. The poem operates as a personal criticism of Wayne, but, more than that, it also highlights the hypocrisy and duplicity of all those Americans eager for their country to go to war but not so keen to go themselves.

The poets, then, suggest that it is important to consider "how larger cultural frames of meaning might have shaped . . . decision making on Vietnam."[153] Perhaps culture simply reflected American society, and so blame should be directed there rather than toward its simulacrum. Yet, even if culture merely acts as a mirror, without critiquing or questioning, then it becomes complicit by promulgating and reinforcing the beliefs and values of society. Moreover, if culture has the potential, as it surely does, not just to mirror but also to influence society, then its burden of responsibility is even greater. By mapping the connections between American culture and the society and the violence with which it is deeply entangled, the poets recognize that "the pinball heart of America" is also "the heart of / a military empire."[154] In doing so, they demand that American culture be included on the scales of accountability for the war in Vietnam. It is no coincidence that John Wayne appears as often in the poetic record, and is regarded with as much disapproval, as Johnson or Nixon—it was his war, too.

The failure of generational responsibility that the war embodied, as young Americans were sacrificed by the older generation, is another significant and frequently discussed issue in the poetic examination of responsibility. "What shall we give our children?" is a question the poets often ask.[155] They may hope for peace, but they angrily acknowledge that what people commonly give their children is war, a seemingly perpetual phenomenon in which each generation is betrayed by the one before. Ehrhart's account of the belated "Welcome Home" parade for American veterans who fought in Vietnam, held in New York City on 7 May 1985, "ten years after the last rooftop / chopper out of Saigon," examines this failure of generational responsibility:

> I saw one man in camouflaged utilities;
> a boy, his son, dressed like dad;
> both proudly marching.
>
> How many wounded generations,
> touched with fire, have offered up

their children to the gods of fire?
Even now, new flames are burning,
and the gods of fire call for more,
and the new recruits keep coming.

What fire will burn that small
boy marching with his father?
What parade will heal
his father's wounds?[156]

Thus, even though a generation may itself have been wounded by war and failed by its parent generation, it is nonetheless still willing to offer up its own children to be wounded by war, who may, in turn, offer up their children and so on, in an endless chain of war perpetuated by each generation's failure of responsibility. Given their own personal wounding by war, it might be assumed that veterans would—should, perhaps—wish for their children to avoid the same fiery fate. "You'd think that any self-respecting / vet would give the middle finger / to the folks who thought of it," Ehrhart suggests of the parade.[157] A particularly disturbing image in this poem is that of the son as he marches by his veteran father's side, only a child yet already dressed as a soldier, another sacrifice readied to be "offered up . . . to the gods of fire." Parents may not make the final decision to go to war, but by preparing and delivering their children to be used by political and military leaders, they are just as responsible for the harms they suffer as these "gods of fire." As Ehrhart writes in another poem:

. . . you offer your children up
without so much as a whimper,
believing in God
knows what:

Whose side are you on, anyway?[158]

In "Allegory for L.B.J.," Barth, in his typically succinct style, captures this confluence of the filicidal and the political during the American war in Vietnam: "So many Isaacs, Abraham! / You needn't even lash

/ Poor boys to altars; seek no ram; / Just raise your knife and slash."[159]

Ehrhart's parade poem also offers an insight into the importance of memory and memorialization with regard to war. Events such as this parade promote a simplified and sanitized version of history that distorts and censors the past in order to make war seem honorable, necessary, and justified, and thus make war more acceptable and more probable in the future. Yet, the poetry, including this particular poem, is itself proof that a different story can be told, one that refuses to glorify war, one that refrains from an abdication of generational responsibility, one that hopes for a more peaceful future, however remote that hope may be. "Above all, Ehrhart's poems warn, we are accountable to future generations," Lorrie Smith argues, "we have a choice about which values we will pass on and which stories we will tell."[160] The same applies to many of the other poets. An important part of this transmission of values and stories, to return to the climatic conditions of America, is supporting and contributing to a climate in which questioning and critical thinking are encouraged and not denigrated—just as the poets do through their poetic production. For Ehrhart, who works as a teacher, this is a particularly pressing and ever-present issue. In "Coaching Winter Track in Time of War," published in the midst of the conflicts in Afghanistan and Iraq, he wonders how he can ensure that his students are aware of the need to engage in a critical examination of their country and the world, especially when it comes to war:

> How do you tell them it's not that simple?
> How do you tell them: question it all.
> Question everything. Even a coach.
> Even a president. How do you tell them:
> ask the young dead soldiers coming home
> each night in aluminum boxes
> none of us is allowed to see,
> an army of shades.[161]

Through this concern to warn and teach the next generation, Ehrhart accepts and enacts the generational responsibility that failed him. Indeed, by rebelling, by bearing witness, by writing about and against the war through poetry, the poets simultaneously reveal the failure of responsibility that their war represented and fulfill their own generational responsibility.

Moreover, the enactment of generational responsibility is a motivating factor in the writing of the poetry itself. "What animates Connolly," Ehrhart suggests, in a statement that could equally apply to himself and a number of the other poets, "is the desire to teach others—especially young people—what he has learned, so that another generation might not have to learn the same lessons all over again."[162] These are poems, then, written "in the fervent if futile hope that governments and nations might one day learn that armies are made of children, and that children are the only future we have."[163]

The poetic position on generational and national responsibility is perhaps best summarized by Ehrhart in "A Relative Thing." The poem—the title itself indicating a familial focus—begins with an angry accusation: "We are the ones you sent to fight a war / You didn't know a thing about." Ehrhart and his fellow veterans "have to live / With the memory that we were the instruments / Of your pigeon-breasted fantasies." He continues with an admittance of soldier responsibility that, as the next section discusses, represents a relatively radical departure from orthodox understandings of soldier responsibility: "We are inextricable accomplices / In this travesty of dreams; / But we are not alone." There is an ambiguity in this last line, in which Ehrhart could be referring to a sense of solidarity among veterans or the complicity of the people to whom the poem is addressed. Either way, in the tone and direction of the poem, and in its final verse, it is clear that Ehrhart is speaking to and indicting the nation and the generation that failed him and his fellow veterans and subsequently ignored and disowned them in the war's aftermath: "We are your sons, America, / And you cannot change that. / When you awake, / We will still be here."[164]

It should be noted that one of the key reasons the poets offer such an expansive and critical account of national responsibility that includes so many culprits is because they refuse to exonerate "bystanders." Implicitly at least, they largely disregard the acts and omissions doctrine and suggest instead that the various inactions, as much as actions, of the American people during the war matter a great deal in any assessment of moral accountability. For the poets, bystander apathy was a crucial contributing factor in the conflict, especially in its lengthy continuance. As

Glover argues, "bystanders look away," and the poets indicate that the American people did just that: "Comfortable people do not look. / Murder is not nice business. / Let soldiers do your work."[165] This indifference and inattention is often depicted in the poetry as a soporific and soundless acquiescence. "Sleep, America," Gustav Hasford writes in a poem in the anthology *Winning Hearts and Minds.* "Silence is a warm bed."[166] In the same collection, another veteran expresses a desire to bring home the horror of the war to the American people in their "quiet" streets and "quiet dignified houses," to shake the country from its slumber:

> If only a trade could be made
> Send the garbage and leaves to Nam
> Send the corpses to suburbia.
>
> Take the war out of the T.V.s and put it in the
> complacent streets
> Kick Amerika awake
> Before it dies in its sleep.[167]

Steve Hassett echoes this concern with complacency when he writes about "the silence of our fathers," as does Frank A. Cross Jr. in his recollection of his muted family:

> I think of relatives,
> Long ago, asking
> A small boy:
> "And what are you going to be
> When you grow up?"
>
> I think the small boy
> Snarls back: "I'll probably
> Be dead in The Nam!"
> The relatives are shocked and frightened,
> But they remain silent.[168]

Viewed from this poetic perspective, in which the portrayal of silence implies and condemns bystanders, Nixon's famous phrase "the great silent majority" can be reconsidered as a particularly precise identification of those apathetic Americans who share considerable responsibility for the war, for allowing American boys to kill and to die in Vietnam.[169] As Connolly suggests, "there's so many sheep that are willing to stand by and let them be sent, and not open their mouths." These bystanders, he continues, were the "silent majority that Nixon talked about . . . I see them as really existing but I use the term in a different way, he thought the silent majority was all in support of him but I see the silent majority as being complicit morons."[170] What people fail to do matters. As Ehrhart notes: "silence to injustice / large or small is simply cowardice."[171]

Of course, not all Americans merit blame for the war's harms. As the conflict continued, public support for the military intervention declined.[172] Moreover, there were those who refused to be silent bystanders and chose instead to oppose the war. In the poetry, this vocal minority of antiwar activists is rarely condemned as complicit in the war's harms. Rather, it is more often pictured as the group of Americans who actually fulfilled their responsibility by attempting to end the war. There is a moral duty to oppose an unjust war, or, more specifically, to oppose a war that one has good reason to believe unjust. As Walzer argues, "we commonly say that if it is possible to do good, without risk or great cost, one ought to do good." This obligation is even stronger in the case of war, "for it is not a question of doing good, but of preventing serious harm, and harm that will be done in the name of my own political community—hence, in some sense, in my own name." In the event of an unjust war, therefore, a citizen "must do all he can, short of accepting frightening risks, to prevent or stop the war." Certainly, it is important to make "allowances for false beliefs, misinformation, and honest mistakes. But there comes a time in any tale of aggression and atrocity when such allowances can no longer be made."[173] As the legal scholar Richard A. Falk stressed during the war: "anyone who believes or has reason to believe that a war is being waged in violation of minimal canons of law and morality has an obligation of conscience to resist participation in and support of that war effort by every means at his disposal . . . The circle of responsibility is drawn around all who have or should have knowledge of the illegal and immoral character of the war . . . The imperatives of personal responsibility call upon each of us to search for effective means to bring the war to an immediate end."[174]

By questioning, challenging, resisting, assembling, marching, demonstrating, and protesting, members of the antiwar movement accepted, acted on, and fulfilled this responsibility. Understandably, given that many of them were actively involved in Vietnam Veterans Against the War, the poets focus on the role of veterans in the antiwar movement: "the burning faces of our sad boy warriors / throwing their medals over the White House fence."[175] Still, they also suggest that all those who battled against the war undertook an important and virtuous task, especially given the above-mentioned structures and apathy that supported the weight of the war. In a poem about the killings at Kent State, for example, Coleman writes bitterly:

> And, yeah, those kids were fools,
> some of them, believing in democracy
> and free speech and other book stuff
> as if it belonged in the real world.
> . . .
> Reminding *you* that
> Something's wrong & some one has
> to do something . . .[176]

If some Americans share blame for the harms caused by the war, then other Americans—and perhaps some belong to both groups—share praise for at least attempting to bring the war to an end. The poets commend this endeavor and, in doing so, bear witness to those who struggled for peace in a time of war. As Barry muses:

> When will people put up statues to those
> who kept the peace? Honor
> those who sacrificed to stop the slaughter?
>
> When will hometowns list local heroes who refused
> to join the last great lust for killing
> when it swept half the world like a plague?
>
> Where are the statues to those brave souls
> who kept the peace, however much provoked
> by those who make a profession of destruction?[177]

Soldiers and Veterans

While politicians, profiteers, and the American nation share significantly in the blame for the harms caused by the American war in Vietnam, ultimately it could not have been fought without soldiers. The "triggermen" are tied together in culpability with those whose actions and inactions put them in a warzone on the other side of the world.[178] As Ehrhart, one of the preeminent poets on this aspect of responsibility as well, writes in "A Relative Thing": "*We* are the ones *you* sent."[179] In early versions of this poem, one of the lines reads: "We have *seen* Democracy on Zippo raids."[180] But when the poem was included in his 1984 collection *To Those Who Have Gone Home Tired,* and in versions reprinted since then, this line became: "We have *been* Democracy on Zippo raids."[181] Typographically, it is a small difference; just one letter changes just one word. Morally, it is a significant alteration, for Ehrhart and his fellow soldiers are now represented as perpetrators rather than witnesses, as agents of American violence rather than mere observers. Such a recognition of the perpetrator status of American soldiers is not, however, a rarity in Ehrhart's poetry, nor is it uncommon in the poetic body of works by veterans as a whole. The poets' strong criticisms of a number of other agents and issues are not part of an attempt to direct blame away from themselves. There is no evasion or self-exculpation; these former soldiers acknowledge that they and their fellow soldiers share significant responsibility for the war and its harms. Theirs is an important and interesting stance on soldier responsibility, but in order to fully understand and explore its significance, it is first necessary to outline the standard philosophical position as well as recent developments in moral philosophy.

Soldier responsibility is a concept currently undergoing a sizable shift within the realm of moral philosophy. "Can a soldier be held responsible for fighting in a war that is illegal or unjust?" David Rodin and Henry Shue ask in *Just and Unjust Warriors: The Moral and Legal Status of Soldiers,* a groundbreaking collection of essays on this issue. It is a question that is "at the heart of a new debate that has the potential to profoundly change our understanding of the moral and legal status of warriors, wars, and indeed of moral agency itself." The "widely shared and legally endorsed conviction about war" is that soldiers "have equal rights and responsibilities irrespective of whether they are fighting in a war that is just or unjust." This "moral equality of soldiers" is expounded and endorsed by Walzer in *Just and Unjust Wars* and is a position that "is rooted in the shared experience of soldiers as victims, compelled to fight by the actions of their enemy and the coercive instruments of their own state."[182] As a result of this mutual victimhood, a combatant senses that "the enemy soldier, though his war may well be criminal, is nevertheless as blameless as oneself."[183] Hence, Walzer posits "a separation between the rules governing the justice of going to war (the *jus ad bellum*) and the rules governing what combatants can do in war (the *jus in bello*)," thus drawing "a line between the war itself, for which soldiers are not responsible, and the conduct of the war, for which they are responsible, at least within their own sphere of activity."[184] Two important consequences follow from this viewpoint. First, "soldiers have an equal right to kill" each other, and so a combatant who kills an enemy soldier "does not wrong him or violate his rights, even if the soldier killed was fighting a legitimate war of self-defence."[185] Second, those outside of the category of soldier, that is, noncombatants, "retain their title to life and liberty and may not be attacked." Yet, while this collection of moral beliefs is "widely accepted and legally sanctioned" and forms "the 'common sense' ethics of war," it is one that has recently been challenged and criticized.[186]

Recent debates in moral philosophy have suggested that *jus ad bellum* and *jus in bello* could indeed be connected, and, consequently, "many aspects of just war theory and laws of war would have to be rethought and perhaps reformed."[187] Of particular relevance here, this coupling could alter our understanding of the moral responsibility of "unjust warriors"—those soldiers who fight in unjust wars—with potential ramifications for American soldiers who fought in Vietnam. To take a key moral question of war: Given that killing is usually deemed to be immoral, why is it justifiable to kill in a time of war? Walzer's argument, and the orthodox just war explanation, is that since enemy soldiers pose a threat to the self and others, it is permissible to kill them, an idea often seen as analogous to the right of self- and other-defense. Yet, this position, Rodin and Shue highlight, "seems false by the standards of normal morality and individual self-defence."[188] As Jeff McMahan explains:

> It is not true, for example, that one makes oneself liable to defensive attack simply by posing a threat to another. If that were true, those who

> engage in justified self-defence against a culpable attacker would then lose their right not to be attacked by him or her. And police would forfeit their right not to be attacked by criminals they justifiably threatened. The correct criterion of liability to attack in these cases is not posing a threat, nor even posing an unjust threat, but moral responsibility for an unjust threat. According to this criterion, just combatants cannot be liable to attack by their unjust adversaries. As in the case of an individual who engages in justified self-defence, a combatant who takes up arms in self-defence or in defence of other innocent people against an unjust threat does nothing to lose his or her moral right not to be attacked or to make himself or herself liable to attack.[189]

As argued throughout this study, the poets indicate that they believe the American war in Vietnam was immoral in a number of ways and strongly suggest that it failed on almost every possible just war principle. So, whether one thinks the Vietnamese revolutionaries were "just combatants" or not, it seems clear that, for the poets at least, the American military posed an "unjust threat," and even though the idea of the "unjust warrior" has only started to gain traction relatively recently in moral philosophy, it is a concept that the poets, as soldiers who fought in what they deem to be an unjust war, have been exploring since their earliest poetic productions.

In their examination of their own role in the war, the poets reflect on what it means to be a soldier and, more specifically with regard to their participation in the war in Vietnam, what it means to be an "unjust warrior." Soldiers, Walzer argues, "are not responsible for the overall justice of the wars they fight; their responsibility is limited by the range of their own activity and authority."[190] The poets, however, suggest otherwise. "When I enlisted, I thought I was doing a good thing—a *cosmically* good thing," Ehrhart says, but after the war he admits: "What I saw and did in Asia in thirteen months was unspeakably evil and immoral."[191] Crucially, the poets identify American soldiers, themselves, as immoral perpetrators not solely as a result of the way in which the war was fought—although, as highlighted in the previous chapter, they do address such issues—but also quite simply because they fought in an unjust war. In other words, even if they did not violate any of the "rules of war," as implementers of what they saw as a wrong war, the poets consider themselves culpable of wrongdoing:

Yea as I walk through the valley of death
I shall fear no evil
For the valleys are gone
And only death awaits

And I am the evil[192]

Against the orthodox understanding of soldier responsibility that decouples the justness of a war from the participating combatants, this group of veteran-poets radically suggest instead that the two can be connected, that soldiers can bear some responsibility for the cause they fight for as well as their own individual conduct within the warzone. In doing so, the poets question a deeply entrenched assumption that has only recently been examined and challenged within moral philosophy. Indeed, they have been reflecting critically on their own role in the war's immorality for decades. The 1972 anthology *Winning Hearts and Minds* firmly set the tone for a sense of personal soldier responsibility that the poets have engaged with and espoused ever since: "The outrage has been too much, and still it goes on. This poetry is an attempt to grapple with a nightmare, a national madness. It is poetry written out of fire and under fire. The war still goes on. We were, and are, a part of the evil. And the fire still burns."[193]

Numerous poems demonstrate an awareness and acceptance of this broader and more demanding understanding of soldier responsibility. A poem by Basil T. Paquet, one of the editors of that early anthology, describes "Mourning The Death, By Hemorrhage, Of A Child From Honai." The Vietnamese child's left arm was shot off by a round from an M-16, and although Paquet did not kill the child, he acknowledges his own complicity in her death: "Small, denuded, one-armed thing, I too was violator."[194] As Barry summarizes in a short piece: "If war is hell / (as General Sherman spat) / then we who were soldiers / created it."[195] Hence, the poets suggest that all members of the military, not just its leaders, are accountable for the harms caused by war. Hansen writes:

To
    lethal lieutenants,
    ambitious captains
    and mad majors,
I add
    callous colonels,
    gung-ho generals,
    hard-boiled sergeants
    and cocksure privates.

The poem concludes with Hansen's realization that he cannot escape from his own complicity in the military web: "The poems / always set up confessional."[196] By acknowledging their own extended culpability, the poets refuse to draw the line that separates responsibility for war itself from the soldier's personal responsibility for his own role in war. Thus, throughout the poetry, these veterans suggest that soldiers, while certainly victims of war, are also perpetrators.

This particular dual moral status of soldiers is succinctly captured by Ehrhart in "What I Know About Myself," a poem dedicated to the author Gloria Emerson.[197] A friend of Ehrhart's, possibly Emerson herself, picks up "a book of photographs / from Vietnam" and says, "Look how young / you are. How innocent. How evil." Ehrhart agrees with her assessment of these youthful American soldiers as both innocent and evil, victims of a war they perpetrated: "She knew I knew what she meant, / and she was right."[198] In this admission and understanding, Ehrhart both signals his acceptance of his own soldier responsibility and hints that the position of perpetrator is one that could apply to all "unjust warriors."

Another way in which the poets address the issue of soldier responsibility is through their rejection of the violence and killing discussed in the previous chapter. Implicitly, this moral stance is displayed in all of their stark and unflinching portrayals of the horrific devastation and destruction of the war, "that mutilated child in its mother's arms" or those "kids not twenty / years old and dead in ricefields; / brain-dead, soul-dead, half-dead / in wheelchairs."[199] Explicitly, it is evidenced by their open expressions of regret, as in, for example, Ehrhart's poem "A Warning to My Students":

> If I were young again,
> I could do it all
> differently: go to college,
> go to Canada, live underground
> on the lam in basement apartments
> in strange cities—anything
> but kill
> somebody else's enemies
> for somebody else's reasons.[200]

This declaration of regret operates as a moral intervention into the past, in which the suggestion that he "could do it all / differently" implies that he *should* have done it all differently. Furthermore, it is also a moral exhortation in the present—and an act of generational responsibility—since it is intended to be a warning to his students, who may one day have to face a similar choice themselves. "The next time they come looking / for soldiers, they'll come looking / for you," he cautions them.[201] This regret is also tinged with a profound sense of sorrow for his participation in war: "once I dreamed a man / with a rifle refused to take aim; / I awoke to a sadness / deeper than dreams."[202] In a poem that reflects on his postwar returns to Vietnam, Ehrhart distances himself from the process of violence that he, and his adversaries, participated in during the war. He meets a young Vietnamese soldier and ponders: "Years ago in another life, / I had killed young men like him / and they had tried to kill me. / But not today. I'm tired of fighting."[203]

In poems such as these, Ehrhart firmly rejects the violence of war. He acknowledges his own prior position as a perpetrator while simultaneously denouncing the act of killing in war and, in doing so, demonstrates a strong sense of postwar soldier responsibility. It is important to note here that Ehrhart's rejection of killing is not purely unconditional, for he is not an absolute pacifist: "I think there are legitimate wars."[204] And if there can be just wars, it follows that there can be "just warriors." Still, for Ehrhart, it is vital that the soldier fights for justifications that are his own and not simply some cause that is deemed just by political leaders: "if I'm ordered to kill anybody, I'm going to kill my enemies for my reasons and not because someone in Washington, D.C. says kill them."[205] Hence, Ehrhart presents an understanding of moral responsibility and war that suggests that soldiers are not only responsible for their own conduct within the warzone but also, to a certain extent, responsible for the war itself.

For those who fight in wars and survive, moreover, their war-related responsibilities do not end once they leave the warzone or even after their war ends. Rather, as veterans, they face an additional aspect of moral responsibility directly linked to their wartime experiences: to bear witness. As witnesses to war, they have two key obligations: the responsibility of remembering a past that is often in danger of being forgotten, distorted, or sanitized and the responsibility of warning, of sounding a cautionary alarm to both the present and the future. Yet, as Janis Haswell highlights, although American soldiers are often glorified as heroes, as veterans they are frequently "marginalized insofar as they are witnesses to a reality the public cannot face and war-makers deny." This is a great moral loss, for it is precisely those who have been to war who "are in a position to articulate the need for a higher morality . . . that determines *when* their country goes to war and *how* war is conducted."[206] In other words, veterans can offer significant insights into both *jus ad bellum* and *jus in bello,* for those willing to listen. As Ehrhart writes in "The Teacher": "I know things / worth knowing."[207]

Veterans can enact the responsibility to bear witness in a number of ways. Most obviously, they can tell others about their war, speak out about their experiences, like Ehrhart who came "back home from Vietnam insisting it was / all just bullshit, just a lethal scam / that only proves how gullible / each generation's cannon fodder is."[208] "So maybe the first responsibility is to create a voice," Komunyakaa suggests, "a personal voice where one begins to question things with a certain kind of . . . understanding."[209] Veterans can bear witness by resisting attempts to distort or sanitize the memory of their war, such as the above-mentioned "Welcome Home" parade, and by challenging uncritical patriotic myths and state-sanctioned stories—indeed, any problematic prowar narratives—to present instead an uncensored version of the past. They can engage in political activism, like those who joined Vietnam Veterans Against the War, as John O'Neill reports:

> Marching through the rain, down Main,
> from a cemetery in Buffalo,
> Vietnam Veterans marching to end the war . . .

Before, just three years ago,
we marched through the rain
of Indochina.
We marched for other reasons,
did other things,
to other people.
These people are now dead.
So we march for them,
the people of Indochina,
the people we killed,
on Veterans day, three years ago.

One hundred veterans marching,
they say we don't represent the majority,
they are wrong.
There would have been more of us,
but it is raining,
and many have grown tired of fighting.
There are others who would have marched with us,
but they have died.[210]

At its peak, Vietnam Veterans Against the War "attracted between twenty-five thousand and thirty thousand members," the historian Andrew E. Hunt notes, and the group's activism had a significant, transformative impact on the antiwar movement in America "by placing Vietnam veterans in the forefront of the nationwide struggle to end the Vietnam War."[211]

Of course, one possibility for veterans is to bear witness through artistic commitment, by writing, for example, plays, memoirs, novels, or poems. "I decided never to war in another jungle," Mason declares, "and to take the fight into the streets as a poet."[212] In his account of democratic responsibility, Walzer outlines the obligations of antiwar movements and suggests one duty that the poets certainly fulfill: "one must describe as graphically as one can the moral reality of war, talk about what it means to force people to fight, analyze the nature of democratic responsibilities."[213] The poets do this, even though people do not always want to hear what they have to say. "You don't want me to tell you about death, / but I'm going to tell you anyway," Ehrhart avows in "All About Death."[214] In the twin poem "All About Love," he writes: "Everybody loves to hear about love, / but I don't feel like talking about that. / Gimme a break. You seen the news lately?"[215] Moreover, bearing witness to the world is also an important aspect of poetic responsibility. Thus, the poets, through their insistence on writing, through their emphasis on an uncensored poetics, through their committed rebellion, and through their "gaze falling on horror, withstanding it, and in unalleviated consciousness of negativity holding fast to the possibility of what is better," fulfill their duty as both veterans and poets.[216] Additionally, being a poetic witness is a way of living with the tension of having been both a victim and a perpetrator, it is an embodiment of what Frankl describes as "the human capacity to creatively turn life's negative aspects into something positive or constructive."[217] As Ehrhart states: "my poetry is an ongoing attempt to atone for the unethical, for my loss of a moral compass when I was a young man."[218]

Perpetual War

The poets' demanding account of moral responsibility, and the fulfillment of their desire and duty to bear witness, extends beyond their own war to the many military actions America has undertaken since then. As Ehrhart highlights in a 2007 essay, the conflict in Vietnam was just one in a long sequence of American wars: "My grandfather's generation fought in the war to end all wars. My father's generation fought in the war to rid the world of fascism. My generation fought in Vietnam to—to what? What was it for that time? Nothing that mattered, we came to realize, but only after the damage had been done. And the killing just goes on and on. Since my generation stopped dying in Vietnam, American soldiers have died in Cambodia, Iran, Lebanon, Grenada, El Salvador, Panama, Kuwait, Iraq, Somalia, Yemen, Afghanistan, and now Iraq again."[219] The poets write about, and often against, these processes of violence, too. Although such poems cannot offer a firsthand account of these conflicts, they are nonetheless filtered through each poet's own direct experience of war and, as such, provide valuable insights into how they understand both the war in Vietnam and America's subsequent military endeavors. Interestingly, the poets suggest that many of the groups and factors responsible for their war are also responsible for these later wars. They also indicate that the seemingly perpetual nature of armed conflict is part of a large interconnected web of other moral failures. Moreover, by bearing witness to and rebelling against not just their own war but the sad succession of American wars that followed, the poets have continued to fulfill their national, generational, veteran, and poetic responsibility.

America's first major military operation after the war in Vietnam was the invasion of Grenada in 1983. If some of the core lessons that could have been learned in Vietnam included "never again," deeper awareness of the potential problems of using military might as a foreign policy tool, greater caution in interfering in the affairs of other countries, and perhaps even just a little more humility, they were lessons soon forgotten or ignored. In his poem "The Invasion of Grenada," Ehrhart writes dejectedly:

> I didn't want a monument,
> not even one as sober as that
> vast black wall of broken lives.
> I didn't want a postage stamp.
> I didn't want a road beside the Delaware
> River with a sign proclaiming:
> "Vietnam Veterans Memorial Highway."
>
> What I wanted was a simple recognition
> of the limits of our power as a nation
> to inflict our will on others.
> What I wanted was an understanding
> that the world is neither black-and-white
> nor ours.
>
> What I wanted
> was an end to monuments.[220]

Within a decade, Ehrhart laments, the memory of his war had been rendered impotent, locked away in an undemanding and passive national remembering extant only in objects such as monuments, stamps, and roads. He had, perhaps, hoped instead for a living memory, a more demanding and moral remembering not consigned or confined to a hermetically sealed and sanitized past but alive and active in the present. Such a hope, however, was shattered as, yet again, America resorted to military power "to inflict our will on others."

For Ehrhart, this disappointment was compounded by America's involvement in the violent events that occurred in certain parts of Central America throughout the 1980s. During a resurgent Cold War climate and under the reign of Ronald Reagan, American military expenditure rose dramatically, and "support for military intervention in defense of traditional allies increased," as "the nation embarked on a new global offensive against the Soviet Union and its clients."[221] On this militarized fear of the Soviet Union and communism, Ehrhart remarks mockingly:

> In Russia, everyone drinks vodka.
> They all wear furry hats, and worship
> at the tomb of Lenin. Godless,
> every last one of them, and hell-bent
> on conquering the world. Yesterday
> Afghanistan; today Nicaragua; tomorrow
> New Jersey. Atlantic City! Sweet
> Jesus, all those elegant casinos
> in the hands of Reds. That's why
> we need missiles. MX missiles.
> Cruise missiles. Pershing missiles.
> Let'em try to take the Boardwalk;
> we'll blow their godless hats off.[222]

Ehrhart also notes the similarities between the American interventions in Vietnam and Central America: "in El Salvador, another / petty upper-class junta / needs American aid / to fight the communists."[223] In "Not Your Problem," he speaks as the victims in a grim echo of Vietnam:

> Here our children will never learn
> to read or write; their teeth
> will rot from their heads;
> they will join the army, or die
> like us beneath foreign bombs.[224]

As in Vietnam, American actions in El Salvador, and in Nicaragua, opposed the forces of change and supported those willing to use violence to maintain control and ensure the status quo: "fuck with how it is and die."[225] Awakened by his own experience of war, Ehrhart sides with the cause of change. "Call it revolution, / if you like," he writes in "Nicaragua Libre," "I call it freedom."[226] Throughout the 1980s, then, Ehrhart refused to forget his war or ignore America's persistent warring in the world. In doing so, he fulfilled the two duties at the heart of bearing witness: to remember and to warn.[227]

During the 1990s, Ehrhart and several other poets, provoked in particular by the Gulf War, continued to write about America's use of military force. In Operation Desert Storm, executed in early 1991, America led a coalition of countries, in the air and on land, against Iraq in response to Iraqi actions in Kuwait. The ghost of the poets' war haunted this conflict. George H. W. Bush insisted that this "would not be another Vietnam" and, after the Gulf War's seemingly swift conclusion, declared: "By God, we've kicked the Vietnam syndrome once and for all!"[228] The poets, however, were less convinced. In "An Open Letter to President Bush," Quintana describes "how much / I wept, / these past months, / so full of rage, another war."[229] Connolly, too, in a poem written "For DC: Corporal, D Company, 41st Infantry, Operation Desert Storm," is distressed that "friends and enemies alike, / will once again / have lungs and limbs shredded, / lose heads and hearts and hands," and expresses concern about the long-term impact of war on another generation of veterans: "And you'll wake and shake / as we all do, / wondering if for you / the war will ever end."[230] Similarly, the Gulf War reminded Ehrhart of his own attempt to cope with the aftermath of the war in Vietnam, a struggle amplified by dashed expectations and the ever-rising toll of war dead:

> On the radio news, nothing but war.
> American planes are bombing Baghdad.
>
> . . . you remember
> the nameless dead you carried home.
> You remember you promised to bury them.
> You thought you could. You didn't know
> there'd be more than you ever imagined.[231]

In another poem, Ehrhart wonders what happened to "Never again. // Never."[232] As Thomas E. Barden notes in "The Fog of War": "nothing ever learned except / nothing ever changes." Barden's piece, "written during Desert Storm" as a note under the title highlights, aptly summarizes the poetic response to the Gulf War, as well as the poets' negation of yet more war and their continued affirmation of life:

So now we're off to harvest
a new crop of humanity
like wheat in the techno-military combine
but no matter
it will be little more than a juice spill
on the slaughterhouse floor of this
criminal century

And I wish this were a better poem
I wish it were a poem that could say
in words of mysterious power

        it is good to live
        it is good to let live

and say it night and day
and deliver its heavy ordnance
in countless endless sorties
in laser guided crosshairs
into the hearts of the masters of war
    until their eyes just opened
    and the fog of war lifted

    and it was so[233]

The wars in Afghanistan and Iraq in the 2000s also stimulated a powerful and prolific poetic response. On 11 September 2001, al-Qaeda terrorists hijacked four American passenger planes—one crashed into a field in Pennsylvania, one into the Pentagon, and two into the North and South Towers of the World Trade Center in New York City, collapsing both buildings. Almost three thousand people were killed in the deadliest-ever foreign attack on American soil. The violence itself was shocking, but as the historian John W. Dower suggests, "For Americans, what was truly original in the horror of September 11 was the spectacle of being the bombed rather than the bomber."[234] "The day the towers came down, goggle-eyed / we stared in disbelief at death for once / so close to home we couldn't hide / our terror in the rubble of Manhattan," Ehrhart writes.[235] Furthermore, the poets understood that, in some ways, the attack was a reverberation of the violence America had perpetrated abroad for years. As Ehrhart acknowledges, "anyone with any grasp of real history can understand why there's a lot of people out there who don't like this country."[236] In his poignant poem "September 11th," Ehrhart adopts the voice of "Aysha Rahim," an Iraqi woman whose life has been blighted by American foreign policy stretching back to the Gulf War:

> I have heard what happened in your country.
> We have all heard, here in Abul Khasib.
> How many died, did you say?
> Not enough, I tell you,
> not nearly enough.[237]

Yet, America's response to the terrorist attack was not to try to understand where such burning hatred had come from or to examine its own complicity in such loathing and such acts but to meet violence with violence.

Less than a month after 9/11, America went to war in Afghanistan, with the stated aim of destroying al-Qaeda and removing the Taliban regime from power.[238] On 20 March 2003, America went to war in Iraq, supposedly to "disarm Iraq of weapons of mass destruction; to end Saddam Hussein's support for terrorism; and to free the Iraqi people."[239] These military operations were part of an even broader worldwide "war on terror," "virtually a global counterinsurgency campaign" that continues to this day.[240] For the poets, the conflicts in Afghanistan and Iraq were sickeningly reminiscent of their own war—seemingly interminable quagmires with questionable causes, fought against deeply entrenched insurgencies with passionately held ideologies, in places and amongst peoples of "otherness," with severe difficulties in discriminating between friend and foe, producing a high number of military and civilian casualties, all set against a backdrop of failed nation building.[241] Weigl describes watching "the one thousandth dead soldier's face / on the color television" and, his usual careful eloquence replaced by unrestrained anger, suggests:

> With the promise of the liars on his lips,
> he died in the liar's war. To die alone in the desert,
> far from home, far from the people who love you,
> is not ever a glorious thing, and I don't give a fuck
> what my government says otherwise. Sacrifice and slaughter
> are not the same things . . .[242]

In another poem, Weigl echoes Ehrhart's above-mentioned piece on the Gulf War, with the increasing number of war dead weighing heavily on him:

> I hear the screams of children
> blown to pieces by bombs
> guided precisely to a room
> in the house next door
> where a "target" lived, or
> didn't; that kind of thing.
>
> The deaths pile up
> as if on my shoulders;
> this is no metaphor;
> the pile grows and grows.
> We can't keep up with the names anymore.
> I am pulled inside the war. I am pulled inside the war.
> Nothing I can do
> can stop even one fucking death; not one.[243]

Connolly succinctly captures the pathos of the poets' reaction to America's latest wars in a poem consisting of only six words: "Dead, Iraq / just eighteen / never voted."[244]

As the violence in Afghanistan and Iraq carried over into a new decade, the poets continued to bear witness. In the 2011 issue of the journal *War, Literature & the Arts,* for example, Dale Ritterbusch published several powerful poems that draw threads between horrors past and present, Vietnam and Iraq. Like many of the poets, he wonders how yet another wave of veterans will grapple with the aftermath of a war that, for them, will never really be over:

> Weeks later the sergeant lies on his couch
> taking a mid-morning nap; he wakes
> to the concussion wave of exploding ordnance,
> a mortar round close and as real as anything
> he's ever known. Thinking his ears are blown
> he reaches up, softly, gently, pats the side of his face,
> feeling for a warm trickle of blood.[245]

Thus, in the years since the end of the war in Vietnam, as America continued to pursue a path of violence in the world, the poets have both remembered their own past war and warned of the present wars. Indeed, the unfolding of current events has reinforced the poets' sense that "The past is always here," a constant and endless intrusion into the present: "memory's phantoms circle the track / like weary athletes running a race / without a finish line."[246] Like the new veteran in Ritterbusch's poem, they still feel the blood.

Who, then, do the poets deem responsible for these conflicts "fought around the globe for forty years, / the millions dead and maimed and dispossessed," for this perpetual cycle of wars?[247] Many of the above-mentioned groups and factors identified by the poets as responsible for the American war in Vietnam also appear in the poets' accounts of these subsequent military interventions. They denounce the usual suspects again, those political and military leaders who make the final decisions to go to war. At the highest levels of power, these two groups seem almost inseparable, and in the poem "High Country," from his 1984 collection *To Those Who Have Gone Home Tired,* Ehrhart suggests that this union is at the heart of war's endless cycle. In his war, "calculating / men in three-piece suits and uniforms / with stars called firestorms down upon / the heads of people with conical hats." Ten years later,

"Calculating men in three-piece suits / and uniforms with stars are calling down / firestorms upon the heads of peasants / in Central America now."[248] It is possible to imagine a repetition of these lines for each of the following decades, as a series of "men in three-piece suits and uniforms" continue to choose war, with the only differences being the place and the people these masters of war call their "firestorms down upon." In each case, a large degree of moral responsibility for the harms caused by these wars, the poets intimate, should be shared by those "in quiet rooms / pouring over maps and plotting fire."[249]

Furthermore, the poets apply their broader and more demanding understanding of responsibility to these later wars. They condemn those who make money from these conflicts, the "crazy rich men / murder on their lips like salt."[250] They also continue to hold the American people to account. The poets rebuke the role of unquestioned ideology and the fear of communism that still hypnotized many in the 1980s, replaced more recently by the fear of terrorism. Ehrhart writes:

> Barbarism, communism, terrorism,
> name your ism, something's always out there
> in the darkness wanting in. You'd think
> by now—we're talking generations here,
> millennia, the whole of human time—
> we'd figure out we're all in this together
> and it's time to learn to share . . .[251]

Similarly, the poets are particularly critical of the persistent power of unreflective patriotism. "I see it all / coming," Ehrhart remarks in a piece from the 1980s, "one more time; one / by one, all the old flags / resurrected," and in his poem on the Gulf War, Barden states: "I don't even have a flag / to join the sea of flags."[252] In his recent poetic productions, Ritterbusch reflects on the hollowness of this patriotism, as he depicts his reaction to a yellow "support our troops" ribbon on a car: "half-assed support for the troops / on the back ass end of his car. / I wonder if the bastard ever thought to enlist, / my anger rising."[253] Unsurprisingly, the poets also highlight the failure of generational responsibility that these wars represented. In "Notes for Veteran's War Protest," Coleman details a number of surreal plans for a march of his generation of veteran dissenters and then finishes with the postscript: "Save the instructions for your grandkids. They'll come in handy."[254] This prophetic statement proved accurate, as America entered, again and again, into "another war in another place," Ehrhart writes, "where yet another generation / is rudely about to discover / what their fathers never told them."[255]

Awakened by their own experiences in Vietnam, some poets also consider the part played by us-them barriers in this succession of wars. In "The Fog of War," Barden suggests sardonically:

> maybe if we bow down
> before the cruise missile
> it will love us and only kill
> sandniggers
> towel-heads
> reds, dinks, slopes[256]

Likewise, in his meditations on the more recent conflict in Iraq, Komunyakaa wonders about the role of race—as well as the desire for revenge and the disproportionate use of force—in American military action:

> Why is our enemy
> always dark-skinned,
> always surrendering an arm
> & a leg for a tooth,
> a child for an eye?[257]

Ehrhart summarizes the poetic position on this aspect of war when he expresses deep disappointment "that we should not find this odd, / that we should so believe our otherness / that we would rather kill and die / than search for common ground."[258]

Hence, as with their depictions of the war in Vietnam, the poets' portrayals of subsequent wars present a comprehensive examination of accountability. They hint, too, that the perpetual cycle of war continues, in part, because of a weakness in fully facing our own guilt, our own complicity in "the thousand torn hearts," as Weigl writes: "and what do we say to them, / and what do we say to the faces we see in our own mirrors, / the ones who still want answers, even as we turn away."[259]

Additionally, there are suggestions in the poetry that the ostensibly perpetual nature of war is part of a vast network of other moral failures. Again, Ehrhart is a particularly perceptive voice on this issue. Perhaps the best example from his early work is "To Those Who Have Gone Home Tired," in which he connects "his evolving perception of American misjudgment and wrongdoing in Vietnam to larger political issues":

> After the streets fall silent
> After the bruises and the tear-gassed eyes are healed
> After the concensus [*sic*] has returned
> After the memories of Kent and My Lai and Hiroshima
> Lose their power
> And their connections with each other
> And the sweaters labeled Made In Taiwan
> After the last American dies in Canada
> And the last Korean in prison
> And the last Indian at Pine Ridge
> After the last whale is emptied from the sea
> And the last leopard emptied from its skin
> And the last drop of blood refined by Exxon
> After the last iron door clangs shut
> Behind the last conscience
> And the last loaf of bread is hammered into bullets
> And the bullets
> Scattered among the hungry
>
> What answers will you find
> What armor will protect you
> When your children ask you
>
> Why?[260]

Here, war is situated alongside and connected with the suppression of dissent, collective amnesia, sweatshop capitalism, the exile of conscientious objectors, the genocide of Native Americans, environmental devastation, and hunger. These are all, the poem suggests, part of the same interconnected structure of moral failure. In the final lines, Ehrhart confronts readers with their own role of responsibility within this entangled web, as he wonders what excuses and explanations we will offer to the next generation for our acts and omissions that contribute to such a world. In doing so, he emphasizes the complicity of all of us while simultaneously stressing, as Kalí Tal notes, "the responsibility of the individual to resist such evils."[261]

Such moral failures are our responsibility because, ultimately, they are caused by the choices we make. In another early poem, "The Eruption of Mount St. Helens," Ehrhart draws a distinction between natural and man-made disasters:

> Nature's fury lacks the tragedy
> of seashore wildlife sanctuaries
> smothering in oil from sinking tankers,
> or an Indochinese village disappearing
> in an orange ball of napalm, or a lake
> dying from the mills in Buffalo,
> or the slums of Baltimore.[262]

In this piece, Ehrhart identifies and links what may be our three greatest moral failures: war, environmental destruction, and poverty. They are deeply intertwined, and the cord that binds together "the hollow stalker / war," "the scarred carcasses / of salmon floating in still pools," and "the starving angry / voices shouting for bread" is human choice, is us.[263]

In his more recent works, Ehrhart continues to map this network of moral failures. "On the Eve of Destruction," produced four decades after "To Those Who Have Gone Home Tired," echoes this earlier poem's connective gaze. Ehrhart remembers that "weekend Watts went up in flames" and recalls his teenage reflections:

What did riots in a Negro ghetto
have to do with me? What could cause
such savage rage? I didn't know
and didn't think about it much.
The Eve of Destruction was just a song.
Surf was up at Pendleton. The war in Vietnam
was still a sideshow half a world away,
a world that hadn't heard of Ia Drang or Tet,
James Earl Ray, Sirhan Sirhan, Black Panthers,
Spiro Agnew, Sandy Scheuer, Watergate.[264]

Violence, politics, domestic discord, and international conflict are all entangled. The Watts Riots prefigure the violence that would soon unfold in Vietnam, and, in turn, the war in Vietnam is connected to assassinations in America, racial problems in American society, corrupt and criminal politicians, the violent crushing of dissent and killing of students, and yet more corrupt and criminal politicians. All of these factors contribute to the fabric of moral failure, and as Ehrhart traces these linkages it appears as though America is as much at war with itself as it is with the Vietnamese revolutionaries. The title of the poem and the allusion to the song "Eve of Destruction" is particularly revealing, for it underlines the apocalyptic quality of these connections. Yet, Ehrhart, in his youthful naïveté, and the apathetic and silent majority of Americans seem unaware of the impending maelstrom of violence. Crucially, ignorance and inaction are an integral part of this interconnected web. A common answer to the question of "Why?" that concludes "To Those Who Have Gone Home Tired," therefore, might be Ehrhart's own explanation—understandable for a teenager, maybe less so for an adult—that "I didn't know / and didn't think about it much."

Even though war seems perpetual and deeply entangled in a number of other moral problems, the poets have continued to speak out. Perhaps their poems are just "a last plea to no one / for some peace."[265] Certainly, the poets recognize the almost futile effort of warning in a global climate so full of war. "I have few expectations the world will change," Ritterbusch writes in his recent batch of poems.[266] As Ehrhart states:

What hurts most
is the plodding sameness
of cruelty, a circular world
impervious to change,
the grinding erosion of hope
stripping the soul.[267]

Often, these are poems "Pressed down by the weight / of despair," by the thought of "the convoluted paths / we have followed into this morass / of disasters just waiting to happen."[268] There is even a suspicion in the poetry that there might be something deep in human nature, or at least in human history, that makes war inescapable. For example, when Ehrhart pictures two victims of war's violence in "The Bodies Beneath the Table," he records the location as "Hue City, 1968 (or was it Fallujah, Stalingrad, or Ur?)."[269] Such scenes of death are not unique to the conflict in Vietnam, Ehrhart emphasizes, but occur in all wars and in all parts of our past, from Iraq to the Second World War to the very origins of human "civilization" itself. "Ur is the first great city of the first great civilization," Ehrhart explains, "and I included it to suggest that war and the death of innocents have been going on for a very long time."[270] The history of violence and war, he intimates, is as old as the history of humanity.

Yet, despite all this, the poets still write. As Ehrhart suggests, "if I have failed, in the words of Ngan Vin Le, 'to rouse the conscience of the people of the world in the cause of peace' (and it seems fairly certain that I have)—well, there are worse things one might fail at. And even worse ways to succeed."[271] Their warning might be drowned out by the din of ongoing wars, and their remembering marginalized or ignored, but the rebellion and witness of their poetry, infused with a strong sense of responsibility, are as important and necessary as ever—for them, as poets and veterans, and for us, as readers and citizens. "I'm grateful that I can address some of the truly moral issues in my life," Brown declared in a symposium on "War, Poetry & Ethics," held in 1998. "It's the way I stay alive. I don't want to shut up: I want to be pissy about it until I'm dead, and I want to be cranky and I don't want to forget because it's dangerous when we start to forget things that we are capable of doing."[272] Above all, the poets have written and continue to write because, as the author and Holocaust survivor Elie Wiesel stresses, the moral witness "cannot do otherwise . . . he may no longer choose not to sing, whether his song is heard or not. What matters is to struggle against silence with words."[273]

The poetic portrayal of moral responsibility for the American war in Vietnam is extensive and uncompromising. The poets condemn politicians and military leaders, as well as businesses that contributed to and profited from the conflict. They highlight how votes, taxes, and certain structures of class, gender, religion, ideology, patriotism, culture, and generation helped to support the weight of the war, while also emphasizing the significance of silence, inaction, and apathy. Through this broad picture of national responsibility, the poets indict the American people for their part in the harms caused by the war. Furthermore, these former soldiers acknowledge that the war could not have been waged without their own participation, and in assessing their own complicity they offer a radical understanding of soldier responsibility in which combatants can be held accountable not just for their conduct within the warzone but also for the war itself. For the poets, then, few are unmarked by guilt. Still, as the historian John Prados notes, "There is responsibility enough for Vietnam that it can be shared."[274]

The poets, moreover, do not just identify and condemn those responsible for the harms of the war—by bearing rebellious witness, they fulfill their generational, veteran, and poetic responsibility. Additionally, in accepting and enacting this difficult task to speak, "to struggle against silence with words," the poets remind us of our own responsibility.[275] Their poems compel us to confront and reflect on our complicity, to consider demanding and daunting questions like those in Ehrhart's "To Those Who Have Gone Home Tired": "What answers will *you* find / What armor will protect *you* / When your children ask *you* // Why?"[276] Jay Winter, writing about Henri Barbusse's classic First World War novel, *Under Fire,* suggests that Barbusse felt as though he "had blood on his hands" and "had to find some way to escape from the moral quicksand of war. Telling the story was his way. Reading it may be ours."[277] The same is true of the poems explored in this study, "these shards of penetrating clarity . . . that force us to question ourselves."[278]

Furthermore, although the poets do hold on to "the possibility of what is better"—"I want to think we'll be okay / if only we can touch the best / in others and ourselves," Ehrhart writes—there is a thread of tragic inevitability that runs throughout the poetry with regard to our frequent, repeated, and interconnected failures of moral responsibility.[279] Nonetheless, for these poets, who have "no use for comfortable hypocrisies / or delicate interpretations / meant to keep the world the way it is," this does not preclude an acceptance of responsibility or prevent us from attempting to alter the way of the world and the way of war.[280] Ehrhart's aforementioned friend, who identifies American soldiers in Vietnam as both innocent and evil, perfectly encapsulates the poetic attitude toward the moral responsibility that we all share: "'Our hands will never be clean,' / she said, 'but we must try.' // And so I do."[281]

WRECKAGE

In "Answering Adorno," Doug Anderson writes:

> Since you doomed poetry nothing has changed.
> People are the same, maybe worse.
> In Bosnia they have raped by battalions,
> nailed children to doors, rubbled fine old Europe
> block by block, and new evil pours into the deep cup
> with the evil I have already seen, overflowing.
> Convention demands that I mortify something.
> My flesh. My heart. Any joy I might have
> on this April day with forsythia suddenly everywhere
> and the willows aching green gold.
> Adorno, your words are like snow lingering
> where shade and wind hold out against the sun.[1]

The poem is prefaced with Theodor Adorno's famous declaration that "To write poetry after Auschwitz is barbaric." It is a stark statement, but it can be better understood in the light of Adorno's assertion that "there is no longer beauty or consolation except in the gaze falling on horror, withstanding it, and in unalleviated consciousness of negativity holding fast to the possibility of what is better."[2] If poetry written in the aftermath of terrible events, such as Auschwitz or, indeed, the

American war in Vietnam, averts its gaze from that wreckage, then it is not beautiful—it is barbaric. Adorno's words stand as a warning against looking away. Here, beauty stems from an unflinching examination of horror; sanitization is an obscenity. As Steve Mason declares: "No one should write bloodlessly / of spilled blood."[3]

Throughout this book, we have seen how a group of American soldiers who fought in Vietnam, and then chose to bear witness to that experience through poetry, answer Adorno's requirement of beauty. These soldier-poets highlight the moral significance of surroundings, from the climates of childhood through the bewildering, arduous, and frightening experience of fighting in a seemingly otherworldly place to the difficulty of returning "home" from the warzone. They describe and dismantle the American-Vietnamese us-them moral barrier that existed during the war and, in doing so, negate the false and dangerous separations upon which war relies and affirm instead our common humanity. Through their uncompromising representations of the devastating impact of violence on the human body, the dehumanization of killing in war, atrocities, and technological violence, the poets present a firm moral rejection of the war's process of injuring and killing. And, they argue that responsibility for the harms caused by the conflict must be shared by a number of groups, including politicians, military leaders, businesses, the American people, and themselves and their fellow soldiers. Good poems, W. D. Ehrhart suggests, "offer us the world with eyes renewed."[4] By maintaining Adorno's gaze, the soldier-poets produce just such works. They enable us to see war from the perspective of those who have fought, to view crucial moral issues from the standpoint of those who have confronted them directly. The poets look and they allow—urge—us to look. Their gaze becomes ours.

Furthermore, through this poetic witness, the poets embody Albert Camus's conception of the rebel. In his poem "The Teacher," Ehrhart describes how he emerged from the experience of war carrying

> anger like a torch
> to keep my heart from freezing,
> and a strange new thing called
> love
> to keep me sane.[5]

This is the poets' rebellion—a moral imagination burning with anger yet anchored in love. As rebels who negate war and affirm life, the poets also satisfy Camus's requirement of beauty, which, like Adorno's, demands that artists "simultaneously reject reality and exalt certain of its aspects. Art disputes reality, but does not hide from it."[6] Moreover, in their willingness and ability to bear witness, to combine a strong moral stance with a determined artistic commitment, the poets epitomize Viktor E. Frankl's belief in the "the human capacity to creatively turn life's negative aspects into something positive or constructive."[7] As Ehrhart states, the poets represent "the terrible beauty that Vietnam engendered in sensitive hearts, the curious grace with which the human spirit can endow even the ugliest of realities."[8]

The American soldier-poets of the war in Vietnam, then, have produced both artistic and moral beauty. Yet, although their rebellious poetic witness points to "the possibility of what is better," this positive potentiality exists only in the present and in the future, not in the past. We can pretend, as in Bruce Weigl's "Song of Napalm," that the girl running down the road with "napalm / Stuck to her dress like jelly" has wings that "Beat inside her until she rises / Above the stinking jungle and her pain / Eases, and your pain, and mine." But it is a lie. The grim actuality, like so many other horrors, is forever locked away in lost time, unalterable by beautiful poetry or beautiful morality:

> The lie works only as long as it takes to speak
> And the girl runs only as far
> As the napalm allows
> Until her burning tendons and crackling
> Muscles draw her up
> Into that final position
> Burning bodies so perfectly assume. Nothing
> Can change that; she is burned behind my eyes
> And not your good love and not the rain-swept air
> And not the jungle green
> Pasture unfolding before us can deny it.[9]

The poets in this book, through the utilization of literary imagination rooted in firsthand experience, may make something beautiful—

artistically and morally—out of the wreckage of the war. But that does not change the wreckage itself. It remains wreckage; it always will. It can never be beautiful. The past is set. The flesh is cut. The heart is hurt. And nothing can bring back the dead.

> What if I didn't shoot the old lady
> running away from our patrol,
> or the old man in the back of the head,
> or the boy in the marketplace?
>
> Or what if the boy—but he didn't
> have a grenade, and the woman in Hue
> didn't lie in the rain in a mortar pit
> with seven Marines just for food,
>
> Gaffney didn't get hit in the knee,
> Ames didn't die in the river, Ski
> didn't die in a medevac chopper
> between Con Thien and Da Nang.
>
> In Vietnamese, Con Thien means
> *place of angels.* What if it really was
> instead of the place of rotting sandbags,
> incoming heavy artillery, rats and mud.
>
> What if the angels were Ames and Ski,
> or the lady, the man, and the boy,
> and they lifted Gaffney out of the mud
> and healed his shattered knee?
>
> What if none of it happened the way I said?
> Would it all be a lie?
> Would the wreckage be suddenly beautiful?
> Would the dead rise up and walk?[10]

APPENDIX A
THE POETS

Listed below are the poets to whom I have referred most often in this book, along with the details, where available, of their branch of service and the years they were in that service, followed by their service in Vietnam and the years they were there.

DOUG ANDERSON, Navy. Corpsman, 3rd Battalion, 1st Marines, 1967–68.

JAN BARRY, Army, 1962–65. Radio specialist, 18th Aviation Company, 1962–63.

R. L. BARTH, Marines, 1966–69. Patrol leader, 1st Reconnaissance Battalion, 1968–69.

D. C. BERRY, Army, 1966–69. Medical Service Corps, 1967–68.

KEVIN BOWEN, Army. 1st Air Cavalry Division, 1968–69.

D. F. BROWN, Army, 1968–77. Medic, 1st Battalion, 14th Infantry Regiment, 4th Infantry Division, 1969–70.

MICHAEL CASEY, Army, 1968–70. Military policeman, Americal Division, 1969–70.

HORACE COLEMAN, Air Force, 1965–70. Air traffic controller–intercept director, 1967–68.

DAVID CONNOLLY, Army. Small arms infantryman, track security, 11th Armored Cavalry Regiment, 1968–69.

FRANK A. CROSS JR., Army, 1969–70. Radioman, reconnaissance platoon, 3rd Battalion, 1st Infantry, 11th Brigade, Americal Division, 1969–70.

W. D. EHRHART, Marines, 1966–69. Assistant intelligence chief, 1st Battalion, 1st Marines, 1967–68.

DAVID HALL, Army, 1966–69. Artillery forward observer, 9th Infantry Division, 1968–69.

J. VINCENT HANSEN, Army. Machine-gunner, 101st Airborne Division, 1966–67.

YUSEF KOMUNYAKAA, Army, 1968–71. Information specialist, combat correspondent and publication editor for the *Southern Cross,* Americal Division, 1969–70.

MCAVOY LAYNE, Marines, 1966–67. Infantryman, 1966–67.

STEVE MASON, Army, 1960–69. Special Forces, 1966–67.

GERALD MCCARTHY, Marines, 1965–68. 1st Combat Engineer Battalion, 1966–67. Deserted after tour and served time in military prison and civilian jail.

JIM NYE, Army. Served two tours: platoon leader, 101st Airborne Division, 1966–67; 5th Special Forces Group, 1969–70.

BASIL T. PAQUET, Army, 1966–68 (drafted as a conscientious objector). Medic, 24th Evacuation Hospital, 1967–68.

LEROY V. QUINTANA, Army. Long-range reconnaissance patrol unit, 101st Airborne Division, 1967–68.

DALE RITTERBUSCH, Army, 1966–69. Liaison officer, coordinated a program for the aerial mining of the Ho Chi Minh Trail, Joint United States Military Assistance Advisory Group/Military Assistance Command—Thailand, 1968–69.

DICK SHEA, Navy, 1961–65. SEAL detachment, 1965.

JAMES SOULAR, Army. Helicopter crew chief, 1st Air Cavalry Division, 1966–67.

LAMONT B. STEPTOE, Army. Scout dog handler, 25th Infantry Division, 1969–70.

BRUCE WEIGL, Army, 1967–70. 1st Air Cavalry Division, 1967–68.

APPENDIX B
THE POEMS

DOUG ANDERSON, "Free Fire Zone," "Infantry Assault," "Mine," "Short Timer," "The Wall," in *The Moon Reflected Fire* (Cambridge, MA: Alice James Books, 1994); "Answering Adorno," in *Blues for Unemployed Secret Police* (Willimantic, CT: Curbstone Press, 2000). Used by permission of the author.

BRUCE ANELLO, untitled ("April 8"), untitled ("February 12"), untitled ("February 19"), in *Peace Is Our Profession: Poems and Passages of War Protest,* edited by Jan Barry (Montclair, NJ: East River Anthology, 1981). Used by permission of the publisher.

RICHARD E. BAKER, "Burying the Children," "Interrogation," "There Are no Sins Inside The Gates of Eden," in *Shell Burst Pond* (1980, 2nd ed., Tacoma, WA: Vardaman Press, 1982). Used by permission of the author.

TOM BARDEN, "The Fog of War," in *Long Time Passing: Poems, Songs & Reflections on the Vietnam War after 20 Years,* edited by Thomas E. Barden (Toledo, OH: Radio Room Press, 1995). Used by permission of the author.

JAN BARRY, "Green Hell, Green Death," "Memorial For Man In Black Pajamas," in *Winning Hearts and Minds: War Poems by Vietnam Veterans,* edited by Larry Rottmann, Jan Barry, and Basil T. Paquet (New York: McGraw-Hill, 1972); "Viet Nam," in *Demilitarized Zones: Veterans after Vietnam,* edited by Jan Barry and W. D. Ehrhart (Perkasie, PA: East River Anthology, 1976); "If war is hell," in *Peace Is Our Profession: Poems and Passages of War Protest,* edited by Jan Barry (Montclair, NJ: East River Anthology, 1981); "In the Footsteps of Genghis Khan," "The Peace Monument," in *Veterans Day* (Richford, VT: Samisdat, 1983); "Gifts," "Lessons," "War Baby," in *War Baby* (Richford, VT: Samisdat, 1983). Used by permission of the author.

R. L. BARTH, "Chaplain to Bishop," "A Letter from An Hoc (4), by a Seedbed," "'The Lighter That Never Fails,'" "M.I.A.," "The Movies Are a State of Mind," in *A Soldier's Time: Vietnam War Poems* (Santa Barbara, CA: John Daniel, 1987); "A Brief History of the Vietnam War," "Why We Fight," in *Simonides in Vietnam* (n.p., 1990); "1992: Consolation," in *Small Arms Fire* (n.p., 1994); "Allegory for L.B.J.," "A Child Accidentally Napalmed," "Epitaph," "Grunt Fantasy," "A Little Elegy for Jimmy Stewart," "Meditations After Battle," "One Way to Carry the Dead," "POWs," "Proem," "Social Darwinism," "'Tonight you bitch, under too many drinks,'" in *Deeply Dug In* (Albuquerque: University of New Mexico Press, 2003). Used by permission of the author.

BILL BAUER, "Worst in Memory," in *The Eye of the Ghost: Vietnam Poems* (Kansas City: BkMk Press, 1986); "Agent Ash," "Benediction," "Moonlight and a Breeze," in *Last Lambs: New and Selected Poems of Vietnam* (Kansas City: BkMk Press, 1997).

PETER BERENBAK, "The Game," in *Peace Is Our Profession: Poems and Passages of War Protest,* edited by Jan Barry (Montclair, NJ: East River Anthology, 1981). Used by permission of the publisher.

D. C. BERRY, untitled ("The gasping redness touches"), untitled ("A poem ought to be a salt lick"), untitled ("The sun goes"), untitled ("Tangerines and white"), untitled ("This is the end where the begin"), untitled ("The way popcorn pops is"), in *saigon cemetery* (Athens: University of Georgia Press, 1972); "Gulf of Tonkin," in *From Both Sides Now: The Poetry of the Vietnam War and Its Aftermath,* edited by Phillip Mahony (New York: Scribner, 1998).

KEVIN BOWEN, "The Arts of Love and Hydrology as Practiced in Hà Nội," "President Diem's Motorcade," "Temple at Quan Loi, 1969," in *Playing Basketball with the Viet Cong* (Willimantic, CT: Curbstone Press, 1994). Copyright 1994 by Kevin Bowen. All rights reserved. Published by Curbstone Press. Used by permission of the publisher.

D. F. BROWN, "Eating the Forest," "Still Later There Are War Stories," in *Unaccustomed Mercy: Soldier-Poets of the Vietnam War,* edited by W. D. Ehrhart (Lubbock: Texas Tech University Press, 1989); "The First Law of Landscaping/May 30, 1990," *War, Literature & the Arts* 10.2 (Fall–Winter 1998); "Even the Spoon is a Weapon," "The Other Half of Everything," "Poem (Westmoreland)," in "Assuming Blue: or The Other Half of Everything" (manuscript, Imaginative Representations of the Vietnam War Collection,

Connelly Library, La Salle University, Philadelphia, 1999). Used by permission of the author.

MICHAEL CASEY, "A Bummer," "Road Hazard," in *Obscenities* (New Haven, CT: Yale University Press, 1972). Used by permission of the author.

HORACE COLEMAN, "Bring Your Lunch!," "D-Day + 50; Tet + 25," "I don't suppose I'll ever forget," "It Was Jane Fonda's Fault!," "Night Flare Drop, Tan Son Nhut," "Notes for Veteran's War Protest," "People's War, People's Army," "The Raid Near Saigon," "Saigon Warrior," "Still Life With Dead Hippie," "War Stories," "You Can't Tell The Players Without A Scorecard," in *In the Grass* (Woodbridge, CT: Viet Nam Generation, Inc. & Burning Cities Press, 1995).

DAVID CONNOLLY, "Brotherhood," "Death by Friendly Fire," "The Michelin," "We're Still Here, America," in "Illumination Rounds: A Collection of Thoughts By a Survivor of the War in Vietnam" (manuscript, Imaginative Representations of the Vietnam War Collection, Connelly Library, La Salle University, Philadelphia, n.d.); "All the Stars Do Not Spangle," "Christmas Standdown," "Corporal Thach: First Confirmed NVA Kill," "Dreams of the Fight," "For DC," "The Guerrilla," "Reconciliation," "Tet, Plus Twenty Four," "Thoughts on a Monsoon Morning," "To the Irish Americans Who Fought the Last War," in *Lost in America* (Woodbridge, CT: Viet Nam Generation, Inc. & Burning Cities Press, 1994); "Building A Raft At The Pond," "Collage On the Cusp of the Century," "Heart Attack," "My Rights," "War Song," "What Was Lost," in *Finding My Way* (Boston: David Connolly and the South Boston Literary Gazette Press, 2005); "Into the Michelin Rubber Plantations," *South Boston Literary Gazette* 16 (Fall 2005); untitled ("Dead, Iraq"), *South Boston Literary Gazette* 22 (Winter 2010); "War Wisdom, for What It's Worth," interview by author, Boston, 15 March 2010. Used by permission of the author.

FRANK A. CROSS JR., "After The Ambush," in *Winning Hearts and Minds: War Poems by Vietnam Veterans,* edited by Larry Rottmann, Jan Barry, and Basil T. Paquet (New York: McGraw-Hill, 1972), used by permission of the publisher; "Heat Casualties," "Jungle Rot," "The Light Colonel," "What Are You Going to Be?," in *Reminders* (Big Timber, MT: Seven Buffaloes Press, 1986).

MARK DOWNEY, "Dutyhonorcountry," in *Winning Hearts and Minds: War Poems by Vietnam Veterans,* edited by Larry Rottmann, Jan Barry, and Basil T. Paquet (New York: McGraw-Hill, 1972). Used by permission of the publisher.

W. D. EHRHART, "Hunting," in *Winning Hearts and Minds: War Poems by Vietnam Veterans,* edited by Larry Rottmann, Jan Barry, and Basil T. Paquet (New York: McGraw-Hill, 1972); "Another Life," "The Bob Hope Christmas Special," "Coming Home," "Farmer Nguyen," "Guerrilla War," "The Next Step," "Perimeter Guard," "A Relative Thing," "Time on Target," in *A Generation of Peace* (New

York: New Voices, 1975); "To Maynard on the Long Road Home," "To Those Who Have Gone Home Tired," "Vietnam Veterans, After All," in *Demilitarized Zones: Veterans after Vietnam,* edited by Jan Barry and W. D. Ehrhart (Perkasie, PA: East River Anthology, 1976); "The Teacher," in *The Samisdat Poems* (Richford, VT: Samisdat, 1980); "The Eruption of Mount St. Helens," "Fog," "Near-Sighted," in *Matters of the Heart* (Easthampton, MA: Adastra Press, 1981); "Cry Wolf," in *Peace Is Our Profession: Poems and Passages of War Protest,* edited by Jan Barry (Montclair, NJ: East River Anthology, 1981); "'. . . the light that cannot fade . . . ,'" "Responsibility," "Sound Advice," "A Warning to My Students," in *The Outer Banks & Other Poems* (Easthampton, MA: Adastra Press, 1984); "High Country," "The Invasion of Grenada," "Letter to the Survivors," "The Reason Why," "A Relative Thing," in *To Those Who Have Gone Home Tired: New and Selected Poems* (New York: Thunder's Mouth Press, 1984); "Nicaragua Libre," "Parade Rest," "What Keeps Me Going," "Why I Don't Mind Rocking Leela to Sleep," in *Winter Bells* (Easthampton, MA: Adastra Press, 1988); "Chasing Locomotives," "In the Valley of the Shadow," "Just for Laughs," "Keeping My Distance," "Not Your Problem," "The Poet as Athlete," "Some Other World," "Song for Leela, Bobby and Me," "Starting Over," "Unaccustomed Mercies," "What We're Buying," "Who Did What to Whom," in *Just for Laughs* (Silver Spring, MD: Viet Nam Generation, Inc. & Burning Cities Press, 1990); "The Cradle of Civilization," "For a Coming Extinction," "Governor Rhodes Keeps His Word," "Guns," "More Than You Ever Imagined," "Sleeping with General Chi," "What War Does," "Why the Kurds Die in the Mountains," in *The Distance We Travel* (Easthampton, MA: Adastra Press, 1993); *Mostly Nothing Happens: A Poem* (Easthampton, MA: Adastra Press, 1996); "Beautiful Wreckage," "Letter," "Making the Children Behave," "Visiting My Parents' Grave," "What I Know About Myself," in *Beautiful Wreckage: New & Selected Poems* (Easthampton, MA: Adastra Press, 1999); "All About Death," "All About Love," "Home Before Morning," "Manning the Walls," in *Sleeping with the Dead* (Easthampton, MA: Adastra Press, 2006); "The Bodies Beneath the Table," "Coaching Winter Track in Time of War," "On the Eve of Destruction," "The Secret Lives of Boys," "September 11th," "What Better Way to Begin," "What Makes a Man," in *The Bodies Beneath the Table* (Easthampton, MA: Adastra Press, 2010). Used by permission of the author.

LARRY FRIES, "From Viet Nam 68–69," in *Winning Hearts and Minds: War Poems by Vietnam Veterans,* edited by Larry Rottmann, Jan Barry, and Basil T. Paquet (New York: McGraw-Hill, 1972). Used by permission of the publisher.

ANDREW GETTLER, "the old guard," "redeye special," in *Footsteps of a Ghost: Poems from Viet Nam* (New Brunswick, NJ: Iniquity Press/Vendetta Books, 1991).

GIS OF THE 1ST AIR CAVALRY DIVISION, "We shoot the sick, the young, the lame," in *Peace Is Our Profession: Poems and Passages of War Protest,* edited by

Jan Barry (Montclair, NJ: East River Anthology, 1981). Used by permission of the publisher.

JON FORREST GLADE, "Blood Trail," "Freedom Bird," in *Photographs of the Jungle* (St. John, KS: Chiron Review Press, 1990).

DAVID HALL, "The Ambush of the Fourth Platoon," "Military Training in the Very Young," "The Pepsi Generation," in *Werewolf and Other Poems* (Fort Collins, CO: Bald Mountain Press, 1981).

J. VINCENT HANSEN, "1965," "Bad Semantics (B.S.)," "Bernard," "Casualties," "The Generals," "Hate," "It Ain't Good, What We Done," "On Belonging," "A Pinch of Salt," "Sgt. Royster Meets Pvt. Stanley," "'Snips and Snails and Puppy Dog Tails,'" "Still Life," "A Thousand Words of Hate," "A Tidy List," "To Lenny and Simon," "Tyus," "Uncertain Notions," "Wallowing at Tuy Hoa," "We Take Him Along," in *Blessed Are the Piecemakers: A Collection of Poems And Uncertain Notions* (St. Cloud, MN: North Star Press of St. Cloud, 1989). Used by permission of the publisher.

GUSTAV HASFORD, "Bedtime Story," in *Winning Hearts and Minds: War Poems by Vietnam Veterans,* edited by Larry Rottmann, Jan Barry, and Basil T. Paquet (New York: McGraw-Hill, 1972). Used by permission of the publisher.

STEVE HASSETT, "Patriot's Day," "Thanksgiving," in *Carrying the Darkness: The Poetry of the Vietnam War,* edited by W. D. Ehrhart (1985; Lubbock: Texas Tech University Press, 1989).

STEVEN HASSNA, "Saturday Rip-Off Blues," in *Peace Is Our Profession: Poems and Passages of War Protest,* edited by Jan Barry (Montclair, NJ: East River Anthology, 1981). Used by permission of the publisher.

STEPHEN R. HATCH, "Vietnam Clouds," in *Winning Hearts and Minds: War Poems by Vietnam Veterans,* edited by Larry Rottmann, Jan Barry, and Basil T. Paquet (New York: McGraw-Hill, 1972). Used by permission of the publisher.

PETER HOLLENBECK, "Anorexia," in *Carrying the Darkness: The Poetry of the Vietnam War,* edited by W. D. Ehrhart (1985; Lubbock: Texas Tech University Press, 1989).

JOHN F. HOWE, "The Land," in *Carrying the Darkness: The Poetry of the Vietnam War,* edited by W. D. Ehrhart (1985; Lubbock: Texas Tech University Press, 1989).

DAVID HUDDLE, "Entry," "Revelation," in *Stopping by Home* (Salt Lake City: Peregrine Smith Books, 1988). Used by permission of the author.

RANDALL JARRELL, "The Death of the Ball Turret Gunner," in *The Complete Poems* (New York: Farrar, Straus and Giroux, 1969). Used by permission of the publisher.

G. P. JOHNSON, "Fighting for Those," "Power, Politics, and Profit," "Power, Politics, and Profit II," in *I Was Fighting for Peace, but, Lord, There Was Much More* (Hicksville, NY: Exposition Press, 1979).

HARRISON KOHLER, "The Cheerleaders," in *Winning Hearts and Minds: War Poems by Vietnam Veterans,* edited by Larry Rottmann, Jan Barry, and Basil T. Paquet (New York: McGraw-Hill, 1972). Used by permission of the publisher.

YUSEF KOMUNYAKAA, "2527th Birthday of the Buddha," "Camouflaging the Chimera," "Fragging," "Hanoi Hannah," "Jungle Surrender," "The One-legged Stool," "Report from the Skull's Diorama," "Starlight Scope Myopia," "Thanks," "Tu Do Street," "We Never Know," in *Dien Cai Dau* (Middletown, CT: Wesleyan University Press, 1988); "Phantasmagoria," in *Thieves of Paradise* (Hanover, NH: Wesleyan University Press, 1998); "Autobiography of My Alter Ego," in *Warhorses* (New York: Farrar, Straus and Giroux, 2008). Used by permission of the publishers.

JAMES D. LANGE, "Violence," in *Peace Is Our Profession: Poems and Passages of War Protest,* edited by Jan Barry (Montclair, NJ: East River Anthology, 1981). Used by permission of the publisher.

MCAVOY LAYNE, "Conclusions on courage," "Eleven October," "Guns," "The mob," "The nickname Night Train," "On deference," "On free haircuts," "On lima beans," in *How Audie Murphy Died in Vietnam* (Garden City, NY: Anchor Books, 1973). Used by permission of the author.

D. S. LLITERAS, "Booby-Trap," in *In A Warrior's Romance* (Norfolk, VA: Hampton Roads, 1991). Used by permission of the author.

PETER P. MAHONEY, "The Airport," in *Demilitarized Zones: Veterans after Vietnam,* edited by Jan Barry and W. D. Ehrhart (Perkasie, PA: East River Anthology, 1976). Used by permission of the author.

STEVE MASON, "Angry Little Poem of Spring," "The Casualty," "The Children of the Sun," "Founding Convention Poem," "A History Lesson," in *Johnny's Song* (Toronto: Bantam Books, 1987); "Death Is A Lady," "In Victory Or Defeat," "Only One Mother," "Portrait Of A Man," "Somewhere, A Woman," in *Warrior for Peace* (New York: Touchstone, 1988).

GERALD MCCARTHY, "War Story," in *War Story: Vietnam War Poems* (Trumansburg, NY: Crossing Press, 1977). Used by permission of the author.

JAMES MCLEROY, "Ambush," in *Dear America: Letters Home from Vietnam,* edited by Bernard Edelman (1985; New York: W. W. Norton, 2002). Used by permission of the editor.

GEORGE MIZO, untitled ("You"), in Jim Willingham, "Ground Zero 9/11/02," *Veteran* 32.2 (Fall 2002). Used by permission of the author's estate.

ROBERT A. MOORE, "I'm home, America," in *Demilitarized Zones: Veterans after Vietnam,* edited by Jan Barry and W. D. Ehrhart (Perkasie, PA: East River Anthology, 1976). Used by permission of the publisher.

JIM NORTHRUP, "The Duke," in *The Rez Road Follies: Canoes, Casinos, Computers, and Birch Bark Baskets* (Minneapolis: University of Minnesota Press, 1999).

JIM NYE, "It's Too Late," "Peace," "This Ground Is Indifferent," "You Gotta Have Heart," in *Aftershock: Poems and Prose from the Vietnam War* (El Paso, TX: Cinco Puntos Press, 1991). Used by permission of the author.

PERRY OLDHAM, "And Now," in *Demilitarized Zones: Veterans after Vietnam,* edited by Jan Barry and W. D. Ehrhart (Perkasie, PA: East River Anthology, 1976); "Epilogue," "Red Madonna," in *Vinh Long* (Meadows of Dan, VA: Northwoods Press, 1976). Used by permission of the author.

JOHN O'NEILL, "Veterans Day, 1972," in *Demilitarized Zones: Veterans after Vietnam,* edited by Jan Barry and W. D. Ehrhart (Perkasie, PA: East River Anthology, 1976). Used by permission of the publisher.

BASIL T. PAQUET, "Graves Registration," "In A Plantation," "It Is Monsoon At Last," "Morning—A Death," "Mourning The Death, By Hemorrhage, Of A Child From Honai," "They Do Not Go Gentle," in *Winning Hearts and Minds: War Poems by Vietnam Veterans,* edited by Larry Rottmann, Jan Barry, and Basil T. Paquet (New York: McGraw-Hill, 1972). Used by permission of the publisher.

MARION PARKER [pseud.], "The Children," in *Demilitarized Zones: Veterans after Vietnam,* edited by Jan Barry and W. D. Ehrhart (Perkasie, PA: East River Anthology, 1976). Used by permission of the publisher.

STAN PLATKE, "And Then There Were None," "Gut Catcher," in *Winning Hearts and Minds: War Poems by Vietnam Veterans,* edited by Larry Rottmann, Jan Barry, and Basil T. Paquet (New York: McGraw-Hill, 1972); "Postface," in *Peace Is Our Profession: Poems and Passages of War Protest,* edited by Jan Barry (Montclair, NJ: East River Anthology, 1981). Used by permission of the publishers.

CHARLES M. PURCELL, "The Walk," in *Winning Hearts and Minds: War Poems by Vietnam Veterans,* edited by Larry Rottmann, Jan Barry, and Basil T. Paquet (New York: McGraw-Hill, 1972). Used by permission of the publisher.

LEROY V. QUINTANA, "ARVN Rangers," "Bates," "Interrogations," "Major Gordon Granger," "Natural History," "An Open Letter to President Bush," in *Interrogations* (Chevy Chase, MD: Viet Nam Generation, Inc. & Burning Cities Press, 1990); "At the New Mexico Viet Nam Veterans' Memorial," "Poem for Our Dog Afraid of Thunder on a Rainy Day," "That Country," in *The Great Whirl of Exile* (Willimantic, CT: Curbstone Press, 1999). Used by permission of the author.

GARY RAFFERTY, "Last Asylum," "Twins," in *From Both Sides Now: The Poetry of the Vietnam War and Its Aftermath,* edited by Phillip Mahony (New York: Scribner, 1998).

DALE RITTERBUSCH, "Choppers," "Geography Lesson," in *Lessons Learned: Poetry of the Vietnam War and Its Aftermath* (Woodbridge, CT: Viet Nam Generation, Inc. & Burning Cities Press, 1995); "Literary Determinism," "Probably Not the Final Destination," *War, Literature & the Arts* 23.1–2 (2011). Used by permission of the author.

SERIGO [IGOR BOBROWSKY], "Hue City," "I Hate You . . . ," in *Winning Hearts and Minds: War Poems by Vietnam Veterans,* edited by Larry Rottmann, Jan Barry, and Basil T. Paquet (New York: McGraw-Hill, 1972). Used by permission of the publisher.

DICK SHEA, "am alone in room," "americans have big heads," "a dead man was on the beach today," "democracy is fighting with money," "everything in house," "i am shitfaced," "i like the vietnamese," "in john one morning," "in reflection," "in the papers you see many photographs of rank officers," "it is detrimental to morale," "met a vietnamese officer today," "on road of holes," "orient is strange," "the people here are simple," "so for some unknown reason," "spent night," "there's no war here," "went fishing with some vietnamese military," "went to vietnamese party," "went with a cab driver," in *vietnam simply* (Coronado, CA: Pro Tem, 1967).

JOSEPH M. SHEA, "Comfortable people do not look," in *Peace Is Our Profession: Poems and Passages of War Protest,* edited by Jan Barry (Montclair, NJ: East River Anthology, 1981). Used by permission of the publisher.

JAMES SOULAR, "The Agent," "The Burning," "Choking," "First Kill," "Letter to Billy," "Numbah One," "Terminus Ad Quem, 1967," "The Thousand-Yard Stare," "The Tunnel," "Voices," in *The Thousand-Yard Stare* (Canton, CT: Singular Speech Press, 1997); "Lines," in *The Thousand-Yard Stare* (1997; 2nd ed., n.p.: 1st Books Library, 2004). Used by permission of the author.

LAMONT B. STEPTOE, "Before Going," "A Circle of Red," "Gulf of Tonkin," "Mad Minute," "Returnee," "A Second Wall," "Toxic Waste," in *Mad Minute* (1990; Camden, NJ: Whirlwind Press, 1993); "letter to momma #2," "they want to take my life," "uncle's south china sea blue nightmare," in *Uncle's South China Sea Blue Nightmare* (1995; 2nd ed., Philadelphia: Plan B Press, 2003). Used by permission of the author.

LANDON THORNE, "Brothers," "On Passing Graves Registration—Dong Ha," in *Winning Hearts and Minds: War Poems by Vietnam Veterans,* edited by Larry Rottmann, Jan Barry, and Basil T. Paquet (New York: McGraw-Hill, 1972). Used by permission of the publisher.

B. D. TRAIL, "The Grenading," *Viet Nam Generation* 4.3–4 (Summer–Fall 1992); "With My Shield or On It," in David Willson, "A Few Well-Chosen Words: Extraordinary, Neglected Vietnam War Poets," *VVA Veteran* 31.1 (January–February 2011).

PETER ULISSE, "Captain Windslow," "Chaplain Flanagan," "Doctor Able," "General Strickland," "Warrant Officer Tadduni," in *Vietnam Voices* (Lewiston, NY: Edwin Mellen Press, 1990). Used by permission of the author.

BRUCE WEIGL, "Eclipse," "Monkey," in *A Romance* (Pittsburgh: University of Pittsburgh Press, 1979); "Amnesia," "Debris," "Girl at the Chu Lai Laundry," "Snowy Egret," "Song of Napalm," "Surrounding Blues on the Way Down," in *The Monkey Wars* (Athens: University of Georgia Press, 1985); "Elegy," "Him, on the Bicycle," "Mines," "On the Anniversary of Her Grace," "When Saigon Was French," in *Song of Napalm* (New York: Atlantic Monthly Press, 1988); "The Impossible," "They Name Heaven," in *What Saves Us* (Evanston, IL: TriQuarterly Books, 1992); "Carp," "For the Novice of Tran Quoc Pagoda," "Meditation at Melville Ave.," "Meditation in Hue," "On the Ambiguity of Injury and Pain," "What I Saw and Did in the Alley," in *Sweet Lorain* (Evanston, IL: TriQuarterly Books, 1996); "And we came home," "The Happy Land," "The Nothing Redemption," "Our Independence Day," in *After the Others* (Evanston, IL: TriQuarterly Books, 1999), "I Put a Shotgun to My Mouth," "Nixon," "Why Plato Left for Megara," in *The Unraveling Strangeness* (New York: Grove Press, 2002); "Apology to No One, November Seventeenth, Two Thousand Four," "Le Filme," "The First Father-Murdered Rabbit," "The One Thousandth," "Patrick, in Memory," "The Prisoner of Ours," in *Declension in the Village of Chung Luong* (Keene, NY: Ausable Press, 2006); "Ice Storm," in *The Abundance of Nothing* (Evanston, IL: TriQuarterly Books, 2012). Used by permission of the author.

NOTES

Introduction

1. W. D. Ehrhart, "Making the Children Behave," in *Beautiful Wreckage: New & Selected Poems* (Easthampton, MA: Adastra Press, 1999), 15. An early version of this poem appears in *Demilitarized Zones: Veterans after Vietnam*, edited by Jan Barry and W. D. Ehrhart (Perkasie, PA: East River Anthology, 1976), 67. For Ehrhart's account of this trip to Vietnam, see W. D. Ehrhart, *Going Back: An Ex-Marine Returns to Vietnam* (Jefferson, NC: McFarland, 1987).
2. W. D. Ehrhart, interview by author, Philadelphia, 2 March 2010.
3. W. D. Ehrhart, "In the Valley of the Shadow," in *Just for Laughs* (Silver Spring, MD: Viet Nam Generation, Inc. & Burning Cities Press, 1990), 14–15.
4. W. D. Ehrhart, "Sound Advice," in *The Outer Banks & Other Poems* (Easthampton, MA: Adastra Press, 1984), 25.
5. W. D. Ehrhart, introduction to *Unaccustomed Mercy: Soldier-Poets of the Vietnam War*, edited by W. D. Ehrhart (Lubbock: Texas Tech University Press, 1989), 5.
6. Ehrhart interview.
7. W. D. Ehrhart, in "War, Poetry & Ethics: A Symposium," *War, Literature & the Arts* 10.2 (Fall–Winter 1998): 29.
8. Theresa L. Brown and Vince Gotera, introduction to *Journal of American Culture* 16.3 (September 1993): 1.
9. W. D. Ehrhart, foreword to *Carrying the Darkness: The Poetry of the Vietnam War*, edited by W. D. Ehrhart (1985; Lubbock: Texas Tech University Press, 1989), xxvi.
10. In the spring of 2010, I met and interviewed the following poets: Jan Barry, Michael Casey, Horace Coleman, David Connolly, W. D. Ehrhart, Yusef Komunyakaa, Gerald McCarthy, and Bruce Weigl. I also interviewed John Baky, who served as a military policeman in Vietnam and was the director of the Connelly Library at La Salle University in Philadelphia, where the Imaginative Representations of the Vietnam War Collection is held, when I conducted my research there. These meetings and inter-

views considerably aided my understanding of both the poetry and the war. Furthermore, the material gathered during the interviews is a valuable auxiliary source. Certainly, this is not an oral history project, and the poetry is always primary, but the interviews provide a useful supply of additional viewpoints, ideas, contexts, and background information. They are employed here as a supplement to, rather than a replacement of, the poetry. All of the interviews have been transcribed verbatim and are available in the Imaginative Representations of the Vietnam War Collection. With regard to other sources, at La Salle I was fortunate to be able to access the archives of Jan Barry, an influential poet, editor, and cofounder of Vietnam Veterans Against the War. In particular, the contents of the archive assisted in piecing together a history of the publication process of the poetry in the 1970s and 1980s. Occasionally, I use unpublished poems that come from either completely unpublished manuscripts or early manuscript versions of collections that did make it to print but lost some interesting poems along the path to publication. Very rarely, I include song lyrics penned by soldiers, but only when they have been printed as part of a poetry collection. Predominantly, though, I select the most relevant pieces from among the thousands of published poems written by those American soldiers who served in Vietnam. With regard to the source material, I should note that I have not standardized the capitalization of poem and poetry collection titles—as I have done with all other titles—but kept them as they appear in the original source.

11. Christian G. Appy, *Working-Class War: American Combat Soldiers and Vietnam* (Chapel Hill: University of North Carolina Press, 1993); Kyle Longley, *Grunts: The American Combat Soldier in Vietnam* (Armonk, NY: M. E. Sharpe, 2008).
12. George Cotkin, *Morality's Muddy Waters: Ethical Quandaries in Modern America* (Philadelphia: University of Pennsylvania Press, 2010).
13. George Cotkin, "History's Moral Turn," *Journal of the History of Ideas* 69.2 (April 2008): 294.
14. Cotkin, *Morality's Muddy Waters,* 199.
15. Horace Coleman, interview by author, Los Angeles, 3 April 2010.
16. Due to the gendered nature of American military roles in Vietnam, then, this is primarily a story of male experience. American women who served in Vietnam had a fundamentally different moral status from American soldiers. Crucially, they were not perpetrators of violence. Additionally, they were not legitimate targets of violence, either. Certainly, some did fall victim to the war's violence, but from a moral philosophical perspective American women in Vietnam were not liable to attack. This differentiates them not only from combat soldiers but also from many rear-echelon military force personnel who may not have directly occupied the position of perpetrator but who were nonetheless legitimate targets during the war. Simply put, American women were not sent to kill and be killed, and this is a vital consideration given this book's focus on soldiers and morality. Thus, to maintain historical and philosophical precision, this study does not draw on poetry written by women who served in Vietnam, and for the same reason I also avoid using the poetry of men who were far removed from the role of soldier. I should stress, of course, that this is not to suggest that the experiences and writings of these particular participants in the war are in any way less valid than those of soldiers, but they are different in ways that are historically and morally significant. I would add that the poetry of female veterans of the American war in Vietnam deserves its own book that can fully address the particularities of their experiences and writings. For more on female experiences of the war, see Heather Marie Stur, *Beyond Combat: Women and Gender in the Vietnam War Era* (Cambridge: Cambridge University Press, 2011). For a good selection of poetry

written by female veterans, see Lynda Van Devanter and Joan A. Furey, eds., *Visions of War, Dreams of Peace: Writings of Women in the Vietnam War* (New York: Warner Books, 1991). For an overview of poetry written by female veterans and its position in discussions of the war, see Lorrie Smith, "The Subject Makes a Difference: Poetry by Women Veterans of the Vietnam War," *Journal of American Culture* 16.3 (September 1993): 71–79. For an interesting exploration of gender and war poetry, see Susan Schweik, "Writing War Poetry Like a Woman," in *Politics & Poetic Value*, edited by Robert von Hallberg (Chicago: University of Chicago Press, 1987), 159–83. For more on women and the canon of war literature, see Lynne Hanley, *Writing War: Fiction, Gender, and Memory* (Amherst: University of Massachusetts Press, 1991).

17. Ehrhart, in "War, Poetry & Ethics," 10–11, 8.
18. Kalí Tal, *Worlds of Hurt: Reading the Literatures of Trauma* (Cambridge: Cambridge University Press, 1996), 113. Still, even with this emphasis on "the experience of the poet rather than the nominal subject of the poem," I do take care to highlight instances where the identity of the poet and the speaker of the poem clearly diverge.
19. This has meant being as careful as possible with regard to checking the military backgrounds of the poets. For example, there is a degree of uncertainty concerning the veteran status of Bill Shields, so I have avoided using his poetry here. When I found out that the veteran "Ray Catina" is actually the nonveteran Alan Catlin, I removed the one quotation of his that I had used. For more on Shields, see Seth Gotro, "Bill Shields: The SEAL Who Never Was," *Verbicide*, 14 May 2004. On Catina, see W. D. Ehrhart, "Carrying the Ghost of Ray Catina," *War, Literature & the Arts* 16.1–2 (2004): 40–41. It is not that such poets and pseudonyms are without merit, but rather that their experiential base is different from that which provides the primary foundation for this study. Perhaps other "fake" veterans have also slipped through. Nonetheless, I am confident of the authenticity of the poets I refer to most often, and for reference—and reassurance—Appendix A provides the details of the military service of these most frequently mentioned poets.
20. Ehrhart, foreword to *Carrying the Darkness*, xxvi.
21. Ehrhart, introduction to *Unaccustomed Mercy*, 4–5.
22. Jim Nye, *Aftershock: Poems and Prose from the Vietnam War* (El Paso, TX: Cinco Puntos Press, 1991), back cover.
23. While some of the poets, such as Jan Barry, were in Vietnam in the early 1960s, most fought between 1966 and 1970. Additionally, some were drafted and others were volunteers, but because the poets themselves make so little of this distinction, I have not focused on it in this study.
24. It is possible to find a few poets less critical of war and the American involvement in Vietnam. However, they are extreme outliers. In comparison with the vast and prodigious antiwar poetic canon, their poetic production is so minuscule and their publishing footprint so negligible that it would be an unnecessary distraction to include them in this study and a significant distortion to include them in the grouping "the poets" or "the poetry." Indeed, there are really only two noncritical poetic productions worth mentioning. One is a prowar, patriotic anthology published by *Pacific Stars and Stripes* during the war: Forest L. Kimler, ed., *Boondock Bards* (San Francisco: Pacific Stars and Stripes, 1968). The other is *DEROS*, a quarterly journal devoted to poetry written by veterans, published between December 1981 and September 1987.
25. Simon Blackburn, *Being Good: A Short Introduction to Ethics* (Oxford: Oxford University Press, 2001), 59.
26. "A Conversation with W. D. Ehrhart," *War, Literature & the Arts* 8.2 (Fall–Winter 1996): 150.

27. W. D. Ehrhart, "Fog," in *Matters of the Heart* (Easthampton, MA: Adastra Press, 1981), 14.
28. Mark Atwood Lawrence, *The Vietnam War: A Concise International History* (Oxford: Oxford University Press, 2008), 1.
29. With regard to other terminological considerations, I use the single-word "Vietnam" rather than "Viet Nam" purely for ease of reading. References to "south Vietnam" and "north Vietnam," without capitalization of either geographical designation, reflect the widespread view in the poetry that America was involved in a war between people of the same country, not a war between two different and legitimately established states. For more on the idea of south Vietnam as a "state," see James M. Carter, *Inventing Vietnam: The United States and State Building, 1954–1968* (Cambridge: Cambridge University Press, 2008). Although it is now more common, and perhaps correct, to call America's military adversaries from the north the People's Army of Vietnam (PAVN), and those from the south the People's Liberation Armed Forces (PLAF) or perhaps the National Liberation Front (NLF), to maintain consistency with the poets, and to minimize confusion, I use the names most frequently employed in the poetry: the North Vietnamese Army (NVA) and the Vietcong (VC), respectively. Additionally, despite their differences, it is often helpful to refer to the entire grouping of America's Vietnamese opponents as one entity. Here, there is a slight difficulty, since any appellation necessarily attaches a cause to that grouping. For example, to use "communists" would omit the core aim of national liberation and unification. "Nationalists" would be even more problematic, for it would overlook the considerable role of communism in the struggle and ignore the opposing nationalistic claims of America's Vietnamese allies. Hence, I refer to the combined forces of America's Vietnamese opponents, and the eventual victors of the war, simply as the "Vietnamese revolutionaries," but with the awareness that these people fought, as Ho Chi Minh stated, "for the cause of national liberation and the ideal of Communism" (quoted in James Pinckney Harrison, *The Endless War: Fifty Years of Struggle in Vietnam* [New York: Free Press; London: Collier Macmillan, 1982]).
30. For example, Ehrhart appears in Stanley Karnow, *Vietnam: A History* (1983; 2nd ed., London: Penguin Books, 1997), 480–87. However, he is included solely as "a former marine sergeant" and not as a poet. Ehrhart also features in the associated television series *Vietnam: A Television History* (PBS, 1983). A poem by Ehrhart and a poem by Frank A. Cross Jr. are quoted in James William Gibson, *The Perfect War: Technowar in Vietnam* (Boston: Atlantic Monthly Press, 1986), 473–74. Several poems are used by Marilyn B. Young in her epilogue to *The Vietnam Wars, 1945–1990* (New York: HarperPerennial, 1991), 322–27. A poem by David Connolly serves as the afterword to John Prados, *The Blood Road: The Ho Chi Minh Trail and the Vietnam War* (New York: John Wiley & Sons, 1999), 381. A few poets and poems are included in Gerard J. DeGroot, *A Noble Cause? America and the Vietnam War* (Harlow: Longman, 2000). Of course, the focus of broad surveys is not on cultural representations of the war. Nonetheless, given the immensity of the poetic production, the relative absence of the poetry from general historical accounts is something of an oversight.
31. Milton J. Bates, *The Wars We Took to Vietnam: Cultural Conflict and Storytelling* (Berkeley: University of California Press, 1996). The literature on the films is particularly copious. See, for example, Gilbert Adair, *Hollywood's Vietnam: From "The Green Berets" to "Full Metal Jacket"* (London: Heinemann, 1989); Linda Dittmar and Gene Michaud, eds., *From Hanoi to Hollywood: The Vietnam War in American Film* (New Brunswick, NJ: Rutgers University Press, 1990); Michael Anderegg, ed., *Inventing Vietnam: The War in Film and Television* (Philadelphia: Temple University Press,

1991); Jeremy M. Devine, *Vietnam at 24 Frames a Second: A Critical and Thematic Analysis of over 400 Films about the Vietnam War* (Jefferson, NC: McFarland, 1995); Eben J. Muse, *The Land of Nam: The Vietnam War in American Film* (Lanham, MD: Scarecrow Press, 1995); and Frank McAdams, *The American War Film: History and Hollywood* (Westport, CT: Praeger, 2002).

32. Philip D. Beidler, *American Literature and the Experience of Vietnam* (Athens: University of Georgia Press, 1982); Philip K. Jason, *Acts and Shadows: The Vietnam War in American Literary Culture* (Lanham, MD: Rowman & Littlefield, 2000); Donald Ringnalda, *Fighting and Writing the Vietnam War* (Jackson: University Press of Mississippi, 1994). Beidler's other relevant works include *Re-writing America: Vietnam Authors in Their Generation* (Athens: University of Georgia Press, 1991) and *Late Thoughts on an Old War: The Legacy of Vietnam* (Athens: University of Georgia Press, 2004). Jason also edits *Fourteen Landing Zones: Approaches to Vietnam War Literature* (Iowa City: University of Iowa Press, 1991), which contains some helpful and insightful essays covering the poetry, as does the more recent collection edited by Mark Heberle, *Thirty Years After: New Essays on Vietnam War Literature, Film, and Art* (Newcastle upon Tyne: Cambridge Scholars, 2009). Another interesting work that examines the poetry in places is Renny Christopher, *The Viet Nam War / The American War: Images and Representations in Euro-American and Vietnamese Exile Narratives* (Amherst: University of Massachusetts Press, 1995).
33. Beidler, *American Literature and the Experience of Vietnam*, 16.
34. Tal, *Worlds of Hurt*, 78, 114. The chapter mentioned is "The Farmer of Dreams: The Writings of W. D. Ehrhart," 77–114.
35. Michael Bibby, *Hearts and Minds: Bodies, Poetry, and Resistance in the Vietnam Era* (New Brunswick, NJ: Rutgers University Press, 1996), 147. The chapter mentioned is "'Fragging the Chain(s) of Command': Mutilation and GI Resistance Poetry," 123–72.
36. Lorrie Goldensohn, *Dismantling Glory: Twentieth-Century Soldier Poetry* (New York: Columbia University Press, 2003). The chapter mentioned is "American Poets of the Vietnam War," 235–340.
37. James F. Mersmann, *Out of the Vietnam Vortex: A Study of Poets and Poetry against the War* (Lawrence: University Press of Kansas, 1974). For more on stateside protest poetry, see Philip Metres, *Behind the Lines: War Resistance Poetry on the American Homefront since 1941* (Iowa City: University of Iowa Press, 2007).
38. Vince Gotera, *Radical Visions: Poetry by Vietnam Veterans* (Athens: University of Georgia Press, 1994), xii–xiv.
39. W. D. Ehrhart, "'What Grace Is Found in So Much Loss?,'" *Virginia Quarterly Review* 73.1 (Winter 1997): 99–111, http://www.vqronline.org/essay/what-grace-found-so-much-loss.
40. Subarno Chattarji, *Memories of a Lost War: American Poetic Responses to the Vietnam War* (Oxford: Oxford University Press, 2001), 200.
41. Edward Miller, "War Stories: The Taylor-Buzzanco Debate and How We Think about the Vietnam War," *Journal of Vietnamese Studies* 1.1–2 (February–August 2006): 454.
42. Fredrik Logevall, *Choosing War: The Lost Chance for Peace and the Escalation of War in Vietnam* (Berkeley: University of California Press, 1999), xiii. McNamara's admission is from Robert S. McNamara with Brian VanDeMark, *In Retrospect: The Tragedy and Lessons of Vietnam* (New York: Times Books, 1995), xvi.
43. Ronald Reagan, "Peace: Restoring the Margin of Safety," Veterans of Foreign Wars Convention, Chicago, 18 August 1980, https://reaganlibrary.archives.gov/archives/reference/8.18.80.html.
44. There is one work that focuses on morality and the war: Paul T. Menzel, ed., *Moral*

Argument and the War in Vietnam: A Collection of Essays (Nashville: Aurora, 1971). However, this is essentially a primary source collection of wartime political debates, published while the conflict was still ongoing, rather than a moral history of the war.

45. Kendrick Oliver, "Towards a New Moral History of the Vietnam War?," *Historical Journal* 47.3 (September 2004): 757.
46. Kendrick Oliver, *The My Lai Massacre in American History and Memory* (Manchester: Manchester University Press, 2006).
47. Oliver, "Towards a New Moral History of the Vietnam War?," 757.
48. Cotkin, "History's Moral Turn," 294. See also Neil Jumonville, "The Complexity of Moral History: Response to Cotkin," *Journal of the History of Ideas* 69.2 (April 2008): 317–22.
49. Cotkin, "History's Moral Turn," 312.
50. Cotkin, *Morality's Muddy Waters*, 204.
51. See Mark Philip Bradley and Marilyn B. Young, eds., *Making Sense of the Vietnam Wars: Local, National, and Transnational Perspectives* (Oxford: Oxford University Press, 2008). Particularly original and illuminating studies of the war in recent years include Heonik Kwon, *Ghosts of War in Vietnam* (Cambridge: Cambridge University Press, 2008); and Jonathan Tran, *The Vietnam War and Theologies of Memory: Time and Eternity in the Far Country* (Chichester: Wiley-Blackwell, 2010).
52. Jonathan Glover, *Humanity: A Moral History of the Twentieth Century* (New Haven, CT: Yale University Press, 2001), x, 2. The chapter mentioned is "The Case of My Lai," 58–63, which appears in "Part Two: The Moral Psychology of Waging War," 45–116.
53. Ibid., 372, 4.
54. Ibid., 22–30 (emphases added).
55. I am not suggesting either way that morality is or is not dependent on metaphysical or religious justifications, only that in a historical account it is helpful to have a non-metaphysical and non-religious grounding for moral analysis.
56. Ibid., 7.
57. I use the term "just war thinking," rather than the more commonly used "just war tradition," in order to emphasize that it stems from and feeds into a number of different traditions, not just the central Christian strand; that even within the Christian strand there are large-enough chronological gaps between developments to suggest that it is more a system of thought with echoed similarities than a continuous and uninterrupted "tradition"; and, most of all, that it is an active approach and a dynamic process, a mode of *thinking* about war. See Richard Sorabji and David Rodin, eds., *The Ethics of War: Shared Problems in Different Traditions* (Aldershot: Ashgate, 2006).
58. Richard B. Miller, *Interpretations of Conflict: Ethics, Pacifism, and the Just-War Tradition* (Chicago: University of Chicago Press, 1991), 13.
59. Charles Guthrie and Michael Quinlan, *Just War: The Just War Tradition: Ethics in Modern Warfare* (London: Bloomsbury, 2007), 14.
60. See Brian Orend, "Justice after War," *Ethics & International Affairs* 16.1 (March 2002): 43–56.
61. Sorabji and Rodin, introduction to *Ethics of War*, 2. On the assimilation of just war thinking into modern international law, see Karma Nabulsi, "Conceptions of Justice in War: From Grotius to Modern Times," in *Ethics of War*, edited by Sorabji and Rodin, 44–60.
62. Michael Walzer, *Just and Unjust Wars: A Moral Argument with Historical Illustrations* (1977; 4th ed., New York: Basic Books, 2006).
63. The recent renewed attention to just war thinking has been such that in 2011, the

Journal of Moral Philosophy dedicated a special issue to the topic, and in the same year *Ethics* devoted a symposium to the discussion of Jeff McMahan's *Killing in War,* likely to become a classic work on the morality of war. *Journal of Moral Philosophy* 8.4 (November 2011); *Ethics* 122.1 (October 2011); Jeff McMahan, *Killing in War* (Oxford: Clarendon Press, 2009).

64. Two particularly important recent works that challenge orthodox just war thinking are McMahan, *Killing in War;* and David Rodin and Henry Shue, eds., *Just and Unjust Warriors: The Moral and Legal Status of Soldiers* (Oxford: Oxford University Press, 2008).
65. Steve Mason, "A History Lesson," in *Johnny's Song* (Toronto: Bantam Books, 1987), 49.
66. Albert Schweitzer, *The Philosophy of Civilization,* translated by C. T. Campion (Buffalo, NY: Prometheus Books, 1987), 79.
67. Ernest Hemingway, foreword to *Treasury for the Free World,* edited by Ben Raeburn (New York: Arco, 1946), xv.
68. Simon Critchley, *Infinitely Demanding: Ethics of Commitment, Politics of Resistance* (London: Verso, 2008), 55.
69. Viktor E. Frankl, *Man's Search for Meaning,* translated by Ilse Lasch (1946; London: Rider, 2004).
70. Albert Camus, *The Rebel,* translated by Anthony Bower (1951; London: Penguin Books, 2000), 19, 217 (emphasis added).
71. Ibid., 19–20. As Camus notes, the idea of an "awakening" and "the conception of values as pre-existent to any kind of action runs counter to the purely historical schools of philosophy in which values are established (if they are ever established) by action itself. An analysis of rebellion leads us to the suspicion that, contrary to the postulates of contemporary thought, a human nature does exist, as the Greeks believed. Why rebel if there is nothing worth preserving in oneself? The slave asserts himself for the sake of everyone in the world when he comes to the conclusion that a command has infringed on something inside him that does not belong to him alone, but which he has in common with other men—even with the man who insults and oppresses him" (21–22). Thus, Camus's understanding of rebellion contradicts Jean-Paul Sartre's existentialist postulation that existence precedes essence: "man first of all exists, encounters himself, surges up in the world—and defines himself afterwards" (*Existentialism and Humanism,* translated by Philip Mairet [1946; rev. ed., London: Methuen, 2007], 30).
72. Camus, *The Rebel,* 20, 267, 224.
73. The phrasing here borrows from Oscar Wilde's declaration that "vice and virtue are to the artist materials for an art" (*The Picture of Dorian Gray* [1891; London: Penguin Books, 2003], 4).
74. Camus, *The Rebel,* 234, 237, 262.
75. The phrasing here borrows from the title of Albert Camus, *Neither Victims nor Executioners: An Ethic Superior to Murder,* translated by Dwight Macdonald (1946; Eugene, OR: Wipf and Stock, 2007).
76. Camus, *The Rebel,* 250.
77. For more on the nuances of Camus's understanding of violence, see John Foley, "Albert Camus and Political Violence," in *Albert Camus in the 21st Century: A Reassessment of His Thinking at the Dawn of the New Millennium,* edited by Christine Margerrison, Mark Orme, and Lissa Lincoln (Amsterdam: Rodopi, 2008), 207–22. See also Peter Klotz-Chamberlin and Scott Kennedy, "Introduction: An Ethic Superior to Murder," in *Neither Victims nor Executioners,* by Camus, 1–23.

78. Camus, *The Rebel,* 256. As Foley suggests, "Camus's primary claim is that political violence must not be granted institutionalized legitimacy" ("Albert Camus and Political Violence," 219).
79. Horace Coleman, "Notes for Veteran's War Protest," in *In the Grass* (Woodbridge, CT: Viet Nam Generation, Inc. & Burning Cities Press, 1995), 51.
80. Camus, *The Rebel,* 21–22, 216–18.
81. Ibid., 236.
82. I add "and remain" here because Vietnam Veterans Against the War is still running. This declaration on the back cover of one of the key works of poetry summarizes the stance of many of the poets: "He takes pride in having been—and continuing to be—a Vietnam Veteran Against the War" (David Connolly, *Lost in America* [Woodbridge, CT: Viet Nam Generation, Inc. & Burning Cities Press, 1994]).
83. Carolyn Forché, introduction to *Against Forgetting: Twentieth-Century Poetry of Witness,* edited by Carolyn Forché (New York: W. W. Norton, 1993), 29–30. For an examination of poetry of witness by one of the soldier-poets, see James Soular, "American and Vietnamese Poetry of Witness: Bridge over Troubled Waters," in *America's Wars in Asia: A Cultural Approach to History and Memory,* edited by Philip West, Steven I. Levine, and Jackie Hiltz (Armonk, NY: M. E. Sharpe, 1998), 100–123.
84. Carl Gustav Jung, *The Undiscovered Self,* translated by R. F. C. Hull (1958; London: Routledge, 2002), 68–69.
85. Wilfred Owen, "Preface," in *The Poems of Wilfred Owen,* edited by Jon Stallworthy (London: Chatto & Windus, 1990), 192.
86. Forché, introduction to *Against Forgetting,* 34–35.
87. James Aitken, "Lederer's Legacy," in *Free Fire Zone: Short Stories by Vietnam Veterans,* edited by Wayne Karlin, Basil T. Paquet, and Larry Rottmann (New York: McGraw-Hill, 1973), 92.
88. Forché, introduction to *Against Forgetting,* 32.
89. Avishai Margalit, *The Ethics of Memory* (Cambridge, MA: Harvard University Press, 2004), 148–50.
90. Ibid., 151. In his reflections on moral history, Cotkin draws on Margalit's *The Ethics of Memory* to suggest that in "their work at interpreting the past, historians and philosophers are part of this moral witnessing process" ("History's Moral Turn," 312).
91. Margalit, *The Ethics of Memory,* 171.
92. Forché, introduction to *Against Forgetting,* 46.
93. Ibid.
94. For an examination of Camus's own witness, see Shoshana Felman and Dori Laub, *Testimony: Crises of Witnessing in Literature, Psychoanalysis, and History* (New York: Routledge, 1992).
95. Frankl, *Man's Search for Meaning,* 116, 139.
96. Lamont B. Steptoe, "Mad Minute," in *Mad Minute* (1990; Camden, NJ: Whirlwind Press, 1993), 69. As Bruce Weigl notes in his introduction to this collection, Steptoe's work indicates that "in spite of our huge moral transgressions in Vietnam and in our own country, it is possible, through the honorable act of the poem, to survive, to go forward" (viii).
97. Frankl, *Man's Search for Meaning,* 124.
98. Theodor Adorno's initial "poetry after Auschwitz" comment appears in "Cultural Criticism and Society," an essay written in 1949 and first published in 1951 (in *Prisms,* translated by Samuel Weber and Shierry Weber [Cambridge, MA: MIT Press, 1981], 34). The latter remark is from Adorno's 1966 work *Negative Dialectics,* and the full quotation reveals that this was not a complete retraction: "Perennial suffering has as

much right to expression as a tortured man has to scream; hence it may have been wrong to say that after Auschwitz you could no longer write poems. But it is not wrong to raise the less cultural question whether after Auschwitz you can go on living—especially whether one who escaped by accident, one who by rights should have been killed, may go on living. His mere survival calls for the coldness, the basic principle of bourgeois subjectivity, without which there could have been no Auschwitz; this is the drastic guilt of him who was spared" (translated by E. B. Ashton [1966; New York: Seabury Press, 1973], 362–63). Just four years prior to this, Adorno had confined his famous assertion to include only "lyric poetry," but nevertheless reiterated his original position: "I have no wish to soften the saying that to write lyric poetry after Auschwitz is barbaric; it expresses in negative form the impulse which inspires committed literature" ("Commitment," in *Aesthetics and Politics: Theodor Adorno, Walter Benjamin, Ernst Bloch, Bertolt Brecht, Georg Lukács*, by Ernst Bloch et al., edited and translated by Ronald Taylor [London: Verso, 1980], 188). For more on the labyrinthine history of Adorno's comment, see Nouri Gana, "War, Poetry, Mourning: Darwish, Adonis, Iraq," *Public Culture* 22.1 (Winter 2010): 33–65. See also Michael Rothberg, "After Adorno: Culture in the Wake of Catastrophe," *New German Critique* 72 (Autumn 1997): 45–81.

99. Forché, introduction to *Against Forgetting*, 41; Theodor Adorno, *Minima Moralia: Reflections from Damaged Life*, translated by E. F. N. Jephcott (1951; London: Verso, 2005), 25 (emphasis added).
100. Bruce Weigl, "I Put a Shotgun to My Mouth," in *The Unraveling Strangeness* (New York: Grove Press, 2002), 10.
101. Ehrhart, "Visiting My Parents' Graves," in *Beautiful Wreckage*, 220.
102. There are a wide variety of reasons that motivate these veterans to write poetry. Stephen P. Hidalgo suggests that much of the poetry, particularly in the early works, "is therapeutic in the original motive," written to "assuage the unheeded anguish of veterans and to overcome symptoms like the long-term traumatic amnesia characteristic of many cases of Vietnam PTSD, and perhaps most importantly, to come to terms with guilt—either 'survivor guilt' or the guilt incurred by deeds of violence, culpable or not as acts of war" ("Agendas for Vietnam War Poetry: Reading the War as Art, History, Therapy, and Politics," *Journal of American Culture* 16.3 [September 1993]: 7). As the veteran and author David Willson recalls, "There was no counseling for us, nobody to talk to. So many of us wrote poetry. Poured out our souls" ("The Aftermath: Vietnam War Poetry," *VVA Veteran* 34.4 [July–August 2014]: http://vvaveteran.org/34-4/34-4_poetry.html). Some of the poets, however, resist this explanation of a cathartic motivation. Bruce Weigl, for example, states: "I never liked the idea of art as therapy. Maybe it works for some people, but I don't like the idea of poetry as a therapeutic" (in Eric James Schroeder, "Bruce Weigl: 'Poetry Grabbed Me by the Throat,'" in *Vietnam, We've All Been There: Interviews with American Writers* [Westport, CT: Praeger, 1992], 182). Still, even for Weigl there is a sense that the writing of poetry, if not a form of therapy, is nonetheless a form of atonement: "Once I found poetry, I began to see that I could also repair some wrongs simply by telling the truth about my experiences in the war" (in Douglas Valentine, "War, Poetry and Reconciliation: An Interview with Bruce Weigl," *CounterPunch*, 18 October 2013, http://www.counterpunch.org/2013/10/18/war-poetry-and-reconciliation/). As W. D. Ehrhart notes: "my poetry is an ongoing attempt to atone for the unethical, for my loss of a moral compass when I was a young man" (in "War, Poetry & Ethics," 31). Besides therapy, the other "agendas" for the poetry that Hidalgo highlights are art, history, and politics. Hidalgo's group of motives is summarized by David Connolly: "what

I write about is what hurts me, what has woken me up over the years, what I feel needs to be explained to those of you who didn't go through this, and as a political activist . . . my secondary goal is to spur you into getting out from in front of that fucking TV and go stop the current war" (interview by author, Boston, 15 March 2010). There are, of course, plenty more reasons these veterans write poetry, and the precise combination and importance of these motivating factors is unique to each particular poet. However, the central motive that unifies the American soldier-poets of the war in Vietnam, and which itself encompasses and enables many of these other motives, is to bear witness.

103. Bruce Weigl, interview by author, Oberlin, OH, 18 March 2010.
104. Weigl, in Valentine, "War, Poetry and Reconciliation."
105. David Connolly, "My Rights," in *Finding My Way* (Boston: David Connolly and the South Boston Literary Gazette Press, 2005), n.p.
106. Albert Camus, "The Artist and His Time," in *The Myth of Sisyphus,* translated by Justin O'Brien (1942; London: Penguin Books, 2000), 191–92.
107. Denise Levertov, "Statement for a Television Program," in *The Poet in the World* (New York: New Directions, 1973), 123.
108. Denise Levertov, quoted in Mersmann, *Out of the Vietnam Vortex,* 26.
109. Ehrhart, foreword to *Carrying the Darkness,* xxvi.
110. Larry Rottmann, Jan Barry, and Basil T. Paquet, eds., *Winning Hearts and Minds: War Poems by Vietnam Veterans* (New York: McGraw-Hill, 1972). For more on this remarkable anthology and the early publication history of the poetry, see Adam Gilbert, "'And the fire still burns': Vietnam War Poetry, Moral Witness, and *Winning Hearts and Minds,*" *War, Literature & the Arts* 25.1–2 (2013), http://wlajournal.com/wlaarchive/25_1/Gilbert.pdf.
111. See, for example, Robert Bly, *The Light around the Body* (London: Rapp and Whiting, 1968) and *The Teeth-Mother Naked at Last* (San Francisco: City Lights Books, 1970); Allen Ginsberg, *Wichita Vortex Sutra* (London: Housmans, 1966); and Denise Levertov, *The Sorrow Dance* (New York: New Directions, 1967). For more on these poets, see Mersmann, *Out of the Vietnam Vortex.* Pacifist activists, such as Daniel Berrigan, were also writing and publishing poetry during this period: Daniel Berrigan, *Night Flight to Hanoi: War Diary with 11 Poems* (New York: Macmillan, 1968) and *Selected and New Poems* (Garden City, NY: Doubleday, 1973). See also Harry J. Cargas, *Daniel Berrigan and Contemporary Protest Poetry* (New Haven, CT: College & University Press, 1972). Edited volumes of protest poetry supported and promulgated these literary voices, such as Robert Bly and David Ray, eds., *A Poetry Reading against the Vietnam War* (Madison, MN: American Writers Against the Vietnam War, the Sixties Press, 1966); and Walter Lowenfels, ed., *Where Is Vietnam? American Poets Respond* (Garden City, NY: Anchor Books, Doubleday, 1967). Additionally, translations of Vietnamese poetry appeared during the war: Thich Nhat Hanh, *The Cry of Vietnam,* translated by Thich Nhat Hanh and Helen Coutant (Santa Barbara, CA: Unicorn Press, 1968); and Don Luce, John C. Schafer, and Jacquelyn Chagnon, eds., *We Promise One Another: Poems from an Asian War* (Washington, DC: Indochina Mobile Education Project, 1971). For more on the stateside poetry, see Chattarji, *Memories of a Lost War,* 26–97.
112. Kimler, *Boondock Bards.*
113. Chattarji, *Memories of a Lost War,* 103; John Baky, interview by author, Philadelphia, 1 March 2010; Ehrhart interview. For more on *Boondock Bards,* see Chattarji, *Memories of a Lost War,* 103–6.
114. Dick Shea, *vietnam simply* (Coronado, CA: Pro Tem, 1967); Timothy Clover, *The*

Leaves of My Trees, Still Green (Chicago: Adams Press, 1970); Earl E. Martin, *A Poet Goes to War* (Bozeman, MT: Big Sky Books, 1970).

115. Caroline Slocock, "Winning Hearts and Minds: The 1st Casualty Press," *Journal of American Studies* 16.1 (April 1982): 107. Slocock suggests that this lack of interest from publishers was more likely to have been a result of commercial considerations than political reservations and censorship, although one does not have to subscribe to Marxist theories of literary production to understand that the two issues are undoubtedly connected (112–14).
116. Bibby, *Hearts and Minds,* 147.
117. Slocock, "Winning Hearts and Minds," 115. See, for example, "A picture and four poems from the war," *New York Times,* 31 March 1972.
118. Slocock, "Winning Hearts and Minds," 115; John Seelye, review of *Winning Hearts and Minds, New York Times Book Review,* 14 May 1972.
119. Jan Barry, interview by author, South Bound Brook, NJ, 8 March 2010; Jan Barry and W. D. Ehrhart, untitled letter, 23 August 1978, in the Jan Barry Archive (Philadelphia: Imaginative Representations of the Vietnam War Collection, Connelly Library, La Salle University), box 1, folder 16. The exact sales figures of *Winning Hearts and Minds* are unclear. While this particular letter indicates fifty thousand, several other letters in the Barry Archive estimate forty thousand, and Slocock suggests forty-five thousand. Nonetheless, all of these figures are impressive.
120. Slocock, "Winning Hearts and Minds," 116. Slocock writes: "That publishers were initially reluctant to take [*Winning Hearts and Minds*] for commercial rather than political reasons is indicated by the ease with which the 1st Casualty secured a contract of joint publication with McGraw-Hill once they had proved the anthology's potential for success" (112).
121. W. D. Ehrhart, "Soldier-Poets of the Vietnam War," *Virginia Quarterly Review* 63.2 (Spring 1987): 246–65, http://www.vqronline.org/essay/soldier-poets-vietnam-war.
122. D. C. Berry, *saigon cemetery* (Athens: University of Georgia Press, 1972); Michael Casey, *Obscenities* (New Haven, CT: Yale University Press, 1972).
123. Review of *The Million Dollar Hole,* by Michael Casey, *Publishers Weekly,* 1 January 2001.
124. Stephen Spender, "Poetry of the Unspeakable," *New York Review of Books,* 8 February 1973. The two books were also reviewed side by side in the *New York Times Book Review,* 14 May 1972, with Daniel Hoffman's review of Casey's *Obscenities* next to Seelye's above-mentioned review of *Winning Hearts and Minds.*
125. Barry and Ehrhart, *Demilitarized Zones,* iii. There was a poetry anthology published between *Winning Hearts and Minds* and *Demilitarized Zones:* Fred Kiley and Tony Dater, eds., *Listen. The War: A Collection of Poetry about the Viet-Nam War* (Colorado Springs: United States Air Force Academy Association of Graduates, 1973). However, the collection contains no information about individual contributors, so it is not possible to identify which of the poets served in the war. Moreover, it lacks the connections, and the tone, to be considered a sequel to *Winning Hearts and Minds,* even if it does contain a number of poems by Ehrhart.
126. Barry and Ehrhart, introduction to *Demilitarized Zones,* ix.
127. McAvoy Layne, *How Audie Murphy Died in Vietnam* (Garden City, NY: Anchor Books, 1973); Perry Oldham, *Vinh Long* (Meadows of Dan, VA: Northwoods Press, 1976); Gerald McCarthy, *War Story: Vietnam War Poems* (Trumansburg, NY: Crossing Press, 1977).
128. W. D. Ehrhart, *A Generation of Peace* (New York: New Voices, 1975); Stephen P. Hidalgo, "Poetry," in *Vietnam War Literature: An Annotated Bibliography of*

Imaginative Works about Americans Fighting in Vietnam, by John Newman with David A. Willson et al. (1982; 3rd ed., Lanham, MD: Scarecrow Press, 1996), 506.
129. Other works by Ehrhart in the 1970s include *A Generation of Peace* (1975; rev ed., San Jose, CA: Samisdat, 1977), *Rootless* (San Jose, CA: Samisdat, 1977), and *Empire* (Richford, VT: Samisdat, 1978).
130. Bruce Weigl, *A Sack Full of Old Quarrels* (Cleveland: Cleveland State University Poetry Center, 1976), *Executioner* (Tucson, AZ: Ironwood Press, 1976), and *A Romance* (Pittsburgh: University of Pittsburgh Press, 1979).
131. Bruce Weigl, "The Impossible," in *What Saves Us* (Evanston, IL: TriQuarterly Books, 1992), 68.
132. Adorno, *Minima Moralia*, 25.
133. Jan Barry, ed., *Peace Is Our Profession: Poems and Passages of War Protest* (Montclair, NJ: East River Anthology, 1981).
134. Ehrhart, foreword to *Carrying the Darkness*, xxvi. The original title of the anthology, before its 1989 reprint, was *Carrying the Darkness: American Indochina—The Poetry of the Vietnam War* (New York: Avon Books, 1985).
135. The only one missing is Michael Casey, who did not want his poems included in the collection. All the other key poets are represented: Jan Barry, R. L. Barth, D. C. Berry, D. F. Brown, Horace Coleman, Frank A. Cross Jr., W. D. Ehrhart, David Hall, Steve Hassett, David Huddle, Yusef Komunyakaa, McAvoy Layne, Gerald McCarthy, Walter McDonald, Perry Oldham, Basil T. Paquet, Larry Rottmann, and Bruce Weigl. There is, it should be noted, an absence of female writers in *Carrying the Darkness*. See W. D. Ehrhart, foreword to *Visions of War, Dreams of Peace*, edited by Van Devanter and Furey, xvii–xx.
136. Ehrhart interview.
137. Ehrhart, introduction to *Unaccustomed Mercy*, 4. The twelve poets included in *Unaccustomed Mercy* are John Balaban, Jan Barry, D. F. Brown, Michael Casey, Horace Coleman, W. D. Ehrhart, Bryan Alec Floyd, Yusef Komunyakaa, Gerald McCarthy, Walter McDonald, Basil T. Paquet, and Bruce Weigl. Eight of them appear in either *Winning Hearts and Minds* or its sequel, *Demilitarized Zones*.
138. Ehrhart's works in the 1980s include *The Awkward Silence* (Stafford, VA: Northwoods Press, 1980); *The Samisdat Poems* (Richford, VT: Samisdat, 1980); *Matters of the Heart* (Easthampton, MA: Adastra Press, 1981); *Channel Fever* (Port Jefferson, NY: Backstreet Editions, 1982); *Outer Banks; To Those Who Have Gone Home Tired: New and Selected Poems* (New York: Thunder's Mouth Press, 1984); and *Winter Bells* (Easthampton, MA: Adastra Press, 1988). Weigl's two key works in this decade are *The Monkey Wars* (Athens: University of Georgia Press, 1985) and *Song of Napalm* (New York: Atlantic Monthly Press, 1988).
139. Robert Stone, introduction to Weigl, *Song of Napalm*, n.p. Many of the poems in this collection appear in Weigl's earlier work *The Monkey Wars*.
140. Richard E. Baker, *Shell Burst Pond* (Tacoma, WA: Rapier Press, 1980) and *Shell Burst Pond* (1980; 2nd ed., Tacoma, WA: Vardaman Press, 1982); R. L. Barth, *Forced-Marching to the Styx: Vietnam War Poems* (Van Nuys, CA: Perivale Press, 1983), *Looking for Peace* (Omaha: University of Nebraska at Omaha Fine Arts Press, 1985), and *A Soldier's Time: Vietnam War Poems* (Santa Barbara, CA: John Daniel, 1987); Bill Bauer, *The Eye of the Ghost: Vietnam Poems* (Kansas City: BkMk Press, 1986); D. F. Brown, *Returning Fire* (San Francisco: San Francisco State University Poetry Chapbook, 1984); Jabiya Dragonsun, *Hit Parade: Poems* (Philadelphia: In the Tradition Press, 1989); David Hall, *Werewolf and Other Poems* (Fort Collins, CO: Bald Mountain Press, 1981); J. Vincent Hansen, *Blessed Are the Piecemakers: A Collection of Poems And Uncertain Notions* (St. Cloud, MN: North Star Press of St. Cloud,

1989); David Huddle, *Stopping by Home* (Salt Lake City: Peregrine Smith Books, 1988); Steve Mason, *Johnny's Song* (Toronto: Bantam Books, 1987) and *Warrior for Peace* (New York: Touchstone, 1988).

141. Yusef Komunyakaa, *Dien Cai Dau* (Middletown, CT: Wesleyan University Press, 1988).
142. Yusef Komunyakaa, *Neon Vernacular: New and Selected Poems* (Hanover, NH: Wesleyan University Press, 1993).
143. Ehrhart, *Going Back*.
144. As John Baky suggests, "There's a good chance that . . . the Vietnam War genre let's call it, would not be where it is today without Kalí Tal and the establishment of Viet Nam Generation" (interview).
145. Doug Anderson, *Bamboo Bridge* (Amherst, MA: Amherst Writers & Artists Press, 1991) and *The Moon Reflected Fire* (Cambridge, MA: Alice James Books, 1994); Kevin Bowen, *Playing Basketball with the Viet Cong* (Willimantic, CT: Curbstone Press, 1994) and *Forms of Prayer at the Hotel Edison* (Willimantic, CT: Curbstone Press, 1998); Connolly, *Lost in America;* Dale Ritterbusch, *Lessons Learned: Poetry of the Vietnam War and Its Aftermath* (Woodbridge, CT: Viet Nam Generation, Inc. & Burning Cities Press, 1995). These are the four core new poets of the 1990s identified by Ehrhart in his 1997 survey of the poetry, "'What Grace Is Found in So Much Loss?'" Other individual collections published in the 1990s include Bill Bauer, *Last Lambs: New and Selected Poems of Vietnam* (Kansas City: BkMk Press, 1997); Coleman, *In the Grass;* Andrew Gettler, *Footsteps of a Ghost: Poems from Viet Nam* (New Brunswick, NJ: Iniquity Press/Vendetta Books, 1991); H. Palmer Hall, *From the Periphery: Poems and Essays* (San Antonio, TX: Chili Verde Press, 1994); Steve Mason, *The Human Being: A Warrior's Journey Toward Peace and Mutual Healing* (New York: Touchstone, 1990); Gerald McCarthy, *Shoetown* (Bristol, IN: Cloverdale Library, 1992); Nye, *Aftershock;* Leroy V. Quintana, *Interrogations* (Chevy Chase, MD: Viet Nam Generation, Inc. & Burning Cities Press, 1990) and *The Great Whirl of Exile* (Willimantic, CT: Curbstone Press, 1999); Larry Rottmann, *Voices From The Ho Chi Minh Trail: Poetry of America and Vietnam, 1965–1993* (Desert Hot Springs, CA: Event Horizon Press, 1993); James Soular, *The Thousand-Yard Stare* (Canton, CT: Singular Speech Press, 1997); Steptoe, *Mad Minute* and *Uncle's South China Sea Blue Nightmare* (1995; 2nd ed., Philadelphia: Plan B Press, 2003); Peter Ulisse, *Vietnam Voices* (Lewiston, NY: Edwin Mellen Press, 1990); and David Vancil, *The Homesick Patrol* (Woodbridge, CT: Viet Nam Generation, Inc. & Burning Cities Press, 1995). In 1993, the *Journal of American Culture* dedicated an entire issue to the poetry "in an effort to gauge and communicate the continuing vitality of Vietnam War poetry" (Brown and Gotera, introduction to *Journal of American Culture,* 1).
146. Phillip Mahony, ed., *From Both Sides Now: The Poetry of the Vietnam War and Its Aftermath* (New York: Scribner, 1998).
147. Ehrhart, *Beautiful Wreckage;* Bruce Weigl, *Archeology of the Circle: New and Selected Poems* (New York: Grove Press, 1999). Ehrhart's poetic productions in the 1990s include *Just for Laughs; The Distance We Travel* (Easthampton, MA: Adastra Press, 1993); and *Mostly Nothing Happens: A Poem* (Easthampton, MA: Adastra Press, 1996). Weigl's works in this decade include *What Saves Us; Sweet Lorain* (Evanston, IL: TriQuarterly Books, 1996); and *After the Others* (Evanston, IL: TriQuarterly Books, 1999).
148. Doug Anderson, *Blues for Unemployed Secret Police* (Willimantic, CT: Curbstone Press, 2000); Kevin Bowen, *Thai Binh: Great Peace* (Boston: Pressed Wafer, 2009); Connolly, *Finding My Way;* Dale Ritterbusch, *Far From the Temple of Heaven*

(Windsor, ON: Black Moss Press, 2005); Jan Barry, *Earth Songs: New & Selected Poems* (Lincoln, NE: iUniverse, 2003); Michael Casey, *The Million Dollar Hole* (Alexandria, VA: Orchises Press, 2001), *Raiding a Whorehouse* (Easthampton, MA: Adastra Press, 2004), and *Permanent Party* (Greensboro, NC: March Street Press, 2005); W. D. Ehrhart, *Sleeping with the Dead* (Easthampton, MA: Adastra Press, 2006); Gerald McCarthy, *Trouble Light* (Albuquerque, NM: West End Press, 2008); Weigl, *The Unraveling Strangeness* and *Declension in the Village of Chung Luong* (Keene, NY: Ausable Press, 2006). While Horace Coleman has not published a collection since *In the Grass,* he has been a regular contributor to Vietnam Veterans Against the War's publication the *Veteran,* and several of his poems were published there, among other places, in the 2000s. Also in this decade, Yusef Komunyakaa returned to the theme of war with his collection *Warhorses* (New York: Farrar, Straus and Giroux, 2008).

149. W. D. Ehrhart, *The Bodies Beneath the Table* (Easthampton, MA: Adastra Press, 2010); Bruce Weigl, *The Abundance of Nothing* (Evanston, IL: TriQuarterly Books, 2012).
150. Weigl, "Ice Storm," in *The Abundance of Nothing,* 13. In addition to the biblical reference, the first line could allude to the film *Jacob's Ladder,* in which the protagonist is a haunted American veteran of the war in Vietnam (directed by Adrian Lyne [TriStar Pictures, 1990]).
151. W. D. Ehrhart, back cover of Steptoe, *Uncle's South China Sea Blue Nightmare.*

Chapter 1: Climates

1. Dick Shea, "so for some unknown reason," in *vietnam simply* (Coronado, CA: Pro Tem, 1967), n.p.
2. Shea's initial impression notes several concerns that many of the poets engage with, especially in their earlier works: the hostility of Vietnam to the American presence, indicated by the sarcastic welcome; the roughness of the American intervention, echoed by the bumpy landing; the landscape scarred by the American involvement, reflected by the pockmarked runway; the omnipresent danger of a war without fronts, signaled by the heavy security presence on the ground; and the color and warmth of Vietnam. And all this before Shea had even set foot on Vietnamese soil.
3. Gilbert Harman, "Moral Philosophy Meets Social Psychology: Virtue Ethics and the Fundamental Attribution Error," *Proceedings of the Aristotelian Society* 99 (1999): 315. The seminal work that established the term "fundamental attribution error" is Lee Ross, "The Intuitive Psychologist and His Shortcomings: Distortions in the Attribution Process," *Advances in Experimental Social Psychology* 10 (1977): 173–220. This expanded on an important earlier work: Edward E. Jones and Victor A. Harris, "The Attribution of Attitudes," *Journal of Experimental Social Psychology* 3 (1967): 1–24. See also Lee Ross and Richard E. Nisbett, *The Person and the Situation: Perspectives of Social Psychology* (Philadelphia: Temple University Press, 1991).
4. John M. Doris, *Lack of Character: Personality and Moral Behavior* (Cambridge: Cambridge University Press, 2002), 93. It should be noted that this tendency does vary across cultures. Doris suggests that "affection for dispositional interpretation exhibits substantial cultural variation; perhaps Eastern cultures are less prone to overattribution than Western ones" (103). He writes that "it is widely argued that non-Westerners such as the Japanese interpret behavior more in terms of situations and less in terms of personal dispositions than is typical in the West" (105).
5. Edward E. Jones and Richard E. Nisbett, "The Actor and the Observer: Divergent Perceptions of the Causes of Behavior," in *Attribution: Perceiving the Causes*

of Behavior, edited by Edward E. Jones et al. (Morristown, NJ: General Learning Press, 1971), 80.

6. See Bertram F. Malle, "The Actor-Observer Asymmetry in Attribution: A (Surprising) Meta-Analysis," *Psychological Bulletin* 132.6 (2006): 895–919; and Bertram F. Malle, Joshua M. Knobe, and Sarah E. Nelson, "Actor-Observer Asymmetries in Explanations of Behavior: New Answers to an Old Question," *Journal of Personality and Social Psychology* 93.4 (October 2007): 491–514.
7. Jonathan Glover, *Humanity: A Moral History of the Twentieth Century* (New Haven, CT: Yale University Press, 2001), 402.
8. Doris, *Lack of Character,* 2.
9. Harman, "Moral Philosophy Meets Social Psychology," 316.
10. Aleksandr Solzhenitsyn, *The Gulag Archipelago, 1918–56: An Experiment in Literary Investigation,* translated by Thomas P. Whitney and Harry Willets (1973; London: Harvill Press, 2007), 75. Solzhenitsyn also writes: "And just so we don't go around flaunting too proudly the white mantle of the just, let everyone ask himself: 'If my life had turned out differently, might I myself not have become just such an executioner?' It is a dreadful question if one really answers it honestly" (73). Solzhenitsyn's statement is discussed in Glover, *Humanity,* 401–2.
11. Thomas Nagel, "Moral Luck," in *Mortal Questions* (1979; Cambridge: Cambridge University Press, 1997), 25–26. For Nagel, the paradoxical character of moral luck means that "in a sense the problem has no solution" (37).
12. Richard J. Ford III, in Wallace Terry, *Bloods: An Oral History of the Vietnam War by Black Veterans* (New York: Ballantine Books, 1985), 42. This story also appears in Samuel Hynes, *The Soldiers' Tale: Bearing Witness to Modern War* (London: Pimlico, 1998), 195. On moral luck and the My Lai massacre, see George Cotkin, "History's Moral Turn," *Journal of the History of Ideas* 69.2 (April 2008): 309–12.
13. Glover, *Humanity,* 99, 42; James Joll, quoted in Glover, *Humanity,* 194; Simon Blackburn, *Being Good: A Short Introduction to Ethics* (Oxford: Oxford University Press, 2001), 5. For an interesting examination of how time constraints can alter helping behavior, see John M. Darley and C. Daniel Batson, "'From Jerusalem to Jericho': A Study of Situational and Dispositional Variables in Helping Behavior," *Journal of Personality and Social Psychology* 27.1 (July 1973): 100–108. For a starting point on roles, obedience, and conformity, see the following seminal studies: Craig Haney, Curtis Banks, and Philip Zimbardo, "A Study of Prisoners and Guards in a Simulated Prison," *Naval Research Reviews* (September 1973): 1–17; Stanley Milgram, "Behavioral Study of Obedience," *Journal of Abnormal and Social Psychology* 67.4 (October 1963): 371–78; Stanley Milgram, *Obedience to Authority: An Experimental View* (London: Tavistock, 1974); and Solomon E. Asch, "Effects of Group Pressure upon the Modification and Distortion of Judgment," in *Groups, Leadership and Men: Research in Human Relations,* edited by Harold Guetzkow (Pittsburgh: Carnegie Press, 1951), 177–90.
14. Glover, *Humanity,* 48. Glover's short section on unreality in the warzone is titled "'A Plain without a Feature,'" after this particular line from Auden's poem. A verse of this poem also serves as the epigraph for the chapter "Close Combat," in which this section appears.
15. Ibid., 408, 48.
16. Ibid., 408.
17. Ibid., 402.
18. Viktor E. Frankl, *Man's Search for Meaning,* translated by Ilse Lasch (1946; London: Rider, 2004), 75, 133–34.

19. Anthony Burgess, *A Clockwork Orange* (1962; London: Penguin Books, 2000), 63.
20. David Hall, "Military Training in the Very Young," in *Werewolf and Other Poems* (Fort Collins, CO: Bald Mountain Press, 1981), 23.
21. Lamont B. Steptoe, "A Circle of Red," in *Mad Minute* (1990; Camden, NJ: Whirlwind Press, 1993), 1.
22. J. Vincent Hansen, "Bernard," in *Blessed Are the Piecemakers: A Collection of Poems And Uncertain Notions* (St. Cloud, MN: North Star Press of St. Cloud, 1989), 71.
23. William Golding, *Lord of the Flies* (London: Faber and Faber, 1954); Bruce Weigl, "Carp," in *Sweet Lorain* (Evanston, IL: TriQuarterly Books, 1996), 30.
24. For a brief discussion of birds in Weigl's poetry, see Edward J. Rielly, "Bruce Weigl: Out of the Landscape of His Past," *Journal of American Culture* 16.3 (September 1993): 50.
25. Bruce Weigl, "Snowy Egret," in *The Monkey Wars* (Athens: University of Georgia Press, 1985), 44–45. The poem also appears in Weigl's collection *Song of Napalm* (New York: Atlantic Monthly Press, 1988), 48–49.
26. Rielly, "Bruce Weigl," 48; Weigl, "Debris," in *The Monkey Wars,* 3.
27. Weigl, "What I Saw and Did in the Alley," in *Sweet Lorain,* 8
28. Bruce Weigl, "The Happy Land," in *After the Others* (Evanston, IL: TriQuarterly Books, 1999), 8.
29. Weigl, "Song of Napalm," in *The Monkey Wars,* 46–47.
30. James Soular, "The Burning," in *The Thousand-Yard Stare* (Canton, CT: Singular Speech Press, 1997), 49. For more on Kim Phuc and that famous photograph, see Denise Chong, *The Girl in the Picture: The Remarkable Story of Vietnam's Most Famous Casualty* (London: Scribner, 2001).
31. For an interesting filmic exploration of the war and birds, which also seems to picture them as a potential source of salvation, see *Birdy,* directed by Alan Parker (TriStar Pictures, 1984).
32. Soular, "First Kill," in *The Thousand-Yard Stare,* 37–38. See also Soular, "Deerkill," in *The Thousand-Yard Stare,* 61.
33. Bruce Weigl, "The First Father-Murdered Rabbit," in *Declension in the Village of Chung Luong* (Keene, NY: Ausable Press, 2006), 47.
34. Steven Hassna, "Saturday Rip-Off Blues," in *Peace Is Our Profession: Poems and Passages of War Protest,* edited by Jan Barry (Montclair, NJ: East River Anthology, 1981), 101.
35. Rielly, "Bruce Weigl," 48.
36. W. D. Ehrhart, "Just for Laughs," in *Just for Laughs* (Silver Spring, MD: Viet Nam Generation, Inc. & Burning Cities Press, 1990), 12–13.
37. Rielly, "Bruce Weigl," 48.
38. Jan Barry, "War Baby," in *War Baby* (Richford, VT: Samisdat, 1983), 3; David Connolly, interview by author, Boston, 15 March 2010; Bruce Weigl, interview by author, Oberlin, OH, 18 March 2010.
39. Weigl interview. Weigl then reflects on the cultural specificity—or not—of violence and war: "it's the American culture, but it's not just American culture . . . every culture, every historical period, has their own war, and interestingly they each talk about it as if it were an anomaly, even when it's not been the first war . . . how often does it have to happen before you stop calling it an anomaly? How often does it have to happen before you can say, 'you know what, this must be part of who we are'?"
40. Bruce Weigl, "Monkey," in *A Romance* (Pittsburgh: University of Pittsburgh Press, 1979), 17. See Philip D. Beidler, *American Literature and the Experience of Vietnam* (Athens: University of Georgia Press, 1982), 186–87.

41. Hall, "The Ambush of the Fourth Platoon," in *Werewolf*, 20.
42. Hall, "The Pepsi Generation," in *Werewolf*, 27.
43. W. D. Ehrhart, "The Secret Lives of Boys," in *The Bodies Beneath the Table* (Easthampton, MA: Adastra Press, 2010), 14–15. See also Weigl's poem "Eclipse," in which he remembers "playing a silent war game with myself" while wearing "my WW II leather pilot's hat" (in *A Romance*, 34).
44. Randall Jarrell, "The Death of the Ball Turret Gunner," in *The Complete Poems* (New York: Farrar, Straus and Giroux, 1969), 144.
45. D. F. Brown, in "War, Poetry & Ethics: A Symposium," *War, Literature & the Arts* 10.2 (Fall–Winter 1998): 29–30.
46. Barry, "Lessons," in *War Baby*, 11; David Connolly, "All the Stars Do Not Spangle," in *Lost in America* (Woodbridge, CT: Viet Nam Generation, Inc. & Burning Cities Press, 1994), 9.
47. William Powers, "Truth," in *Peace Is Our Profession*, edited by Barry, 92.
48. Steve Mason, "In Victory Or Defeat," in *Warrior for Peace* (New York: Touchstone, 1988), 102.
49. Weigl, "Carp," in *Sweet Lorain*, 30.
50. Don Duncan, "Closing Statement," in *The Winter Soldier Investigation: An Inquiry into American War Crimes*, by Vietnam Veterans Against the War (Boston: Beacon Press, 1972), 167.
51. Brown, in "War, Poetry & Ethics," 30.
52. Barry, "Gifts," in *War Baby*, 2.
53. Glover, *Humanity*, 401; Beidler, *American Literature and the Experience of Vietnam*, 113.
54. McAvoy Layne, "On free haircuts," in *How Audie Murphy Died in Vietnam* (Garden City, NY: Anchor Books, 1973), n.p.
55. Steptoe, "Before Going," in *Mad Minute*, 2.
56. Peter P. Mahoney, "Calley and That Old Bitterness," *New York Times*, 9 January 1974. This also appears in *Peace Is Our Profession*, edited by Barry, 104.
57. Layne, "The mob," in *How Audie Murphy Died in Vietnam;* David Widup, "Red Horse," in *From Both Sides Now: The Poetry of the Vietnam War and Its Aftermath*, edited by Phillip Mahony (New York: Scribner, 1998), 38.
58. Glover, *Humanity*, 48, 51.
59. Mahoney, "Calley and That Old Bitterness," 35.
60. Weigl, "The Nothing Redemption," in *After the Others*, 45.
61. Horace Coleman, "Bring Your Lunch!," in *In the Grass* (Woodbridge, CT: Viet Nam Generation, Inc. & Burning Cities Press, 1995), 10.
62. Lamont B. Steptoe, "uncle's south china sea blue nightmare," in *Uncle's South China Sea Blue Nightmare* (1995; 2nd ed., Philadelphia: Plan B Press, 2003), 49. There is a slight discrepancy in the titling of Steptoe's poem. The title in the contents follows that of the collection itself and is the one I have used here, but on the opening page of the poem two of the words are switched so that it reads instead "uncle's south sea china blue nightmare." It is worth noting that both the country and the people encountered by American soldiers, especially those who fought in the latter part of the war, had been dramatically altered by a long period of American intervention that had seemingly turned Vietnam into a physical and moral wasteland. It was, therefore, a version of Vietnam heavily influenced by American involvement that many soldiers recoiled from—"the rage of Caliban seeing his own face in a glass" (Oscar Wilde, *The Picture of Dorian Gray* [1891; London: Penguin Books, 2003], 3).

63. Weigl uses the phrase "the green war" in several poems, especially in his collection *Sweet Lorain.* See, for instance, "Sitting with the Buddhist Monks, Hue, 1967" (1); "Meditation at Melville Ave." (47); and "Words Like Cold Whiskey between Us and Pain" (57).
64. Shea, "so for some unknown reason," in *vietnam simply.*
65. Perry Oldham, "Epilogue," in *Vinh Long* (Meadows of Dan, VA: Northwoods Press, 1976), 54.
66. David Huddle, "Entry," in *Stopping by Home* (Salt Lake City: Peregrine Smith Books, 1988), 3.
67. Christian G. Appy, *Working-Class War: American Combat Soldiers and Vietnam* (Chapel Hill: University of North Carolina Press, 1993), 27. Although the most commonly reported figure for the average age of Americans serving in Vietnam is nineteen, some sources dispute this and suggest instead the higher but still youthful age of twenty-two. See Patrick Hagopian, *The Vietnam War in American Memory: Veterans, Memorials, and the Politics of Healing* (Amherst: University of Massachusetts Press, 2009), 298, 505n90.
68. Weigl interview. Weigl uses the phrase "the green place" in several poems. See, for instance, "Cleaning out the Shaker Gears, Elyria Foundry, Elyria, Ohio, 1971," in *Sweet Lorain,* 24; and "What He Said When They Made Him Tell Them Everything," in *After the Others,* 14. It also appears several times in his book *The Circle of Hanh: A Memoir* (New York: Grove Press, 2000).
69. Weigl interview.
70. Donald Ringnalda, *Fighting and Writing the Vietnam War* (Jackson: University Press of Mississippi, 1994), 51; Jan Barry, "Green Hell, Green Death," in *Winning Hearts and Minds: War Poems by Vietnam Veterans,* edited by Larry Rottmann, Jan Barry, and Basil T. Paquet (New York: McGraw-Hill, 1972), 65.
71. Beidler, *American Literature and the Experience of Vietnam,* 155.
72. Mostly, the poets focus on the heat of Vietnam, although some do note that it could, at particular times and in certain areas, also become uncomfortably cool. See, for instance, W. D. Ehrhart, "Perimeter Guard," in *A Generation of Peace* (New York: New Voices, 1975), 11.
73. Steve Hassett, "Thanksgiving," in *Carrying the Darkness: The Poetry of the Vietnam War,* edited by W. D. Ehrhart (1985; Lubbock: Texas Tech University Press, 1989), 128–29.
74. Stephen R. Hatch, "Vietnam Clouds," in *Winning Hearts and Minds,* edited by Rottmann, Barry, and Paquet, 74.
75. Weigl, "Monkey," in *A Romance,* 15; Weigl, "Girl at the Chu Lai Laundry," in *The Monkey Wars,* 2; Weigl, "Amnesia," in *The Monkey Wars,* 1. All three poems are reprinted in Weigl's collection *Song of Napalm.*
76. Hall, "The Ambush of the Fourth Platoon," in *Werewolf,* 16.
77. W. D. Ehrhart, interview by author, Philadelphia, 2 March 2010.
78. Beidler, *American Literature and the Experience of Vietnam,* 155–56.
79. Gustav Hasford, *The Short-Timers* (New York: Harper & Row, 1979), 104. See also Beidler, *American Literature and the Experience of Vietnam,* 170.
80. Hassett, "Thanksgiving," in *Carrying the Darkness,* edited by Ehrhart, 128.
81. W. D. Ehrhart and Philip K. Jason, introduction to *Retrieving Bones: Stories and Poems of the Korean War,* edited by W. D. Ehrhart and Philip K. Jason (New Brunswick, NJ: Rutgers University Press, 1999), xviii. For an excellent filmic representation of the relationship between nature, American soldiers, and the war in the Pacific, see *The Thin Red Line,* directed by Terrence Malick (Twentieth Century Fox, 1998).

82. Ehrhart and Jason, introduction to *Retrieving Bones,* xvii–xviii. If the American war in Vietnam, a limited conflict against communists in a faraway and apparently strange Asian land, seemed like an excursion into the unfamiliar, it should not have. The parallels between the war in Vietnam and the war in Korea are numerous and at times quite startling. In their introduction, Ehrhart and Jason offer a good summary of the similarities between the two wars and consider the lessons that the American military should have learned in Korea but did not.
83. Ringnalda, *Fighting and Writing the Vietnam War,* 51.
84. Subarno Chattarji, *Memories of a Lost War: American Poetic Responses to the Vietnam War* (Oxford: Oxford University Press, 2001), 129.
85. Leroy V. Quintana, "Natural History," in *Interrogations* (Chevy Chase, MD: Viet Nam Generation, Inc. & Burning Cities Press, 1990), 62–63.
86. John F. Howe, "The Land," in *Carrying the Darkness,* edited by Ehrhart, 138–39.
87. Connolly interview. That is not to say that there are no disadvantages to fighting on home soil, of course. Still, tactically, the benefits are significant.
88. James D. Lange, "Violence," in *Peace Is Our Profession,* edited by Barry, 14; Ringnalda, *Fighting and Writing the Vietnam War,* 51.
89. Quintana, "Natural History," in *Interrogations,* 62.
90. Steptoe, "uncle's south china sea blue nightmare," in *Uncle's South China Sea Blue Nightmare,* 54.
91. Hansen, "Wallowing at Tuy Hoa," in *Blessed Are the Piecemakers,* 26.
92. John Balaban, quoted in Renny Christopher, *The Viet Nam War / The American War: Images and Representations in Euro-American and Vietnamese Exile Narratives* (Amherst: University of Massachusetts Press, 1995), 246–47. For more on Balaban's fascinating experiences in Vietnam, see his book *Remembering Heaven's Face: A Moral Witness in Vietnam* (New York: Poseidon Press, 1991), reprinted as *Remembering Heaven's Face: A Story of Rescue in Wartime Vietnam* (Athens: University of Georgia Press, 2002). See also John Balaban, *Ca Dao Viet Nam: Vietnamese Folk Poetry* (1974; rev. ed., Port Townsend, WA: Copper Canyon Press, 2003).
93. Bruce Anello, untitled ("April 8"), in *Peace Is Our Profession,* edited by Barry, 26. Anello was killed in Vietnam on 31 May 1968. His name is on Panel 62W, Line 4, of the Vietnam Veterans Memorial in Washington, DC.
94. Chattarji, *Memories of a Lost War,* 134, 129.
95. Yusef Komunyakaa, "Camouflaging the Chimera," in *Dien Cai Dau* (Middletown, CT: Wesleyan University Press, 1988), 3–4.
96. Komunyakaa, "Thanks," in *Dien Cai Dau,* 44.
97. Yusef Komunyakaa, "Autobiography of My Alter Ego," in *Warhorses* (New York: Farrar, Straus and Giroux, 2008), 61, 56.
98. Yusef Komunyakaa, interview by author, New York City, 11 March 2010.
99. See Christopher, *Viet Nam War / American War,* 246–53.
100. Komunyakaa, "Autobiography of My Alter Ego," in *Warhorses,* 58.
101. Steve Mason, "The Casualty," in *Johnny's Song* (Toronto: Bantam Books, 1987), 76.
102. Michael Casey, interview by author, Boston, 13 March 2010. It should be noted that Casey continues: "I don't think it [the climate of fear] entered into some of my friends at all." He suggests, though, "This might be just my reaction and my not seeing through their acting."
103. Steptoe, "letter to momma #2," in *Uncle's South China Sea Blue Nightmare,* 13.
104. Hassett, "Thanksgiving," in *Carrying the Darkness,* edited by Ehrhart, 129.
105. Hall, "The Ambush of the Fourth Platoon," in *Werewolf,* 18.
106. Ehrhart, "In the Valley of the Shadow," in *Just for Laughs,* 15.

107. John Baky, interview by author, Philadelphia, 1 March 2010.
108. Ehrhart, "The Next Step," in *A Generation of Peace,* 14.
109. Weigl, "Mines," in *Song of Napalm,* 43. This is one of Weigl's earliest poems, and a version of it appears in his first collection, *Executioner* (Tucson, AZ: Ironwood Press, 1976).
110. Quintana, "Natural History," in *Interrogations,* 63.
111. Ehrhart, "In the Valley of the Shadow," in *Just for Laughs,* 14–15.
112. Michael Casey, "Road Hazard," in *Obscenities* (New Haven, CT: Yale University Press, 1972), 54.
113. Tim O'Brien, *The Things They Carried* (London: Flamingo, 1991), 17–18.
114. Weigl, "Patrick, in Memory," in *Declension in the Village of Chung Luong,* 43. Other poems that examine this phrase include Kevin Bowen, "First Casualty," in *Playing Basketball with the Viet Cong* (Willimantic, CT: Curbstone Press, 1994), 13; Connolly, "It Don't Mean Nothin," in *Lost in America,* 10; Jim Nye, "Don't Mean Nuthin," in *Aftershock: Poems and Prose from the Vietnam War* (El Paso, TX: Cinco Puntos Press, 1991), 30; and Weigl, "Our Independence Day," in *After the Others,* 61–62. Connolly describes the phrase as "sort of like a self-hypnosis and very necessary if you're going to keep putting one foot in front of the other and not dwell on what just happened five minutes ago and maybe die in the next five minutes because you're not paying attention" (interview).
115. Layne, "Conclusions on courage," in *How Audie Murphy Died in Vietnam.*
116. Horace Coleman, "Twenty-Five Years Ago Today," *Veteran* 30.1 (Spring–Summer 2000), http://www.vvaw.org/veteran/article/?id=139. These two quotes come from a list that begins, "I learned a lot in 'Nam. Namely, that . . ." In our interview, Coleman expands on this: "it's easy sometimes to do something physical, and it's harder to . . . do something that is morally right." Using the example of the civil rights movement and the Freedom Summer, he stresses that moral courage is often linked to not being a bystander (interview by author, Los Angeles, 3 April 2010).
117. David Connolly, "War Wisdom, for What It's Worth" (Connolly interview).
118. James Soular, "Lines," in *The Thousand-Yard Stare* (1997; 2nd ed., n.p.: 1st Books Library, 2004), 81. With the exception of this particular poem, all citations for Soular's *The Thousand-Yard Stare* refer to the original edition of the book.
119. Of course, this is not to suggest that those on military bases had it particularly easy either. See, for instance, Appy, *Working-Class War,* 239.
120. Jim Northrup, *The Rez Road Follies: Canoes, Casinos, Computers, and Birch Bark Baskets* (Minneapolis: University of Minnesota Press, 1999), 202. The situation was slightly different for those soldiers out in the field with mechanized operations. See Philip D. Beidler, *Late Thoughts on an Old War: The Legacy of Vietnam* (Athens: University of Georgia Press, 2004), 83.
121. Hassett, "Thanksgiving," in *Carrying the Darkness,* edited by Ehrhart, 129.
122. Robert E. Peavey, *Praying for Slack: A Marine Corps Tank Commander in Vietnam* (St. Paul, MN: Zenith Press, 2004), 189; Layne, "On lima beans," in *How Audie Murphy Died in Vietnam.* See also Quintana, "Birdshit, Ham and Lima Beans and Heroism," in *Interrogations,* 81.
123. Northrup, *Rez Road Follies,* 202.
124. O'Brien, *The Things They Carried,* 6–17.
125. Frank A. Cross Jr., "Heat Casualties," in *Reminders* (Big Timber, MT: Seven Buffaloes Press, 1986), 8.
126. Cross, "Jungle Rot," in *Reminders,* 14.
127. Cross, "The Light Colonel," in *Reminders,* 6.

128. Ehrhart, "The Bob Hope Christmas Special," in *A Generation of Peace*, 12.
129. Ehrhart, "Another Life," in *A Generation of Peace*, 22.
130. This is similar to what C. D. B. Bryan identifies as the "Generic Vietnam War Narrative," which "charts the gradual deterioration of order, the disintegration of idealism, the breakdown of character, the alienation from those at home, and, finally, the loss of all sensibility save the will to survive" ("Barely Suppressed Screams: Getting a Bead on Vietnam War Literature," *Harper's* 268 [June 1984]: 68–69). See also Fred Turner, *Echoes of Combat: The Vietnam War in American Memory* (New York: Anchor Books, 1996), 133–34.
131. See chapter 4 for more on the poetic account of responsibility.
132. Appy, *Working-Class War*, 117.
133. Shea, "it is detrimental to morale," in *vietnam simply*.
134. W. D. Ehrhart, "Soldier-Poets of the Vietnam War," *Virginia Quarterly Review* 63.2 (Spring 1987): 246–65, http://www.vqronline.org/essay/soldier-poets-vietnam-war.
135. Shea, "i am shitfaced," in *vietnam simply*.
136. Appy, *Working-Class War*, 207–8.
137. Ehrhart, "Soldier-Poets of the Vietnam War."
138. Mason, "The Casualty," in *Johnny's Song*, 78.
139. Connolly interview; Connolly, "Tet, Plus Twenty Four," in *Lost in America*, 40. This poem is dedicated to Ehrhart.
140. Steptoe, "letter to momma #2," in *Uncle's South China Sea Blue Nightmare*, 13; Hall, "The Ambush of the Fourth Platoon," in *Werewolf*, 15.
141. D. F. Brown, "The First Law of Landscaping/May 30, 1990," *War, Literature & the Arts* 10.2 (Fall–Winter 1998): 42.
142. Hall, "The Ambush of the Fourth Platoon," in *Werewolf*, 17.
143. Hansen, "Uncertain Notions," in *Blessed Are the Piecemakers*, 85.
144. Hall, "The Ambush of the Fourth Platoon," in *Werewolf*, 18.
145. Steptoe, "letter to momma #2," in *Uncle's South China Sea Blue Nightmare*, 13; Hall, "The Ambush of the Fourth Platoon," in *Werewolf*, 15.
146. Layne, "On deference," in *How Audie Murphy Died in Vietnam;* Marion Parker [pseud.], "The Children," in *Demilitarized Zones: Veterans after Vietnam*, edited by Jan Barry and W. D. Ehrhart (Perkasie, PA: East River Anthology, 1976), 31; Steptoe, "Gulf of Tonkin," in *Mad Minute*, 28; Cross, "What Are You Going to Be?," in *Reminders*, 1; Hall, "The Ambush of the Fourth Platoon," in *Werewolf*, 20; Ehrhart, "In the Valley of the Shadow," in *Just for Laughs*, 14.
147. Perry Oldham, "And Now," in *Demilitarized Zones*, edited by Barry and Ehrhart, 21; W. D. Ehrhart, quoted in Stanley Karnow, *Vietnam: A History* (1983; 2nd ed., London: Penguin Books, 1997), 487.
148. Ehrhart interview.
149. David Cortright, *Soldiers in Revolt: GI Resistance during the Vietnam War* (1975; rev. ed., Chicago: Haymarket Books, 2005).
150. D. F. Brown, "Still Later There Are War Stories," in *Unaccustomed Mercy: Soldier-Poets of the Vietnam War*, edited by W. D. Ehrhart (Lubbock: Texas Tech University Press, 1989), 42; Glover, *Humanity*, 158. Glover discusses soldiers' experiences of feeling trapped during the First World War and here, in this quote about "helpless resignation," is referring to the poet Siegfried Sassoon.
151. Mason, "The Casualty," in *Johnny's Song*, 77.
152. Kyle Longley, *Grunts: The American Combat Soldier in Vietnam* (Armonk, NY: M. E. Sharpe, 2008), 80.
153. Mason, "The Casualty," in *Johnny's Song*, 75; Karnow, *Vietnam*, 486.

154. Mason, "The Casualty," in *Johnny's Song,* 86.
155. R. L. Barth, "1992: Consolation," in *Small Arms Fire* (n.p., 1994), 19. The phrase "fear of censure" alludes to Ezra Pound, "Hugh Selwyn Mauberley," in *Selected Poems and Translations,* edited by Richard Sieburth (London: Faber and Faber, 2011), 112–13.
156. R. L. Barth, "Why We Fight," in *Simonides in Vietnam* (n.p., 1990), 9.
157. R. L. Barth, "Epitaph," in *Deeply Dug In* (Albuquerque: University of New Mexico Press, 2003), 20.
158. W. D. Ehrhart, in "War, Poetry & Ethics," 8.
159. Gerald McCarthy, interview by author, New York City, 10 March 2010.
160. Albert Camus, *The Rebel,* translated by Anthony Bower (1951; London: Penguin Books, 2000), 20.
161. Ehrhart interview.
162. Barry and Ehrhart, introduction to *Demilitarized Zones*, ix.
163. Soular, "Terminus Ad Quem, 1967," in *The Thousand-Yard Stare,* 35. As indicated previously, the tour of a Marine was thirteen months. Also, some soldiers extended their tour, sometimes, as with Connolly, in the hope of a quicker discharge from the military once they returned to America (interview).
164. Beidler, *American Literature and the Experience of Vietnam,* 6.
165. Soular, "Terminus Ad Quem, 1967," in *The Thousand-Yard Stare,* 35.
166. Peter Ulisse, "Captain Windslow," in *Vietnam Voices* (Lewiston, NY: Edwin Mellen Press, 1990), 75.
167. Andrew Gettler, "redeye special," in *Footsteps of a Ghost: Poems from Viet Nam* (New Brunswick, NJ: Iniquity Press / Vendetta Books, 1991), n.p.
168. B. D. Trail, "With My Shield or On It," quoted in David Willson, "A Few Well-Chosen Words: Extraordinary, Neglected Vietnam War Poets," *VVA Veteran* 31.1 (January–February 2011): 34.
169. Soular, "The Tunnel," in *The Thousand-Yard Stare,* 31.
170. Siegfried Sassoon, "Prelude: The Troops," in *The War Poems,* arranged by Rupert Hart-Davis (1983; London: Faber and Faber, 2006), 93. Here, Sassoon also hints that war kills youth even in those who make it back alive.
171. Gettler, "redeye special," in *Footsteps of a Ghost.*
172. Jon Forrest Glade, "Freedom Bird," in *Photographs of the Jungle* (St. John, KS: Chiron Review Press, 1990), 37.
173. Ulisse, "Captain Windslow," in *Vietnam Voices,* 75.
174. Ehrhart, "Coming Home," in *A Generation of Peace,* 24. See also Gerald McCarthy, "War Story," in *War Story: Vietnam War Poems* (Trumansburg, NY: Crossing Press, 1977), 23.
175. Soular, "Terminus Ad Quem, 1967," in *The Thousand-Yard Stare,* 35–36.
176. Coleman, "D-Day + 50; Tet + 25," in *In the Grass,* 43.
177. Longley, *Grunts,* 159–60.
178. The homecoming problems faced by American veterans of the Second World War, including the feeling of resentment and the difficulty of reintegration that have so burdened the identity of American veterans of the war in Vietnam, are expertly explored in Kenneth D. Rose, *Myth and the Greatest Generation: A Social History of Americans in World War II* (New York: Routledge, 2008), 225–50.
179. Longley, *Grunts,* 160.
180. Soular, "Terminus Ad Quem, 1967," in *The Thousand-Yard Stare,* 35.
181. For a neat summary of the "spitting image" problem and encounters between returning soldiers and antiwar activists, see Longley, *Grunts,* 160–61. The classic

work on this issue is Jerry Lembcke, *The Spitting Image: Myth, Memory, and the Legacy of Vietnam* (New York: New York University Press, 1998).

182. Soular, "Terminus Ad Quem, 1967," in *The Thousand-Yard Stare*, 35.
183. George C. Herring, *America's Longest War: The United States and Vietnam, 1950–1975* (1979; 3rd ed., New York: McGraw-Hill, 1996), 306.
184. Baky interview.
185. Robert A. Moore, "I'm home, America," in *Demilitarized Zones*, edited by Barry and Ehrhart, 45 (ellipses in original).
186. Decades later, on 7 March 2011, the Senate passed by unanimous consent a resolution expressing support for the designation of 30 March, the date on which American troops were withdrawn from Vietnam in 1973, as "Welcome Home Vietnam Veterans Day" (https://www.govtrack.us/congress/bills/112/sres55).
187. Steptoe, "Returnee," in *Mad Minute*, 14.
188. Ehrhart interview.
189. Gettler, "the old guard," in *Footsteps of a Ghost*.
190. William Jayne, "Immigrants from the Combat Zone," in *The Wounded Generation: America after Vietnam*, edited by A. D. Horne (Englewood Cliffs, NJ: Prentice-Hall, 1981), 161.
191. Jonathan Tran, *The Vietnam War and Theologies of Memory: Time and Eternity in the Far Country* (Chichester: Wiley-Blackwell, 2010), 189.
192. Weigl, "And we came home," in *After the Others*, 37.
193. Ibid., 38.
194. W. D. Ehrhart, "Letter," in *Beautiful Wreckage: New & Selected Poems* (Easthampton, MA: Adastra Press, 1999), 30. This poem, which originally appears in Ehrhart's collection *Empire* (Richford, VT: Samisdat, 1978), is addressed "to a North Vietnamese soldier whose life crossed paths with mine in Hue City, February 5th, 1968."
195. Richard E. Baker, "There Are no Sins Inside The Gates of Eden," in *Shell Burst Pond* (1980; 2nd ed., Tacoma, WA: Vardaman Press, 1982), 17, 19.
196. Peter P. Mahoney, "The Airport," in *Demilitarized Zones*, edited by Barry and Ehrhart, 13.
197. Gary Rafferty, "Twins," in *From Both Sides Now*, edited by Mahony, 217.
198. McCarthy, "War Story," in *War Story*, 26.
199. Quoted in John Clark Pratt, preface to *Vietnam Voices: Perspectives on the War Years, 1941–1975*, edited by John Clark Pratt (1984; Athens: University of Georgia Press, 1999), v.
200. Hansen, "On Belonging," in *Blessed Are the Piecemakers*, 64–65.
201. Weigl, "On the Anniversary of Her Grace," in *Song of Napalm*, 54.
202. Weigl, "Our Independence Day," in *After the Others*, 61.
203. Kalí Tal, *Worlds of Hurt: Reading the Literatures of Trauma* (Cambridge: Cambridge University Press, 1996), 87.
204. Bill Bauer, "Agent Ash," in *Last Lambs: New and Selected Poems of Vietnam* (Kansas City: BkMk Press, 1997), 39.
205. Bruce Weigl, foreword to Larry Rottmann, *Voices From The Ho Chi Minh Trail: Poetry of America and Vietnam, 1965–1993* (Desert Hot Springs, CA: Event Horizon Press, 1993), n.p.
206. Mason, "In Victory Or Defeat," in *Warrior for Peace*, 101.
207. Ibid., 103.
208. Weigl, foreword to Rottmann, *Voices From The Ho Chi Minh Trail*.
209. W. D. Ehrhart, "Vietnam Veterans, After All," in *Demilitarized Zones*, edited by Barry and Ehrhart, 126. Of course, almost immediately veterans disagreed with

each other over the meaning and morality of the war. For example, Vietnam Veterans Against the War, which many of the poets joined, was opposed by Vietnam Veterans for a Just Peace, which defended government policy on the war and attacked antiwar veterans. However, it should be noted that the latter group was set up by the Nixon administration and, as Andrew E. Hunt suggests, "consisted of nothing more than a desk in the White House and one prowar veteran, John O'Neill" (*The Turning: A History of Vietnam Veterans Against the War* [New York: New York University Press, 1999], 90). See also Rick Perlstein, *Nixonland: The Rise of a President and the Fracturing of America* (New York: Scribner, 2008), 576.

210. Ehrhart, "A Relative Thing," in *A Generation of Peace*, 28.
211. Landon Thorne, "Brothers," in *Winning Hearts and Minds*, edited by Rottmann, Barry, and Paquet, 105.
212. Stan Platke, "Postface," in *Peace Is Our Profession*, edited by Barry, 291.
213. Ehrhart interview.
214. Dale Ritterbusch, "Geography Lesson," in *Lessons Learned: Poetry of the Vietnam War and Its Aftermath* (Woodbridge, CT: Viet Nam Generation, Inc. & Burning Cities Press, 1995), 15. Such homecoming issues are still with Ritterbusch as he picks through the debris of the war in Iraq, an observer of the repeatability of history. See the section "Perpetual War" in chapter 4. For more on representations of homecoming and the home front, see Maureen Ryan, *The Other Side of Grief: The Home Front and the Aftermath in American Narratives of the Vietnam War* (Amherst: University of Massachusetts Press, 2008). For an insightful overview of how the poets have portrayed life after the war in the long term, see David Willson, "The Aftermath: Vietnam War Poetry," *VVA Veteran* 34.4 (July–August 2014), http://vvaveteran.org/34-4/34-4_poetry.html.

Chapter 2: Others

1. Jim Nye, "This Ground Is Indifferent," in *Aftershock: Poems and Prose from the Vietnam War* (El Paso, TX: Cinco Puntos Press, 1991), 24.
2. Jonathan Glover, *Humanity: A Moral History of the Twentieth Century* (New Haven, CT: Yale University Press, 2001), 28.
3. Peter Gay, *Freud: A Life for Our Time* (1988; New York: W. W. Norton, 1998), 281.
4. Julia Kristeva, *Strangers to Ourselves*, translated by Leon S. Roudiez (New York: Columbia University Press, 1991), 1, 191.
5. Carl Gustav Jung, *The Undiscovered Self*, translated by R. F. C. Hull (1958; London: Routledge, 2002), 71.
6. Glover, *Humanity*, 28.
7. Simon Blackburn, *Being Good: A Short Introduction to Ethics* (Oxford: Oxford University Press, 2001), 8.
8. Paul Fussell, *The Great War and Modern Memory* (London: Oxford University Press, 1977), 75.
9. Janis Haswell, "The Lesson Unlearned: Moral Trauma in Andrew Jolly's *A Time of Soldiers*," in *Thirty Years After: New Essays on Vietnam War Literature, Film, and Art*, edited by Mark Heberle (Newcastle upon Tyne: Cambridge Scholars, 2009), 451.
10. Simone Weil, "The *Iliad* or the Poem of Force," in *An Anthology*, edited by Siân Miles (London: Penguin Books, 2005), 183.
11. Yusef Komunyakaa, interview by author, New York City, 11 March 2010.
12. David Connolly, interview by author, Boston, 15 March 2010.

13. Che Guevara, *Guerrilla Warfare* (1961; Harmondsworth: Penguin Books, 1970), 18.
14. Peter Singer, *The Life You Can Save: Acting Now to End World Poverty* (London: Picador, 2009), 16.
15. Komunyakaa interview.
16. To use Martin Buber's terminology, this is not an *I-It* but an *I-Thou* relation: "If I face a human being as my *Thou* . . . he is not a thing among things, and does not consist of things" (*I and Thou,* translated by Ronald Gregor Smith [1923; 2nd ed., London: Continuum, 2004], 15).
17. Kristeva, *Strangers to Ourselves,* 1.
18. Harper Lee, *To Kill a Mockingbird* (1960; London: Vintage, 2004), 31.
19. Rollo May, *The Courage to Create* (1975; New York: W. W. Norton, 1994), 16–17.
20. Simon Baron-Cohen, *Zero Degrees of Empathy: A New Theory of Human Cruelty* (London: Allen Lane, 2011).
21. Robert S. McNamara et al., *Argument without End: In Search of Answers to the Vietnam Tragedy* (New York: PublicAffairs, 1999), 376, 390.
22. *The Fog of War: Eleven Lessons from the Life of Robert S. McNamara,* directed by Errol Morris (Sony Pictures Classics, 2003).
23. Simon Critchley, "Calm—On Terrence Malick's *The Thin Red Line,*" in *The Thin Red Line,* edited by David Davies (London: Routledge, 2009), 20–21.
24. James F. Mersmann, *Out of the Vietnam Vortex: A Study of Poets and Poetry against the War* (Lawrence: University Press of Kansas, 1974), 23, 28–29. In "A Supermarket in California," Allen Ginsberg asks Walt Whitman: "Are you my Angel?" (in *Howl and Other Poems* [1956; San Francisco: City Lights Books, 2006], 29). With regard to Whitman's "all-embracing love," it should be noted that this did not extend to everyone: "Whitman's all-embracing love for Americans was, in effect, limited to white Americans" (Ken Peeples Jr., "The Paradox of the 'Good Gray Poet' (Walt Whitman on Slavery and the Black Man)," *Phylon* 35.1 [First Quarter 1974]: 22). This is particularly evident in Whitman's prose writings, if not in his poetry: "the explicitly racist (if altogether conventional) attitudes that pervade much of his journalism seem deeply at odds with the egalitarian spirit of his poetry generally and the deeply sympathetic and admiring verse portraits of African Americans he creates" (Paul H. Outka, "Whitman and Race ('He's Queer, He's Unclear, Get Used to It')," *Journal of American Studies* 36.2 [August 2002]: 295).
25. Kate McLoughlin, *Authoring War: The Literary Representation of War from the "Iliad" to Iraq* (Cambridge: Cambridge University Press, 2011), 192–94. See Emmanuel Lévinas, *Totality and Infinity: An Essay on Exteriority,* translated by Alphonso Lingis (1961; Pittsburgh: Duquesne University Press, 1969).
26. Viktor E. Frankl, *Man's Search for Meaning,* translated by Ilse Lasch (1946; London: Rider, 2004), 116.
27. Albert Camus, *The Rebel,* translated by Anthony Bower (1951; London: Penguin Books, 2000), 21–23, 27–28, 240, 216.
28. Don Duncan, "Closing Statement," in *The Winter Soldier Investigation: An Inquiry into American War Crimes,* by Vietnam Veterans Against the War (Boston: Beacon Press, 1972), 167–68.
29. Bruce Weigl, interview by author, Oberlin, OH, 18 March 2010.
30. Connolly interview.
31. Komunyakaa interview.
32. See Henry J. Laskowsky, "*Alamo Bay* and the Gook Syndrome," *Vietnam Generation* 1.2 (Spring 1989): 130–39.
33. W. D. Ehrhart, "Making the Children Behave," in *Beautiful Wreckage: New & Selected*

Poems (Easthampton, MA: Adastra Press, 1999), 15. An early version of this poem appears in *Demilitarized Zones: Veterans after Vietnam*, edited by Jan Barry and W. D. Ehrhart (Perkasie, PA: East River Anthology, 1976), 67.

34. Renny Christopher, *The Viet Nam War / The American War: Images and Representations in Euro-American and Vietnamese Exile Narratives* (Amherst: University of Massachusetts Press, 1995), 250. Christopher offers an excellent overview of the history of American representations of Asians and a noteworthy analysis of literary depictions of the Vietnamese.
35. H. Bruce Franklin, *Vietnam and Other American Fantasies* (Amherst: University of Massachusetts Press, 2000), 33.
36. For more on the idea of "Orientalism," see Edward W. Said, *Orientalism* (London: Routledge & Kegan Paul, 1978). On its opposite, see Ian Buruma and Avishai Margalit, *Occidentalism: The West in the Eyes of Its Enemies* (New York: Penguin Press, 2004). For an examination of "Orientalism" with specific regard to war, see Patrick Porter, *Military Orientalism: Eastern War through Western Eyes* (New York: Columbia University Press, 2009). For an interesting exploration of the role of race in the relationship between America and Asia, see Matthew Jones, *After Hiroshima: The United States, Race and Nuclear Weapons in Asia, 1945–1965* (Cambridge: Cambridge University Press, 2010).
37. Dick Shea, "orient is strange," in *vietnam simply* (Coronado, CA: Pro Tem, 1967), n.p.
38. Robert S. McNamara with Brian VanDeMark, *In Retrospect: The Tragedy and Lessons of Vietnam* (New York: Times Books, 1995), 321–22.
39. George C. Herring, "The Big Muddy," review of *A Time for War: The United States and Vietnam, 1941–1975*, by Robert D. Schulzinger, *Los Angeles Times Book Review*, 11 May 1997.
40. David Connolly, "To the Irish Americans Who Fought the Last War," in *Lost in America* (Woodbridge, CT: Viet Nam Generation, Inc. & Burning Cities Press, 1994), 39.
41. Serigo [Igor Bobrowsky], "I Hate You . . . ," in *Winning Hearts and Minds: War Poems by Vietnam Veterans*, edited by Larry Rottmann, Jan Barry, and Basil T. Paquet (New York: McGraw-Hill, 1972), 86.
42. Subarno Chattarji, *Memories of a Lost War: American Poetic Responses to the Vietnam War* (Oxford: Oxford University Press, 2001), 117–18. Chattarji cites Herbert Marcuse, *An Essay on Liberation* (London: Allen Lane, 1969), 74.
43. Shea, "a dead man was on the beach today," "went fishing with some vietnamese military," and "there's no war here," in *vietnam simply*. This was a view shared by General William Westmoreland, as captured in the Oscar-winning documentary *Hearts and Minds*: "Well, the Oriental doesn't put the same high price on life as does the Westerner. Life is plentiful, life is cheap in the Orient, and as the philosophy of the Orient expresses it, life is not important" (directed by Peter Davis [Warner Bros. Pictures, 1974]).
44. Stanley Karnow, introduction to *From Both Sides Now: The Poetry of the Vietnam War and Its Aftermath*, edited by Phillip Mahony (New York: Scribner, 1998), 23.
45. John Kerry appeared before the Senate Foreign Relations Committee on 22 April 1971, and his testimony was published in the *Congressional Record*. For an accessible print version, see the extract "Statement before the Senate Foreign Affairs Committee," in *The Vietnam Reader*, edited by Walter Capps (New York: Routledge, 1991), 152–56. An excerpt also appears as "Testimony to Congress," in *Peace Is Our Profession: Poems and Passages of War Protest*, edited by Jan Barry (Montclair, NJ: East River Anthology, 1981), 154–57.

46. Komunyakaa interview.
47. W. D. Ehrhart, "Glossary of Unfamiliar Terms," in *Carrying the Darkness: The Poetry of the Vietnam War,* edited by W. D. Ehrhart (1985; Lubbock: Texas Tech University Press, 1989), xxix.
48. For more on the discrimination requirement and the American violation of it in Vietnam, see the section "Distinctions" in this chapter.
49. Gordon S. Livingston, "Letter from a Vietnam Veteran," in *Crimes of War: A Legal, Political-Documentary, and Psychological Inquiry into the Responsibility of Leaders, Citizens, and Soldiers for Criminal Acts in Wars,* edited by Richard A. Falk, Gabriel Kolko, and Robert Jay Lifton (New York: Random House, 1971), 433 (emphasis added).
50. Joseph M. Shea, "Comfortable people do not look," in *Peace Is Our Profession,* edited by Barry, 24.
51. Jan Barry, "Memorial For Man In Black Pajamas," in *Winning Hearts and Minds,* edited by Rottmann, Barry, and Paquet, 94.
52. Yusef Komunyakaa, "Autobiography of My Alter Ego," in *Warhorses* (New York: Farrar, Straus and Giroux, 2008), 66.
53. J. Vincent Hansen, "A Thousand Words of Hate," in *Blessed Are the Piecemakers: A Collection of Poems And Uncertain Notions* (St. Cloud, MN: North Star Press of St. Cloud, 1989), 39.
54. Hansen, "Hate," in *Blessed Are the Piecemakers,* 93.
55. Peter Berenbak, "The Game," in *Peace Is Our Profession,* edited by Barry, 72.
56. Kyle Longley, *Grunts: The American Combat Soldier in Vietnam* (Armonk, NY: M. E. Sharpe, 2008), 28. For more on racial dynamics as portrayed in the poetry, see the section "Race Relations among Americans in Vietnam" in Vince Gotera, *Radical Visions: Poetry by Vietnam Veterans* (Athens: University of Georgia Press, 1994), 152–65; the section "Brothers in the Nam" in Lorrie Goldensohn, *Dismantling Glory: Twentieth-Century Soldier Poetry* (New York: Columbia University Press, 2003), 289–96; Shirley A. J. Hanshaw, "Refusal to Be Can(n)on Fodder: African American Representation of the Vietnam War and Canon Formation," in *Thirty Years After,* edited by Heberle, 123–41; and Catherine Calloway, "In Their Own Voices: The Chicano Experience in Vietnam War Literature," in *Thirty Years After,* edited by Heberle, 142–55.
57. Christian G. Appy, *Working-Class War: American Combat Soldiers and Vietnam* (Chapel Hill: University of North Carolina Press, 1993), 246. See also George Lepre, *Fragging: Why U.S. Soldiers Assaulted Their Officers in Vietnam* (Lubbock: Texas Tech University Press, 2011).
58. For more on issues of class, see Appy, *Working-Class War.*
59. For more on black Americans and the war, see James E. Westheider, *Fighting on Two Fronts: African Americans and the Vietnam War* (New York: New York University Press, 1997); and his more recent book *The African American Experience in Vietnam: Brothers in Arms* (Lanham, MD: Rowman & Littlefield, 2008).
60. Taking stock of the "Book corpus of Vietnam" in 1985, James William Gibson bemoaned the lack of racial minorities in literary representations of the war, in terms of both their depicted presence and their authorship, and suggested that the "present book corpus does not provide adequate accounts of race relations among combat troops and commanders" (*The Perfect War: Technowar in Vietnam* [Boston: Atlantic Monthly Press, 1986], 469). Yet, as this section demonstrates, the poets are sensitive to racial issues in their work, and even at that time two important black poets, Komunyakaa and Horace Coleman, were already writing, and Steptoe would soon

emerge, as would a significant Latino voice, Leroy V. Quintana, and also a Native American veteran poet, Jim Northrup. For more on Coleman's poetic representation of racial issues, see Gotera, *Radical Visions,* 165–69.

61. Lamont B. Steptoe, "they want to take my life," in *Uncle's South China Sea Blue Nightmare* (1995; 2nd ed., Philadelphia: Plan B Press, 2003), 18. In the previous poem in the collection, "street crossings," Steptoe uses the more common spelling "Cu Chi" (17).
62. Steptoe, "they want to take my life," in *Uncle's South China Sea Blue Nightmare,* 18–19.
63. Steptoe, "uncle's south china sea blue nightmare," in *Uncle's South China Sea Blue Nightmare,* 60. There is a slight discrepancy in the titling of this poem. See chapter 1, note 62.
64. Longley, *Grunts,* 128. See also Westheider, *Fighting on Two Fronts,* 12–13; and Westheider, *African American Experience in Vietnam,* 47–49.
65. Steptoe, "uncle's south china sea blue nightmare," in *Uncle's South China Sea Blue Nightmare,* 61.
66. For more on the poetry of Komunyakaa, see Angela M. Salas, *Flashback through the Heart: The Poetry of Yusef Komunyakaa* (Selinsgrove, PA: Susquehanna University Press, 2004), which includes an investigation of his "war poetry" in the chapter "'Condemned to Carry the Weight of Our Own Hearts': Wartime Memories in *Dien Cai Dau,*" 65–87. For a more detailed account of war and race in Komunyakaa's poetry than it is possible to provide here, see Nancy Esposito, "Yusef Komunyakaa, the U.S. Military, the Interracial DMZ," in *Thirty Years After,* edited by Heberle, 110–22.
67. Komunyakaa interview.
68. Ibid.
69. Yusef Komunyakaa, "Hanoi Hannah," in *Dien Cai Dau* (Middletown, CT: Wesleyan University Press, 1988), 13.
70. Komunyakaa, "Report from the Skull's Diorama," in *Dien Cai Dau,* 47.
71. Komunyakaa, "The One-legged Stool," in *Dien Cai Dau,* 40–42.
72. Komunyakaa interview.
73. Komunyakaa, "Starlight Scope Myopia," in *Dien Cai Dau,* 8–9.
74. Komunyakaa, "We Never Know," in *Dien Cai Dau,* 26. As Komunyakaa says, "that is a poem that has been taken both ways. Could be an American soldier . . . Could be an enemy soldier" (interview).
75. Komunyakaa, "Jungle Surrender," in *Dien Cai Dau,* 37. For more on the role of empathy in Komunyakaa's work, see the chapter "Human Empathy and Negative Capability: Yusef Komunyakaa's Poetry," in *Flashback through the Heart,* by Salas, 46–64.
76. Komunyakaa interview.
77. Yusef Komunyakaa, "Phantasmagoria," in *Thieves of Paradise* (Hanover, NH: Wesleyan University Press, 1998), 74.
78. David Connolly, "Brotherhood," in "Illumination Rounds: A Collection of Thoughts By a Survivor of the War in Vietnam" (manuscript, Imaginative Representations of the Vietnam War Collection, Connelly Library, La Salle University, Philadelphia, n.d.), n.p.
79. Connolly interview.
80. Connolly, "Brotherhood," in "Illumination Rounds."
81. Komunyakaa, "Tu Do Street," in *Dien Cai Dau,* 29.
82. Livingston, "Letter from a Vietnam Veteran," in *Crimes of War,* edited by Falk, Kolko, and Lifton, 433.
83. Shea, "the people here are simple," in *vietnam simply.*

84. Shea, "i am shitfaced," in *vietnam simply.*
85. Shea, "it is detrimental to morale," in *vietnam simply.*
86. Shea, "i am shitfaced," in *vietnam simply.*
87. Shea, "it is detrimental to morale," in *vietnam simply.*
88. Shea, "met a vietnamese officer today," in *vietnam simply.*
89. Shea, "went fishing with some vietnamese military," in *vietnam simply.*
90. Horace Coleman, "War Stories," in *In the Grass* (Woodbridge, CT: Viet Nam Generation, Inc. & Burning Cities Press, 1995), 30. Coleman explains that the child "was allergic to penicillin" (interview by author, Los Angeles, 3 April 2010).
91. W. D. Ehrhart, "A Relative Thing," in *A Generation of Peace* (New York: New Voices, 1975), 27.
92. Longley, *Grunts,* 96.
93. Leroy V. Quintana, "ARVN Rangers," in *Interrogations* (Chevy Chase, MD: Viet Nam Generation, Inc. & Burning Cities Press, 1990), 69.
94. Longley, *Grunts,* 96.
95. Kerry, Senate Foreign Relations Committee, 22 April 1971.
96. Shea, "the people here are simple," in *vietnam simply.*
97. Shea, "democracy is fighting with money," in *vietnam simply.*
98. W. D. Ehrhart, interview by author, Philadelphia, 2 March 2010.
99. Ibid.
100. Steve Mason, "The Children of the Sun," in *Johnny's Song* (Toronto: Bantam Books, 1987), 126. It should be noted, though, that in the following lines, Mason fallaciously proclaims: "we fought him on his ground / and we beat him into that ground. / No one here ever lost any war He was in! / Nor even a single battle!!" Perhaps, however, that was because "There was just nothing to be won in Vietnam. / There is just nothing any more to be won in any war."
101. Longley, *Grunts,* 94.
102. W. D. Ehrhart, "Song for Leela, Bobby and Me," in *Just for Laughs* (Silver Spring, MD: Viet Nam Generation, Inc. & Burning Cities Press, 1990), 81. This piece is dedicated to Ehrhart's friend in the poem, Robert Ross, who was killed in Vietnam on 10 May 1967. His name is on Panel 19E, Line 86, of the Vietnam Veterans Memorial in Washington, DC.
103. Connolly interview.
104. Steve Hassett, "Thanksgiving," in *Carrying the Darkness,* edited by Ehrhart, 130.
105. Chattarji, *Memories of a Lost War,* 129.
106. D. F. Brown, "Eating the Forest," in *Unaccustomed Mercy: Soldier-Poets of the Vietnam War,* edited by W. D. Ehrhart (Lubbock: Texas Tech University Press, 1989), 39; David Connolly, "Building A Raft At The Pond," in *Finding My Way* (Boston: David Connolly and the South Boston Literary Gazette Press, 2005), n.p.
107. Ehrhart, "Another Life," in *A Generation of Peace,* 22. For a discussion of the poetic portrayal of the war as hunting, see the section "Killing in War" in chapter 3.
108. Connolly, "Dreams of the Fight," in *Lost in America,* 36.
109. Connolly interview.
110. John F. Howe, "The Land," in *Carrying the Darkness,* edited by Ehrhart, 138.
111. McAvoy Layne, "Eleven October," in *How Audie Murphy Died in Vietnam* (Garden City, NY: Anchor Books, 1973), n.p.
112. Layne, "Guns," in *How Audie Murphy Died in Vietnam.*
113. Layne, "The nickname Night Train," in *How Audie Murphy Died in Vietnam.*
114. David Hall, "The Ambush of the Fourth Platoon," in *Werewolf and Other Poems* (Fort Collins, CO: Bald Mountain Press, 1981), 17.

115. Komunyakaa interview.
116. Hall, "The Ambush of the Fourth Platoon," in *Werewolf and Other Poems,* 19.
117. Doug Anderson, "Free Fire Zone," in *The Moon Reflected Fire* (Cambridge, MA: Alice James Books, 1994), 19; Coleman, "Night Flare Drop, Tan Son Nhut," in *In the Grass,* 29.
118. James Pinckney Harrison, *The Endless War: Fifty Years of Struggle in Vietnam* (New York: Free Press; London: Collier Macmillan, 1982), 316.
119. Longley, *Grunts,* 95; W. D. Ehrhart, "Soldier-Poets of the Vietnam War," *Virginia Quarterly Review* 63.2 (Spring 1987): 246–65, http://www.vqronline.org/essay/soldier-poets-vietnam-war.
120. For a poetic account that displays the various types of interactions and encounters between American soldiers and the people of south Vietnam, see Michael Casey, *Obscenities* (New Haven, CT: Yale University Press, 1972). As Stanley Kunitz highlights, Casey's assignment as a military policeman "brought him into close contact with Vietnamese nationals," and, as a result, his poems offer particularly perceptive insights into this relationship (foreword to Casey, *Obscenities,* x). Casey's work demonstrates that even within the severely strained climate of the war, it was possible for a warm and friendly bond to develop between American soldiers and the Vietnamese people.
121. Frank A. Cross Jr., "After The Ambush," in *Winning Hearts and Minds,* edited by Rottmann, Barry, and Paquet, 82.
122. Connolly interview.
123. Shea, "orient is strange," in *vietnam simply.* In this poem, Shea portrays "the american" as an unsuccessful alien invader, a parasite on an otherwise harmonious organism. And while he states that "the communist . . . clutches" the people "so they know no other way of life / and all they see / is that hated clod / the american," he nonetheless recognizes that the revolutionaries live "with the people," that they are themselves an intrinsic part of the Vietnamese organism.
124. W. D. Ehrhart, *Busted: A Vietnam Veteran in Nixon's America* (Amherst: University of Massachusetts Press, 1995), 13.
125. Casey, "A Bummer," in *Obscenities,* 26. "I do think the last four lines are wonderful," Casey says of this poem, "but I read them on a wall" (interview by author, Boston, 13 March 2010).
126. Connolly, "The Guerrilla," in *Lost in America,* 62. In this poem, Connolly draws parallels between the Irish War for Independence and the Vietnamese revolutionary effort. For Connolly, an Irish American who grew up listening to his "grandfather talk about fighting for Ireland" in their war for national liberation, he quickly "began to understand," he explains, that "I was doing things that were completely against my heritage . . . things that were just too sickeningly reminiscent of my grandfather's stories" (interview). As he writes in his poem "To the Irish Americans Who Fought the Last War": "we became the hated Black and Tan, / and we shamed our ancestry" (*Lost in America,* 39). "I started to think about this role as an Irish American performing counterrevolutionary acts . . . the grandson of a revolutionary," Connolly states. He felt "that in light of my heritage I was on the wrong side, that my country was on the wrong side . . . and that was like a flash . . . it was like, holy shit, I'm a Black and Tan . . . and once you plug yourself into that then why don't I call myself a Nazi" (interview).
127. Kevin Bowen, "Temple at Quan Loi, 1969," in *Playing Basketball with the Viet Cong* (Willimantic, CT: Curbstone Press, 1994), 24.
128. W. D. Ehrhart, "Address to Middle America," in *Peace Is Our Profession,* edited by

Barry, 275. Here, Ehrhart is responding to a question about "whether or not the anti-war movement in the United States had affected my morale while I was fighting in Vietnam." He insists that "it had not, though we could not help being aware of the demonstrations."

129. Charles Guthrie and Michael Quinlan, *Just War: The Just War Tradition: Ethics in Modern Warfare* (London: Bloomsbury, 2007), 14.
130. Jeff McMahan, *Killing in War* (Oxford: Clarendon Press, 2009), 12.
131. Ibid., 14. It is helpful to note McMahan's views on the discrimination requirement, outlined in *Killing in War,* 11–14. According to "mainstream" just war thinking, "the criterion of liability to attack in war is simply posing a threat. Because all combatants pose a threat to another, they are morally liable to attack; because noncombatants do not, they are not liable—that is, they are morally immune from attack." This is the foundation of the orthodox just war approach to "the requirement of discrimination," which "states simply that combatants must confine their intentional attacks to legitimate targets. Among persons, those who are legitimate targets are those who are liable to military attack. If posing a threat is the criterion of liability to attack in war, then combatants are liable but noncombatants are not." It is this line of just war thinking that "underlies the almost universally accepted claim that the distinction between legitimate and illegitimate targets coincides with that between combatants and noncombatants," a claim "so widely accepted that many just war theorists substitute the term 'principle of noncombatant immunity' for 'requirement of discrimination,' on the assumption that they are synonymous." Yet, there are a number of people who could "pose a threat in war who would not be considered combatants by anyone," such as scientists who develop napalm. Conversely, there are some people who would be considered combatants and legitimate targets by just war thinking "but who do not pose a threat to the enemy." There are other problems with the notion that the criterion of liability to attack in war is posing a threat. "The most important of these," McMahan suggests, is the intuitive implausibility of "the idea that one makes oneself liable to defensive attack merely by posing a threat to another." Here, he gives an example in which the only way to stop a rampaging murderer is to kill him. A "police officer who takes aim to shoot him does not thereby make herself morally liable to defensive action, and if the murderer kills her in self-defense, he adds one more murder to the list of his offences." Hence, McMahan argues, "a person can have no right of defense against a threatened harm to which he has made himself liable." In his example, "the murderer has, by wrongfully threatening the lives of further innocent people, made himself liable to be killed in their defense. He therefore has no right of defense against the police, if their only effective defensive option is to kill him." Thus, McMahan concludes, it is "false that by posing a threat to another, one necessarily makes oneself liable to defensive action." When McMahan applies this critique to the situation of war, his example is particularly pertinent to the conflict in Vietnam. He argues that a group of people "who fight solely to defend themselves and other innocent people from a wrongful threat of attack, and who threaten no one but the wrongful aggressors, do not make themselves morally liable to defensive attack." As with the police officer, "By engaging in morally justified self- and other-defense, they do nothing to forfeit their right not to be attacked or killed." So, even though these just combatants pose a threat and are doing harm when they fight against unjust combatants, "they do not thereby become legitimate targets of attack but retain their innocence in the generic sense. Like the police officer, they may not be attacked, even in self-defense." Although this example cannot be mapped precisely onto the

war in Vietnam, and without wishing to overly romanticize the Vietnamese revolutionaries or demonize the Americans, the parallels are nonetheless interesting and thought-provoking. Can the revolutionaries be understood to have engaged, at least partly, in "morally justified self- and other-defense"? Were the Americans "wrongful aggressors"? Overwhelmingly, the poets offer an affirmative answer to both questions.

132. Glover, *Humanity,* 84. As with just war thinking, the doctrine of double effect has links stretching back to Thomas Aquinas: "Nothing hinders one act from having two effects, only one of which is intended, while the other is beside the intention. Now moral acts take their species according to what is intended, and not according to what is beside the intention, since this is accidental . . . Accordingly the act of self-defense may have two effects, one is the saving of one's life, the other is the slaying of the aggressor. Therefore this act, since one's intention is to save one's own life, is not unlawful, seeing that it is natural to everything to keep itself in 'being,' as far as possible. And yet, though proceeding from a good intention, an act may be rendered unlawful, if it be out of proportion to the end" (*Summa Theologica,* translated by Fathers of the English Dominican Province [2nd ed., 1920], II.II.64.7, available online at http://newadvent.org/summa).
133. Peter Singer, for example, suggests that "the distinction between directly intended effect and side-effect is a contrived one. We cannot avoid responsibility simply by directing our intention to one effect rather than another. If we foresee both effects, we must take responsibility for the foreseen effects of what we do" (*Practical Ethics* [1979; 2nd ed., Cambridge: Cambridge University Press, 1993], 210).
134. Glover, *Humanity,* 84.
135. Ehrhart, "Farmer Nguyen," in *A Generation of Peace,* 5.
136. As David Huddle writes: "You got / any idea how many Nguyen's are in Vietnam?" ("Revelation," in *Stopping by Home* [Salt Lake City: Peregrine Smith Books, 1988], 8).
137. Kerry, Senate Foreign Relations Committee, 22 April 1971.
138. R. L. Barth, "POWs," in *Deeply Dug In* (Albuquerque: University of New Mexico Press, 2003), 37. A slightly different version of the same poem appears in R. L. Barth, *A Soldier's Time: Vietnam War Poems* (Santa Barbara, CA: John Daniel Publisher, 1987), 48.
139. Barth, "'The Lighter That Never Fails,'" in *Soldier's Time,* 57.
140. Ehrhart, "A Relative Thing," in *A Generation of Peace,* 27. An explanatory note at the end of the poem defines "hooches" as "houses, huts" (28).
141. Barth, "'The Lighter That Never Fails,'" in *Soldier's Time,* 57.
142. Michael Walzer, *Just and Unjust Wars: A Moral Argument with Historical Illustrations* (1977; 4th ed., New York: Basic Books, 2006), 193.
143. Wayne Karlin, Basil T. Paquet, and Larry Rottmann, eds., *Free Fire Zone: Short Stories by Vietnam Veterans* (New York: McGraw-Hill, 1973), iii.
144. Perry Oldham, "Red Madonna," in *Vinh Long* (Meadows of Dan, VA: Northwoods Press, 1976), 52.
145. Dale Ritterbusch, "Choppers," in *Lessons Learned: Poetry of the Vietnam War and Its Aftermath* (Woodbridge, CT: Viet Nam Generation, Inc. & Burning Cities Press, 1995), 17.
146. Marion Parker [pseud.], "The Children," in *Demilitarized Zones,* edited by Barry and Ehrhart, 31.
147. Kerry, Senate Foreign Relations Committee, 22 April 1971; GIs of the 1st Air Cavalry Division in Vietnam, "We shoot the sick, the young, the lame," in *Peace Is Our Profession,* edited by Barry, 22.

148. Thomas Merton, "War and the Crisis of Language," in *The Nonviolent Alternative*, edited by Gordon C. Zahn (1971; rev. ed., New York: Farrar, Straus and Giroux, 1980), 238–39. The essay was originally published in *The Critique of War: Contemporary Philosophical Explorations*, edited by Robert Ginsberg (Chicago: Henry Regnery, 1969).
149. Connolly interview.
150. W. D. Ehrhart, quoted in Stanley Karnow, *Vietnam: A History* (1983; 2nd ed., London: Penguin Books, 1997), 482.
151. Ehrhart, "Keeping My Distance," in *Just for Laughs*, 16; Peter Ulisse, "General Strickland," in *Vietnam Voices* (Lewiston, NY: Edwin Mellen Press, 1990), 77.
152. Huddle, "Revelation," in *Stopping by Home*, 8.
153. Bruce Weigl, "When Saigon Was French," in *Song of Napalm* (New York: Atlantic Monthly Press, 1988), 44.
154. Ehrhart, "Guerrilla War," in *A Generation of Peace*, 15.
155. McMahan, *Killing in War*, 13; Thomas Nagel, "War and Massacre," in *Mortal Questions* (1979; Cambridge: Cambridge University Press, 1997), 71.
156. Walzer, *Just and Unjust Wars*, 146.
157. McMahan, *Killing in War*, 13. For a detailed philosophical examination of this distinction between military and nonmilitary contributions of civilians, see Cécile Fabre, "Guns, Food, and Liability to Attack in War," *Ethics* 120.1 (October 2009): 36–63.
158. Hugo Slim, *Killing Civilians: Method, Madness and Morality in War* (London: Hurst, 2007), 2.
159. Nagel, "War and Massacre," 70.
160. Karnow, introduction to *From Both Sides Now*, 22. Karnow then quotes part of Ehrhart's poem "Guerrilla War."
161. For more on this, see the section "Atrocities" in chapter 3.
162. Samuel Hynes, *The Soldiers' Tale: Bearing Witness to Modern War* (London: Pimlico, 1998), 194 (emphasis added).
163. W. D. Ehrhart, interview by Amelia Moriarty, 1 April 2008. Ehrhart suggests that this is a significant similarity shared by the war in Vietnam and the war in Iraq.
164. Horace Coleman, in the short documentary *Reminiscences of a War*, directed by Simara Sousa (screened at the Ventura Film Society, Ventura, CA, 2011).
165. Mersmann, *Out of the Vietnam Vortex*, 23.
166. Weigl, "Him, on the Bicycle," in *Song of Napalm*, 9–10. This is one of Weigl's earliest poems, and a version of it appears in his first collection, *Executioner* (Tucson, AZ: Ironwood Press, 1976).
167. Christopher, *Viet Nam War / American War*, 249.
168. Philip D. Beidler, *American Literature and the Experience of Vietnam* (Athens: University of Georgia Press, 1982), 190.
169. Weigl interview.
170. Dalton Trumbo, *Johnny Got His Gun* (1939; London: Penguin Books, 2009), 251.
171. Ehrhart, interview by author.
172. Trumbo, *Johnny Got His Gun*, 251.
173. Connolly interview. During our interview, I outlined, somewhat clumsily, my understanding of cosmopolitanism as it relates to morality—"that all humans come under the same moral standard"—and asked Connolly if that was something he recognized in his own thinking. He replied: "Yeah, yeah, I see a community of man."
174. Kwame Anthony Appiah, *Cosmopolitanism: Ethics in a World of Strangers* (New York: W. W. Norton, 2006), xiv–xv. See also David Held, *Cosmopolitanism: Ideals and Realities* (Cambridge: Polity Press, 2010).

175. Hints of this cosmopolitanism can also be discerned in soldier-poetry from previous wars. For example, in his First World War poem "Break of Day in the Trenches," Isaac Rosenberg considers a rat's "cosmopolitan sympathies. / Now you have touched this English hand / You will do the same to a German" (in *The Collected Poems of Isaac Rosenberg,* edited by Gordon Bottomley and Denys Harding [London: Chatto and Windus, 1977], 73). Also from the First World War, Wilfred Owen writes in "Strange Meeting": "I am the enemy you killed, my friend" (in *The Poems of Wilfred Owen,* edited by Jon Stallworthy [London: Chatto and Windus, 1990], 126). In these "imaginative transactions," such poems depict, and also act out, our "human sameness" (Jahan Ramazani, "'Cosmopolitan Sympathies': Poetry of the First World War," paper presented at "The First World War: Literature, Culture, Modernity," British Academy, London, 12 November 2014).
176. Jan Barry, "Viet Nam," in *Demilitarized Zones,* edited by Barry and Ehrhart, 173. As Benedict de Spinoza suggests: "Hate completely conquered by love passes into love, and the love is therefore greater than if hate had not preceded it" (*Ethics,* edited and translated by Edwin Curley [London: Penguin Books, 1996], 93).
177. Gotera, *Radical Visions,* 263.
178. Steve Mason, *The Human Being: A Warrior's Journey Toward Peace and Mutual Healing* (New York: Touchstone, 1990), 11. In "A History Lesson," Mason writes: "We went to Vietnam / as American fighting men / and came back / as human beings" (in *Johnny's Song,* 52).
179. Frankl, *Man's Search for Meaning,* 139.
180. "Yesterday's Enemies" is the title of a section in Glover, *Humanity,* 159. Here, Glover discusses the breakthrough of the Christmas truce during the First World War and quotes a Scottish soldier who referred to a German soldier as "belonging to one of 'yesterday's enemies.'" For a filmic representation of this remarkable wartime breakthrough, see *Joyeux Noël,* directed by Christian Carion (Sony Pictures Classics, 2005).
181. For Ehrhart's account of this visit, see W. D. Ehrhart, *Going Back: An Ex-Marine Returns to Vietnam* (Jefferson, NC: McFarland, 1987). See also Ehrhart's poems "For Mrs. Na," "Twice Betrayed," "Second Thoughts," and "Who Did What to Whom," in *Just for Laughs,* 23–29. With regard to postwar diplomatic relations between America and Vietnam, George C. Herring notes: "Conflict with Vietnam did not end with the fall of Saigon in 1975. In marked contrast to the magnanimity it showed toward Germany and Japan after World War II, the United States was neither gracious nor generous in defeat. For nearly two decades, it continued to treat Vietnam as an enemy, and sporadic efforts to 'normalize' relations got nowhere" (*America's Longest War: The United States and Vietnam, 1950–1975* [1979; 3rd ed., New York: McGraw-Hill, 1996], 315).
182. Bruce Weigl, in Douglas Valentine, "War, Poetry and Reconciliation: An Interview with Bruce Weigl," *CounterPunch,* 18 October 2013, http://www.counterpunch.org/2013/10/18/war-poetry-and-reconciliation/.
183. For more on this conference, see W. D. Ehrhart, "A Common Language," *Virginia Quarterly Review* 67.3 (Summer 1991): 377–96, http://www.vqronline.org/essay/common-language.
184. Bruce Weigl, in Eric James Schroeder, "Bruce Weigl: 'Poetry Grabbed Me by the Throat,'" in *Vietnam, We've All Been There: Interviews with American Writers* (Westport, CT: Praeger, 1992), 193. In the same interview, Weigl speaks about the POW/MIA issue: "It's become a cottage industry: MIA-izing. It's perfectly clear to anyone with an iota of intelligence that there are no Americans being held prisoner

in Vietnam . . . The MIA issue has been orchestrated in part by members of our government because it's a way to keep us from normalizing relations with Vietnam" (193). For more on the POW/MIA myth, see H. Bruce Franklin, *M.I.A., or, Mythmaking in America* (1992; rev. ed., New Brunswick, NJ: Rutgers University Press, 1993). As Franklin highlights, the supposedly unresolved nature of the POW/MIA issue was the "only official rationale for refusing to recognize and begin normal relations with Vietnam" (4). Franklin's book finishes with Ehrhart's poem "POW/MIA," in *Just for Laughs*, 19–21.

185. Ehrhart, "A Common Language."
186. Carolyn Forché, introduction to Bowen, *Playing Basketball with the Viet Cong*, 7.
187. Larry Rottmann, *Voices From The Ho Chi Minh Trail: Poetry of America and Vietnam, 1965–1993* (Desert Hot Springs, CA: Event Horizon Press, 1993). Unfortunately, Rottmann refused to grant permission for his poems to be used in this book.
188. Christopher, *Viet Nam War / American War*, 323n30.
189. Bruce Weigl, introduction to *Poems from Captured Documents*, selected and translated by Thanh T. Nguyen and Bruce Weigl (Amherst: University of Massachusetts Press, 1994), xiii. See also Kevin Bowen, Nguyen Ba Chung, and Bruce Weigl, eds., *Mountain River: Vietnamese Poetry from the Wars, 1948–1993: A Bilingual Collection* (Amherst: University of Massachusetts Press, 1998); Nguyen Duy, *Distant Road: Selected Poems*, translated by Kevin Bowen and Nguyen Ba Chung (Willimantic, CT: Curbstone Press, 1999); Nguyen Ba Chung and Kevin Bowen, eds., *6 Vietnamese Poets* (Willimantic, CT: Curbstone Press, 2002).
190. Connolly, "Reconciliation," in *Lost in America*, 46. See also Connolly, "Anh Hung," in *Lost in America*, 63.
191. Wayne Karlin, "Reconciliation through Literature: Mirrors and Windows," in *Thirty Years After*, edited by Heberle, 159.
192. Chattarji, *Memories of a Lost War*, 165. For Chattarji's analysis of these poems, see the section "Life after Vietnam: Gestures towards Healing and Solidarity," 162–200.
193. Theodor Adorno, *Minima Moralia: Reflections from Damaged Life*, translated by E. F. N. Jephcott (1951; London: Verso, 2005), 25.
194. Glover, *Humanity*, 22–25.
195. Shea, "am alone in room," in *vietnam simply*.
196. Shea, "went to vietnamese party," in *vietnam simply*. On the following page, Shea expresses his regret at this indulgence: "spent night / in wild painful ecstasy / on white porcelain plumbing / with stomach throbbing / head aching" ("spent night," in *vietnam simply*).
197. Shea, "everything in house," in *vietnam simply*.
198. Shea, "in john one morning," in *vietnam simply*.
199. Shea, "on road of holes," in *vietnam simply*.
200. Gotera, *Radical Visions*, 44.
201. Shea, "in reflection," in *vietnam simply*.
202. Shea, "i like the vietnamese," in *vietnam simply*.
203. Shea, "americans have big heads," in *vietnam simply*.
204. Coleman, "I don't suppose I'll ever forget," in *In the Grass*, 41. "Say-Lems" refers to Salem cigarettes.
205. Frankl, *Man's Search for Meaning*, 93–94.
206. Jean Améry, *At the Mind's Limits: Contemplations by a Survivor on Auschwitz and Its Realities*, translated by Sidney Rosenfeld and Stella P. Rosenfeld (Bloomington: Indiana University Press, 1980), 73. Glover discusses Améry's examples in *Humanity*, 383.
207. Glover, *Humanity*, 383, 393. See also Walzer, *Just and Unjust Wars*, 138–43.

Chapter 3: Violence

1. Dalton Trumbo, "Addendum: 1970," in *Johnny Got His Gun* (1939; London: Penguin Books, 2009), xix.
2. The exact number of American war dead varies slightly depending on the source. There are 58,272 names listed on the Vietnam Veterans Memorial in Washington, DC. See http://thewall-usa.com/information.asp. I have rounded up here simply for the ease of reworking Trumbo's equation.
3. John Prados, *Vietnam: The History of an Unwinnable War, 1945–1975* (Lawrence: University Press of Kansas, 2009), 531. Casualty figures for the war are uncertain and can vary considerably between sources. Since it is a relatively recent work, Prados's summary of the statistics is used here.
4. Theodor Adorno, *Minima Moralia: Reflections from Damaged Life,* translated by E. F. N. Jephcott (1951; London: Verso, 2005), 25.
5. Gordon S. Livingston, "Letter from a Vietnam Veteran," in *Crimes of War: A Legal, Political-Documentary, and Psychological Inquiry into the Responsibility of Leaders, Citizens, and Soldiers for Criminal Acts in War,* edited by Richard A. Falk, Gabriel Kolko, and Robert Jay Lifton (New York: Random House, 1971), 440 (ellipsis in original).
6. Elaine Scarry, *The Body in Pain: The Making and Unmaking of the World* (New York: Oxford University Press, 1985), 63–69.
7. Ibid., 89.
8. W. D. Ehrhart, "The Value of Your Name," in *Dead on a High Hill: Essays on War, Literature and Living, 2002–2012* (Jefferson, NC: McFarland, 2012), 95.
9. Charles Guthrie and Michael Quinlan, *Just War: The Just War Tradition: Ethics in Modern Warfare* (London: Bloomsbury, 2007), 12.
10. Scarry, *Body in Pain,* 81, 89.
11. Jeff McMahan, *Killing in War* (Oxford: Clarendon Press, 2009), vii.
12. Joseph Heller, *Catch-22* (1961; London: Vintage, 2004), 504. After quoting Heller's famous passage, Tobey C. Herzog writes: "Similar symbolic confrontations with death commonly appear in Vietnam narratives as soldiers quickly discover that they are not fearless John Waynes controlling their destiny" (*Vietnam War Stories: Innocence Lost* [London: Routledge, 1992], 36). For more on John Wayne's relationship to the war and the poetry, see the section "America and Americans" in chapter 4.
13. Jean Améry, *At the Mind's Limits: Contemplations by a Survivor on Auschwitz and Its Realities,* translated by Sidney Rosenfeld and Stella P. Rosenfeld (Bloomington: Indiana University Press, 1980), 28. Hence, it is not just trust in the physical world that can be destroyed, but also any trust we might have in any metaphysical world. In this sense, violence can be understood as an attempt to force the primacy of the physical over the metaphysical. This would seem to have implications for violence done in the name of metaphysics.
14. Ibid., 28–29.
15. James W. Douglass, *The Non-violent Cross: A Theology of Revolution and Peace* (London: Geoffrey Chapman, 1968), 13.
16. Stephen King-Hall, *Defence in the Nuclear Age* (3rd ed., London: Gollancz, 1958), 31, quoted in Douglass, *Non-violent Cross,* 13.
17. Douglass, *Non-violent Cross,* 220.
18. Améry, *At the Mind's Limits,* 22; Sidney Rosenfeld, "Afterword: Jean Améry: The Writer in Revolt," in *At the Mind's Limits,* by Améry, 107. As Avishai Margalit, who

briefly examines Améry as "both an expert witness and a moral witness when it comes to torture," suggests: "Mental scars last longer than physical scars, and the effects of insults and humiliation last longer than mere physical pain . . . In remembering torture, the victim dwells on the humiliation, whereas in experiencing torture he dwells on the pain" (*The Ethics of Memory* [Cambridge, MA: Harvard University Press, 2004], 117–19).

19. Hubert Dreyfus and Camilo Salazar Prince, "*The Thin Red Line:* Dying without Demise, Demise without Dying," in *The Thin Red Line,* edited by David Davies (London: Routledge, 2009), 29.
20. Ibid.; Améry, *At the Mind's Limits,* 28. As helpful as these Heideggerian concepts might be, I have experienced a certain discomfort in using them, especially alongside the thoughts of Améry. See Améry, *At the Mind's Limits,* 18–19; and Jonathan Glover, *Humanity: A Moral History of the Twentieth Century* (New Haven, CT: Yale University Press, 2001), 374. For an interesting discussion of "The Case of Martin Heidegger," see Glover, *Humanity,* 367–76.
21. Janis Haswell, "The Lesson Unlearned: Moral Trauma in Andrew Jolly's *A Time of Soldiers,*" in *Thirty Years After: New Essays on Vietnam War Literature, Film, and Art,* edited by Mark Heberle (Newcastle upon Tyne: Cambridge Scholars, 2009), 452.
22. Aphrodite Matsakis, *Vietnam Wives: Facing the Challenges of Life with Veterans Suffering Post-traumatic Stress* (New York: Sidran Press, 1996), 23, quoted in Haswell, "Lesson Unlearned," 453.
23. Haswell, "Lesson Unlearned," 453. Here, Haswell cites Judith Lewis Herman, *Trauma and Recovery* (New York: Basic Books, 1997), 53.
24. Haswell, "Lesson Unlearned," 453.
25. Dreyfus and Prince, "Dying without Demise, Demise without Dying," 31–34.
26. In particular, see the section "Doubt" in chapter 1.
27. Haswell, "Lesson Unlearned," 453.
28. The phrasing here borrows from Améry's description of sadism as "the radical negation of the other" (*At the Mind's Limits,* 35).
29. Tim O'Brien, *The Things They Carried* (London: Flamingo, 1991), 77.
30. Scarry, *Body in Pain,* 122–23.
31. Trumbo, "Addendum: 1970," xix.
32. Ludwig Wittgenstein, *Tractatus Logico-Philosophicus,* translated by D. F. Pears and B. F. McGuinness (1921; rev. ed., London: Routledge, 2001), 87.
33. Albert Camus, *The Myth of Sisyphus,* translated by Justin O'Brien (1942; London: Penguin Books, 2000), 21.
34. Bruce Weigl, in Douglas Valentine, "War, Poetry and Reconciliation: An Interview with Bruce Weigl," *CounterPunch,* 18 October 2013, http://www.counterpunch.org/2013/10/18/war-poetry-and-reconciliation/.
35. Franny Nudelman, *John Brown's Body: Slavery, Violence & the Culture of War* (Chapel Hill: University of North Carolina Press, 2004), 3.
36. Robert Pinsky, "Responsibilities of the Poet," in *Politics & Poetic Value,* edited by Robert von Hallberg (Chicago: University of Chicago Press, 1987), 8. He expands: "It is the nature of poetry to emphasize constantly that the physical sounds of words come from a particular body, one at a time, in a certain order . . . This dual concern, bodily and conceptual, is what Pound means by saying that poetry is a centaur: prose hits the target with its arrow; poetry does the same from horseback. If you are too stupid, or too cerebral, you may miss half of it."
37. David Connolly, interview by author, Boston, 15 March 2010.
38. Serigo [Igor Bobrowsky], "Hue City," in *Winning Hearts and Minds: War Poems by*

Vietnam Veterans, edited by Larry Rottmann, Jan Barry, and Basil T. Paquet (New York: McGraw-Hill, 1972), 40.

39. Bruce Weigl, "Elegy," in *Song of Napalm* (New York: Atlantic Monthly Press, 1988), 70.
40. Bruce Weigl, "On the Ambiguity of Injury and Pain," in *Sweet Lorain* (Evanston, IL: TriQuarterly Books, 1996), 54. This is ostensibly a "nonwar" poem, but since it is a reflection on the nature of injury and pain it nonetheless seems applicable to war.
41. James Soular, "The Thousand-Yard Stare," in *The Thousand-Yard Stare* (Canton, CT: Singular Speech Press, 1997), 53.
42. W. D. Ehrhart, "Basil T. Paquet," in *Unaccustomed Mercy: Soldier-Poets of the Vietnam War,* edited by W. D. Ehrhart (Lubbock: Texas Tech University Press, 1989), 111.
43. Basil T. Paquet, "They Do Not Go Gentle," in *Winning Hearts and Minds,* edited by Rottmann, Barry, and Paquet, 3. This is the first actual poem in the collection; the first piece is the marching cadence "I Wanna Go To Vietnam" (1). For an excellent discussion of bodily mutilation in the soldier-poetry written during the war, with a particular focus on *Winning Hearts and Minds,* see the chapter "'Fragging the Chain(s) of Command': Mutilation and GI Resistance Poetry," in *Hearts and Minds: Bodies, Poetry, and Resistance in the Vietnam Era,* by Michael Bibby (New Brunswick, NJ: Rutgers University Press, 1996), 123–72.
44. Paquet, "They Do Not Go Gentle," in *Winning Hearts and Minds,* edited by Rottmann, Barry, and Paquet, 3.
45. I am not necessarily positing a mind-body dualism, but simply highlighting that what we commonly understand as a mental self is reliant on a body, while a body can live on even when there has been complete mental demise.
46. Bruce Weigl, "Why Plato Left for Megara," in *The Unraveling Strangeness* (New York: Grove Press, 2002), 63.
47. Paquet, "In A Plantation," in *Winning Hearts and Minds,* edited by Rottmann, Barry, and Paquet, 12.
48. This corporeal vulnerability, especially in the midst of the mechanized violence of modern warfare, is also considered in earlier war poetry. For example, in his epic poem about the First World War, David Jones suggests that war is "disproportionate in its violence considering the fragility of us" (*In Parenthesis* [1937; London: Faber and Faber, 2010], 183).
49. Paquet, "Mourning The Death, By Hemorrhage, Of A Child From Honai," in *Winning Hearts and Minds,* edited by Rottmann, Barry, and Paquet, 77.
50. *Notre Musique,* directed by Jean-Luc Godard (Wellspring Media, 2004), quoted in Simon Critchley, *Infinitely Demanding: Ethics of Commitment, Politics of Resistance* (London: Verso, 2008), 146. Critchley also uses this quote in his book *The Faith of the Faithless: Experiments in Political Theology* (London: Verso, 2012), 145. The original line in French is "Tuer un homme pour défendre une idée, n'est pas défendre une idée, c'est tuer un homme," which draws on the sixteenth-century religious reformer Sebastian Castellio's declaration that "to kill a man does not mean to defend a doctrine; it means the death of a man" (quoted in Hans R. Guggisberg, *Sebastian Castellio, 1515–1563: Humanist and Defender of Religious Toleration in a Confessional Age,* edited and translated by Bruce Gordon [Aldershot: Ashgate, 2003], 270).
51. W. D. Ehrhart, "Soldier-Poets of the Vietnam War," *Virginia Quarterly Review* 63.2 (Spring 1987): 246–65, http://www.vqronline.org/essay/soldier-poets-vietnam-war.

52. Paquet, "Morning—A Death," in *Winning Hearts and Minds,* edited by Rottmann, Barry, and Paquet, 22–23.
53. D. C. Berry, untitled ("The sun goes"), in *saigon cemetery* (Athens: University of Georgia Press, 1972), 3.
54. Berry, untitled ("The way popcorn pops is"), in *saigon cemetery,* 41.
55. Berry, untitled ("Tangerines and white"), in *saigon cemetery,* 24.
56. Berry, untitled ("This is the end where the begin"), in *saigon cemetery,* 30.
57. Berry, untitled ("The gasping redness touches"), in *saigon cemetery,* 28.
58. Bibby, *Hearts and Minds,* 164.
59. Ehrhart, "Soldier-Poets of the Vietnam War."
60. Carolyn Forché, introduction to *Against Forgetting: Twentieth-Century Poetry of Witness,* edited by Carolyn Forché (New York: W. W. Norton, 1993), 42.
61. Vince Gotera, *Radical Visions: Poetry by Vietnam Veterans* (Athens: University of Georgia Press, 1994), 57–58.
62. Philip D. Beidler, *American Literature and the Experience of Vietnam* (Athens: University of Georgia Press, 1982), 129. See also Gotera, *Radical Visions,* 58.
63. Berry, untitled ("A poem ought to be a salt lick"), in *saigon cemetery,* 50.
64. Doug Anderson, "Short Timer," in *The Moon Reflected Fire* (Cambridge, MA: Alice James Books, 1994), 21. This poem appears with minor variations—for instance, "brains" instead of "brain"—in Anderson's earlier work *Bamboo Bridge* (Amherst, MA: Amherst Writers & Artists Press, 1991), 13.
65. Anderson, "Mine," in *The Moon Reflected Fire,* 12. This poem also appears in his earlier work *Bamboo Bridge,* 10. For another excellent poetic example of the impact of violence on not only the victim but also the witness, see Dick Shea, "ever seen a man," in *vietnam simply* (Coronado, CA: Pro Tem, 1967), n.p.
66. Anderson, "Mine," in *The Moon Reflected Fire,* 12.
67. R. L. Barth, "One Way to Carry the Dead," in *Deeply Dug In* (Albuquerque: University of New Mexico Press, 2003), 12.
68. Paquet, "Morning—A Death," in *Winning Hearts and Minds,* edited by Rottmann, Barry, and Paquet, 22; Paquet, "It Is Monsoon At Last," in *Winning Hearts and Minds,* edited by Rottmann, Barry, and Paquet, 57.
69. Gerald McCarthy, "War Story," in *War Story: Vietnam War Poems* (Trumansburg, NY: Crossing Press, 1977), 8.
70. Stan Platke, "Gut Catcher," in *Winning Hearts and Minds,* edited by Rottmann, Barry, and Paquet, 21 (ellipsis in original).
71. D. S. Lliteras, "Booby-Trap," in *In A Warrior's Romance* (Norfolk, VA: Hampton Roads, 1991), 59 (ellipsis in original).
72. Weigl, "Mines," in *Song of Napalm,* 43 (ellipsis in original). This is one of Weigl's earliest poems, and a version of it appears in his first collection, *Executioner* (Tucson, AZ: Ironwood Press, 1976).
73. Barth, "Meditations After Battle," in *Deeply Dug In,* 48. For an earlier version of this poem that includes an additional verse, see R. L. Barth, *A Soldier's Time: Vietnam War Poems* (Santa Barbara, CA: John Daniel, 1987), 65–66.
74. Yusef Komunyakaa, "Autobiography of My Alter Ego," in *Warhorses* (New York: Farrar, Straus and Giroux, 2008), 61.
75. Lamont B. Steptoe, "letter to momma #2," in *Uncle's South China Sea Blue Nightmare* (1995; 2nd ed., Philadelphia: Plan B Press, 2003), 13.
76. Nudelman, *John Brown's Body,* 177n3. Here, Nudelman cites the influence of Scarry's *Body in Pain* on her own study of violence.

77. W. D. Ehrhart, "The Bodies Beneath the Table," in *The Bodies Beneath the Table* (Easthampton, MA: Adastra Press, 2010), 67.
78. David Hall, "The Ambush of the Fourth Platoon," in *Werewolf and Other Poems* (Fort Collins, CO: Bald Mountain Press, 1981), 19.
79. Paquet, "Graves Registration," in *Winning Hearts and Minds,* edited by Rottmann, Barry, and Paquet, 64.
80. Ehrhart, "The Bodies Beneath the Table," in *Bodies Beneath the Table,* 67 (emphasis added).
81. Horace Coleman, "State of Disunion," *Veteran* 38.2 (Fall 2008), http://www.vvaw.org/veteran/article/?id=935.
82. Haswell, "Lesson Unlearned," 450.
83. Yusef Komunyakaa, interview by author, New York City, 11 March 2010.
84. This picturing of war as hunting also brings to mind the violence directed toward animals that is so prominent in the poets' depictions of their childhoods. See the section "Making Soldiers" in chapter 1.
85. James McLeroy, "Ambush," in *Dear America: Letters Home from Vietnam,* edited by Bernard Edelman (1985; New York: W. W. Norton, 2002), 65.
86. W. D. Ehrhart, "Hunting," in *Winning Hearts and Minds,* edited by Rottmann, Barry, and Paquet, 33.
87. Jon Forrest Glade, "Blood Trail," in *Photographs of the Jungle* (St. John, KS: Chiron Review Press, 1990), 27 (emphasis added). For more on the moral responsibility of soldiers, see the section "Soldiers and Veterans" in chapter 4.
88. W. D. Ehrhart, "Another Life," in *A Generation of Peace* (New York: New Voices, 1975), 22.
89. Leroy V. Quintana, "Poem for Our Dog Afraid of Thunder on a Rainy Day," in *The Great Whirl of Exile* (Willimantic, CT: Curbstone Press, 1999), 58.
90. McLeroy, "Ambush," in *Dear America,* edited by Edelman, 65–66.
91. Wittgenstein, *Tractatus Logico-Philosophicus,* 87.
92. J. Vincent Hansen, "To Lenny and Simon," in *Blessed Are the Piecemakers: A Collection of Poems And Uncertain Notions* (St. Cloud, MN: North Star Press of St. Cloud, 1989), 113.
93. Dreyfus and Prince, "Dying without Demise, Demise without Dying," 31.
94. Geoffrey Childs, "From a Letter to the Editors," in *Demilitarized Zones: Veterans after Vietnam,* edited by Jan Barry and W. D. Ehrhart (Perkasie, PA: East River Anthology, 1976), 98.
95. McLeroy, "Ambush," in *Dear America,* edited by Edelman, 66.
96. Soular, "First Kill," in *The Thousand-Yard Stare,* 37–38. See the section "Making Soldiers" in chapter 1.
97. Soular, "Letter to Billy," in *The Thousand-Yard Stare,* 7.
98. Haswell, "Lesson Unlearned," 453–54.
99. Scarry, *Body in Pain,* 122. For more on the impact of killing on both the killer and society, see Dave Grossman, *On Killing: The Psychological Cost of Learning to Kill in War and Society* (New York: Back Bay Books, 1996).
100. Bill Bauer, "Moonlight and a Breeze," in *Last Lambs: New and Selected Poems of Vietnam* (Kansas City: BkMk Press, 1997), 19.
101. Lorrie Goldensohn, *Dismantling Glory: Twentieth-Century Soldier Poetry* (New York: Columbia University Press, 2003); McMahan, *Killing in War,* vii. As indicated earlier in this chapter, McMahan argues against the view that different moral principles govern killing in war and killing in other contexts.
102. Peter Klotz-Chamberlin and Scott Kennedy, "Introduction: An Ethic Superior

to Murder," in *Neither Victims nor Executioners: An Ethic Superior to Murder,* by Albert Camus, translated by Dwight Macdonald (1946; Eugene, OR: Wipf and Stock, 2007), 17.

103. McLeroy, "Ambush," in *Dear America,* edited by Edelman, 66.
104. Soular, "Choking," in *The Thousand-Yard Stare,* 41.
105. W. D. Ehrhart, "Keeping My Distance," in *Just for Laughs* (Silver Spring, MD: Viet Nam Generation, Inc. & Burning Cities Press, 1990), 16.
106. For more on the postwar responsibilities of veteran poets, see the section "Soldiers and Veterans" in chapter 4.
107. George Mizo, untitled ("You"), quoted in Jim Willingham, "Ground Zero 9/11/02," *Veteran* 32.2 (Fall 2002), http://www.vvaw.org/veteran/article/?id=16.
108. W. D. Ehrhart, in "War, Poetry & Ethics: A Symposium," *War, Literature & the Arts* 10.2 (Fall–Winter 1998): 31.
109. Peter Ulisse, "Warrant Officer Tadduni," in *Vietnam Voices* (Lewiston, NY: Edwin Mellen Press, 1990), 68.
110. Glover, *Humanity,* 156.
111. Hansen, "1965," in *Blessed Are the Piecemakers,* 7.
112. Bibby, *Hearts and Minds,* 164. For more on the role of the body count in "GI Resistance poetry," see 162–65. As Bibby notes, "promotion, troop rewards such as rest and relaxation (R&R) leaves, and other perks in the military were dependent on the production of high body counts" (162). See James William Gibson, *The Perfect War: Technowar in Vietnam* (Boston: Atlantic Monthly Press, 1986), 112–28.
113. Glover, *Humanity,* 352.
114. Soular, "Letter to Billy," in *The Thousand-Yard Stare,* 7.
115. Barth, "M.I.A.," in *Soldier's Time,* 62.
116. Jim Nye, "You Gotta Have Heart," in *Aftershock: Poems and Prose from the Vietnam War* (El Paso, TX: Cinco Puntos Press, 1991), 47.
117. David Connolly, "Corporal Thach: First Confirmed NVA Kill," in *Lost in America* (Woodbridge, CT: Viet Nam Generation, Inc. & Burning Cities Press, 1994), 12. Stanley Karnow writes of this poem: "while the horrors of Vietnam desensitized many GIs, it also aroused the conscience of some, like David Connolly, and the memory of Thach, a slain North Vietnamese corporal, was to remain with him" (introduction to *From Both Sides Now: The Poetry of the Vietnam War and Its Aftermath,* edited by Phillip Mahony [New York: Scribner, 1998], 23)
118. Connolly interview. Connolly kept "a bunch of his stuff . . . his hat, his belt buckle, bunch of papers, an ID card, a book that I thought was a diary, it turned out to be poetry . . . He was actually found . . . Back in 89, 90, with reconciliation between the two countries there was a program set up by which American veterans of the war could sit down with somebody in each state and say, 'I killed a guy at this trail junction,' and the representative of the joint recovery team would come up with a plat map . . . and I sat down with a guy and I said, 'this road junction right here outside of Gia Re I killed a man named Thach and kicked him back in the hole I saw him climb out of, and left him there, and here's all his shit,' and handed back all of his stuff, and they went and they found him."
119. David Connolly, "Heart Attack," in *Finding My Way* (Boston: David Connolly and the South Boston Literary Gazette Press, 2005), n.p.
120. Connolly interview.
121. Guthrie and Quinlan, *Just War,* 14.
122. Ehrhart, in "War, Poetry & Ethics," 34.
123. Horace Coleman, "You Can't Tell The Players Without A Scorecard," in *In the Grass*

(Woodbridge, CT: Viet Nam Generation, Inc. & Burning Cities Press, 1995), 42; Leroy V. Quintana, "Bates," in *Interrogations* (Chevy Chase, MD: Viet Nam Generation, Inc. & Burning Cities Press, 1990), 56.

124. Anderson, "Infantry Assault," in *The Moon Reflected Fire*, 4. This poem also appears in his earlier work *Bamboo Bridge*, 4.
125. Michael Walzer, *Just and Unjust Wars: A Moral Argument with Historical Illustrations* (1977; 4th ed., New York: Basic Books, 2006), 307.
126. Quoted ibid., 189–90. For Walzer's analysis of the American rules of engagement in Vietnam, see 188–96.
127. Hansen, "It Ain't Good, What We Done," in *Blessed Are the Piecemakers*, 40.
128. Hansen, "Tyus," in *Blessed Are the Piecemakers*, 33.
129. Haswell, "Lesson Unlearned," 453.
130. W. D. Ehrhart, interview by Annalisa Bova, 2003.
131. Barth, "A Letter from An Hoc (4), by a Seedbed," in *Soldier's Time*, 47.
132. Hansen, "'Snips and Snails and Puppy Dog Tails,'" in *Blessed Are the Piecemakers*, 41. Hansen also uses the imagery of food to describe war's violence in another of his poems: "His taut / brown body / erupted / in a hundred places / like / butterscotch pudding / coming to a boil" ("Still Life," in *Blessed Are the Piecemakers*, 52).
133. Soular, "Voices," in *The Thousand-Yard Stare*, 50.
134. Barth, "A Child Accidentally Napalmed," in *Deeply Dug In*, 10.
135. Nye, "It's Too Late," in *Aftershock*, 23.
136. Richard E. Baker, "Burying the Children," in *Shell Burst Pond* (1980; 2nd ed., Tacoma, WA: Vardaman Press, 1982), 2.
137. B. D. Trail, quoted in "Into Memory, B. D. Trail," *Viet Nam Generation* 4.3–4 (Summer–Fall 1992): 30.
138. B. D. Trail, "The Grenading," *Viet Nam Generation* 4.3–4 (Summer–Fall 1992): 30–31.
139. David Willson, "A Few Well-Chosen Words: Extraordinary, Neglected Vietnam War Poets," *VVA Veteran* 31.1 (January–February 2011): 34.
140. McCarthy, "War Story," in *War Story*, 16.
141. Goldensohn, *Dismantling Glory*, 307. For more on misogyny and the war in this context, see Jacqueline E. Lawson, "'She's a Pretty Woman . . . for a Gook': The Misogyny of the Vietnam War," in *Fourteen Landing Zones: Approaches to Vietnam War Literature*, edited by Philip K. Jason (Iowa City: University of Iowa Press, 1991), 15–37. For an overview of sexual violence in filmic representations of the war, see Cynthia J. Fuchs, "'Vietnam and Sexual Violence': The Movie," in *America Rediscovered: Critical Essays on Literature and Film of the Vietnam War*, edited by Owen W. Gilman Jr. and Lorrie Smith (New York: Garland, 1990), 120–33.
142. McCarthy, "War Story," in *War Story*, 18.
143. Shea, "went with a cab driver," in *vietnam simply*.
144. Soular, "Numbah One," in *The Thousand-Yard Stare*, 18.
145. Baker, "Interrogation," in *Shell Burst Pond*, 9.
146. Quintana, "Interrogations," in *Interrogations*, 54. For another poetic depiction of this particular interrogation process, see Richard M. Mishler, "Ceremony," in *Carrying the Darkness: The Poetry of the Vietnam War*, edited by W. D. Ehrhart (1985; Lubbock: Texas Tech University Press, 1989), 199–200.
147. Quintana, "Interrogations," in *Interrogations*, 54–55.
148. This has important implications for national responsibility, as discussed in the section "America and Americans" in chapter 4.
149. Bruce Weigl, "Surrounding Blues on the Way Down," in *The Monkey Wars* (Athens: University of Georgia Press, 1985), 26.

150. Bruce Weigl, interview by author, Oberlin, OH, 18 March 2010.
151. Hansen, "It Ain't Good, What We Done," in *Blessed Are the Piecemakers*, 40.
152. For example, with regard to Nye's poem about the dead child, "It's Too Late," Timothy P. Kinsella argues that Nye "wishes the weeping would stop, because it makes him feel guilty." It is as though Nye, as a soldier, looks away. "The mature poet, however, does not look away," Kinsella continues. "The very act of writing such a poem remembers—*revivifies*—the horror of that day and presents it for the soldier's exorcism and our contemplation" ("A Season in Hell: Art Song and the American War in Vietnam," in *Thirty Years After*, edited by Heberle, 354).
153. Adorno, *Minima Moralia*, 25.
154. Robert Jay Lifton, "Home from the War: The Psychology of Survival," in *The Vietnam Reader*, edited by Walter Capps (New York: Routledge, 1991), 60. See also Robert Jay Lifton, *Home from the War: Vietnam Veterans: Neither Victims nor Executioners* (New York: Simon and Schuster, 1973), 59.
155. William Calley, quoted in Michael Bilton and Kevin Sim, *Four Hours in My Lai* (London: Penguin, 1993), 372.
156. Glover, *Humanity*, 42.
157. Ehrhart, "Value of Your Name," 97.
158. Peter Hollenbeck, "Anorexia," in *Carrying the Darkness*, edited by Ehrhart, 137.
159. Adorno, *Minima Moralia*, 25.
160. Karnow, introduction to *From Both Sides Now*, 21.
161. W. D. Ehrhart, introduction to *In the Shadow of Vietnam: Essays, 1977–1991* (Jefferson, NC: McFarland, 1991), xii.
162. The distance between the Lincoln Memorial and the Capitol is around 2 miles, which is a little over 3 kilometers. If the wall was to "stand nine feet high" (2.7432 meters) for its entire length, then, given that the current wall has approximately 243 names per square meter (its dimensions are such that it can be measured as a rectangle 3.2 meters high and 75 meters long, which is 240 meters squared, and with 58,272 names that works out at just under 243 names per square meter), and using Karnow's rough and possibly low figure of 2 million dead, it would actually measure approximately 3,000 meters long: (2,000,000 ÷ 243) ÷ 2.7432≈3,000. Mathematical thanks to Andrew Povey for double-checking my calculations.
163. Anderson, "The Wall," in *The Moon Reflected Fire*, 62. This poem also appears in his earlier work *Bamboo Bridge*, 31. Anderson also wonders about including "four million Cambodians" on such a wall. For more on the link between the American war in Vietnam and the Cambodian genocide, see note 203 in this chapter.
164. Samuel Hynes, *The Soldiers' Tale: Bearing Witness to Modern War* (London: Pimlico, 1998), 195.
165. Connolly, "To the Irish Americans Who Fought the Last War," in *Lost in America*, 39. The rise in the number of civilian casualties in the wars of the twentieth century—5 percent of casualties in the First World War were civilians, 50 percent in the Second World War, 90 percent in Vietnam—is a key feature of technological warfare: "advances in military technology have invariably served to reduce the number of casualties among those who possess the technology, while causing a concomitant and disproportionate rise in the number of innocent victims" (John Foley, "Albert Camus and Political Violence," in *Albert Camus in the 21st Century: A Reassessment of His Thinking at the Dawn of the New Millennium*, edited by Christine Margerrison, Mark Orme, and Lissa Lincoln [Amsterdam: Rodopi, 2008], 221).
166. Guthrie and Quinlan, *Just War*, 14.
167. Gibson, *Perfect War*, 319. "Estimates on how many bombs were dropped over Southeast Asia differ considerably," Gibson notes, and according to some calculations the

"total tonnage for all of Southeast Asia would tally at least 15 million tons" (495n1). These bombs fell not just on Vietnam but on neighboring countries as well. See, for instance, Karen J. Coates, *Eternal Harvest: The Legacy of American Bombs in Laos,* photos by Jerry Redfern (San Francisco: ThingsAsian Press, 2013).

168. Thomas Hurka, "Proportionality in the Morality of War," *Philosophy & Public Affairs* 33.1 (Winter 2005): 36. Hurka also mentions "the necessity condition, which . . . says that killing soldiers and especially civilians is forbidden if it serves no military purpose; unnecessary force is wrong" (36). Certainly, much of the American bombing could be considered unnecessary, even if one believes the war itself to have been somehow necessary.
169. Ibid., 35. In orthodox just war thinking, there is a disconnect between *jus ad bellum* and *jus in bello.* However, as chapter 4 outlines, this separation has been questioned in recent moral philosophy and in the works of the poets.
170. Charles Hirschman, Samuel Preston, and Vu Manh Loi, "Vietnamese Casualties during the American War: A New Estimate," *Population and Development Review* 21.4 (December 1995): 790. The actual number of civilian casualties remains uncertain, although "Vietnamese government figures released in 1995 estimated approximately 2 million civilian deaths in each of the two regroupment zones of Vietnam" (Prados, *Vietnam,* 531).
171. Ehrhart, in "War, Poetry & Ethics," 33.
172. Kevin Bowen, "The Arts of Love and Hydrology as Practiced in Hà Nội," in *Playing Basketball with the Viet Cong* (Willimantic, CT: Curbstone Press, 1994), 37–38.
173. Coleman, "The Raid Near Saigon," in *In the Grass,* 52.
174. Coleman, "Saigon Warrior," in *In the Grass,* 72 (emphasis added).
175. Horace Coleman, interview by author, Los Angeles, 3 April 2010.
176. Ehrhart, "Time on Target," in *A Generation of Peace,* 16. Ehrhart notes that COC denotes "Command, Operations & Communications bunker."
177. Lorrie Smith, "Resistance and Revision in Poetry by Vietnam War Veterans," in *Fourteen Landing Zones,* edited by Jason, 53–54.
178. For more on the role of distancing in killing, see Grossman, *On Killing.*
179. George Orwell, "Politics and the English Language," *Horizon* 13 (April 1946): 261–62. Years after Orwell wrote this, "pacification" was employed by America during the war in Vietnam. The term essentially came to "encompass the array of things done with Vietnamese villagers as their object" (Prados, *Vietnam,* 322).
180. Connolly interview.
181. Depending on the angle of interpretation, some euphemisms can reveal as much as they conceal. For example, what could be a more accurate descriptor of what happens to life in war than "wasted"?
182. Hansen, "Bad Semantics (B.S.)," in *Blessed Are the Piecemakers,* 92.
183. James Pinckney Harrison, *The Endless War: Fifty Years of Struggle in Vietnam* (New York: Free Press; London: Collier Macmillan, 1982), 192. For an interesting history of napalm, see Robert M. Neer, *Napalm: An American Biography* (Cambridge, MA: Harvard University Press, 2013).
184. Gabriel Kolko, *Vietnam: Anatomy of War, 1940–1975* (London: Unwin, 1987), 145.
185. See David Zierler, *The Invention of Ecocide: Agent Orange, Vietnam, and the Scientists Who Changed the Way We Think about the Environment* (Athens: University of Georgia Press, 2011).
186. See chapter 1, note 63.
187. Hynes, *Soldiers' Tale,* 195.
188. Steptoe, "uncle's south china sea blue nightmare," in *Uncle's South China Sea Blue*

Nightmare, 53–54. There is a slight discrepancy in the titling of this poem. See chapter 1, note 62.

189. Weigl, "Song of Napalm," in *The Monkey Wars*, 46–47.
190. Fred A. Wilcox, *Scorched Earth: Legacies of Chemical Warfare in Vietnam* (New York: Seven Stories Press, 2011), 2.
191. Zierler, *Invention of Ecocide*, 6.
192. Wilcox, *Scorched Earth*, 2–3. For more on the impact of Agent Orange on American veterans, see Fred A. Wilcox, *Waiting for an Army to Die: The Tragedy of Agent Orange* (1983; 2nd ed., New York: Seven Stories Press, 2011). For Vietnamese perspectives, see Charles Waugh and Huy Lien, eds., *Family of Fallen Leaves: Stories of Agent Orange by Vietnamese Writers* (Athens: University of Georgia Press, 2010). For a photographic record, see Philip Jones Griffiths, *Agent Orange: "Collateral Damage" in Viet Nam* (London: Trolley, 2003).
193. Wilcox, *Scorched Earth*, 6, 2–3.
194. Ton That Tung, quoted ibid., 1.
195. Lamont B. Steptoe, "Toxic Waste," in *Mad Minute* (1990; Camden, NJ: Whirlwind Press, 1993), 54–55.
196. Soular, "The Agent," in *The Thousand-Yard Stare*, 46.
197. Quintana, "At the New Mexico Viet Nam Veterans' Memorial," in *Great Whirl of Exile*, 50.
198. David Connolly, "Death by Friendly Fire," in "Illumination Rounds: A Collection of Thoughts By a Survivor of the War in Vietnam" (manuscript, Imaginative Representations of the Vietnam War Collection, Connelly Library, La Salle University, Philadelphia, n.d.), n.p.
199. Steve Mason, "Portrait Of A Man," in *Warrior for Peace* (New York: Touchstone, 1988), 97–98.
200. Steve Mason, "The Casualty," in *Johnny's Song* (Toronto: Bantam Books, 1987), 77–78.
201. Robert Plain, "Mason knows the end is near," *Ashland Daily Tidings*, 16 March 2005.
202. For more on the idea of "slow violence," see Rob Nixon, *Slow Violence and the Environmentalism of the Poor* (Cambridge, MA: Harvard University Press, 2011), especially the chapter "Ecologies of the Aftermath: Precision Warfare and Slow Violence," 199–232.
203. The connection between the American war in Vietnam and the Cambodian genocide is contentious, but Ben Kiernan argues that "Pol Pot's revolution would not have won power without U.S. economic and military destabilization of Cambodia . . . This was probably the most important single factor in Pol Pot's rise" (*The Pol Pot Regime: Race, Power, and Genocide in Cambodia under the Khmer Rouge, 1975–79* [1996; 2nd ed., New Haven, CT: Yale University Press, 2002], 16). See also William Shawcross, *Sideshow: Kissinger, Nixon, and the Destruction of Cambodia* (New York: Simon and Schuster, 1979). Glover briefly discusses the role of America in the rise of the Khmer Rouge in *Humanity*, 300–302.
204. Steptoe, "A Second Wall," in *Mad Minute*, 44–45. On 10 November 2004, a memorial plaque was placed near the Vietnam Veterans Memorial in Washington, DC, inscribed, "In memory of the men and women who served in the Vietnam War and later died as a result of their service. We honor and remember their sacrifice."
205. Hansen, "A Tidy List," in *Blessed Are the Piecemakers*, 63. A note at the top of the page reads: "'*58,132 killed in action.*' U.S. State Department release."
206. Connolly, "What Was Lost," in *Finding My Way*.

207. W. D. Ehrhart, "Who's Responsible?," in *The Madness of It All: Essays on War, Literature and American Life* (Jefferson, NC: McFarland, 2002), 23.
208. D. F. Brown, "Still Later There Are War Stories," in *Unaccustomed Mercy,* edited by Ehrhart, 42.
209. Gary Rafferty, "Last Asylum," in *From Both Sides Now,* edited by Mahony, 215–16.
210. Adorno, *Minima Moralia,* 25; Connolly, "We're Still Here, America," in "Illumination Rounds."
211. Weigl, "For the Novice of Tran Quoc Pagoda," in *Sweet Lorain,* 49.

Chapter 4: Responsibility

1. W. D. Ehrhart, "Who's Responsible?," in *The Madness of It All: Essays on War, Literature and American Life* (Jefferson, NC: McFarland, 2002), 31. This piece was "Originally given as a talk to the Freshman Forum at La Salle University, Philadelphia, Pennsylvania, October 15, 1991" (21). For more on Ehrhart's poetic account of war and responsibility, see Adam Gilbert, "'We are the ones you sent': Moral Responsibility and War in the Poetry of W. D. Ehrhart," in *The Last Time I Dreamed about the War: Essays on the Life and Writing of W. D. Ehrhart,* edited by Jean-Jacques Malo (Jefferson, NC: McFarland, 2014), 59–76.
2. In just war thinking, there might also be a responsibility for war, and not only a responsibility against war. If a war fulfills the just war criteria, then perhaps there is a moral obligation to go to war. In other words, just war thinking is not necessarily set up so as to avoid war.
3. David W. P. Elliott, "Official History, Revisionist History, and Wild History," in *Making Sense of the Vietnam Wars: Local, National, and Transnational Perspectives,* edited by Mark Philip Bradley and Marilyn B. Young (Oxford: Oxford University Press, 2008), 284.
4. W. D. Ehrhart, "Starting Over," in *Just for Laughs* (Silver Spring, MD: Viet Nam Generation, Inc. & Burning Cities Press, 1990), 49.
5. Bruce Anello, untitled ("February 12"), in *Peace Is Our Profession: Poems and Passages of War Protest,* edited by Jan Barry (Montclair, NJ: East River Anthology, 1981), 26.
6. David Connolly, "War Song," in *Finding My Way* (Boston: David Connolly and the South Boston Literary Gazette Press, 2005), n.p.
7. W. D. Ehrhart, "'They Want Enough Rice': Reflections on the Late American War in Vietnam," in *Dead on a High Hill: Essays on War, Literature and Living, 2002–2012* (Jefferson, NC: McFarland, 2012), 120.
8. Larry May, *Sharing Responsibility* (Chicago: University of Chicago Press, 1992), 16.
9. For more on causation and responsibility, see Michael S. Moore, *Causation and Responsibility: An Essay in Law, Morals, and Metaphysics* (Oxford: Oxford University Press, 2009).
10. May, *Sharing Responsibility,* 16. May expands: "Responsibility stems from agency, and yet agency itself begins in the deep recesses of the self. The kind of behavior we engage in does not arise overnight but is normally a function of many successive layers of choosing over the course of a life. For this reason, responsibility is not confined to those isolated actions which have effects on others, but also includes those decisions that form the self into the kind of agent it is and that influence the way that the self then acts in the world" (17).
11. Ibid., 19, 3. Given the importance of Albert Camus in this study, it is worth noting that May explores Camus's work *The Myth of Sisyphus* as an example of personal existentialism (19–21).

12. Viktor E. Frankl, *Man's Search for Meaning,* translated by Ilse Lasch (1946; London: Rider, 2004), 134.
13. Jean-Paul Sartre, *Being and Nothingness,* translated by Hazel E. Barnes (1943; rev. ed., London: Routledge, 2003), 574–75. May also utilizes this example in *Sharing Responsibility,* 21–22.
14. May, *Sharing Responsibility,* 3.
15. Sartre, *Being and Nothingness,* 574. For more on this, see May, *Sharing Responsibility,* 21. As George Cotkin suggests: "We are responsible for our acts. This is a tremendous burden, but one that cannot be avoided. This is why existentialists talk so readily of the dreadful nature of freedom" (*Morality's Muddy Waters: Ethical Quandaries in Modern America* [Philadelphia: University of Pennsylvania Press, 2010], 204).
16. May, *Sharing Responsibility,* 38, 1 (emphases added).
17. Ibid., 38, 5, 47.
18. John Harris, *Violence and Responsibility* (London: Routledge & Kegan Paul, 1980), 1–2.
19. Richard Norman, *Ethics, Killing and War* (Cambridge: Cambridge University Press, 1995), 77. Jonathan Glover offers a more formal definition of the acts and omissions doctrine: "in certain contexts, failure to perform an act, with certain foreseen bad consequences of that failure, is morally less bad than to perform a different act which has the identical foreseen bad consequences" (*Causing Death and Saving Lives* [1977; London: Penguin Books, 1990], 92). See also Tony Honoré, "Are Omissions Less Culpable?," in *Responsibility and Fault* (Oxford: Hart, 1999), 41–66.
20. Harris, *Violence and Responsibility,* 2, 9.
21. May, *Sharing Responsibility,* 1.
22. Glover, *Causing Death and Saving Lives,* 94. See also Peter Singer, *Practical Ethics* (1979; 2nd ed., Cambridge: Cambridge University Press, 1993).
23. Glover, *Causing Death and Saving Lives,* 95.
24. Ibid., 112.
25. Harris, *Violence and Responsibility,* 1.
26. Fyodor Dostoyevsky, *The Brothers Karamazov,* translated by David McDuff (1880; London: Penguin Books, 2003), 374. Later in the novel, Dostoyevsky reiterates this radical conception of responsibility: "take yourself and make yourself a respondent for all human sin . . . for no sooner do you sincerely make yourself the respondent of all creatures and all things than you will immediately see that it is in reality thus and that it is you who are guilty for all creatures and all things" (414). Glover explores Dostoyevsky's expansive understanding of responsibility in a section titled "The View of Father Zossima's Brother, and the Impossibility of Doing All Good Things," in *Causing Death and Saving Lives,* 104–7.
27. May, *Sharing Responsibility,* 10–11. For an example of the good that can occur, even in the midst of extreme and difficult circumstances, when a group of people chooses to work together for a higher morality, see Philip P. Hallie, *Lest Innocent Blood Be Shed: The Story of the Village of Le Chambon and How Goodness Happened There* (1979; New York: HarperPerennial, 1994).
28. Karl Jaspers, *The Question of German Guilt,* translated by E. B. Ashton (1947; New York: Fordham University Press, 2001), 63. This quote serves as an epigraph for Glover's chapter that discusses the acts and omissions doctrine, "Not Striving to Keep Alive," in *Causing Death and Saving Lives,* 92–112. Glover also uses this quote in his more recent work *Humanity: A Moral History of the Twentieth Century* (New Haven, CT: Yale University Press, 2001), 380. In *Humanity,* Glover dedicates a whole chapter to the issue

of "Bystanders" (379–93). For an excellent poetic examination of the bystander issue, see Maurice Ogden, *The Hangman* (Tustin, CA: Media Masters for Regina Publications, 1968). Ogden's poem is also the basis for the short animated film *The Hangman,* directed by Les Goldman and Paul Julian (Contemporary Films, 1964).

29. Glover, *Humanity,* 406.
30. Theodor Adorno, *Minima Moralia: Reflections from Damaged Life,* translated by E. F. N. Jephcott (1951; London: Verso, 2005), 25.
31. Peter Ulisse, "Doctor Able," in *Vietnam Voices* (Lewiston, NY: Edwin Mellen Press, 1990), 3 (ellipsis in original).
32. D. C. Berry, "Gulf of Tonkin," in *From Both Sides Now: The Poetry of the Vietnam War and Its Aftermath,* edited by Phillip Mahony (New York: Scribner, 1998), 29 (ellipsis in original). For a detailed account of the Gulf of Tonkin incident, see Edwin E. Moïse, *Tonkin Gulf and the Escalation of the Vietnam War* (Chapel Hill: University of North Carolina Press, 1996).
33. For an overview of the role of national security officials in the policymaking process with regard to the war, and why it might be an oversimplification to make no distinction between Johnson and his advisers, see Gareth Porter, "Explaining the Vietnam War: Dominant and Contending Paradigms," in *Making Sense of the Vietnam Wars,* edited by Bradley and Young, 67–90. For McNamara's own account, see Robert S. McNamara with Brian VanDeMark, *In Retrospect: The Tragedy and Lessons of Vietnam* (New York: Times Books, 1995). For more on the influence of Bundy and the National Security Council, see Andrew Preston, *The War Council: McGeorge Bundy, the NSC, and Vietnam* (Cambridge, MA: Harvard University Press, 2006).
34. Berry, "Gulf of Tonkin," in *From Both Sides Now,* edited by Mahony, 29.
35. Steven Hassna, "Saturday Rip-Off Blues," in *Peace Is Our Profession,* edited by Barry, 101.
36. Fredrik Logevall, "'There Ain't No Daylight': Lyndon Johnson and the Politics of Escalation," in *Making Sense of the Vietnam Wars,* edited by Bradley and Young, 98. See also Fredrik Logevall, *Choosing War: The Lost Chance for Peace and the Escalation of War in Vietnam* (Berkeley: University of California Press, 1999).
37. Bruce Weigl, "Nixon," in *The Unraveling Strangeness* (New York: Grove Press, 2002), 18–19.
38. Larry Berman, *No Peace, No Honor: Nixon, Kissinger, and Betrayal in Vietnam* (New York: Free Press, 2001); Myra MacPherson, *Long Time Passing: Vietnam and the Haunted Generation* (1984; rev. ed., Bloomington: Indiana University Press, 2001), xxiii. On the link between the American war in Vietnam and the destabilization of Cambodia, see chapter 3, note 203.
39. John Kerry, Senate Foreign Relations Committee, 22 April 1971. See chapter 2, note 45.
40. Hassna, "Saturday Rip-Off Blues," in *Peace Is Our Profession,* edited by Barry, 101.
41. Charles M. Purcell, "The Walk," in *Winning Hearts and Minds: War Poems by Vietnam Veterans,* edited by Larry Rottmann, Jan Barry, and Basil T. Paquet (New York: McGraw-Hill, 1972), 107.
42. Connolly, "My Rights," in *Finding My Way.* On the death of Nixon, D. F. Brown comments: "I wasn't glad when Nixon died. I wanted him to suffer for a long, long time with phlebitis and throw little clots off to his brain" (in "War, Poetry & Ethics: A Symposium," *War, Literature & the Arts* 10.2 [Fall–Winter 1998]: 16).
43. McAvoy Layne, "On deference," in *How Audie Murphy Died in Vietnam* (Garden City, NY: Anchor Books, 1973), n.p.
44. Bill Bauer, "Worst in Memory," in *The Eye of the Ghost: Vietnam Poems* (Kansas City: BkMk Press, 1986), 57.

45. McNamara would eventually admit: "We of the Kennedy and Johnson administrations who participated in the decisions on Vietnam . . . were wrong, terribly wrong" (*In Retrospect,* xvi).
46. V. B. Price, foreword to R. L. Barth, *Deeply Dug In* (Albuquerque: University of New Mexico Press, 2003), xv–xvi.
47. G. P. Johnson, "Fighting for Those," in *I Was Fighting for Peace, but, Lord, There Was Much More* (Hicksville, NY: Exposition Press, 1979), 20.
48. Anello, untitled ("February 19"), in *Peace Is Our Profession,* edited by Barry, 26.
49. Horace Coleman, "People's War, People's Army," in *In the Grass* (Woodbridge, CT: Viet Nam Generation, Inc. & Burning Cities Press, 1995), 56.
50. J. Vincent Hansen, "Casualties," in *Blessed Are the Piecemakers: A Collection of Poems And Uncertain Notions* (St. Cloud, MN: North Star Press of St. Cloud, 1989), 60.
51. W. D. Ehrhart, "Cry Wolf," in *Peace Is Our Profession,* edited by Barry, 272.
52. Lamont B. Steptoe, "Gulf of Tonkin," in *Mad Minute* (1990; Camden, NJ: Whirlwind Press, 1993), 26, 31.
53. Yusef Komunyakaa, "Thanks," in *Dien Cai Dau* (Middletown, CT: Wesleyan University Press, 1988), 44.
54. W. D. Ehrhart, "Home Before Morning," in *Sleeping with the Dead* (Easthampton, MA: Adastra Press, 2006), 17. This poem is dedicated to Lynda Van Devanter, co-editor, along with Joan A. Furey, of an important collection of female poetry from the war: *Visions of War, Dreams of Peace: Writings of Women in the Vietnam War* (New York: Warner Books, 1991). It should be noted that there was some resistance to the war from politicians as well as support. See Randall B. Woods, ed., *Vietnam and the American Political Tradition: The Politics of Dissent* (Cambridge: Cambridge University Press, 2003).
55. Landon Thorne, "On Passing Graves Registration—Dong Ha," in *Winning Hearts and Minds,* edited by Rottmann, Barry, and Paquet, 59.
56. Hansen, "The Generals," in *Blessed Are the Piecemakers,* 37.
57. D. F. Brown, "Poem (Westmoreland)," in "Assuming Blue: or The Other Half of Everything" (manuscript, Imaginative Representations of the Vietnam War Collection, Connelly Library, La Salle University, Philadelphia, 1999), n.p.
58. Barth, "Proem," in *Deeply Dug In,* 2.
59. Dick Shea, "in the papers you see many photographs of rank officers," in *vietnam simply* (Coronado, CA: Pro Tem, 1967), n.p.
60. Leroy V. Quintana, "Major Gordon Granger," in *Interrogations* (Chevy Chase, MD: Viet Nam Generation, Inc. & Burning Cities Press, 1990), 82.
61. Komunyakaa, "Fragging," in *Dien Cai Dau,* 16. For more on the practice of "fragging" in Vietnam, see George Lepre, *Fragging: Why U.S. Soldiers Assaulted Their Officers in Vietnam* (Lubbock: Texas Tech University Press, 2011).
62. David Connolly, "Christmas Standdown," in *Lost in America* (Woodbridge, CT: Viet Nam Generation, Inc. & Burning Cities Press, 1994), 32.
63. David Connolly, interview by author, Boston, 15 March 2010; Connolly, "Christmas Standdown," in *Lost in America,* 32.
64. It is worth noting, though, as the historian Gareth Porter argues, that America, especially in the pre-escalation period from 1953 to 1965, "held a position of strategic dominance over the Soviet Union and China" that "significantly influenced the definition of the situation by U.S. policy makers and the choice of options available to them in regard to Vietnam" ("Explaining the Vietnam War," 84). See also Gareth Porter, *Perils of Dominance: Imbalance of Power and the Road to War in Vietnam* (Berkeley: University of California Press, 2006).
65. Jan Barry, "In the Footsteps of Genghis Khan," in *Veterans Day* (Richford, VT:

Samisdat, 1983), 5. The poem originally appears in *Winning Hearts and Minds,* edited by Rottmann, Barry, and Paquet, 6. There is a slight typographical error in the *Veterans Day* version, where Genghis is spelt "Ghenghis" in the text of the poem, although not in the title. I have adjusted the spelling here to accord with the title of the piece.

66. For a brief overview of the role of profiteering and "nation building" in Vietnam, and also in the war in Iraq, see James M. Carter, "The Merchants of Blood: War Profiteering from Vietnam to Iraq," *CounterPunch,* 11 December 2003, http://www.counterpunch.org/2003/12/11/war-profiteering-from-vietnam-to-iraq. During the war, Bertrand Russell commented on this link between industry and the military: "When we consider that the fantastic sums of money spent on armament are awarded in contracts to the industries on whose boards of directors sit the generals who demand the weapons, we can see that the military and large industry have formed an interlocking alliance for their own profit" (*War Crimes in Vietnam* [New York: Monthly Review Press, 1967], 117).
67. Steve Mason, "Angry Little Poem of Spring," in *Johnny's Song* (Toronto: Bantam Books, 1987), 67–68, 70.
68. Steptoe, "Gulf of Tonkin," in *Mad Minute,* 27–29. The Trilateral Commission is an organization that was formed in 1973 by David Rockefeller to increase cooperation between North America, Western Europe, and Japan. It can be understood as an "alliance between the major capitalist states, with the aim of promoting (or sustaining) a stable form of world order which is congenial to their dominant interests. More specifically, this involves a commitment to a more-or-less liberal international economic order" (Stephen Gill, *American Hegemony and the Trilateral Commission* [Cambridge: Cambridge University Press, 1990], 1). In Steptoe's poem, and in Mason's piece above, the Trilateral Commission is pictured as a symbol and part of the power of state-sponsored international capitalism.
69. Steptoe, "Gulf of Tonkin," in *Mad Minute,* 30–32.
70. Connolly interview.
71. Ibid.
72. David Zierler, *The Invention of Ecocide: Agent Orange, Vietnam, and the Scientists Who Changed the Way We Think about the Environment* (Athens: University of Georgia Press, 2011), 110–11.
73. Howard Zinn, "Dow Shalt Not Kill," first appeared in the *New South Student* in December 1967 and is quoted here from *The Zinn Reader: Writings on Disobedience and Democracy* (New York: Seven Stories Press, 1997), 305–6.
74. Dow Chemical Company, quoted in David Maraniss, *They Marched into Sunlight: War and Peace, Vietnam and America, October 1967* (New York: Simon & Schuster, 2003), 71.
75. GIs of the 1st Air Cavalry Division in Vietnam, "We shoot the sick, the young, the lame," in *Peace Is Our Profession,* edited by Barry, 22.
76. Mason, "The Casualty," in *Johnny's Song,* 78.
77. Glover, *Causing Death and Saving Lives,* 95. From the perspective of just war thinking, it can be understood that a person who contributes to the production of weapons to be used in a just war still shares responsibility for the harms they cause, but that this is *justifiable* harm. Here, it is incumbent on each individual to assess to the best of their ability the justness of any war to which they contribute.
78. Zinn, preamble to "Dow Shalt Not Kill," 302.
79. Larry Fries, "From Viet Nam 68–69," in *Winning Hearts and Minds,* edited by Rottmann, Barry, and Paquet, 66 (ellipsis in original).
80. Tom Barden, "The Fog of War," in *Long Time Passing: Poems, Songs & Reflections on the Vietnam War after 20 Years,* edited by Thomas E. Barden (Toledo, OH: Radio

Room Press, 1995), 31; Jim Nye, "Peace," in *Aftershock: Poems and Prose from the Vietnam War* (El Paso, TX: Cinco Puntos Press, 1991), 77.
81. Mark Downey, "Dutyhonorcountry," in *Winning Hearts and Minds,* edited by Rottmann, Barry, and Paquet, 100.
82. Johnson, "Power, Politics, and Profit," in *I Was Fighting for Peace,* 53.
83. Johnson, "Power, Politics, and Profit II," in *I Was Fighting for Peace,* 76–77.
84. Steve Mason, "In Victory Or Defeat," in *Warrior for Peace* (New York: Touchstone, 1988), 102.
85. It is worth noting that there are no values within capitalism that express a preference for peace rather than war, no intrinsic ethic that asks us to reduce harm or to help others. As Mason indicates, profits matter more than people: "bottom line results / not concerned with / the human condition" ("Founding Convention Poem," in *Johnny's Song,* 115). It is an idea he rails against: "Life is not a business / and cannot be run for profit" ("Angry Little Poem of Spring," in *Johnny's Song,* 68). Moreover, it could be argued that immorality is interior to capitalism. Situated at the heart of morality is an "infinitely demanding" altruism that clashes with the egoism at the center of capitalism (see Simon Critchley, *Infinitely Demanding: Ethics of Commitment, Politics of Resistance* [London: Verso, 2008]). As Terri Murray suggests in her compelling existentialist interpretation of the film *Forrest Gump,* which she regards "as a scathing *critique* of American capitalist values and the profit-driven worldview that underpins them": "as we instinctively know, morality is distinct from self-interest, the cardinal rule of capitalism" ("*Forrest Gump,*" *Philosophy Now* 83 [March–April 2011]: 45). It follows that responsibility is a concern exterior to capitalism. Amendments or additions may attach morality and responsibility to capitalism, but intrinsically capitalism demands no duty toward others, no obligations to attempt to fulfill. To alter, subvert, resist, or negate this cold system, and affirm instead the value of others, is to accept the difficult burden of responsibility that altruism, and perhaps humanity, requires. "We need courage now," Mason writes, "and survival without profit" ("Somewhere, A Woman," in *Warrior for Peace,* 100).
86. Smedley D. Butler, *War Is a Racket* (1935; Los Angeles: Feral House, 2003), 23.
87. Connolly, "Thoughts on a Monsoon Morning," in *Lost in America,* 14.
88. David Connolly, "The Michelin," in "Illumination Rounds: A Collection of Thoughts By a Survivor of the War in Vietnam" (manuscript, Imaginative Representations of the Vietnam War Collection, Connelly Library, La Salle University, Philadelphia, n.d.), n.p.
89. Connolly, "Thoughts on a Monsoon Morning," in *Lost in America,* 14.
90. Connolly, "The Michelin," in "Illumination Rounds."
91. Connolly interview.
92. David Connolly, "Into the Michelin Rubber Plantations," *South Boston Literary Gazette* 16 (Fall 2005): 45. See also David Connolly, "Aftermath: The Michelin," *South Boston Literary Gazette* 16 (Fall 2005): 46.
93. Connolly, "Thoughts on a Monsoon Morning," in *Lost in America,* 14–15.
94. For a fuller account of the issue of national responsibility than it is possible to present here, see David Miller, *National Responsibility and Global Justice* (Oxford: Oxford University Press, 2007). A number of interesting essays on this subject can be found in Tracy Isaacs and Richard Vernon, eds., *Accountability for Collective Wrongdoing* (Cambridge: Cambridge University Press, 2011).
95. Ashley King, "Lesson of Songmy," *New York Times,* 27 March 1970 (emphasis added). The letter is located and dated "New York, March 22, 1970." It also appears in *Crimes of War: A Legal, Political-Documentary, and Psychological Inquiry into the Responsibility of Leaders, Citizens, and Soldiers for Criminal Acts in War,*

edited by Richard A. Falk, Gabriel Kolko, and Robert Jay Lifton (New York: Random House, 1971), 238.

96. Rottmann, Barry, and Paquet, introduction to *Winning Hearts and Minds*, v.
97. Bruce Weigl, "Meditation at Melville Ave.," in *Sweet Lorain* (Evanston, IL: TriQuarterly Books, 1996), 48.
98. Michael Walzer, *Just and Unjust Wars: A Moral Argument with Historical Illustrations* (1977; 4th ed., New York: Basic Books, 2006), 299.
99. W. D. Ehrhart, "Letter to the Survivors," in *To Those Who Have Gone Home Tired: New and Selected Poems* (New York: Thunder's Mouth Press, 1984), 70. For an interesting poem that engages with the issues of voting and empty political promises of peace during the war, in both America and Vietnam, see Michael Casey, "Hoa Binh," in *Obscenities* (New Haven, CT: Yale University Press, 1972), 67.
100. W. D. Ehrhart, "A Relative Thing," in *A Generation of Peace* (New York: New Voices, 1975), 27.
101. Given the link between taxes and war, tax resistance has long been a weapon in the nonviolent arsenal of pacifists. See, for example, Lawrence Rosenwald, "On War Tax Resistance," *Agni* 35 (1992): 27–36. Yet, it should be noted that this position becomes particularly problematic if the acts and omissions doctrine is rejected. Then, the refusal to pay tax may stop money from going toward the harms caused by war, but it may also *allow* other harms to happen; taxes no longer support the military machine, but they are also withheld from state services that prevent, restrict, and lessen harms, such as health care, education, or housing. From a consequentialist perspective, and with the acts and omissions doctrine removed, the overall balance of harm caused and harm prevented by tax contributions—which will vary considerably depending on the spending priorities and efficiencies of a particular state—would be a crucial factor in deciding whether to resist paying tax. But from a deontological viewpoint, such as that suggested by an absolute pacifism that holds nonviolence as a categorical principle, and with the acts and omissions doctrine maintained, the duty to not *do* harm would transcend any such calculation.
102. Arthur S. Blank Jr., "Atrocity," in *Peace Is Our Profession*, edited by Barry, 206.
103. W. D. Ehrhart, "Responsibility," in *The Outer Banks & Other Poems* (Easthampton, MA: Adastra Press, 1984), 34–35 (ellipses in original). For another poem that links the war in El Salvador to taxes, see Ehrhart, "What We're Buying," in *Just for Laughs*, 62.
104. Bruce Weigl, "Apology to No One, November Seventeenth, Two Thousand Four," in *Declension in the Village of Chung Luong* (Keene, NY: Ausable Press, 2006), 58.
105. Christian G. Appy, *Working-Class War: American Combat Soldiers and Vietnam* (Chapel Hill: University of North Carolina Press, 1993), 6.
106. Brown, "The Other Half of Everything," in "Assuming Blue."
107. Connolly, "War Song," in *Finding My Way*. The reference to the IRA is linked to Connolly's Irish American ancestry, and this poem begins: "So I've come to see James Connolly / and Ho Chi Minh as the same."
108. Mason, "The Casualty," in *Johnny's Song*, 76.
109. The poets do not denounce conscientious objectors or those who had "moral qualms against the war." Rather, their ire is directed toward those who only "had qualms against *them[selves]* being in a war, it was okay for somebody else" (Horace Coleman, interview by author, Los Angeles, 3 April 2010).
110. Barth, "Social Darwinism," in *Deeply Dug In*, 53.
111. Barth, "Grunt Fantasy," in *Deeply Dug In*, 56.
112. Barth, "'Tonight you bitch, under too many drinks,'" in *Deeply Dug In*, 64. From the

same collection, see also "After the War," 65; "Epitaph," 70; and "Seeing the Wall, Thinking of Clinton," 71.

113. R. L. Barth, "A Brief History of the Vietnam War," in *Simonides in Vietnam* (n.p., 1990), 13.
114. W. D. Ehrhart, "What Makes a Man," in *The Bodies Beneath the Table* (Easthampton, MA: Adastra Press, 2010), 32–33.
115. Jan Barry, "Gifts," in *War Baby* (Richford, VT: Samisdat, 1983), 2.
116. Mason, "Only One Mother," in *Warrior for Peace*, 39.
117. Ehrhart, "Unaccustomed Mercies," in *Just for Laughs*, 83–84.
118. Kevin Bowen, "President Diem's Motorcade," in *Playing Basketball with the Viet Cong* (Willimantic, CT: Curbstone Press, 1994), 26.
119. Komunyakaa, "2527th Birthday of the Buddha," in *Dien Cai Dau*, 18. Other poems on the self-immolating protests include Richard E. Baker, "Protestor," in *Shell Burst Pond* (1980; 2nd ed., Tacoma, WA: Vardaman Press, 1982), 14; Barry, "A Nun in Ninh Hoa," in *War Baby*, 8; Barth, "For the Memory of Thich Quang Duc," in *Simonides in Vietnam*, 4; H. Palmer Hall, "For My Students in Pleiku," in *From the Periphery: Poems and Essays* (San Antonio, TX: Chili Verde Press, 1994), 27; and Hansen, "When," in *Blessed Are the Piecemakers*, 5.
120. Hansen, "Sgt. Royster Meets Pvt. Stanley," in *Blessed Are the Piecemakers*, 11.
121. Hansen, "We Take Him Along," in *Blessed Are the Piecemakers*, 53.
122. Ulisse, "Chaplain Flanagan," in *Vietnam Voices*, 65. For an investigation of American military chaplains and the war in Vietnam, see Jacqueline E. Whitt, *Bringing God to Men: American Military Chaplains and the Vietnam War* (Chapel Hill: University of North Carolina Press, 2014).
123. R. L. Barth, "Chaplain to Bishop," in *A Soldier's Time: Vietnam War Poems* (Santa Barbara, CA: John Daniel, 1987), 44; Bill Bauer, "Benediction," in *Last Lambs: New and Selected Poems of Vietnam* (Kansas City: BkMk Press, 1997), 38.
124. Weigl, "Meditation in Hue," in *Sweet Lorain*, 50.
125. Bruce Weigl, interview by author, Oberlin, OH, 18 March 2010. After the war, Weigl turned away from the Catholicism he grew up with, toward the Buddhism he had first encountered in Vietnam.
126. Yusef Komunyakaa, interview by author, New York City, 11 March 2010.
127. Barth, "Chaplain to Bishop," in *Soldier's Time*, 44.
128. Of course, there are a wide variety of Christian views on the morality of violence and war. Most obviously, the framework of just war thinking, which allows for the use of violence in certain circumstances, has deep Christian roots. Indeed, the American intervention in Vietnam was supported at the time by some American Christians as a just war. For an important defense of just war thinking, published at the peak of the conflict, see Paul Ramsey, *The Just War: Force and Political Responsibility* (1968; Lanham, MD: University Press of America, 1983). For an opposing view, published in the same year, that supports a Christian ethic of nonviolence, see James W. Douglass, *The Non-violent Cross: A Theology of Revolution and Peace* (London: Geoffrey Chapman, 1968). For an overview of just war thinking and pacifism in relation to Christianity, see John Howard Yoder, *Christian Attitudes to War, Peace, and Revolution*, edited by Theodore J. Koontz and Andy Alexis-Baker (Grand Rapids, MI: Brazos Press, 2009). For more on the various Christian responses to the war in Vietnam, see David E. Settje, *Faith and War: How Christians Debated the Cold and Vietnam Wars* (New York: New York University Press, 2011). It is important to note that numerous Christians "belonged to the Vietnam antiwar movement, in which they picketed, protested, wrote letters to the government, and

generally fought against the war from the very beginning because they thought it unjust and immoral" (Settje, *Faith and War,* 9).

129. Marion Parker [pseud.], "The Children," in *Demilitarized Zones: Veterans after Vietnam,* edited by Jan Barry and W. D. Ehrhart (Perkasie, PA: East River Anthology, 1976), 31.
130. Doug Anderson, "Free Fire Zone," in *The Moon Reflected Fire* (Cambridge, MA: Alice James Books, 1994), 19.
131. David Hall, "The Ambush of the Fourth Platoon," in *Werewolf and Other Poems* (Fort Collins, CO: Bald Mountain Press, 1981), 20.
132. Leroy V. Quintana, "That Country," in *The Great Whirl of Exile* (Willimantic, CT: Curbstone Press, 1999), 53.
133. Steptoe, "Gulf of Tonkin," in *Mad Minute,* 34.
134. W. D. Ehrhart, "To Maynard on the Long Road Home," in *Demilitarized Zones,* edited by Barry and Ehrhart, 109.
135. W. D. Ehrhart, "Guns," in *The Distance We Travel* (Easthampton, MA: Adastra Press, 1993), 42.
136. Ehrhart, "What Better Way to Begin," in *Bodies Beneath the Table,* 11. For more on patriotism and its link to war and peace, see Stephen Nathanson, *Patriotism, Morality, and Peace* (Lanham, MD: Rowman & Littlefield, 1993).
137. Ehrhart, "For a Coming Extinction," in *The Distance We Travel,* 33.
138. Connolly, "War Song," in *Finding My Way.*
139. Adam J. Berinsky, *In Time of War: Understanding American Public Opinion from World War II to Iraq* (Chicago: University of Chicago Press, 2009), 171. Berinsky adds: "In 1965, a shift from the most extreme antiwar position to the most extreme prowar position increased the probability of supporting restrictions on civil liberties by 18 percent; in 1967 a comparable movement on the war-support scale increased support for restrictions by 25 percent."
140. Ehrhart, "Governor Rhodes Keeps His Word," in *The Distance We Travel,* 19.
141. W. D. Ehrhart, "Visiting My Parents' Grave," in *Beautiful Wreckage: New & Selected Poems* (Easthampton, MA: Adastra Press, 1999), 219.
142. Glover, *Humanity,* 229.
143. David Willson, "A Few Well-Chosen Words: Extraordinary, Neglected Vietnam War Poets," *VVA Veteran* 31.1 (January–February 2011): 31. Lorrie Goldensohn refers to John Wayne as "that irrepressible phantom making its derisive appearances throughout Vietnam War literature" (*Dismantling Glory: Twentieth-Century Soldier Poetry* [New York: Columbia University Press, 2003], 285).
144. Ehrhart, "'. . . the light that cannot fade . . . ,'" in *Outer Banks,* 31.
145. Tobey C. Herzog, *Vietnam War Stories: Innocence Lost* (London: Routledge, 1992), 19. See also Kyle Longley, *Grunts: The American Combat Soldier in Vietnam* (Armonk, NY: M. E. Sharpe, 2008), 24–26.
146. Barth, "The Movies Are a State of Mind," in *Soldier's Time,* 45.
147. Barth, "A Little Elegy for Jimmy Stewart," in *Deeply Dug In,* 72.
148. Harrison Kohler, "The Cheerleaders," in *Winning Hearts and Minds,* edited by Rottmann, Barry, and Paquet, 43.
149. Gerald McCarthy, "War Story," in *War Story: Vietnam War Poems* (Trumansburg, NY: Crossing Press, 1977), 28 (ellipsis in original).
150. Willson, "A Few Well-Chosen Words," 31.
151. Jim Northrup, *The Rez Road Follies: Canoes, Casinos, Computers, and Birch Bark Baskets* (Minneapolis: University of Minnesota Press, 1999), 176.
152. Northrup, "The Duke," in *Rez Road Follies,* 176–77.

153. Bradley and Young, "Introduction: Making Sense of the Vietnam Wars," in *Making Sense of the Vietnam Wars,* 9.
154. Brown, "Even the Spoon is a Weapon" and "The Other Half of Everything," in "Assuming Blue."
155. Ehrhart, "Unaccustomed Mercies," in *Just for Laughs,* 84. For an overview of the war's generational issues, see Milton J. Bates, *The Wars We Took to Vietnam: Cultural Conflict and Storytelling* (Berkeley: University of California Press, 1996), 174–213.
156. W. D. Ehrhart, "Parade Rest," in *Winter Bells* (Easthampton, MA: Adastra Press, 1988), 10–11.
157. Ibid. For another important poem on generational responsibility by Ehrhart, see "Guns," in *The Distance We Travel,* 42–43.
158. Ehrhart, "Cry Wolf," in *Peace Is Our Profession,* edited by Barry, 272. A note under the title of the poem reads: "on the re-institution of draft registration: July 21st, 1980." Interestingly, the line break after the word "God" hints at the role of certain religious beliefs in this failure of generational responsibility.
159. Barth, "Allegory for L.B.J.," in *Deeply Dug In,* 5.
160. Lorrie Smith, "Resistance and Revision in Poetry by Vietnam War Veterans," in *Fourteen Landing Zones: Approaches to Vietnam War Literature,* edited by Philip K. Jason (Iowa City: University of Iowa Press, 1991), 54.
161. Ehrhart, "Coaching Winter Track in Time of War," in *Bodies Beneath the Table,* 74.
162. W. D. Ehrhart, "'What Grace Is Found in So Much Loss?,'" *Virginia Quarterly Review* 73.1 (Winter 1997): 99–111, http://www.vqronline.org/essay what-grace-found-so-much-loss.
163. W. D. Ehrhart, foreword to *Carrying the Darkness: The Poetry of the Vietnam War,* edited by W. D. Ehrhart (1985; Lubbock: Texas Tech University Press, 1989), xxiii.
164. Ehrhart, "A Relative Thing," in *A Generation of Peace,* 27–28. For an account of Ehrhart's first reading of this poem, see his book *Passing Time: Memoir of a Vietnam Veteran Against the War* (1986; Jefferson, NC: McFarland, 1989), 247–48. Of course, the American people are not exceptional in this failure of national and generational responsibility. Rather, it is a moral problem common to many wars. A. Golubnichaya's view about the Soviet war in Afghanistan, for example, could apply equally well to the American war in Vietnam or, indeed, any number of other wars: "It's not true that the public didn't know what was going on. Everyone could see parents opening their doors to those zinc coffins or having their sons returned to them broken and crippled . . . What kind of people are we, and what right have we to ask our children to do the things they had to do there? How can we, who stayed at home, claim that our hands are cleaner than theirs? . . . The machine-gunned and abandoned villages and ruined land are not on their consciences but on ours. We were the real murderers, not they, and we murdered our own children as well as others" (in Svetlana Alexievich, *Zinky Boys: Soviet Voices from the Afghanistan War,* translated by Julia Whitby and Robin Whitby [New York: W. W. Norton, 1992], 185–86).
165. Glover, *Humanity,* 406; Joseph M. Shea, "Comfortable people do not look," in *Peace Is Our Profession,* edited by Barry, 24.
166. Gustav Hasford, "Bedtime Story," in *Winning Hearts and Minds,* edited by Rottmann, Barry, and Paquet, 41.
167. Purcell, "The Walk," in *Winning Hearts and Minds,* edited by Rottmann, Barry, and Paquet, 107.
168. Steve Hassett, "Patriot's Day," in *Carrying the Darkness,* edited by Ehrhart, 131;

Frank A. Cross Jr., "What Are You Going to Be?," in *Reminders* (Big Timber, MT: Seven Buffaloes Press, 1986), 1.

169. Richard Nixon, "Address to the Nation on the War in Vietnam," 3 November 1969, American Presidency Project, http://www.presidency.ucsb.edu/ws/?pid=2303. My thanks to David Connolly for calling my attention to this link between American apathy and the silent majority.
170. Connolly interview. For a wartime assessment of the silent majority, see Milton J. Rosenberg, Sidney Verba, and Philip E. Converse, *Vietnam and the Silent Majority: The Dove's Guide* (New York: Harper & Row, 1970).
171. Ehrhart, "Visiting My Parents' Grave," in *Beautiful Wreckage*, 220.
172. Berinsky, *In Time of War*, 20–21. As Berinsky notes, "support for Vietnam seems to have followed a path of slow and steady decline" (20). He also emphasizes that partisanship shaped opinion regarding the conflict (111–18).
173. Walzer, *Just and Unjust Wars*, 300–303.
174. Richard A. Falk, "The Circle of Responsibility," in *Crimes of War*, edited by Falk, Kolko, and Lifton, 230. Walzer also cites part of this quote in *Just and Unjust Wars*, 351n19.
175. Coleman, "Notes for Veteran's War Protest," in *In the Grass*, 51. In another poem about veterans protesting, Coleman writes: "So I led 'em out singing: / '*And it's one, two, three, / what are we fighting for?*' / And we really *knew* this time" ("It Was Jane Fonda's Fault!," in *In the Grass*, 73).
176. Coleman, "Still Life With Dead Hippie," in *In the Grass*, 55.
177. Barry, "The Peace Monument," in *Veterans Day*, 12.
178. Ehrhart, "What War Does," in *The Distance We Travel*, 40. There is an intriguing question with regard to soldier responsibility and military conscription: What impact, if any, does the draft—both being drafted and volunteering under the influence of the draft—have on assessments of the moral responsibility of soldiers? This is an interesting issue, but since it is not one the poets address, it will not be considered further here. See also introduction, note 23.
179. Ehrhart, "A Relative Thing," in *A Generation of Peace*, 27–28 (emphases added).
180. Ibid., 27 (emphasis added). This line reads the same in *Demilitarized Zones*, edited by Barry and Ehrhart, 150; and also in Ehrhart's 1980 collection *The Samisdat Poems* (Richford, VT: Samisdat, 1980), 14.
181. Ehrhart, "A Relative Thing," in *To Those Who Have Gone Home Tired*, 18 (emphasis added).
182. David Rodin and Henry Shue, introduction to *Just and Unjust Warriors: The Moral and Legal Status of Soldiers*, edited by David Rodin and Henry Shue (Oxford: Oxford University Press, 2008), 1–2.
183. Walzer, *Just and Unjust Wars*, 36.
184. Rodin and Shue, introduction to *Just and Unjust Warriors*, 1; Walzer, *Just and Unjust Wars*, 38–39.
185. Walzer, *Just and Unjust Wars*, 41; Rodin and Shue, introduction to *Just and Unjust Warriors*, 2.
186. Rodin and Shue, introduction to *Just and Unjust Warriors*, 2.
187. Ibid., 1.
188. Ibid., 3.
189. Jeff McMahan, "The Morality of War and the Law of War," in *Just and Unjust Warriors*, edited by Rodin and Shue, 21–22. A common objection here is that moral principles differ in the context of war. For more on this, and a strong rebuttal, see Jeff McMahan, *Killing in War* (Oxford: Clarendon Press, 2009), 14–15. See also chapter 2, note 131.

190. Walzer, *Just and Unjust Wars,* 304.
191. W. D. Ehrhart, in "A Conversation with W. D. Ehrhart," *War, Literature & the Arts* 8.2 (Fall–Winter 1996): 151; W. D. Ehrhart, quoted in Timothy J. Lomperis, *"Reading the Wind": The Literature of the Vietnam War: An Interpretative Critique* (Durham, NC: Duke University Press, 1987), 20.
192. Stan Platke, "And Then There Were None," in *Winning Hearts and Minds,* edited by Rottmann, Barry, and Paquet, 101.
193. Rottmann, Barry, and Paquet, introduction to *Winning Hearts and Minds,* v.
194. Basil T. Paquet, "Mourning The Death, By Hemorrhage, Of A Child From Honai," in *Winning Hearts and Minds,* edited by Rottmann, Barry, and Paquet, 77.
195. Jan Barry, "If war is hell," in *Peace Is Our Profession,* edited by Barry, 29.
196. Hansen, "A Pinch of Salt," in *Blessed Are the Piecemakers,* 98.
197. Emerson was a strong supporter of veterans and veteran writers. Indeed, she helped with the publication of the two key early poetry anthologies *Winning Hearts and Minds* and *Demilitarized Zones.* "Her enthusiastic support and networking," Barry recalls, "helped launch *Winning Hearts and Minds: War Poems by Vietnam Veterans* to a national audience" (Marc Leepson, "Gloria Emerson: An Influential Advocate for Vietnam Veterans," *VVA Veteran* 24.5 [August–September 2004], http://archive.vva.org/archive/TheVeteran/2004_08/arts1.htm). "She contributed money to the publication of Jan's and my 1976 anthology *Demilitarized Zones: Veterans After Vietnam,*" Ehrhart writes, and they also corresponded when he was working on the later anthology *Carrying the Darkness.* "And when the Five College Program in Peace and World Security Studies invited her to participate in a scholarly conference called 'Tet Plus Twenty: The Legacy of the Vietnam War,'" Ehrhart continues, "she said she'd do it only if the organizers also invited some Vietnam veteran-poets" (W. D. Ehrhart, Wayne Karlin, and John Balaban, "Gloria Emerson (1929–2004): Remembrances," *War, Literature & the Arts* 18.1–2 [2006]: 13).
198. Ehrhart, "What I Know About Myself," in *Beautiful Wreckage,* 196–97.
199. Ehrhart, "Chasing Locomotives," in *Just for Laughs,* 69; Ehrhart, "Parade Rest," in *Winter Bells,* 10.
200. Ehrhart, "A Warning to My Students," in *Outer Banks,* 23.
201. Ibid., 24.
202. Ehrhart, "Some Other World," in *Just for Laughs,* 40.
203. Ehrhart, "Sleeping with General Chi," in *The Distance We Travel,* 31–32.
204. Ehrhart, in "A Conversation with W. D. Ehrhart," 157.
205. Ibid.
206. Janis Haswell, "The Lesson Unlearned: Moral Trauma in Andrew Jolly's *A Time of Soldiers,*" in *Thirty Years After: New Essays on Vietnam War Literature, Film, and Art,* edited by Mark Heberle (Newcastle upon Tyne: Cambridge Scholars, 2009), 445.
207. Ehrhart, "The Teacher," in *The Samisdat Poems,* 65.
208. Ehrhart, "What Makes a Man," in *Bodies Beneath the Table,* 32. Of course, for a variety of reasons, not all veterans want to or are able to speak about their wartime experiences. Perhaps, in some of these cases, such as with severe trauma, this silence is itself performative and can operate as a mode of witness.
209. Komunyakaa interview.
210. John O'Neill, "Veterans Day, 1972," in *Demilitarized Zones,* edited by Barry and Ehrhart, 71 (ellipsis in original).
211. Andrew E. Hunt, *The Turning: A History of Vietnam Veterans Against the War* (New York: New York University Press, 1999), 2.
212. Mason, "Death Is A Lady," in *Warrior for Peace,* 29.

213. Walzer, *Just and Unjust Wars,* 303.
214. Ehrhart, "All About Death," in *Sleeping with the Dead,* 10.
215. Ehrhart, "All About Love," in *Sleeping with the Dead,* 12.
216. Adorno, *Minima Moralia,* 25.
217. Frankl, *Man's Search for Meaning,* 139.
218. W. D. Ehrhart, in "War, Poetry & Ethics," 31.
219. Ehrhart, "Concerning Memorial Day," in *Dead on a High Hill,* 88.
220. Ehrhart, "The Invasion of Grenada," in *To Those Who Have Gone Home Tired,* 71.
221. George C. Herring, *America's Longest War: The United States and Vietnam, 1950–1975* (1979; 3rd ed., New York: McGraw-Hill, 1996), 308.
222. Ehrhart, "The Reason Why," in *To Those Who Have Gone Home Tired,* 67.
223. Ehrhart, "A Warning to My Students," in *Outer Banks,* 23. For an overview of the links between the wars in Vietnam and El Salvador, see George C. Herring, "Vietnam, El Salvador, and the Uses of History," in *The Central American Crisis: Sources of Conflict and the Failure of U.S. Policy,* edited by Kenneth M. Coleman and George C. Herring (Wilmington, DE: Scholarly Resources, 1985), 97–110.
224. Ehrhart, "Not Your Problem," in *Just for Laughs,* 63. As Stephen P. Hidalgo notes, "in its strong parallel to the Vietnam War" this poem suggests "the progeneration of violence, the parenting of one war by another" ("Agendas for Vietnam War Poetry: Reading the War as Art, History, Therapy, and Politics," *Journal of American Culture* 16.3 [September 1993]: 11).
225. Ehrhart, "What We're Buying," in *Just for Laughs,* 62.
226. Ehrhart, "Nicaragua Libre," in *Winter Bells,* 17.
227. There are pieces by other poets that address America's military actions in the world during the 1980s, but Ehrhart is by far the most prolific on this particular subject, hence the focus here. For a poem on proxy wars during the Cold War, see Hansen, "Superpowers," in *Blessed Are the Piecemakers,* 91. On Central America, see, for example, Bruce Weigl, "On the Dictatorship of the Proletariat," in *What Saves Us* (Evanston, IL: TriQuarterly Books, 1992), 34.
228. George H. W. Bush, quoted in Herring, *America's Longest War,* 311. See also George C. Herring, "Refighting the Last War: The Persian Gulf and the 'Vietnam Syndrome,'" *New Zealand International Review* 16.5 (September–October 1991): 15–19.
229. Quintana, "An Open Letter to President Bush," in *Interrogations,* 100.
230. Connolly, "For DC," in *Lost in America,* 64–65.
231. Ehrhart, "More Than You Ever Imagined," in *The Distance We Travel,* 10.
232. Ehrhart, "Why the Kurds Die in the Mountains," in *The Distance We Travel,* 12.
233. Barden, "The Fog of War," in *Long Time Passing,* edited by Barden, 30–31.
234. John W. Dower, *Cultures of War: Pearl Harbor, Hiroshima, 9–11, Iraq* (New York: W. W. Norton, 2010), 300.
235. Ehrhart, "Manning the Walls," in *Sleeping with the Dead,* 23.
236. W. D. Ehrhart, interview by author, Philadelphia, 2 March 2010.
237. Ehrhart, "September 11th," in *Bodies Beneath the Table,* 70–72.
238. George W. Bush, "Address to the Nation Announcing Strikes against Al Qaida Training Camps and Taliban Military Installations in Afghanistan," 7 October 2001, American Presidency Project, http://www.presidency.ucsb.edu/ws/?pid=65088.
239. George W. Bush, "The President's Radio Address," 22 March 2003, American Presidency Project, http://www.presidency.ucsb.edu/ws/?pid=25127.
240. James Dingeman, "Triumph Impossible," in *Triumph Revisited: Historians Battle for the Vietnam War,* edited by Andrew Wiest and Michael J. Doidge (New York: Routledge, 2010), 75. Dingeman continues: "The U.S. armed forces have had to relearn

the sobering lessons of fighting a counterinsurgency war after decades of deliberately turning away from this kind of warfare after Vietnam. A fierce debate rages about the mindset of our senior policymakers concerning what lessons they did or did not take from the Vietnam War as they crafted our intervention into Iraq."

241. For more on the links between the war in Vietnam and the war in Iraq, see Lloyd C. Gardner and Marilyn B. Young, eds., *Iraq and the Lessons of Vietnam: Or, How Not to Learn from the Past* (New York: New Press, 2007).
242. Weigl, "The One Thousandth," in *Declension in the Village of Chung Luong*, 51.
243. Weigl, "Le Filme," in *Declension in the Village of Chung Luong*, 65.
244. Dave Connolly, untitled ("Dead, Iraq"), *South Boston Literary Gazette* 22 (Winter 2010): 5.
245. Dale Ritterbusch, "Probably Not the Final Destination," *War, Literature & the Arts* 23.1–2 (2011), http://wlajournal.com/wlaarchive/23_1-2/ritterbush.pdf.
246. Connolly, "Collage On the Cusp of the Century," in *Finding My Way*; Ehrhart, "Coaching Winter Track in Time of War," in *Bodies Beneath the Table*, 74. The phrase "The past is always here" begins and ends "Collage On the Cusp of the Century," and repeats throughout the piece, the refrain itself a reminder of the perpetual presence of the past. In a note at the top of the poem, Connolly explains the piece's composition: "This poem is written in the Renga form, using voices gleaned from a Millennium Reconciliation Poetry Project made up of survivors of the Vietnam War who were refugees, former comrades, both Vietnamese and American, and new friends and comrades, whom fate had made former enemies, from the NLF and PAVN. The voices include: Kevin Bowen Dave Connolly Pat DiGregorio Do Vi Ha Frankie Heng Preston Hood III Nguyen Ba Chung Khanh Phuong Paul Shea Richard Lee Sheehan. May our reconciliation put an end to our war, at least between us."
247. Ehrhart, "Manning the Walls," in *Sleeping with the Dead*, 24.
248. Ehrhart, "High Country," in *To Those Who Have Gone Home Tired*, 72.
249. Ehrhart, "Who Did What to Whom," in *Just for Laughs*, 29.
250. Weigl, "They Name Heaven," in *What Saves Us*, 32.
251. Ehrhart, "Manning the Walls," in *Sleeping with the Dead*, 25.
252. Ehrhart, "A Warning to My Students," in *Outer Banks*, 23; Barden, "The Fog of War," in *Long Time Passing*, edited by Barden, 30.
253. Ritterbusch, "Probably Not the Final Destination."
254. Coleman, "Notes for Veteran's War Protest," in *In the Grass*, 51.
255. Ehrhart, "Guns," in *The Distance We Travel*, 43.
256. Barden, "The Fog of War," in *Long Time Passing*, edited by Barden, 30.
257. Yusef Komunyakaa, "Autobiography of My Alter Ego," in *Warhorses* (New York: Farrar, Straus and Giroux, 2008), 82.
258. Ehrhart, "The Cradle of Civilization," in *The Distance We Travel*, 11.
259. Weigl, "The One Thousandth," in *Declension in the Village of Chung Luong*, 51.
260. Kalí Tal, *Worlds of Hurt: Reading the Literatures of Trauma* (Cambridge: Cambridge University Press, 1996), 88; W. D. Ehrhart, "To Those Who Have Gone Home Tired," in *Demilitarized Zones*, edited by Barry and Ehrhart, 177.
261. Tal, *Worlds of Hurt*, 89.
262. W. D. Ehrhart, "The Eruption of Mount St. Helens," in *Matters of the Heart* (Easthampton, MA: Adastra Press, 1981), 17. This poem is dedicated to "Nimimosha of the Bear Tribe Medicine Society."
263. Ehrhart, "Near-Sighted," in *Matters of the Heart*, 10.
264. Ehrhart, "On the Eve of Destruction," in *Bodies Beneath the Table*, 65.
265. Weigl, "The Prisoner of Ours," in *Declension in the Village of Chung Luong*, 42.

266. Dale Ritterbusch, "Literary Determinism," *War, Literature & the Arts* 23.1–2 (2011), http://wlajournal.com/wlaarchive/23_1-2/ritterbush.pdf.
267. Ehrhart, "Why I Don't Mind Rocking Leela to Sleep," in *Winter Bells*, 20.
268. Ehrhart, "What Keeps Me Going," in *Winter Bells*, 22.
269. Ehrhart, "The Bodies Beneath the Table," in *Bodies Beneath the Table*, 67.
270. W. D. Ehrhart, correspondence with author, 29 May 2010.
271. W. D. Ehrhart, "A Common Language," *Virginia Quarterly Review* 67.3 (Summer 1991): 377–96, http://www.vqronline.org/essay/common-language.
272. Brown, in "War, Poetry & Ethics," 11–12.
273. Elie Wiesel, "Why I Write," translated by Rosette C. Lamont, in *Confronting the Holocaust: The Impact of Elie Wiesel*, edited by Alvin H. Rosenfeld and Irvin Greenberg (Bloomington: Indiana University Press, 1978), 205–6. He continues: "What matters is to gather a smile here and there, a tear here and there, a word here and there, and thus justify the faith placed in you, a long time ago, by so many victims. Why I write? To wrench those victims from oblivion. To help the dead vanquish death."
274. John Prados, *The Blood Road: The Ho Chi Minh Trail and the Vietnam War* (New York: John Wiley & Sons, 1999), 375.
275. Wiesel, "Why I Write," 206.
276. Ehrhart, "To Those Who Have Gone Home Tired," in *Demilitarized Zones*, edited by Barry and Ehrhart, 177 (emphases added).
277. Jay Winter, "Introduction: Henri Barbusse and the Birth of the Moral Witness," in *Under Fire*, by Henri Barbusse, translated by Robin Buss (1916; London: Penguin Books, 2003), xviii. As Richard Aldington states in his First World War novel *Death of a Hero*: "How can we atone for the lost millions and millions of years of life, how atone for those lakes and seas of blood? . . . That is why I am writing . . . It is an atonement, a desperate effort to wipe off the blood-guiltiness . . . Perhaps you too must atone" ([1929; Ottawa, ON: Golden Dog Press, 1998], 21–22).
278. Yusef Komunyakaa, introduction to Quintana, *Interrogations*, 9.
279. Adorno, *Minima Moralia*, 25; W. D. Ehrhart, *Mostly Nothing Happens: A Poem* (Easthampton, MA: Adastra Press, 1996), n.p.
280. Ehrhart, "Visiting My Parents' Grave," in *Beautiful Wreckage*, 220.
281. Ehrhart, "What I Know About Myself," in *Beautiful Wreckage*, 197.

Wreckage

1. Doug Anderson, "Answering Adorno," in *Blues for Unemployed Secret Police* (Willimantic, CT: Curbstone Press, 2000), 71.
2. Theodor Adorno, *Minima Moralia: Reflections from Damaged Life*, translated by E. F. N. Jephcott (1951; London: Verso, 2005), 25.
3. Steve Mason, "A History Lesson," in *Johnny's Song* (Toronto: Bantam Books, 1987), 49.
4. W. D. Ehrhart, "The Poet as Athlete," in *Just for Laughs* (Silver Spring, MD: Viet Nam Generation, Inc. & Burning Cities Press, 1990), 53.
5. W. D. Ehrhart, "The Teacher," in *The Samisdat Poems* (Richford, VT: Samisdat, 1980), 65.
6. Albert Camus, *The Rebel*, translated by Anthony Bower (1951; London: Penguin Books, 2000), 224.

7. Viktor E. Frankl, *Man's Search for Meaning*, translated by Ilse Lasch (1946; London: Rider, 2004), 139.
8. W. D. Ehrhart, introduction to *Unaccustomed Mercy: Soldier-Poets of the Vietnam War*, edited by W. D. Ehrhart (Lubbock: Texas Tech University Press, 1989), 4.
9. Bruce Weigl, "Song of Napalm," in *The Monkey Wars* (Athens: University of Georgia Press, 1985), 46–47.
10. W. D. Ehrhart, "Beautiful Wreckage," in *Beautiful Wreckage: New & Selected Poems* (Easthampton, MA: Adastra Press, 1999), 206.

INDEX

ADAM GILBERT studied for his BA and MA at the University of Sheffield before moving to the University of Cambridge, where he completed his PhD in history in 2012. He was then a Leverhulme Early Career Fellow at the University of Sussex, where he combined his interests in history and moral philosophy through his research project "A Moral History of the American War in Vietnam." He now works as a writer and historian. This is his first book.